OUR MORE PERFECT UNION

Tentative

ARTHUR N. HOLCOMBE

OUR MORE PERFECT UNION

FROM EIGHTEENTH-CENTURY PRINCIPLES

TO TWENTIETH-CENTURY PRACTICE

HARVARD UNIVERSITY PRESS

CAMBRIDGE

1950

Copyright, 1950

By the President and Fellows of Harvard College

Distributed in Great Britain by

GEOFFREY CUMBERLEGE

OXFORD UNIVERSITY PRESS

LONDON

Second Printing

Printed in the United States of America

Preface

WE are in the midst of a period of revolutionary change. Since the Bomb fell on Hiroshima it has been evident to all persons of a reflective disposition that the world as a whole was badly organized, and that even in the best-organized parts of the world there was need to reëxamine the established processes of government with a view to reappraising their value under the strenuous conditions of modern times. Decisions of the greatest political importance, depending upon sound judgment in matters of unprecedented technical complexity, are made by statesmen who doubtless possess superior political skill but are handicapped by inferior technological understanding. The question inevitably arises, how best such decisions may be made in a democratic republic. For instance, should the President or the Congress decide whether and when to make a hydrogen bomb? Furthermore, in the light of what considerations and upon what evidence should such decisions be made? Finally, to what extent, if at all, should the people at large be consulted in the process of deciding?

In the United States, political power is exercised in pursuance of a plan originally formed in the eighteenth century. The plan was set forth in a carefully prepared written constitution. In fact, the people of the United States have possessed two written constitutions. The first, framed by the Continental Congress and called the Articles of Confederation and Perpetual Union, was in effect only eight years. It was never repealed, but, having been found unsatisfactory, was quietly ignored and quickly forgotten. The second, framed by the Federal Convention of 1787, proved to be more durable. It is now the oldest written constitution in the world.

Longevity may be an excellent quality in a political constitution. It may help greatly in solving the first problem of government, which is to enable the men at the head of the government to control the governed. In the course of time there develops a habit of obedience to constituted authority upon which men in public office can rely to procure the appearance of consent on the part of the governed to the system of government. When to the intrinsic strength of the constitution is added the force of political inertia, moreover, the men in power have less need to resort to the more objectionable means of maintaining their sway, particularly, unscrupulous propaganda, intimidation, and violence. A long-lived constitution may furnish the foundation for a better as well as for a stronger government. Then too, as a new constitution grows old and gray, feeling and sentiment combine with the force of reason to give vitality to the body politic. As long as the common purposes of the people of the state, notably those set forth in the Preamble to the Constitution of the United States, seem to be served, if not well, at least not too badly, rational grounds of submission to the established authorities will be supplemented by unreflecting, and yet ungrudging, deference to the men in power. The rational springs of orderly political behavior will be sustained by the subconscious and nonrational. An old constitution, if tolerably well implemented, binds the people of the state together, and the governed to their rulers, by the "mystic chords of memory," to which Lincoln appealed so eloquently, and unhappily so ineffectually, in his "First Inaugural."

The mere fact of survival, however, is not necessarily a sign of merit in a constitution. In a changing world the demands of the people upon their government also change. The modern trend is toward more numerous and more costly services by the government to the people. A more serviceable government means a stronger and wiser government, but to make a government both stronger and at the same time wiser is not easy. That all power corrupts and absolute power corrupts absolutely is a political truth the importance of which becomes more evident as the growing strength of the men in power calls for a corresponding growth in wisdom. A solution of the second problem of government, which is to compel the men in power to control themselves, becomes both more urgent and more difficult. Modern history repeats with fresh emphasis ancient tales of the tyranny of men with too much power and too little wisdom. Yet the price of power enough to fulfill the purposes of the state includes the risk of its abuse by men with too little understanding of the need for self-control.

A government is more than an arrangement of the offices of the state for the service of the people. It is a means of adjusting the relations between the individual and the whole body of people. The individual wants liberty as well as justice, and the body politic needs capacity for growth as well as order. Since the individual belongs, by necessity or by choice, to associations of many different kinds, economic, social, and cultural, as well as to the state itself, the proper adjustment of the relations between the individual and the state involves the adjustment also of the relations between the various kinds of associations and the state. There is an economic, a social, and a cultural, as well as a political basis of a constitution.

Economic, social and cultural forces exert their characteristic influences, which the government must keep in balance at the peril of its good name, if not of its life. A good constitution means at least for a time a stable equilibrium of forces. The best constitution would provide an opportunity also for the gradual readjustment of the balance between forces, changing in strength at different rates and in different directions, without ever disturbing too much the general equilibrium. It is essential for a well-constituted commonwealth not to permit a dictatorship of any part over the rest of the organized community, neither a dictatorship of the rich nor of the poor, nor of any minority, nor even of the majority itself. It is desirable also that some part of the people should be able to act as freely and as vigorously as if they were the whole body of people, for in a modern state there must be a division of labor, if the people are to be served. The ultimate test of goodness is practical capacity to act intelligently and energetically in the public interest.

The framers of the Constitution of 1787 were aware of these perennial problems of government. Some of them had given much thought to their solution. Their conclusions were embodied in political principles to which they were devoted. Not all the leading principles upon which the framers acted may properly be described as principles of 1787. The two most fundamental principles of American government — the sovereignty of the people and the reign of law — must be assigned to the original state constitutions, but there are three important principles of government which were first recognized as basic or received their first systematic application in the Federal Convention at Philadelphia. These are principles which have become of major interest to people of a reflective turn of mind everywhere, both in explaining the stability and capacity for growth of "the more perfect Union," as the new model of the United States was described by the framers in the Preamble of the Constitution, and in discussing plans for the organization of a suitable international government under the strenuous conditions of the modern world.

The practical business, however, of forming a plan for a system of government, upon which not only the members of the Convention but also the states of the Union and the people of the United States could agree, compelled the acceptance of many compromises. The principles upon which the plan was prepared were obscured by details which it was difficult to explain in terms of any recognizable principle. General Washington, transmitting the finished document to the President of the Congress under the Articles of Confederation, did not claim that anybody liked it exactly as it was. He contended only that it would have been worse, if it had been made more pleasing to the special interests of particular states. He hoped and believed that it was "liable to as few exceptions as could reasonably have been expected."

In the course of the Constitution's comparatively long life the opinion of it, formed by those it was designed to serve, has undergone great changes. In the beginning it was accepted reluctantly and with misgiving. A generation passed before there was general confidence in its suitability for the purposes of a people who looked forward to an extraordinary growth in numbers, wealth, and power. A century passed before the whole body of the people gave their definitive consent to the political system which had been established under its authority. There has never been a time when the Government of the Union was not challenged by some problem which tested its structure and powers. Yet popular approval of the principles upon which it was supposed to rest has long been taken for granted. The people have seemed generally to believe that the principles of 1787 furnished unquestionable answers to the problems of government to which they were applied.

In our time a fresh challenge to the traditional principles has come from a new quarter. The totalitarian political systems, both Fascist and Communist, have not only contended with the American for influence in the modern world, but their sponsors have also attacked the principles which Americans have offered in explanation and justification of their political way of life. Among these the principles of 1787 form an important part. Their interpretation in terms of contemporary politics and their evaluation under the strenuous conditions of the modern world are the topics of this book. It is written in the belief that the principles of 1787, as they have come to be applied in American politics, are sound, and capable of affording comfort, not only to Americans interested primarily in the preservation and further development of their own way of life, but also to all peoples everywhere who feel the need for a better political order in the world as a whole and seek a way to establish such an order. I do not contend, however, that the present application of these principles leaves nothing further to be done in order to preserve the American way of government against its enemies. On the contrary, it seems to me clear that the Constitution of "the more perfect Union" must still be regarded as an unfinished experiment in government and that the further extension of these principles is essential for the maintenance of a satisfactory position for the American people in the modern world.

This is, in short, a critical essay on the Constitution of the United States. For the statements and opinions of other writers, which I have had occasion to quote, whether with approval or disapproval, I have cited the authority. But my own conclusions have been greatly influenced by opinions which cannot conveniently be quoted, either because they were expressed informally without a view to publication or in some cases because their authors would prefer to remain anonymous. Among those to whom I am indebted more deeply than I can indicate here are my colleagues at Harvard, with whom I have often over many years discussed the principles and problems of American government; numerous fellow members of my profession in other institutions; and others, connected in one way or another with the Government of the United States. I have been particularly fortunate in my associates in the United States Bureau of Efficiency during World War I, on the staff of President Roosevelt's Committee on Administrative Management in 1936–1937, and in the War Production Board during World War II when I was chairman of its Appeals Board. The fact that I could not always agree with those for whose judgment I felt the deepest respect does not diminish my sense of obligation to them. For invaluable aid in research and in the preparation of the manuscript for the press, I am greatly indebted to my research secretaries, Mrs. Nancy W. Wheat, Miss Helen B. Poland, and Mrs. Sadi Sakai. I am glad to be able to express my gratitude here.

A. N. H.

Harvard University
Cambridge, Massachusetts

CONTENTS

Contents

OUR MORE
PERFECT
UNION

"In our complex society, there is a great variety of limited loyalties, but the overriding loyalty of all is to our country and to the institutions under which a particular interest may be pursued."

Chief Justice Fred M. Vinson
(*United States* v. *United Mine Workers*, March 6, 1947)

CHAPTER ONE

To Form
A More Perfect Union

PRELUDE TO WORLD FEDERATION?

THE vision of a universal reign of law, based on the consent of the governed and sustained by the organized opinion of mankind, is not new. It has been beheld by generations of men in different parts of the world. It is a vision which in the nature of things must make a strong appeal to the rational mind. Nor is it surprising that in modern times there should have been a ready response to this appeal among the American people. For the experience of Americans under their Constitution encourages the belief that, by taking due thought, it is possible to establish a durable harmony between the processes of law and right principles of justice and liberty.

A nation without a national government, the American people were told in the midst of the struggle for the adoption of their Constitution, is "an awful spectacle." [1] Believing themselves to be a nation, they gave their consent to what was represented to them as a suitable form of union. This Federal Union still exists, sustained by the organized opinion of the people. The blessings of liberty and justice, it seems, are the natural fruits of a well-constituted commonwealth. Since under the changed conditions of modern times a world without a world government is also an awful spectacle, American experience, both in forming a more perfect Union and in maintaining it, may be regarded, in Carl Van Doren's expressive phrase, as a "great rehearsal" [2] of an eventual act on the broad stage of world history.

The significance of the work of the Federal Convention, from the viewpoint of better international relations, was immediately perceived by the wisest of its members. Benjamin Franklin wrote to an old friend in France, October 22, 1787, barely a month after the adjournment of

1

the Convention, enclosing a copy of the proposed Federal Constitution, and remarking that he had spent four months in the Convention which prepared it. "If it succeeds," he added, "I do not see why you might not in Europe carry the project of good Henry the Fourth into execution, by forming a Federal Union and One Grand Republic of all its different States and Kingdoms, by means of a like Convention; for we had many interests to reconcile." [3] Franklin's comment identifies the essential problem in organizing a reign of law to supersede the appeal to arms in world politics — not the simple vindication of right against wrong, but the reconciliation of conflicting interests. Important interests, he understood, must be respected like veritable rights. A durable international organization, Franklin knew, must rest upon the consent of the interested peoples and be sustained by a general conviction that their various interests will be duly considered in the management of its affairs.

The framers of the American Constitution, finding a practical solution of the problem of interstate organization, gave the world its finest example of a society of men forming a more perfect Union by rational adjustment of conflicts of interest so as to promote the common interests felt by them to be fundamental and durable. Alexander Hamilton, like Franklin, did not like the final product of this process of compromise in all respects, though its faults seemed very different in his eyes than in Franklin's, but he also understood clearly how great was the Convention's achievement. "It has been frequently remarked," he wrote in the first number of *The Federalist*,[4] "that it seems to have been reserved for the people of this country, by their conduct and example, to decide the important question, whether societies of men are really capable or not of establishing good government from reflection and choice, or whether they are forever destined to depend for their political constitutions on accident and force." Hamilton was writing as the advocate of an imperfect plan of government, which he had reluctantly decided to support, rather than as the expounder of one which he could regard as thoroughly desirable, and, again like Franklin, he was not sure that it would prove to be a successful solution of the problem of government in America. He continued prudently in the first number of *The Federalist*: "If there be any truth in the remark, the crisis at which we are arrived may with propriety be regarded as the era in which that decision is to be made; and a wrong election of the part we shall act may, in this view, deserve to be considered as the general misfortune of mankind."

2

The Federal Constitution, though a better instrument of government than Hamilton believed, did not prevent one great civil war. Yet it has served the American people more than tolerably well for above a century and a half, and the decision reached by them when it was submitted by the Convention for their approval does deserve to be considered as fortunate not only for themselves but also for mankind. It was a great achievement of rational reflection and deliberate choice, and rightly encourages the belief that mankind is not destined to depend forever for a solution of the problem of world government upon either accident or force.

The spirit of the proceedings in the Federal Convention was best reflected in the famous little speech by Benjamin Franklin on the last day of its deliberations.[5] The stage had been reached when the finished text of the Constitution lay before the delegates and the question was whether those who doubted its suitability for forming a more perfect Union would sign their names to it. Gouverneur Morris had proposed, as a means of making it easier for the doubters to attach their signatures, that they should sign as witnesses to the fact that the Constitution had been adopted by the unanimous consent of the States present. Franklin supported this ambiguous formula in the hope of diminishing the appearance of dissension among the delegates. "I confess that there are several parts of this constitution which I do not at present approve," he declared, "but I am not sure that I shall never approve them: for having lived long, I have experienced many instances of being obliged by better information, or fuller consideration, to change opinions even on important subjects, which I once thought right, but found to be otherwise. It is, therefore, that the older I grow, the more apt I am to doubt my own judgment, and to pay more respect to the judgment of others . . . I doubt too whether any other Convention we can obtain may be able to make a better Constitution. For when you assemble a number of men to have the advantage of their joint wisdom, you inevitably assemble with those men all their prejudices, their passions, their errors of opinion, their local interests, and their selfish views. From such an assembly can a perfect production be expected? It therefore astonishes me, Sir," addressing General Washington, who was presiding, "to find this system approaching so near to perfection as it does; and I think it will astonish our enemies, who are waiting with confidence to hear that our councils are confounded like those of the Builders of Babel; and that our States are on the point of separation, only to meet hereafter for the purpose of cutting one another's throats.

3

Thus I consent, Sir, to this Constitution, because I expect no better, and because I am not sure, that it is not the best. The opinions I have had of its errors, I sacrifice to the public good . . ." Hamilton put the same thought even more emphatically. "No man's ideas," he confessed, "were more remote from the plan than his own were known to be; but is it possible to deliberate between anarchy and convulsion on one side, and the chance of good to be expected from the plan on the other." [6]

All but three of the delegates who were present at the close of the Convention were ready to act in the spirit of Franklin and Hamilton. These closing proceedings illustrated the democratic-republican political process at its best. This is the process of adjusting conflicts of interest by reasonable men of moderate temper, determined to make the general interests of the whole body of people prevail over the special interests of any particular part. The proceedings of the Federal Convention show clearly that such a body of men can compromise their differences with satisfactory results. Where such a spirit of compromise is absent, satisfactory results become more difficult and a durable achievement may become impossible. There have been many examples since 1787 of unsuccessful attempts to establish democratic republics where the political process was not at its best. It is evident why the study of the Federal Convention's proceedings will continue to be of extraordinary interest to intelligent people everywhere who may be concerned with the basic problems of government in the modern world.

THE THREE PRINCIPLES OF THE AMERICAN FEDERAL UNION

The decision of the American people to form a more perfect Union was doubtless, as Hamilton intimated, an act of choice and reflection. But the actual framing of the Constitution was a process in which the give-and-take of practical politicians, representing different groups of people, produced a plan of Union not anticipated by any of them. The case for the adoption of this plan was presented by its framers to the people in various ways. James Madison, the framer with the most philosophical mind, offered three main reasons for his belief that the original Constitution would furnish a framework for a stable and durable system of national government. These reasons are set forth with masterly logic in the fifty-first number of *The Federalist*.[7] They offer the most convenient point of departure for any searching analysis of the principles upon which the more perfect Union was founded. If these principles are sound, the argument is convincing that study of

4

the "great rehearsal" can contribute to the solution of the problem of a world without a world government.

Madison's first reason for faith in the Constitution was his belief in the principle of the separation of powers, upon which the government planned by the Convention had been constructed. This principle meant to him that "the interior structure of the government" had been so contrived "that its several constituent parts may, by their mutual relations, be the means of keeping each other in their proper places." A well-contrived interior structure, Madison believed, would maintain the partition of power among the several departments of the government necessary for preventing a consolidation of power in any single officer or organ of government and the consequent development of a tyranny. "Were this principle rigorously adhered to," Madison observed, "it would require that all the appointments for the supreme executive, legislative, and judiciary magistracies should be drawn from the same fountain of authority, the people, through channels having no communication whatever with one another." This, he recognized, was impracticable under the conditions of that time. Therefore some deviations from the strict logic of the principle had to be admitted. It was also desirable that the members of each department of the government should be as little dependent as possible on those of the other departments for their official salaries. "But the great security against a gradual concentration of the several powers in the same department," Madison declared, "consists in giving to those who administer each department the necessary constitutional means and personal motives to resist encroachments of the others." Madison had given much thought to this problem. "The provision for defense," he urged, "must in this, as in all other cases, be made commensurate with the danger of attack. Ambition must be made to counteract ambition. The interests of the man must be connected with the constitutional rights of the place."

Madison conceded that the principle of the separation of powers had been only imperfectly embodied in the Constitution. It was possible, he thought, to give to each department an equal power of self-defense. In a republican form of government, he was convinced, the legislative authority necessarily predominated. Even if the legislature were weakened by division into two distinct branches, organized upon different principles of representation, it would be difficult, he feared, to insure the independence of the executive and judiciary. The executive, he suggested, should possess for its protection an absolute power of veto over legislative acts, but such a provision had proved to be impracti-

5

cable. The executive might have been strengthened, he believed, by joining the judges with the chief executive in the exercise of the veto, but this too had proved impracticable. In short, Madison evidently feared that both the executive and the judicial powers might prove unequal to the task of checking the legislature and keeping the system of government in balance. However, he was sure that the proposed Federal Constitution was better balanced than the several state constitutions, with which it might then be compared.

Madison's confidence in the internal structure of the proposed system of government was fortified by two considerations which, he wrote, "place that system in a very interesting point of view." One of these was the principle of federalism. This was not a principle which, in the form in which it appears in the Constitution, had originally commended itself to Madison. He would have preferred a system of national government operating directly upon the people without any dependence whatever upon the agency of the state governments. The opposition of the delegates from the smaller states, many of whom desired a national government as strong in other respects as was desired by Madison himself, forced the acceptance of the principle, most vigorously urged in the Federal Convention by the delegates from Connecticut, that a national government could be strong enough only if supported as firmly as possible on the governments of the states. "In the compound republic of America," Madison concluded, "the power surrendered by the people is first divided between two independent governments, and then the portion allotted to each subdivided among distinct and separate departments. Hence a double security arises to the rights of the people. The different governments will control each other, at the same time that each will be controlled by itself."

The final consideration, fortifying Madison's faith in the stability of the proposed government under the Constitution, was the great diversification of interests in a country as extensive as the United States. This, he believed, would enhance the difficulties standing in the way of the abuse of power by factious majorities in the national legislature. "It is of great importance in a republic," Madison opined, "not only to guard the society against the oppression of its rulers, but to guard one part of the society against the injustice of the other part." This seemed to him a matter of such great importance that he took pains to make his meaning as clear as possible. "Different interests," he wrote, "necessarily exist in different classes of citizens. If a majority be united by a common interest, the rights of the minority will be insecure. There are but two methods of providing against this evil: the one by creating a will in the community independent of a majority — that is, of the society itself; the other, by comprehending in the society so many separate descriptions of citizens as will render an unjust combination of a majority of the whole very improbable, if not impracticable."

"The first method," Madison continued, "prevails in all governments possessing an hereditary or self-appointed authority." Such a method is exemplified, not only by the European monarchies with which Madison's generation was familiar, but also by the party dictatorships of our own time, characterized by a resolute purpose of the men at the helm to keep the majority of the people in tutelage by force, if necessary, until the foundations of their own power may be made otherwise secure. "This," Madison declared, "at best, is but a precarious security; because a power independent of the society may as well espouse the unjust views of the major, as the rightful interests of the minor party, and may possibly be turned against both parties." The second method, he was happy to report, "will be exemplified in the federal republic of the United States. Whilst all authority in it will be derived from and dependent on the society, the society itself will be broken into so many parts, interests and classes of citizens, that the rights of individuals, or of the minority, will be in little danger from interested combinations of the majority. In a free government the security for civil rights . . . consists . . . in the multiplicity of interests . . . and this may be presumed to depend on the extent of country and number of people comprehended under the same government." Thus Madison reached the comfortable conclusion that the larger the more perfect Union, and the greater the diversity of interests among the people, the more secure would be their rights and the more stable their Constitution.

This is an interesting argument in favor of a Constitution which Madison obviously feared might be excessively democratic. The principle on which it rests, that of the natural limits to the power of numerical majorities, if sound, must be more important now than in Madison's time, since the internal structure of the national government has become more democratic than in 1787 and the concentration of authority in the central government at Washington has become much greater. To determine whether it be sound calls for an inquiry into an aspect of government to which Madison gave little attention, and most of his contemporaries less — the nature and functions of political parties in a federal republic. The government of the United States is a kind of dual government. There is constitutional government, though not exactly as

7

planned by the framers, and there is also party government. The government of the more perfect Union has gradually developed into a combination of the two, not anticipated by the framers, and not to be judged exclusively upon the principles approved by them. Analysis of the political system which has developed in the United States must begin with an inquiry into the nature of the framers' principles, but it cannot be completed without inquiry also into their practical operation, and particularly into the party system, by means of which, in unexpected ways, the original principles have been put into practice.

REASON AND NATURE IN THE POLITICAL ORDER

The further development of the original frame of government, by the adoption of constitutional amendments, by the cumulative effect of judicial decisions, and by the gradual growth of political customs, particularly those embodied in the operation of the party system, has produced in our own time a form of union not contemplated by the generation of Americans which took the original decision. Moreover, accident and force as well as reflection and choice have played an important part in the development of the contemporary political system, and the result suggests that the explanation of a stable and durable constitution is more complex than Hamilton seemed to think. So important do the former factors appear to have been in determining the present form of the more perfect Union of the American people that the value of the "great rehearsal" to the people of our time, who would form a more perfect Union of mankind, may be challenged by those who pride themselves upon their objectivity and realism. What is the significance of the formation of the American Union in the political experience of the nations? What are the factors which may be expected to exert the greatest influence on human behavior in the field of politics on the great stage of the modern world?

Some observations by A. Lawrence Lowell suggest that reflection and choice may exert at least a greater influence than meets the casual eye. At the celebration of the Harvard Tercentenary he was discussing the factors determining political behavior and offered what he called an example from the evidence of history.[8] Lowell was a great admirer of the British system of parliamentary government, believing that system to be "singularly self-consistent and harmonious in its operation, more so than any other now existing or perhaps that ever did exist." He did not contend, however, that it had been planned to operate in

8

that way. On the contrary, he was of the opinion "that the parliamentary system, as it now stands, was by no means contemplated by the men who brought it about; that it was in fact quite contrary to their theories of government; that the steps they took were consciously and rationally taken to meet certain immediate needs without thought of possible ultimate consequences; but that they naturally led to the system finally evolved." It was "by a happy accident" that "the parliamentary form of government proved well suited to the temperament of the English people." Thus Lowell reached the somewhat mystical conclusion that "men, like animals, may attain a self-consistent and harmonious system of conducting their affairs by a process of striving for immediate intentional objects, if the conditions happen to be such as to lead to a system of that kind; and this although the actors themselves do not contemplate it, or even if the result is quite contrary to their preconceived ideas."

It might seem that, if such a satisfactory result could be achieved with so little intelligent foresight and deliberate planning, there would be slight inducement for men to study the form of the American Union with a view to forming on similar principles and by similar methods a more perfect general international organization. Why not rather be content to meet the political problems of the day by such expedients as should be most convenient from time to time? Why try to form a union of all the nations, if a temporary coalition of a few powers with common, though limited, interests should seem to serve the immediate purpose better or at least well enough? Why seek to establish world government, when that end may as well be attained by means which in the minds of those who employ them are consciously devised to make the world safe merely for some particular part of mankind? Why follow the example of the framers of the American Constitution, if that of the British statesmen noted by Lowell is as likely to lead to a more perfect union of the nations?

It is beside the point to argue, as capable students of the science of government have done, that the British Constitution is not superior to the American, or, more precisely, that the British parliamentary system is not superior to the American system of checks and balances. To be sure, some discerning British observers of their own political system have not shared Lowell's opinion of its excellence, or at least of its durability without change. Bryce, writing more than half a century ago,[9] expressed the opinion that "even in England it is impossible to feel confident that any one of the existing institutions of the country will be standing fifty years hence." The event would have justified a more sanguine view, though it is clear that the British monarchy under George VI is in many ways profoundly different from what it was at the time of Queen Victoria's golden jubilee. Harold J. Laski was not perhaps the most authoritative expositor of the institutions of contemporary Britain, but his analysis of the parliamentary system on the eve of World War II suggests that there are solid reasons for its lowered prestige.[10] The point is that in Britain a political system, deemed by some of the most competent professional critics to be most excellent, was brought about without deliberate contrivance, and that in the United States a carefully contrived frame of government, which is still cherished as a monument to the wisdom of the framers, developed through more than a century and a half under the influence of other factors as well as systematic reflection and purposeful choice. The question still remains, how significant is the development of the American Constitution to those who feel strongly that a world without a world government is an awful spectacle.

There is an incidental remark among Lowell's observations that merits further consideration. This is that steps taken to meet certain immediate needs "naturally led to the system finally evolved." The course of political development may not have been logical, but it was natural. Lowell did not choose to explain more explicitly what he meant by natural. It is, however, an idea of the highest importance to those who deplore the lack in the modern world of a satisfactory general international organization. It is an idea which should enable men to know what they may hope to accomplish by deliberate reflection and rational choice in the field of world politics. It is an idea which should encourage men to strive to choose the right part in the present political scene with a view to putting an end to the awful spectacle of a world without a world government.

The natural principle of the political order was a topic to which Immanuel Kant gave much thought.[11] His conclusion was that the history of the human race, viewed as a whole, may be regarded as the realization of a hidden plan of nature, to bring about a perfect political constitution as the only state in which all the capacities implanted by her in mankind can be fully developed. He was convinced that the full development of all the capacities implanted by nature in her creatures was "natural," but that in man as the highest of the creatures such a development could not be achieved within the lifetime of a single individual. It could be achieved, he thought, only in the species. In other

10

words, the full development of man would require as a necessary condition the perfection of the organized state in which he lived. Since there could be no such perfection short of a satisfactory organization of the whole world, the development of a general international organization was also "natural." To put it still differently, the full development of the human individual would require the progress of mankind, which could not be fully accomplished without a solution of the problem of world government. Since the full development of man is "natural," the eventual establishment of a suitable form of world government is inevitable.[12]

From such a theory of progress certain conclusions follow. If "by a happy accident" the British people found themselves provided with a form of government well suited to their temperament, that might well be in harmony with the natural course of political development, as Lowell implied. The results of such a happy accident were no doubt more likely to prove durable than any result of an unhappy accident. But how much better to promote the good fortune of mankind by deliberate reflection and rational choice, as Hamilton argued, through a right "election of the part we shall act." From this point of view the decision of the American people to form a more perfect Union becomes a more significant fact in the natural course of political development.

Confidence in the practical capacity of mankind to make right decisions in the field of national and international politics must rest upon the record. If the reasons were sound for thinking that the form of the more perfect Union was good, confidence in the political behavior of a thoughtful people will be strengthened. If the development of the more perfect Union, accidental in part and influenced by force though it may have been, seems to be in line with the "natural" trend, trust in the value of well-laid plans will be confirmed. Whether Madison's three reasons were sound, for believing that the form of the more perfect Union was suited to the needs and temperament of the American people, is a matter to be investigated in the light of the record. Whether the principles of government, which furnished the grounds for Madison's confidence, are still suited to the needs and temperament of the American people, or would be applicable to the problem of world government, are other questions on which the record of the "great rehearsal" and its consequences should throw much light.

CHAPTER TWO

The Political Principles of 1787

FEDERALISM

JAMES MADISON's three reasons for believing that the Constitution submitted to the people of the United States by the Convention of 1787 was an acceptable solution of the problem of a more perfect Union furnish the clews to three major principles of American constitutional government. The first in importance in his opinion was the principle of the separation of powers. The second was that of the natural limits to the power of numerical majorities of the people in a representative system of popular government. The third, which Madison had accepted in the Convention with great reluctance, was that of federalism. But in the actual framing of the Constitution the last came first and the first was last.

The framers of the Constitution for the more perfect Union called it a Federal Constitution and the Union itself came to be known as the Federal Union.[1] The leaders in the struggle for the ratification of the Constitution called themselves Federalists and the leaders in the first government under the Constitution operated under the same title. But they were not the original Federalists and if such a title had been offered them at the opening of the Constitutional Convention in 1787 they would have rejected it with indignation. The original Federalists preferred a less perfect form of Union and some of them withdrew from the Convention rather than take part in framing such a Constitution as was eventually adopted. Those among the framers who took the lead at the opening of the Convention proposed to establish a national government, consisting of a national legislature, a national executive, and a national judiciary. They wished the government of the more perfect Union to represent as directly as possible the whole body of the

12

people, and to depend as little as possible upon the governments of the states. They took care to explain the distinction between a federal and a national government and contended for a government of the latter description, capable of operating directly upon individuals regardless of their distribution among the states. They would have preferred to be called Nationalists.[2] The later change of name was dictated by considerations of policy rather than of principle and throws more light on the nature of the American way in politics than on that of the more perfect Union.

The Nationalists comprised approximately one-third of the total number of delegates to the Constitutional Convention. But they actually controlled only two of the twelve delegations which attended the Convention during the course of its deliberations. Most of the Nationalists were members of the large delegations sent by the great states of Virginia and Pennsylvania. The former delegation was dominated by wealthy planters and by professional men connected with wealthy landholding families residing in the tidewater region where tobacco was the staple crop. General Washington and Governor Randolph were able representatives of this leading element in the American people at the time of the Revolution and impressive symbols of the power and prestige of old Virginia. They were accustomed to leadership in the most populous and richest state of the Union and looked forward with confidence to creating a more perfect Union in which they and their kind could continue to play a leading part. They had utilized the time, while awaiting the arrival of enough delegations to make a quorum, to prepare a plan for submission to the Convention, the famous Virginia plan.[3]

The Pennsylvania delegation was dominated by leading Philadelphia merchants and by Philadelphia lawyers with a flourishing mercantile practice. Robert Morris was the richest and most influential of these merchants, but was content to leave the speechmaking on the floor of the Convention to his business partner, Gouverneur Morris, and to his lawyer, James Wilson, who were the two most frequent speakers in the Convention's debates. Among the Pennsylvania delegates there was no representative of the farmers in the back country or of the pioneers on the frontier, unless Franklin, who had been added to the delegation out of respect for his position rather than for his political ideas, can be regarded as the special representative of the common man in Pennsylvania politics. But Franklin's stature was too great for him to be the special representative of a faction in the politics

13

of any state. At times he could speak for the American people more convincingly than any other member of the Convention, but he could not speak for the Pennsylvania delegation with the same assurance. The leading Pennsylvania delegates were doubtless consulted by the Virginians in the preparation of their plan. In fact, Washington himself resided throughout the sittings of the Convention in Robert Morris's commodious town house, where the two Nationalist leaders maintained their political headquarters. Their customary silence during the long debates on the Convention floor enabled them to keep their own counsel, while their vigilant and tireless lieutenants expounded the preconcerted plan, pushed forward with the development of the enterprise, and explored, when necessary, the possibilities of a suitable compromise.

Outside the Virginia and Pennsylvania delegations the Nationalists were distinguished more for their extraordinary intellectual quality and legislative skill than for their numbers. Prominent among them were several brilliant young men, notably Alexander Hamilton of New York, Rufus King of Massachusetts, and Charles Pinckney of South Carolina, who shone brightly in debate without being able to deliver the votes of their delegations. Hamilton left the Convention early in its course, frustrated by the opposition of the other New York delegates, and did not return to stay until near its end. Pinckney preferred to play a lone hand rather than serve as the political aide of any of the Convention's leaders and.contributed to its work less than might have been expected from so talented a young man. King, however, qualified for an important place in the little band of brain trusters, foremost among whom were Madison and Gouverneur Morris, who supported Washington's leadership at every crisis of the Convention and at the end enjoyed the solid satisfaction of signing their names to a Constitution which their great chieftain, despite grave misgivings at certain concessions to the opposition, was willing to recommend to his countrymen.

In the light of events it is hard to believe that such intelligent and experienced politicians as the Nationalist· leaders could have seriously supposed the American people would approve so highly centralized a system of government as was embodied in the Virginia plan. The plan provided [4] that the national legislature should have power to legislate in all cases in which the several states might be incompetent, whatever that might mean, or in which the harmony of the United States might be interrupted by the legislative activity of the state governments. To make the supremacy of the national government more secure, the

Nationalists' plan further provided that the national legislature should have power to veto all laws passed by the state legislatures which, in the opinion of the national legislature, would contravene the Articles of Union. Thus the national legislature was to be the judge of the extent of its own powers. Finally, the national legislature was to have power to authorize the use of military force against any state which should fail to fulfill its obligations under the Articles of Union. The provision for the coercion of the states by military force was quickly dropped by the Nationalist leaders.[5] They perceived the repugnance of many delegates to so offensive a proposal and came to understand more clearly the superiority of a national government operating directly upon the people of the Union rather than indirectly through the state governments. Madison and Pinckney would have liked to extend the authority of the national legislature to review state legislation [6] in order to include the power to veto state laws which might be found to conflict with the policies of the national government as well as with the principles of the national constitution, but this was going too far even for many of the Nationalists. Hamilton and Pinckney would have been willing to go further [7] and authorize the national executive to appoint the state governors. They apparently had in mind the way in which the British Crown dealt with colonial legislation through the colonial governors before the Revolution, but the Convention would not even consider such a proposal. Whether these proposals were trial balloons, sent up to discover how far the Convention would go in supporting a Nationalist program, or were unauthorized excursions by ebullient brain trusters, does not appear from the records of the Convention or from the private papers of its members. Though there is no evidence that the Nationalist leaders countenanced such extreme proposals, it is clear that the Nationalist program contemplated a greater concentration of political power in the national government than would have been acceptable to the American people.

The original Federalists, like the Nationalists, wished to form a stronger Union than that created by the unsatisfactory Articles of Confederation. They felt the need for a more powerful Congress and for an independent executive and judiciary. They were generally prepared to revise the Articles of Confederation so as to render what they already called the Federal Constitution adequate to the exigencies of government and the preservation of the Union. But they were unwilling to change the structure of the Congress or to give the federal government authority to determine the extent of its own powers. They insisted that the additional powers of the Congress be strictly limited to those made necessary by the acknowledged deficiencies of the existing government, that they be clearly expressed in the new Articles of Union, and that the government of the Union depend upon those of the states as under the Articles of Confederation.[8] The original Federalists might well be termed Confederationists, or more simply Confederates, if that name had not become the property of a later movement in American politics. There were in fact few genuine Confederationists in the Convention of 1787. The ablest and most active among them was Roger Sherman of Connecticut. The most dogmatic and clamorous was Luther Martin of Maryland. The only delegation which they actually controlled at the opening of the Convention was that of New York.

The numbers of the original Federalists were swelled by the addition of delegates from certain of the smaller states who were prepared to support a strong national government, provided that each state continued to have an equal voice in the Congress.[9] But they preferred a weak government for the Union to a strong government in which the small states were deprived of their equal representation in the legislative department. They did not share Luther Martin's addiction to the principle of state sovereignty, or Roger Sherman's faith in the state governments as the best possible servants of the people within the field of their competence, or the New York delegates' antipathy to any kind of general government capable of regulating interstate commerce to the detriment of their own advantageous position in the national economy. But they would join with these stubborn Confederationists in opposing the plans of the Nationalists rather than submit to the authority of a strong national government in which their little states might exert no more than a negligible influence. These recruits to original Federalism controlled the delegations from two states, New Jersey and Delaware. The original Federalists altogether numbered fewer delegates than the Nationalists, but they controlled a greater number of delegations in the Convention.

The New Jersey plan, which the original Federalists offered as an alternative to that of the Nationalists, contained some features which found favor with the Convention and eventually filled an important place in the finished Constitution. It contained more precise definitions of the additional legislative powers to be granted to the general government. It provided a more independent judiciary and apparently contemplated a judicial rather than a legislative process for the review of state legislation which might seem to trespass upon the constitutional authority of the general government. But it offered only a weak executive and it made no provision for the representation of the people of the United States in the general government. From the viewpoint of most advocates of a more perfect Union the former was a serious and the latter a fatal defect in the plan of the original Federalists.

William Paterson of New Jersey, the leading advocate of the New Jersey plan on the floor of the Convention and a lawyer of superior ability, did not emphasize the merits of the plan in his statement of the case for its adoption. He stressed rather his objections to the plan of the Nationalists.[10] The people, he declared, were not ready for so great a change in the character of their Union and would not approve the highly centralized form of government proposed by the Nationalists. Moreover, he added, the Convention was not authorized to set aside the Articles of Confederation and could not frame a government based upon the Virginia plan without exceeding its legal powers. He did not attempt to justify the retention of a purely federal form of government as an adequate response to the need for a more perfect Union. He was obviously influenced by counsels of expediency, particularly as the expedient might be viewed by the people of a small state. But he was also a politician of conciliatory disposition genuinely devoted to the task of forming a more perfect Union. It is not surprising to find him in later years a leading member of the United States Supreme Court by appointment of President Washington.

The Nationalists and original Federalists together accounted for a majority of the delegates to the Convention of 1787, but they did not control a majority of the delegations. The New England delegations and those from the three most southerly states were controlled by members who rejected the original Federalists' view that the Union could be made strong enough without changing its essential character, but were unwilling to accept, without important modifications, the Nationalists' plan for a highly centralized national government. They agreed with the Nationalists that the people of the United States should be represented in a national legislature, but they could not approve the proposition that the national government should depend for its existence as little as possible upon the governments of the states. They agreed with the original Federalists that the states should be represented in the general government, but they could not admit that the general government should continue to be wholly dependent upon the states for its existence. These delegates wanted a more perfect Union

17

than the original Federalists were ready to accept, but they feared a National Union in which the states would be reduced to the level of mere organs of local government. They prepared no common plan like the Nationalists and the original Federalists, and history has no name for them. It is convenient, however, despite their lack of a common organization or program, to give them a name, and none is more suitable than that of Unionists.

The Unionists could easily have dominated the Convention, if they could have agreed, like the other two factions, upon a plan. They controlled a majority of the delegations. They held an intermediate position between the Nationalists and the original Federalists. Each of these factions could more easily come to terms with the Unionists than with one another. But the differences among the Unionists were numerous and controversial, and agreement was difficult. The foremost obstacle to agreement was the position of the states in the more perfect Union. John Rutledge, the leading representative of the prosperous planters in the Lower South, and Nathaniel Gorham, the leading representative of the successful New England merchants, could agree with John Dickinson, the leading representative of the substantial landowners in the Middle States, that neither the position of the states in the National Union proposed in the Virginia plan, nor that of the nation in the improved Federation proposed in the New Jersey plan, was sufficiently secure. But Rutledge and Gorham could not agree with Dickinson that equal representation for all the states in one branch of a Union legislature would afford proper protection for the special interests of states as important as theirs. Nor could they readily agree with one another on any other plan for the special security of interests as diverse as those of the big New England merchants and the great planters of the Lower South.

Many of the Unionists, like most of the Nationalists and not a few of the original Federalists, believed that the principal problem in a popular government is to prevent numerical majorities of the people from abusing their power and oppressing the minorities. But there were deep differences of opinion among these Unionists concerning the kind of minorities that would most need protection and the most suitable methods of protecting them. The great planters and big merchants would naturally feel most secure, if protected against the abuse of power by the representatives of the middle and lower classes of the people in the popular branch of the Union legislature through the establishment of property qualifications for membership in the other branch.

In most of the states there were property qualifications of various kinds for membership in the state legislatures, and in many of them these qualifications were so much higher for the upper house of the legislature than for the lower as to make it a special bulwark of upper-class interests. The more opulent Unionists, regardless of the section of the country from which they came, would generally have preferred to organize the upper branch of the Union legislature on similar principles. But the great planters would want the ownership of land to be the test of qualification for membership and the big merchants would prefer a different kind of test. The various kinds of Unionists were divided against themselves in a matter which they were generally disposed to regard as one of prime importance. They agreed that the Union legislature should be divided into two branches and that one of the two should be utilized for the purpose of protecting the interests of minorities, but beyond that point there was no unity among the Unionists.

The divisions among the Unionists were further complicated by the differences in size of the states which they represented in the Convention. The possibility of protecting minorities against oppression on the part of the representatives of numerical majorities of the people, by utilizing one of the branches of the Union legislature as an instrument of minority representation, was particularly attractive to minorities which could dominate individual states and thus control their representation in that branch of the Union legislature designed to represent the states. If the state were small, there could be no better protection for such special interests than to secure an equal vote for their state in the appropriate branch of the Union legislature. Some of the Unionists supported proposals for equal representation of the states in the Senate of the United States on this ground. Others, representing larger and more important states, were reluctant to surrender the advantages of superior population or importance. They could not agree that the states should have an equal voice in the Senate. All the delegations from New England and from the Lower South were inclined toward a middle way between the plans of the Nationalists and of the original Federalists, but the middle way was broad and there was room for much diversity of opinion among the members of these delegations. The large-state Unionists and the small-state Unionists were bound to make uneasy allies.

The Unionists from states of the middle rank occupied a different position. Whether the system of voting in the Senate gave an equal voice to all the states or adjusted their votes in proportion to their population and wealth might seem to be a matter of indifference to a state which would possess a vote equal to the average in either case. But equal representation for the states in the Senate could be more favorable to the dignity and authority of the average state than a system of proportional representation. Oliver Ellsworth of Connecticut, who led the fight for the Connecticut Compromise in its later stages, was strongly of this opinion.[11] He was the most active and influential spokesman for those Unionist delegates who believed that the state governments were the best servants of the people within their proper sphere of action. He was not as much interested as many of the delegates in establishing a stronger general government for the purpose of protecting the peoples of the states against the abuse of power by their own state governments. He was more concerned with preserving the authority of the states for the purpose of protecting the interests of their peoples against the abuse of power by a stronger general government. It was upon his motion that the Convention struck out the word "national" wherever it appeared in the text of the Virginia plan and substituted an expression which was more ambiguous but not on that account less appropriate for its purpose. Thus the proposed National Government became the Government of the United States. The prime function of the Senate, according to Ellsworth's view, should be not to protect minorities of the people against popular majorities, but to help maintain a political system in which both national majorities and state majorities would play their appropriate parts. There should be neither a National Union nor a Federal Union, but a combination of the two for which there was no specific name. He would be content to call it simply a more perfect Union.

What has come to be known as American federalism is not a product of any preconceived and approved principle. The Connecticut Compromise was only one feature of the system, but it was a feature the acceptance of which made the adoption of the rest possible. It combined a legislative body based on the federal principle with one based on the principle of nationalism. Consent to this combination of principles was extorted from a reluctant Convention by imperative necessity. But it was not a true compromise in the sense that it was freely accepted by all the parties to the controversy. Several of the original Federalists refused to accept it and left the Convention rather than acquiesce in the consequences of their defeat. Many of the Unionists voted against it, but readily accepted the result. Most of the National-

20

ists fought the Compromise to the bitter end and only acquiesced in the result because the alternative of breaking up the Convention seemed the greater of two evils.[12] The final adoption of the so-called compromise by a close vote of five states to four, with one state delegation divided and three states absent and not voting, was made possible by the switch of the North Carolina delegation and of two of the four Massachusetts delegates. The number of delegates who actually changed their votes in order to make possible the triumph of the so-called compromise was a very small minority of the total. To the bulk of the Nationalists the adoption of the compromise was a crushing defeat to which they became reconciled only slowly and with great reluctance. To a few of the original Federalists it was also a crushing defeat, to which they refused to become reconciled. They continued to resist its consequences until, despite their opposition, the new Constitution was finally approved by the people of the United States.

The winning of the little handful of Unionist votes needed for the adoption of the Connecticut Compromise was accomplished by the addition of what may be conveniently called the Franklin proviso. Benjamin Franklin had been an early and persistent advocate of a compromise between the Nationalists and the original Federalists. He himself did not share the original Federalists' distrust of a national government, nor did he share the Nationalists' distrust of popular majorities and of state legislatures under the influence of such majorities. He was a Nationalist, but a democratic Nationalist, the first great democratic Nationalist in American politics. A majority of the Convention eventually came round to his opinion, that compromise was desirable, and a committee was appointed to work out an acceptable scheme. Its report included a provision, ascribed to his influence,[13] reserving to the popular branch of the Union legislature the exclusive right to initiate money bills of every kind, including bills creating offices which would become a charge on the public revenues. The other branch of the Union legislature, in which the representatives of each state would possess an equal voice, would have power to accept or reject such bills, but not to amend them. This proviso was obviously intended to strengthen the popular branch so that it would be the preponderant branch of the Union legislature. When objection was made that the other branch would be too weak, Franklin replied that he personally would be willing to dispense with it entirely.[14]

The Franklin proviso was a shrewd attempt to utilize the conflict between the Nationalists and the original Federalists in order to make a more democratic frame of government than most of the delegates really wanted. To the other Nationalists this provision of the committee's report made the Connecticut Compromise more objectionable than before. It accomplished its immediate purpose of procuring a majority for the report, but it failed in its ulterior purpose of making a more democratic Constitution than most of the delegates wanted for the more perfect Union. Later in the proceedings of the Convention many of the original Federalists, who had joined Franklin and a majority of the Unionists in approving the Connecticut Compromise with the Franklin proviso, shifted their position and joined the Nationalists in striking out most of the proviso and leaving the so-called compromise in more nearly its original form. This turn of affairs was denounced by several of the delegates, who had supported the Compromise only because of the addition of the proviso, as a breach of trust.[15] For this reason, among others, Randolph and Mason of Virginia and Gerry of Massachusetts eventually refused to sign the finished Constitution. Franklin himself found his patience sorely tried, but his determination to set an example of good temper and political moderation prevented him from repudiating the final result of the Convention's work.

The Federal Union, as the final product of the first of the great compromises continues to be called, was the creature of expediency rather than of principle. It was the empirical solution of a dangerous conflict between the two rival principles of nationalism and federalism. Its form originated in a casual adjustment of the differences between factions in the Convention favoring a centralized and a decentralized government for the more perfect Union. The justification of the particular mixture of nationalism and federalism, which was finally adopted, depended upon its practical capacity to furnish a durable foundation for the continuous collaboration of these same factions in framing a government for the more perfect Union. The bicameral national-federal Congress would have to fit into a suitable place in the general system of government contrived by the Convention. Its value cannot be appraised without considering the other principal features of the system. Indeed, its essential nature cannot be rightly understood without analyzing the relations between the legislative department of the Union government, which was the immediate product of the Connecticut Compromise and modified Franklin proviso, and the other departments of the government of the more perfect Union, into the construction of which other principles besides nationalism and federalism also entered.

22

The first test of the plan for a National-Federal Union — to give the Federal Union its proper name — was its acceptance by the state ratifying conventions. The record of the proceedings in these conventions shows that the plan was not equally acceptable to the large and the small states.[16] The latter, on the whole, seemed much the better pleased with their bargain. Delaware was the first state to ratify, and New Jersey, Georgia, and Connecticut quickly followed. In the first three of these state conventions ratification was accomplished after only a short debate and by a unanimous vote. In all the large states, on the other hand, except Pennsylvania, the debate was long and doubtful, and the result close. In Pennsylvania, which was the second state to ratify, the opponents of unconditional ratification complained that the friends of the new Constitution had acted without due notice and had rushed the opposition off their feet. For years after the new Constitution went into effect, and long after Pennsylvania had joined Virginia in the Democratic-Republican opposition, Delaware and New Jersey remained loyal supporters of the Federalist Party. Delaware continued one of its most devoted adherents until the end. There were, of course, various reasons for these later political differences, but there can be no doubt that the people of the small states believed their special interests had been well served by the action of the Philadelphia Convention. The ratification of the new Constitution, however, was a victory neither for the principle of federalism, in the proper sense of that term, nor for that of nationalism. The Unionist delegations had done their work well in forcing the adoption of a mixture of both principles. Ratification was a triumph for temporizing leadership, enlightened opportunism, and a sound spirit of moderation in politics.

NATURAL LIMITS TO THE POWER OF NUMERICAL MAJORITIES

Madison's principle of the natural limits to the power of numerical majorities in a popular government was derived from what he believed to be the facts of human nature.[17] Men were prone to disagree with one another, he had observed, for reasons of many different kinds or even for no reason at all. But the most important cause of disagreement, he was convinced, was "the various and unequal distribution of property." He cited an impressive variety of special interests among property owners which could produce political conflicts in any state where all kinds of people were free to pursue their happiness with the aid of governmental power. First, however, among the causes of political

23

conflict in free states he put the distinction between those who hold property, regardless of its form or amount, and those who are without property.

This economic interpretation of politics was endorsed and emphasized during the debates in the Convention of 1787 by two of Madison's closest associates among the National leaders. Alexander Hamilton gave the theory of economic determinism its most lucid and vigorous expression.[18] "In every community where industry is encouraged," he declared, according to Madison's report, in an elaborate speech on June 18th expounding his political philosophy, "there will be a division of it into the few and the many. Hence separate interests will arise . . . Give all power to the many, they will oppress the few. Give all power to the few, they will oppress the many." According to Judge Yates's report, Hamilton was more explicit. "All communities divide themselves into the few and the many. The first are the rich and wellborn, the other the mass of the people." Gouverneur Morris, in an extended speech on July 2nd, committed himself to the same conception of the class structure of the American economy.[19] These aristocratic young Nationalists developed their whole system of political ideas from the assumption that there were two and only two principal divisions of the people, the upper classes and the masses, and that this social dichotomy was the basic fact of politics.

Hamilton and Morris drew from their simple theory of class struggle the conclusion that one of the branches of the Congress should be an organ for the special representation of the rich. They wished the Senate to be capable of checking the abuse of power by the representatives of the "masses" in the popular branch of the national legislature. "The aristocratic body," Morris declared, "should be as independent and firm as the democratic." To this end he urged that its membership should possess "great personal property," that it should have "the aristocratic spirit," and that "it must love to lord it through pride." He expressed these extreme aristocratic notions with astonishing candor. "The rich," he declared, "will strive to establish their dominion and enslave the rest. They always did. They always will." The proper security against an abuse of their power, he believed, was "to form them into a separate interest. The two forces will then control each other." The stubborn opposition by all the aristocratic Nationalist delegates to the equal representation of the states in the Senate may be at least partly explained by their desire to establish the upper branch of the Congress upon the principles avowed by Hamilton and

Morris. Several of the leading Nationalists advocated special representation for wealth in the organization of the Senate and none of them expressly repudiated the aristocratic theory of class struggle.

The representatives of the rich in the Convention of 1787 were apparently in a position to frame a government which would give them assurance of protection against the poor, if they had deemed it politic to do so. Two-thirds of the delegates were wealthy landowners or merchants, or professional men connected with the families of wealthy landowners and merchants and largely dependent upon these classes for clients and professional success. They composed a clear majority of the delegations from nine of the states represented in the Convention. If these delegates had wished to act as Gouverneur Morris asserted that the rich were universally disposed to do, they could easily have dominated the proceedings in their own interest. In fact, Hamilton's and Morris's schemes for the organization of the Senate were rejected by the Convention and their arguments seemed to have fallen on deaf ears. Either the aristocratic members of the Convention were not so devoted to the interests of their class as Morris supposed, or considerations of political expediency persuaded them to seek the desired protection in some other way than by establishing an avowedly aristocratic senate to balance the power of the more popular branch of the Congress. The delegates generally did not choose to discuss the theory of the class struggle and the extent of their class consciousness must be inferred from their votes rather than from their speeches.

The approximately one-third of the delegates who did not qualify as aristocrats by the nature of their occupation and family connections consisted chiefly of lawyers. Most of them had been born in humble circumstances, had been forced to struggle against adversity for their educations, and were practicing their profession in small country towns, where they were dependent on local tradesmen and neighboring farmers or planters for their clients. Of these James Wilson had attained the greatest professional success, advancing from an obscure practice on the Pennsylvania frontier to a leading place at the Philadelphia bar. But Wilson retained the democratic principles of his youth and became an outspoken advocate on the floor of the Convention of the rights of the common man.[20] He declared that "all men wherever placed have equal rights and are equally entitled to confidence." He insisted that "the majority of people wherever found ought in all questions to govern the minority." He could not agree that "property was the sole or the primary object of government and society." On the contrary, "the culti-

25

vation and improvement of the human mind was the most noble object." These country lawyers, however, cannot fairly be described as members of the "masses." They belonged definitely to that characteristically American social phenomenon, the middle class. They furnished competent and effective spokesmen for what was in 1787 the largest and most important element in the structure of the American economy, the rural middle class.[21]

The outstanding representative of the urban middle class in the Convention of 1787 was Benjamin Franklin.[22] This sensationally successful printer and publisher had accumulated substantial wealth by his enterprise and thrift and in his old age could easily qualify as a member of the aristocracy, if the test of membership be the ownership of property. But he began his career as a humble printer's apprentice and steadily followed his trade as long as he was actively engaged in business. In colonial politics he was long associated with the opposition to the Pennsylvania proprietors and big merchants and he retained to the close of his life his warm sympathies with the common man. In the Convention he led the fight against property qualifications for voting and holding office under the Constitution. He was too big a man to devote himself to any interest short of that of the public, as he understood it. If he must be classified politically, it cannot be as a conventional aristocrat. His uniformly even temper and conciliatory deportment and consistent adherence to moderate measures marked him as an excellent specimen of the typical middle-class politician.

Middle-class politicians were scattered among the delegations from most of the states. Virginia and South Carolina were the conspicuous exceptions. But only the Connecticut and New York delegations were controlled by their middle-class members. Of the other delegations, that from North Carolina seemed most responsive to middle-class points of view. The middle-class delegations were in no position to challenge the leadership of the aristocrats in the Convention. But at the greatest crisis of the Convention, that over the basis of representation in the Senate, middle-class delegates held the balance of power. Their influence on the character of the Constitution was greater than their numbers.

The disproportionate influence of the middle-class delegates is more clearly disclosed by their distribution among the three great factions in the Convention. Among the Nationalists their numbers were few, but these few included Franklin and Wilson. Among the original Federalists they were more numerous, accounting for half of the total membership of this faction. Among them were its most active members, Sherman, Paterson, and Luther Martin. But the influence of the middle-class delegates was greatest among the Unionists, who held the balance of power in the Convention and contributed most to the solution of its greatest crisis. Oliver Ellsworth, whose leadership of the fight for the Connecticut Compromise marked the turning-point in the framing of the Constitution, was an outstanding member of this faction. A majority of the delegates who changed their votes in order to make possible the adoption of the Connecticut Compromise with the Franklin proviso were middle-class Unionists. Probably no members of the Convention were better satisfied with the final draft of the Constitution than these same middle-class Unionists.

In the light of these facts it becomes possible to appraise more accurately the contributions of the three great factions to the framing of the Constitution. The aristocratic Nationalists are entitled to the credit for taking the lead in the production of the Virginia plan and indeed in the whole course of the struggle to form a stronger Union. The original Federalists, both the aristocratic and the middle-class members of the faction, are entitled to the credit for forcing the issue when the aristocratic Nationalists strove to carry their plan for a high-toned centralized government too far. But it was the middle-class Unionists together with the middle-class Nationalist, Franklin, who are entitled to the chief credit for working out the first great compromise which made possible the eventual success of the Convention of 1787. These are conclusions which make it impossible to accept the simple aristocratic theory of the class struggle propounded by Hamilton and Gouverneur Morris.

Madison's theory of the natural limits to the power of numerical majorities of the people offered an alternative to the special representation of the rich in the Senate as a means of assuring some protection for that particular minority against the abuse of power in the special interest of the "masses." He was not as anxious as Morris and Hamilton to secure for the great landowners and big merchants a preferred position in one branch of the Congress. He was less sure that the danger of oppression by the representatives of the "indigent" in the other branch was so great as to make necessary a special organ of government for the protection of the "opulent." The diversification of interests in a large country would put substantial obstacles in the way of joint action for common ends by all the various factions which would be needed to form a majority party capable of dictating the laws and ex-

27

ploiting the rest of the people. In short, he believed that what has become known as sectionalism would mitigate the violence of the class struggle in national politics and make for a salutary moderation in the use of power by the government of the more perfect Union.

The leading form of sectionalism in the politics of the original states was that of the East against the West. The East began at the seaboard and extended as far beyond tidewater as navigable rivers supplied cheap and easy transportation for the products of the farm and plantation. The lack of good roads hindered the development of the more distant lands and only extraordinary fertility of the soil and a most favorable terrain could compensate for the disadvantages of the back country. The merchants in the seaports and the farmers and planters in the more accessible rural areas were prone to align themselves against the settlers in the less favored rural areas and the pioneers on the frontier. But the struggle to subdue the wilderness stimulated the development of a vigorous and enterprising rural population which would not tamely submit to domination by the representatives of the "rich and wellborn." The eventual removal of the state capitals from the seaports to the interior in most of the larger states attested both the severity of the struggle and the generally westward course of political power.

In the Convention of 1787 the West was greatly underrepresented. The seaboard merchants managed to control the delegations in two of the largest states, Massachusetts and Pennsylvania, as well as in New Hampshire, and the great planters were in full control in Virginia and South Carolina. The New York delegation was the only one clearly dominated by the representatives of the local "West." The influence of the "West" was strong in the North Carolina delegation and for a part of the time also in that of Maryland. But all the members of the Convention knew that the various local "Wests" would be strongly represented in the state ratifying conventions, particularly in the larger states. The knowledge that the Constitution must be made acceptable to a substantial portion of the smaller independent farmers and planters, in order to be ratified, weighed heavily in the minds of the leaders of the Convention and sustained the efforts of middle-class delegates to make it more democratic than was originally intended by the aristocratic Nationalists. The conflict of interest between East and West burst into the open in the Convention only occasionally, notably in connection with the debates over the basis of representation in the House of Representatives [23] and over the admission of new states,[24] but it had much to do with the later insistence on the addition of a bill of rights to the original Constitution, particularly in the ratifying conventions of Massachusetts, New Hampshire, New York, Virginia, and the two Carolinas.

In the Philadelphia Convention the most important form of sectionalism was the division between North and South. Madison himself thought that these two sections were the major sections in national politics [25] and the course of the debates in the Convention supported this opinion.[26] The unequal distribution of slaves between the Northern and Southern states was indeed, as Madison asserted, the greatest single cause of conflict in the Convention. It afforded a striking illustration of his dictum that the primary source of faction in politics was the unequal distribution of property. The division between North and South existed in all three of the major political factions in the Convention and clearly demonstrated how even the divisions between the major social classes would yield to the demands of sectionalism in the broad field of national politics. So easy it appeared to be to form two major parties in national politics on the basis of an alignment of the North against the South, which would have constituted a perpetual threat of intolerable oppression of one section by the other, that nearly all the delegates, regardless of their various interests and prejudices, were willing to join in supporting the most generally acceptable measures designed to keep the slavery issue, if possible, out of national politics. The greatest of all the compromises, that over the representation of the states in the Senate, was influenced by the desire to maintain an equal balance between North and South in one branch of the Congress. A good constitution, in the opinion of the Convention leaders of all factions, was evidently one in which the division between the two most equally matched major sections would be subordinated to the less dangerous divisions between the more numerous minor sections. The great compromise over the basis of representation in the House of Representatives furnishes the most conclusive evidence of the determination of the Convention leaders to form a more perfect Union and of their skill in the management of pressures so strong as to threaten the very existence of any kind of Union.

The kind of sectionalism which the Convention considered most favorable to a sound system of national politics was that reflected in the composition of its most important select committee, the Committee of Detail. For working out the great compromises the Convention preferred the so-called grand committees, or committees of the states, consisting of one member from each state. There were altogether six of these grand committees, beginning with the Committee on the Organization of the Senate, which planned the first great compromise, providing for equal representation of the states in the upper branch of the Congress, and ending with the Committee on Postponed Matters and Unfinished Business, which planned the last great compromise on the organization of the executive and judicial departments of government. But for working out the details of the proposed Articles of Union, as the resolutions referred to the Committee of Detail were called, the Convention preferred a smaller committee, representing the principal sections within the main divisions of North against South and East against West. For this purpose a committee of five was deemed most suitable.

The composition of the Committee of Detail is of unique significance. In this committee not only was the first draft of the Constitution actually prepared, but also the foundation was laid for a lasting alignment of parties in national politics. The strategy of the Convention leaders was to form a Constitution which could command the support of all its principal factions and thereby provide a firm basis for the government of a stronger Union. This strategy attained its primary objective, since the committee did represent all the principal sections as well as the two principal classes, which were represented in the Convention itself, and it was able to bring in a unanimous report. But not all its members were equally pleased with the report and the division of opinion within the committee forecast the later divisions among the people of the country which underlay the permanent two-party system in national politics.

The Chairman of the Committee of Detail was John Rutledge of South Carolina. He had been the outstanding political leader of the Lower South in the Revolution and was the most vigorous of its spokesmen in the Convention. An able lawyer and a resolute politician, he commanded the confidence of the great planters throughout his section of the country and was determined to protect its interests, as understood by them, in devising a system of government for a more perfect Union. The Lower South was the least populous and important of the sections in 1787, but its people looked forward to a rapid growth in numbers and wealth and were not disposed to make what they considered excessive sacrifices for the sake of a stronger Union. Proximity to the Spanish Empire made the people of the Lower South desire a strong general government capable of providing for the common defense, but the apparent dependence of their prosperity upon the expansion of Negro slavery made them appreciate the importance of their peculiar sectional interests.

The Upper South was represented on the Committee of Detail by Edmund Randolph. He was a member of one of the first families in tidewater Virginia and thoroughly familiar with the problems of the aristocratic tobacco planters, whose major money crop formed the foundation for the prosperity of the section and who regarded themselves as mainly responsible for the protection of its interests. But his service as governor of his state had made him better acquainted than most members of the old aristocratic families with the needs and hopes of the plain farmers back from the coast and of the pioneers on the frontier. These new elements in the population of the Upper South were growing rapidly and were already formidable competitors for power in Maryland and Virginia and definitely in the ascendant in North Carolina. This section as a whole was the largest and most populous in the Union, but its influence in the Convention was weakened by the lack of solidarity among its three delegations. Governor Randolph reflected, in the vacillation and indecisiveness which marked his own course in the Convention, the conflicting interests of the people of the Upper South.

The Middle States were represented on the Committee of Detail by James Wilson. As a successful Philadelphia lawyer, he was qualified to speak for the big merchants who controlled the Pennsylvania delegation and, as a former practitioner in a small town in the back country, he could not be unmindful of the interests of the small farmers and frontier folk. But the open conflict between town and country in state politics put him in an equivocal position and made it difficult for him to represent effectively either the urban aristocracy or the rural middle class. As in the Upper South, the lack of sectional solidarity, enhanced by the disparity of size between Pennsylvania on the one hand, and New Jersey and Delaware on the other, made the three delegations from the Middle States less effective than might have been expected from the importance of their agriculture and commerce in the economy of the nation. This prosperous grain-growing section was well situated to hold the balance of power between North and South, but Wilson needed more than his great learning and firm democratic principles in order to make the most of his opportunity.

The North, like the South, was divided into two parts for the purpose of representation in the Committee of Detail. Oliver Ellsworth, represented the rural North, while the urban North was represented by Nathaniel Gorham. The former was well qualified to speak for the independent middle-class farmers whose sturdy self-reliance made the New England town meeting a symbol of popular government in revolutionary America and whose spirited enterprise sparked the development of rural New England and New York. But the political influence of rural New England was impaired by the recent uprising of the Shaysites in Massachusetts and the general disaffection of the farmers on the poorer and less accessible soils, and that of rural New York by the uncoöperative attitude of Governor Clinton at the head of the dominant upstate faction in state politics. Ellsworth's political shrewdness and parliamentary skill made him a more important factor in the sectional and class struggles within the Convention than might have been expected under the circumstances and enabled him to play perhaps the decisive role in the deliberations of the Committee of Detail.

The success of the New England merchants in getting control of the delegations from both Massachusetts and New Hampshire gave them a disproportionate influence in the Convention. Gorham was not the foremost representative of the commercial interests in the Convention, but he was thoroughly familiar with the problems of maritime New England, had gained useful experience in Massachusetts politics, and enjoyed considerable prestige among the delegates from all sections as the most recent President of the Continental Congress. His election by the Convention as chairman of its Committee of the Whole was a mark of respect for his state as well as for himself, but his personal abilities were adequate to justify his selection for one of the five places on the Committee of Detail. Since he must be classified as a Unionist and an upper-class delegate, his selection for this important committee gave the Unionists a majority of three votes against two for the Nationalists in its membership, and gave its upper-class members the same preponderance over its middle-class members. Gorham and Rutledge alone belonged to both majorities, a circumstance favorable to the famous combination between Massachusetts and South Carolina which took the lead in the sectional conflicts within the Convention during its later stages.

The pattern of sectional politics, as it developed in the Convention, was determined by the support of the Massachusetts–South Carolina combination by Connecticut. The great problem of the Committee of Detail was the definition of the powers of the Congress. A logical combination would seem to have been one between the two Northern

32

sections and the Middle States against the South. Great efforts, how-ever, had been made before the appointment of the Committee of Detail to prevent such an alignment of sections by timely compromises over the basis of representation in both branches of the Congress, and the Committee of Detail was doubtless expected to adhere to the spirit of these compromises. Moreover, Ellsworth and Wilson, middle-class delegates who might have made common cause with each other on issues affecting the social basis of the Constitution, were divided by their different views concerning the place of the states in the more perfect Union. Thus it became easier for the middle-class Unionist, Ellsworth, to join the two upper-class Unionists in defining the powers of the Congress than for the middle-class Nationalist, Wilson, to effect a combination of three sections in which he could take a satisfactory part.

The adjustment of conflicts of interest between minor sections of the country in such a way as to avoid precipitating disruptive conflicts between major sections is best illustrated by the controversy over the powers of the Congress to lay taxes and to regulate commerce. The Committee of Detail agreed that both the tax power and the commerce power should be granted to the government of the more perfect Union. But the interests of different sections in the use of these great powers differed sharply and the Committee sought to moderate future inter-sectional conflicts by limiting the powers to be granted so as to prevent their abuse by factious majorities. No navigation act, to promote the welfare of the maritime interests, was to be adopted by less than a two-thirds majority in each branch of the Congress, and no act to prohibit the slave trade, or even to tax it, was to be adopted by any majority, nor was any tax to be paid on articles exported from any state. The interest of the producers of the leading export crops, particularly tobacco, in the last provision was obvious, and that of the great planters of the Lower South in the prevention of interference with the importa-tion of slaves was even more manifest. All the producers of articles for export naturally would dislike a navigation act. The importance of guarding against the development of these various sources of local grievances into a major intersectional conflict was clearly understood by the leaders of the Convention.

The particular combination of concessions to special interests, recommended by the Committee of Detail, presumably at the instance of its New England and South Carolina members, did not meet with the approval of a majority of the Convention. The whole question of a

33

more suitable compromise was recommitted to a new Grand Committee and a new basis of intersectional adjustment was worked out. The
Middle States took the lead in making the details of the proposed compromise somewhat more favorable to the Northern maritime interests
and less agreeable to the Southern planters. Most of the Southern delegations resisted the new compromise to the last, but South Carolina
continued to adhere to its bargain with New England. None of the
minor sections was altogether satisfied with the final arrangement. Indeed, such active and influential sectional politicians as Edmund
Randolph and George Mason of Virginia were seriously disaffected by
the outcome. But a sharp alignment of the major sections against one
another was successfully avoided and all the delegations remaining in
the Convention were able to move on to other problems with unimpaired capacity for fruitful deliberation.

This outcome of the factional disputes within the Convention vindicated Madison's confidence that in a large country the variety of interests, growing particularly out of the ownership of property of different kinds, would produce such a development of sectionalism in
national politics as to make difficult the formation of great factions,
supported by popular majorities infused with a single-minded purpose
to pursue their own special interests, regardless of injury to others,
and able to control the use of the legislative power. It strengthened his
argument that all kinds of minorities could venture to enter the more
perfect Union without fear of exposure with inadequate means of self-
protection to oppression by adverse majorities. It seemed to sustain his
principle of the natural limits to the power of numerical majorities in
a popular government.

When Governor Randolph, on behalf of the Nationalist leaders,
agreed to drop the word "national" from the Virginia plan and these
leaders presently began to call themselves also Federalists, they were
not aware that they were laying the foundation of the party system
in national politics. Their object was to find a basis for agreement, not
only among all the leading political factions in the Convention, but
also among all the leading economic interests. General Washington's
abhorrence of "the alternate domination of one faction over another,"
as he described the two-party system in his "Farewell Address," may
have been strengthened by his experience in the presidency, but it was
consistent with his policy in the Convention. He already recognized
the danger of founding parties on geographical discriminations and
had no intention of organizing a partial combination of sectional in-

terests for the purpose of framing a constitution which would enable the dominant combination of interests to control the government of the more perfect Union for its own particular advantage. He sincerely wanted a constitution which would serve the public interest. Gouverneur Morris, in his funeral oration after the death of Washington, said the purpose was to "raise a standard to which the wise and honest can repair." The plan was to provide for government not by parties, but by superior persons — an aristocracy.

The event was not in accordance with the plan. The finished Constitution was acceptable to all the factions in the Convention, but it was not equally acceptable to them. It was not acceptable at all, or at least not without significant changes, to the most powerful class not adequately represented in the Convention — the rural middle class. In order to procure its ratification and put it into effective operation it was necessary to form a party from the sectional and class interests which had worked together in the Convention. As Madison had predicted, it was difficult to bring together a harmonious combination of such various and conflicting interests. It was impossible to hold them all together for the purpose of governing under the Constitution. The representatives of sectional and class interests who continued to work together in national politics formed a political party in spite of themselves, which under Washington's reluctant leadership made the unplanned institution of organized partisanship an essential feature of the Constitution of the more perfect Union.

It is not surprising that people of the "middling sort," particularly the rural middle class, should have been slow to appreciate the merits of the new Constitution.[27] They were naturally suspicious of a plan, prepared by a convention composed chiefly of the "opulent" and recommended by avowed spokesmen for the upper classes, on the ground, among others, that the proposed government was one which a numerical majority of the people would find it difficult to control through their chosen representatives. They would naturally have put greater trust in a government made by politicians expressing more confidence in the plain people. But they were aware that proposals to establish property qualifications for voting and office-holding under the new Constitution, and to give greater weight to wealth in the apportionment of Congressmen, had been rejected by the Convention. The decisions on these basic issues, actually taken by the Convention, were less objectionable than the language of its more aristocratic leaders. The Unionists, who talked less of principles than either the Nationalists or the original Federalists, had used their superiority in numbers and delegations to good advantage. The new Constitution was a kind of peace treaty between the sections, or at least between all of them except the various local "Wests," on which the "middling sort" of people as well as "superior" persons could take their stand together. The eventual addition of the Bill of Rights must be regarded as a further concession to the "middling sort" of people in fulfillment of promises to the representatives of the rural middle class in the state ratifying conventions. The adoption of the new Constitution, including the Bill of Rights, was a great triumph, not for the "opulent" alone, but, under the circumstances, especially for the middle classes.

THE SEPARATION OF POWERS

Madison's political thinking, like that of a majority of his associates in the Constitutional Convention, was profoundly influenced by the favorite political idea of the eighteenth century in the English-speaking part of the world. It is the experience of the ages, the scholarly Montesquieu had written,[28] that every man who attains power is prone to abuse it. He goes forward until he finds his limit. If power is not to be abused, Montesquieu concluded, then it is necessary in the nature of things that power be made a check to power. The American Revolutionists had reason enough, they felt, to believe that their own experience was in harmony with that of the ages. To Madison and most of his fellow framers, the maxim of statecraft which Montesquieu derived from that experience seemed thoroughly consistent with the nature of things. The most satisfactory form of government, they were convinced, would be a system of checks and balances based upon the principle of the separation of powers.

The framers were not disposed to make any exception for a government conducted in the name of the people themselves. In a popular government, as in other kinds of government, some body or bodies in particular would have to be entrusted with the power to govern. Even a majority of the people, like lesser portions of mankind, could abuse their power, and, the framers generally believed, were likely to do so unless effectively restrained by suitable constitutional limitations. Most of the framers, though born loyal subjects of a king, had come to believe in popular government. Few, however, believed that a sovereign people would be wholly free from the natural faults associated with all possessors of governmental powers. As Madison put it,[29] "you must first enable the government to control the governed; and in the next place oblige it to control itself." His conclusion followed with exemplary logic. "A dependence on the people is, no doubt, the primary control on the government; but experience has taught mankind the necessity of auxiliary precautions."

The authors of the Virginia plan, which was the original blueprint for the frame of government of the more perfect Union, proceeded upon the assumption that the primary seat of power in a national government would be the popular branch of the national legislature. The House of Representatives therefore would be the governmental organ most likely to abuse its power. The problem of the planners was to devise checks upon the authority of those speaking in the name of a majority of the people that would be capable of keeping them from usurping the authority of other branches of the government and thereby upsetting the balance of the system. To this end the Virginia plan provided for three main checks: first, a second branch of the national legislature, designed to represent the minorities deemed most in danger of oppression at the hands of the representatives of popular majorities; second, an independent executive, armed with a veto against legislation threatening either his own independence or the national interest, if in his judgment a measure upon which both branches of the national legislature agreed should still fall dangerously short of serving the general public interest; and third, an independent judiciary, authorized to administer justice according to law and incidentally, if possible, to keep legislators and executive officers from encroaching upon the province of the judges. Madison, fortified by his faith in the natural limits to the power of popular majorities in an extensive democratic republic, expressed great confidence in the practical capacity of suitable constitutional limitations to keep the House of Representatives within bounds and thereby to maintain the supremacy of the general public interest over the various special interests, which might be tempted to combine forces in the House of Representatives for the advancement of their private ends.

The Virginia planners' scheme for a second chamber, consisting of persons elected by the first, seems ill-designed to accomplish its purpose. If its probable operation is viewed in the light of the development of the two-party system in national politics, such a second chamber would seem incapable of checking the activities of the majority party in the House of Representatives. Presumably the aristocratic Nationalists, who drew up the Virginia plan, had in mind the fixing of high property qualifications for election to the Senate, in order that it might have the will to protect the interests of that minority which they feared would most need protection, namely, the "opulent." The action of the Convention, in promptly rejecting this feature of the plan and substituting the system of election by the state legislatures, would not necessarily have made a less aristocratic Senate than the Virginians wanted. Indeed, some of the original state legislatures, with their own aristocratic senates, were likely to elect senators more acceptable to the "opulent" than those that might have been elected by the national House of Representatives. The objection of the aristocratic Nationalists to the method of electing senators by the state legislatures arose rather from their justified apprehension that this method of election would facilitate the retention of what they regarded as the vicious system of equal representation for the states in the Senate.[30] Nevertheless, the Senate, as finally established, must have seemed to them a body capable of giving an amount of protection to the interests of the "opulent" which would contribute substantially toward maintaining what they would have regarded as a healthy balance in the government of the more perfect Union.[31]

The organization of an executive department, which would be strong enough to check the House of Representatives, and if necessary the Senate also, without becoming too strong and tipping the balance too much against the Congress, gave the framers of the Constitution their most perplexing problem.[32] The Virginia planners could not agree among themselves on the details of this part of their plan, but proposed the election of an executive, to consist of an undetermined number of persons and to serve for an undetermined number of years, by the legislative department of the government. Washington and Madison preferred that a single person should be the chief executive, that he should be armed with an effective veto against objectionable legislation, and that he should serve for a long term of years or be eligible for reëlection without any limit to the number of terms. Randolph and Mason feared that such a powerful and independent chief executive would become too powerful and independent and would upset the balance of the system. They favored a plural executive and a short term of service with a prohibition against reëlection. Other Nationalists, however, favored even greater authority and security of tenure for the chief executive. Wilson wanted to secure his independence by some system of popular election. Hamilton wanted him to serve for life, or at least during good behavior, and to possess an absolute veto over objectionable legislation. These Nationalists deplored the consequences of electing the executive by the legislative department, since such an electoral process would make the former dependent on the latter, at least at the beginning of his term, and the possibility of reëlection would make for a perpetual dependence.

The original Federalists, on the other hand, proposed a weak executive. They seemed to want that department of the government to be dependent on the Congress and to care less than the Nationalists for the principle of the separation of powers. The most democratic views were expressed by Franklin. He had no liking for the principle of the separation of powers, as expounded by British political theorists, or for the practice of government under the British Constitution, as he had observed it at the Court of St. James's. He would have preferred something like the present British system, in which the House of Commons chooses the Ministers and supervises, if it does not actually direct, the processes of government. Some of the framers understood the importance of the Ministers in the British system of parliamentary government, but none of them foresaw the development of British democracy under the forms of a limited monarchy. Only a few of them understood the importance of the power vested in the Crown to dissolve the Parliament and recognized that the relationship which they were trying to establish between the President and the Congress was not the same as that which then existed between the King, the Lords, and the Commons.

The Convention changed its mind several times concerning the organization of the executive, and not until near the end of its deliberations was it able to agree upon the plan which was finally adopted. The details were worked out in the Committee on Postponed Matters and Unfinished Business as a part of the last great compromise between the Nationalists and the original Federalists. It was a compromise which sought to freeze the relationship between the President and the Congress in a form which was supposed to reproduce the essentials of the contemporary British system. In fact, it did not correspond to the British system in any phase of its modern development. It was in 1784 that the modern form of cabinet government really began, when Parliament was dissolved in order that the younger Pitt might appeal to the people to give him a majority in the House of Commons. The relationship between the President and the Congress, established by this compromise, made the development of a more democratic system of government through the agency of political parties more difficult in

America than in Great Britain. It made the democratization of what were supposed to be similar systems of checks and balances contingent upon the development of different techniques in the two countries.

The final plan for the organization of the executive was part of a compromise which included also a plan for the organization of the judiciary.[33] The Virginia plan originally provided for the election of the judges by the legislative department of the national government. The Nationalist leaders, however, seem to have really preferred the election of judges by the more aristocratic branch of that department and, when the opportunity arose, they promptly accepted an amendment to their plan, providing for the election of a Supreme Court by the Senate. The original Federalists, on the other hand, proposed the appointment of Supreme Court judges by the executive department of the government. Both factions agreed that the Supreme Court judges should hold office during good behavior and should have jurisdiction over cases of impeachment as well as over cases arising in the ordinary course of the judicial process. Both wanted an independent judiciary, but there was no agreement upon a logical method of achieving independence. In applying the principle of the separation of powers, the various state delegations seemed to be influenced less by political theory than by the actual practice in the state governments with which they were most familiar or which they deemed most successful.

More important in the development of a system of checks and balances than the differences over the organization of the judiciary were those over its powers.[34] The Nationalists, relying upon the use of political processes for maintaining a balance between the three departments as well as for maintaining the superiority of the Union over the states, wished to join the judges with the executive in the exercise of the veto over legislation. The actual proposal in the Virginia plan was that "the executive and a convenient number of the judiciary ought to compose a Council of Revision with authority to examine every act of the national legislature before it shall operate, and every act of a particular [that is, state] legislature before a negative thereon [that is, by the national legislature] shall be final; and that the dissent of the said Council shall amount to a rejection," unless overridden by the national legislature. The original Federalists, on the other hand, made no provision in the New Jersey plan for an executive or joint executive-judicial veto of legislative bills before their final enactment into law. Their plan, however, contained the significant proposals (1) that all acts of the Congress, made "by virtue and in pursuance of" its constitu-

40

tional powers, and all treaties made and ratified "under the authority of the United States," should be "the supreme law" of the states, in so far as they might be applicable to the states or the people thereof; (2) that the state judges should be bound to observe the supreme law, regardless of conflicting provisions in the laws of the states; and (3) that the federal executive should have power to enforce such law, if necessary by calling out the state militia. It is clear that the original Federalists were more interested than the Nationalists in establishing a reign of law in the government of the more perfect Union. They relied primarily upon judicial processes for the maintenance of the supremacy of the Union and the authority of its laws, and their emphasis on the constitutional limitations on the powers of the Congress would necessarily enhance the influence of the judges in the whole system of checks and balances.

There has been much controversy over the origin of the American doctrine of judicial review. During periods of discontent with the exercise of the judicial veto by the Supreme Court there have been charges (1) that the power to declare laws unconstitutional was not a part of the judicial power, as understood by the framers; (2) that it was not vested in the Supreme Court under the Constitution; and (3) that the practice of declaring legislative acts, especially acts of Congress, null and void after they had gone into operation involved a usurpation of power by the judiciary. The record of the debates in the Convention does not support these charges.[35] The Nationalists' proposal for a Council of Revision, in which the judges would be joined with the executive in the exercise of the veto power, was opposed not only by the original Federalists, but also by leading Unionists and even by some of the Nationalists themselves. Though it was submitted three times to the Convention for approval, it was consistently rejected. The discussions disclosed a general conviction that the judges should be kept out of politics as much as possible by excluding them from any connection with the making of the laws. The unshakeable conclusion was that they should be limited to interpreting the laws that were brought before them in the ordinary course of litigation.

The members of the Convention understood that the power of the judges to interpret the laws was broad enough to include a power to disapprove and refuse to enforce ordinary legislative acts found to be in conflict with the fundamental law set forth in the Constitution. This was stated explicitly in the debate on the Nationalists' proposal to give the Congress power to set aside state legislation found by it to be in conflict with the authority of the Union.[36] It was clearly implied in the debate over their proposal to join the judges with the executive in the exercise of a veto against acts of the Congress.[37] Only one member of the Convention, John F. Mercer of Maryland, one of the least influential of all the delegates, expressly repudiated the exercise of a judicial veto as an incident of the judicial process.[38] He disapproved of "the doctrine that the judges, as expositors of the Constitution, should have authority to declare a law void." He thought laws "ought to be well and cautiously made," according to Madison's report, "and then to be uncontrollable." John Dickinson, a much more important delegate, thereupon observed that he "was strongly impressed with the remark of Mr. Mercer as to the power of the judges to set aside the law. He thought no such power ought to exist." But he proceeded to make a further comment of great significance. "He was at the same time," he declared, "at a loss what expedient to substitute." Those other delegates, if any, who shared Mr. Dickinson's feelings were similarly at a loss. No other expedient was suggested. A strong and preponderant majority of the delegates were certainly satisfied with the role assigned to the judges in maintaining both the supremacy of the Union and the balance of the political system established by the Constitution.

The doctrine of judicial review, as understood by the framers, was most clearly expressed by Oliver Ellsworth in the Connecticut ratifying convention.[39] "This Constitution," he explained, "defines the extent of the powers of the general government. If the general legislature should at any time overleap their limits, the judicial department is a constitutional check. If the United States go beyond their powers, if they make a law which the Constitution does not authorize, it is void and the judicial power, the national judges, who, to secure their impartiality, are to be made independent, will declare it to be void. On the other hand, if the states go beyond their limits, if they make a law which is a usurpation upon the general government, the law is void; and upright independent judges will declare it to be so."

Some of the leading Nationalists remained to the end unconvinced that an independent judicial process was superior to the mixing of the judges with the executive for preserving the supremacy of the Union and maintaining a suitable system of checks and balances. The power of the judges, Wilson believed,[40] "did not go far enough. Laws may be unjust, may be unwise, may be dangerous, may be destructive; and yet may not be so unconstitutional as to justify the judges in refusing to give them effect. Let them have a share in the revisionary power, and they will have an opportunity of taking notice of these characters of a law, and of counteracting by the weight of their opinions the improper views of the Legislature." Madison held similar views.[41] But the judgment of most of the delegates is clear. "No maxim," one of them declared,[42] "was better established" than that which led to the separation of the judicial veto from that of the executive.

The last of the great compromises between the Nationalists and the original Federalists, unlike the first, was a genuine compromise. Madison, Gouverneur Morris, and Rufus King, who represented the aristocratic Nationalists as well as the three largest states on the Committee on Postponed Matters and Unfinished Business, wanted a strong and independent chief executive. Sherman of Connecticut and Brearley of New Jersey, who represented the original Federalists, wanted a strong and independent judiciary. These two experienced state judges understood as well as any members of the Convention the importance of a strong and independent judiciary in a durable system of constitutional government. Brearley, indeed, was a member of a state court which had actually declared a legislative act unconstitutional. John Dickinson was the leading Unionist on the committee, but the Unionists, though in a majority, did not dominate the committee's proceedings. Moreover, the middle-class members of the Convention were not as strongly represented on this committee as on the first of the grand committees and did not exert as great an influence as before on the outcome of its deliberations. The reported plan was clearly the result of the give-and-take between the aristocratic Nationalists and the original Federalists. The Unionists were content to contribute a political atmosphere favorable to compromise.

The complicated system of interdepartmental relationships upon which the Committee on Postponed Matters and Unfinished Business finally succeeded in agreeing was a masterpiece of checks and balances. The aristocratic Nationalists were delighted with the establishment of a more independent and powerful executive than they had ventured to propose in their original plan. The original Federalists must have been equally delighted with the establishment of a more independent and powerful judiciary than had been originally contemplated. But the independence of the executive was compromised by the establishment of a process of impeachment, and the authority of the judiciary by the removal of the trial of impeachments from the courts to the Senate. The authority of the executive was strengthened by the rejection of all projects for the establishment of an executive council, but it was weakened by the requirement that important appointments, though to be made on the nomination of the President, should be subject to confirmation by the Senate. The arrangements for the election of the chief executive gave the large states a substantial advantage in the selection of candidates, but insured to the small states a disproportionate voice in the final election, unless the large states should be able to take concerted measures for the purpose of keeping the elections out of the House of Representatives. Whether this would be possible would depend upon the development of organized parties, and what form an unplanned institution of organized partisanship might take was beyond the range of vision in 1787.

It is evident that this complicated system of checks and balances was not based upon any logical application of the principle of the separation of powers. The President would have an important share in the legislative power through his possession of the veto and the Senate would have an important share in the executive power through its control over appointments. The conduct of foreign affairs was sharply separated from that of domestic affairs and the exclusion of the House of Representatives from any share in the treaty-making power, except as its coöperation might be required for carrying treaties into effect by appropriating money, imposed an additional and unpredictable check upon the power of numerical majorities of the people under the new political system. If the primary objects of the system were to prevent the representatives of the people from abusing their powers and to protect minorities against "the turbulence and follies of democracy," as Randolph put it in one of his speeches,[43] the disregard of logic in the construction of the system might be justified by the better balance to be expected from the multiplication of checks. But not all the framers believed in a system of checks and balances,[44] and some of those who shared that belief feared that the multiplication of checks had been carried too far and that the system would become unbalanced and end in either aristocracy or monarchy.[45]

The last of the great compromises, like its predecessors, was not altogether satisfactory to the Convention. There was still complaint that the Senate, though stripped of some of its great authority under the previous unsatisfactory arrangement, remained too strong, and that the plan as a whole continued to be too aristocratic. The final decision in presidential elections was therefore transferred from the Senate to the House of Representatives, but despite James Wilson's forceful arguments all efforts to give the House an equal voice in the treaty-making process failed. In this instance a narrow sectionalism turned the scale against a more democratic nationalism. No delegate would have contended that the final result represented a logical application of the principle of the separation of powers, or, it may be surmised, that a suitable system of checks and balances could have been based on such an application of the principle.

The most serious defect in the actual system of checks and balances, from the standpoint of the delegates who believed in the principle of a separation of powers, was the absence of a bill of rights.[46] Repeated efforts were made toward the end of the Convention to secure the addition of a bill of rights to the draft constitution. They all failed, either because delegates had little faith in the practical efficacy of declarations of general principles or because they believed that the fundamental rights of Americans were sufficiently protected by the declarations in the state constitutions and by the incorporation in the Federal Constitution of provisions protecting the most important rights against abridgment by the Congress. The delegates were practical men and tended to regard the state declarations of rights as educational papers, addressed to the peoples of the states and to their representatives in the legislatures and on the juries, rather than as legal documents, addressed to the judges and designed for their guidance in the formal administration of justice. The provisions inserted in the body of the draft constitution were, to be sure, more practical. The prohibition of the passage of any bill of attainder or *ex post facto* law was of this character. As Dr. Hugh Williamson of North Carolina said,[47] such a prohibitory clause "may do good here, because the judges can take hold of it." It might be supposed that the thought would have occurred to the delegates that the judges would be able to take hold of other provisions in a suitable bill of rights and make them the basis for a more effective use of the judicial power in defense of the rights of the people. But the delegates were too impatient or too weary at the close of the Convention to give due thought to such a possibility. They adjourned without doing what they might have done to improve the system of checks and balances by strengthening in this way the judicial power.

The last of the great compromises completed the Convention's response to Madison's challenge to all framers of constitutions. The challenge set up two main tests of success in framing a constitution: (1) to enable the government to control the governed; and (2) to oblige it to control itself. The response was based on an agreement that

45

the government must be a popular government. The primary responsibility for conducting public affairs under the proposed constitution, therefore, was vested in the House of Representatives, but the only powers vested exclusively in the House were to judge the elections and qualifications of its members, choose its officers, adopt rules of procedure, and adjourn from day to day. All other powers vested in the House were divided between it and the other branches and departments of the government. Moreover, a sharp distinction was made between the fields of domestic and foreign affairs, and the authority of the House in the latter field was greatly inferior to its authority in the former. Whether these arrangements would furnish a satisfactory basis for a government deriving its just powers, in Jefferson's memorable phrase, from the consent of the governed would be for history to tell.

Madison's tests of good constitutional government put in general terms the perennial problem of popular government. This is, how to reconcile the right of popular majorities to rule as they please with the rights of minorities and of individuals to be ruled in a manner satisfactory to themselves. The clash of majority and minority interests creates a need for ascertaining, protecting, and promoting the general public interest. As Jefferson put it in his "First Inaugural": "Though the will of the majority is in all cases to prevail, that will, to be rightful, must be reasonable; . . . the minority possess their equal rights . . . to violate which would be oppression." Madison's three principles of government provided three different ways of adjusting majority and minority interests and of reconciling the various kinds of private interests with the public interest. The Convention deliberately adopted two of Madison's principles. The third was plainly implicit in its proceedings, though no effort was made to explore the implications of an unpredictable system of national parties.

No delegate was fully satisfied with the solution reached by the Convention. Franklin was the most conspicuous of its members who feared that the authority of the popular branch of the Congress was insufficient for its essential function. Washington was the most conspicuous among those who would have been better pleased with greater checks upon the authority of the House. Both agreed that not logic but only experience could give an acceptable answer to these doubts. Both felt that the acceptance of the Convention's plan by most of the members of all factions in the Convention was the best guaranty of future success and were more than willing that the experiment should be tried.

The process of ratifying the proposed Constitution supplied the best commentary on the performance of the Convention of 1787. The state ratifying conventions represented the people more adequately than the Federal Convention, since the delegates were more numerous and more fairly distributed among the various sections and classes of people. In general the various local "Wests" were duly represented, and the "middling sort" of persons, particularly the small independent farmers and country lawyers dependent upon such farmers for their professional success, were present in large, if not always preponderant, numbers. The contest was closest in the large states, particularly Massachusetts and Virginia, and in those which, though not yet among the largest, expected to grow rapidly, above all New York. The adherence of these states to the new Constitution was essential for the success of the more perfect Union. The support of substantial numbers of middle-class farmers and others of the "middling sort" was indispensable. The balance of power in these important ratifying conventions lay in the rural middle class. John Adams's theory,[48] that "the triple balance is so established by Providence in the constitution of nature that order without it can never be brought out of confusion and anarchy," was known to leading middle-class members of these state conventions,[49] though not always clearly understood by them. The fate of the more perfect Union, planned largely by upper-class statesmen, was determined by the middle class.

There was little objection on the part of middle-class delegates in the ratifying conventions to the principle of the separation of powers. There was not much objection to specific details of the proposed system of checks and balances. More objectionable was the small size of the House of Representatives. It seemed to some of the country lawyers and other middle-class spokesmen that a larger number of representatives, elected in smaller districts, would afford better representation to the kind of people for whom they spoke. It was evident that Washington had shown sound political sense at the close of the Convention, when he took the floor in person in order to recommend a reduction in the minimum size of a congressional district.[50] A widespread opinion was that a larger House of Representatives, the members of which would be closer to their constituents, would be a stronger House. The objection to the proposed system of checks and balances seemed to be, not that the Senate, the President, and the Supreme Court would be too strong, but that the popular branch of the Congress would be too weak.

Among these large-state middle-class delegates there was a strong demand for a national bill of rights. There seemed little awareness of the practical utility of a bill of rights as a basis for the protection of human rights by the Supreme Court, though Jefferson, writing from Paris,[51] had emphasized the possibility and the value of such a development of the judicial power. Middle-class spokesmen in the state conventions put their trust in juries rather than in judges. It was the educational value of bills of rights that seemed to weigh heavily in their minds. A national bill of rights would contribute to the political education of the people and of their representatives on federal juries and in the popular branch of the Congress. The promise of such a bill by the upper-class delegates in the state conventions seemed a significant mark of sympathy on their part with the aspirations of the common man. The fulfillment of the promise stood as a symbol of the unity of all classes in the more perfect Union. Thus the completion of the Constitution by the eventual addition of the Bill of Rights, though an actual triumph for the middle class, was also an expression of faith in the ideal of a classless people.

The ratification of the new Constitution and Bill of Rights by the necessary numbers of states attested the excellence of the American political way as well as the acceptability of the principles of government embodied in these documents. The essence of the former was well expressed by Franklin in his famous speech at the end of the Convention.[52] He did not claim that he was pleased with all the details of the Constitution, though the plan as a whole was certainly more satisfactory to him than were the original Nationalist and Federalist plans. But he was able to argue strongly that the Convention should not repudiate its own work. He closed his speech with a plea for a united front on the part of all the factions. "Much of the strength and efficiency of any government in procuring and securing happiness to the people," he observed, "depends on opinion — on the general opinion of the goodness of the government as well as of the wisdom and integrity of the governors." He hoped, therefore, that the members of the Convention would act heartily and unanimously in recommending the Constitution, wherever their influence might extend, and would turn their future thoughts and endeavors to the means of having it well administered. He wished that every delegate who might still have objections to it would, like himself on this occasion, "doubt a little of his own infallibility." Thus by precept and example Franklin extolled the middle way as the proper American way in politics.

48

The result of the whole process of constitution-making, including the adoption of the Bill of Rights, was an impressive demonstration of the political skill of the leading framers and of the good sense and moderate tempers of those associated with them throughout the enterprise. It also served to demonstrate that the leading principles of American politics were not derived, as Hamilton had intimated, from the division of the people into two main classes of rich and poor and the alleged supreme necessity of protecting each against the other, but rather from the existence of a powerful middle class and the likelihood that its special interests would ordinarily coincide with those of the whole body of people. Investigation of the political basis of the great compromises confirms the inferences drawn from that of the social and economic bases. The economic interests of the dominant elements in the politics of the several states tended to prevail in the framing of the Constitution without, however, resulting in the definitive establishment of an upper-class instrument of government. The Constitution of the more perfect Union was indeed, as the leading Unionists intended it to be, the framework for a union both of people and of states. It was a National as well as a Federal Union. Above all, it was a middle-class Union as well as, or even more than, an upper-class Union.

CHAPTER THREE

The Ordeal of the Constitution

THE UNEXPECTED DURABILITY OF THE CONSTITUTION

Looking back upon the framing of the Constitution with the advantage of political experience gained under eighty-one Congresses, thirty-two different Presidents, and thirteen Chief Justices, it is evident that the framers built better than they knew. Most of them would have claimed no great merit for many of its essential provisions, since they rested upon compromises dictated by political expediency rather than principle. The nature of the institutions created by such compromises could not be clearly explained. Much less could the institutions be fully justified upon any principles of government generally recognized and respected in 1787. Yet the Constitution still stands, the oldest written constitution in the world today.

It is not surprising that many of the framers had grave doubts about the Constitution and that few were ready to predict a long and useful life for the new instrument of national government. The debates in the Convention showed that its members knew the America of their own time well. But they could catch only uncertain glimpses of the America that was to come. What those glimpses revealed was not liked by all of them. Some shrank from the vision of an expanding West, opened to settlement by rugged and independent pioneers and filling up with men of vigorous and purposeful enterprise. Such men could not be kept down. But when they should take possession of the government of the more perfect Union, would they transform it into something very different, not only from what had been originally planned by the big planters and merchants, but also from what had been finally approved and adopted by the littler men in the state conventions and legislatures? Others shuddered at the fancied spectacle of great cities crowded with landless laborers, bent on measures for winning their bread and passing their time that would be utterly alien and perhaps hostile to the agrarian interests and rustic pleasures of the American people they knew. Would not such landless laborers, if they should become sufficiently numerous, be a menace, not only to the successors of the big planters and merchants in the original states, but also to the pioneers and settlers of the West and all those who might cherish the original American way? In short, how could the framers of a Constitution for a simple and mainly rural body politic expect that it would serve also the needs of a distant and perhaps fantastic future?

Grievous trials, which, if anticipated, would have made the framers of the Constitution even less confident of its future, were to be encountered in the years ahead. It nearly broke down in the midst of the first strenuous conflict over the presidency, and had to be amended before its true nature was clearly understood by the politicians who were trying to govern under it. It did break down under the strains and stresses of the great struggle over slavery, and was radically altered in the process of reconstructing a Union which might really become more perfect than before. The revolutions of the business cycle brought other stresses and strains which, if predictable, the framers might well have viewed with alarm. The years 1837, 1857, 1873, 1893, 1907, and 1929 mark crises of government as well as of business. Greater emergencies were created by the impact of foreign wars. The expansion of governmental authority during the recent World Wars was not marked by such outbursts of criticism as the Virginia and Kentucky resolutions or those of the Hartford Convention, but the necessity of tremendous national efforts demanded a concentration of power which put the serviceability of the Constitution to the severest tests.

Despite the misgivings of the framers, the Constitution was an immediate and impressive success. When unforeseen difficulties forced the adoption of the Eleventh and Twelfth Amendments, the lawmakers were careful to disturb the original frame of government as little as possible. The Congress which submitted the Twelfth Amendment might have gone further in revising the process of electing the presidents, since greater improvements could easily have been devised and might have been adopted under the pressure of the emergency. But already respect for an established and effective system of government was changing into reverence for institutions under which the country seemed to be rapidly growing prosperous and powerful. It was no longer good form to question the details of a constitution already credited with the qualities which command the success it had demonstrably achieved.

How much of its astonishing success was, in reality, the achievement of the extraordinary statesmen who first took the responsibility of governing under it is a question which cannot now be answered with useful exactitude. Washington and Jefferson could have governed wisely and perhaps well under constitutions greatly inferior to that under which they actually held power. Even John Adams, though he permitted the Congress to abuse its power with its Alien and Sedition Acts, had the good sense to keep the country out of war, when that was possible, notwithstanding great pressure from warmongers. None of these statesmen was entirely satisfied with the Constitution. But they were able to make the people of the United States feel satisfied with it, and that feeling of satisfaction has endured through great vicissitudes of fortune and great changes in the people themselves.

THE POLITICAL EFFECTS OF THE GROWTH OF CITIES

The changes in the character and condition of the people have been as spectacular as the vicissitudes of fortune under the instrument of government framed in 1787. The more perfect Union was designed to unite at the beginning fewer than four million persons and only thirteen states. It has come to be a Union of more than one hundred fifty millions of persons and forty-eight states. Nine of the present states contain a greater number of inhabitants each than the whole Union contained in 1787. But these numerical changes are trivial compared with the changes in the state of mind of the people and in their way of life.

The most spectacular and politically the most important of the changes in the American way of life has been the growth of cities. In 1787 there were only two urban centers in the United States large enough to be entitled to a representative of their own in Congress under the constitutional rule of apportionment. Besides Philadelphia and New York there were three other towns, Boston, Baltimore, and Charleston, which, though not possessing the number of inhabitants prescribed by the Constitution as the minimum for a representative in Congress, might have dominated the districts in which they were situated. In eight of the original thirteen states there was no town of as many as eight thousand inhabitants, and no congressional district

52

not controlled by rural voters. Of the 106 representatives under the first apportionment following the census of 1790, no fewer than 101 were elected mainly by farmers and planters.

At the present time the people of the United States are piled up in cities in the very manner which caused Jefferson, when writing in 1787 from Paris to his friend Madison, to view the plight of the people of Europe with grave alarm. The census of 1940 showed that 56.5 per cent of the total population lived in what were defined as urban areas, that is, in incorporated cities and villages of more than 2500 inhabitants. There were more than a thousand cities of at least 10,000 inhabitants each. So much of the urban population had spilled over into adjacent rural territory that the Census Bureau had devised a new kind of district to measure the growth of the major urban centers of the country. These so-called metropolitan districts consisted of a central city of at least 50,000 inhabitants, together with the inhabitants of all contiguous territory containing not fewer than 150 persons per square mile. There were 140 such metropolitan districts in the United States, containing altogether 47.8 per cent of the total population. The rural population was reported to be 43.5 per cent of the total. But only 23 per cent actually lived on farms. The other 20.5 per cent lived in villages of fewer than 2500 inhabitants, or, if in the open country, at least not on farms. The agrarian economy of 1787 had definitely passed away.

The congressional representation of the urban and rural population is distorted by the vagaries of a representative system which is territorial instead of personal. The urban population is mainly concentrated in the metropolitan districts; the rural population is dispersed throughout the country, swamping that part of the urban population which resides in the smaller cities and villages. The unplanned discrimination against the urban population, which necessarily results from a territorial system of representation, is exaggerated by the deliberate discrimination of the districting laws in states where rural members dominate the legislatures. If the 435 representatives in Congress under the apportionment following the census of 1940 were distributed between the urban and rural populations in proportion to their respective numbers, the people in the metropolitan districts would have 208 representatives, the people in smaller urban areas would have 38 representatives, and the people in the rural areas would have 189 representatives. Actually, as nearly as can be conveniently reckoned, there were only 130 congressional districts under the state districting

53

laws in effect following the congressional reapportionment of 1941 which can be described as strictly metropolitan in character. There were 125 other districts in which metropolitan and rural populations were mixed together in various proportions, and there were 180 congressional districts which contained no city of as many as 50,000 inhabitants and no part of any metropolitan district. These congressional districts must have been predominantly rural. Neither the urban nor the rural population possessed a definite ascendancy in the national House of Representatives.

In the Senate, the overrepresentation of the rural population is more striking, because of the concentration of the urban population in the industrial states. In 1940 there were only twelve states in which the inhabitants of the metropolitan districts comprised a clear majority of the total population. There were eight others in which the total urban population exceeded the rural population, as defined by the Census Bureau, though in most of them by no more than a narrow margin. In twenty-eight states the rural population was in the majority. Under the system of representation in the Senate, the rural voters are in a position to exert an unduly powerful, if not predominant, influence in that body.

It is in presidential elections that the urban population appears at an advantage. The practice of choosing presidential electors on general tickets in state-wide elections gives the majority of the voters in each state the whole of the electoral vote for the state. If the urban voters in the twenty states where they are in a majority should vote for electors pledged to support the same candidate for the presidency, they could choose the President regardless of the wishes of all the rural voters and of a majority of the states. This is the situation which would cause a modern Jefferson to dread lest the people "go to eating one another as in Europe." [1] It is a situation which raises the question more insistently than ever before, whether a frame of government designed for a predominantly rural people can be expected to work as satisfactorily in the future as in the past.

In Jefferson's time the predominance of the rural part of the population meant the domination of agricultural interests in national politics. The inhabitants of the commercial cities, he observed in a letter written while he was President,[2] "are as different in sentiment and character from the country people as any two distinct nations, and are clamorous against the order of things established by the agricultural interest." He had in mind the measures of his own administration

54

when he referred to the order of things established by the agricultural interest, and he was doubtless writing in a mood of exasperation at his critics when he added, "Though by the command of newspapers they make a great deal of noise, they have little effect on the direction of policy." Doubtless also there was some exaggeration in his estimate of the differences between the country people and the inhabitants of the cities. After all, he had been popular among the urban mechanics and the small tradesmen as well as among the plain folks in the country. Nevertheless there can be no question of the essential accuracy of Jefferson's opinion concerning the paramount importance of the small farmers and planters in national politics after he had organized them so as to make their numbers effective in national elections.

The time has long since passed away when national leaders could speak so contemptuously of the character and influence of the urban population. Among the male population old enough to form part of the labor force, as defined by the Census Bureau in 1940, the employed workers in agriculture, forestry, and fishery together were outnumbered by those employed in manufactures. The total number of employed workers in commerce (trade, wholesale and retail, and transportation), together with those employed by public utilities, also exceeded the number in agriculture, forestry, and fishery. In 1787 the workers in agriculture, forestry, and fishery must have far exceeded workers of all other kinds combined. By the census of 1820, when the occupations of the people were first reported, such workers were more than twice as numerous as all the others. Years later Emerson could still write in his "Boston Hymn" with no more than a reasonable degree of poetic license that "fishers and choppers and ploughmen shall constitute a state." Now the original body politic, with its rural habitat, agrarian pursuits, and rustic way of life, has yielded to a new species of body politic with a predominantly urban habitat, urban occupations, and presumably urban point of view. Unresolved doubt whether such a body politic is also more urbane, or, as many of the framers of the Constitution feared, is a grave menace to the order of things, including the Constitution itself, established by the agricultural interest, is an outstanding characteristic of contemporary American politics.

The growth of the cities and the growing ascendancy of urban interests in national politics test the present value of the principles of government upon which Madison relied for his confidence in the stability and durability of the Constitution. The principle of the separation of powers seems to have been shrewdly designed for the

55

purpose of establishing a balance between the conflicting interests of the comparatively simple and predominantly agrarian economy of 1787. Can it serve equally well under the more complex industrialized economy of the present age? Federalism was an ingenious and convenient solution of the problem of adjusting conflicts between the major interests of the nation and the minor interests of its various regions and sections as revealed in the debates of the Federal Convention. Is it still well suited to the task of reconciling national and local interests in an age when a city dweller's world is often sharply arrayed against the producers of foodstuffs and the raw materials of industry in the rural areas of the country and is far more capable than one hundred and sixty years ago of making its influence felt in the conduct of public affairs? The natural limits to the political power of numerical majorities of the people were readily discernible under a political system in which there were few institutional rivals to the constitutional bodies provided for the representation of the interests and the organization of the will of the people. Are such limits likely to be efficacious at a time when the competitive loyalties originally associated with a few religious and social communities such as the Anglican and Puritan churches and the Society of the Cincinnati have given place to a great variety of limited and distracting loyalties attached to a multitude of organizations within the common country?

The growth of cities and of urban industry has caused a prodigious proliferation of organizations actively engaged in representing the special interests of their members in direct competition with constitutional representatives of the same persons in the legislative bodies of the nation. The organized urban industrial interests are much more numerous and complex than the agrarian organizations, which are their counterparts in the rural areas, and much more formidable competitors of the official representative bodies under the Constitution. It was not difficult for an alert Congressman to represent all the important interests in a typical rural district of the late eighteenth century, but it has become practically impossible for any single Congressman to represent adequately the huge variety of interests to be found among the residents of one of the highly industrialized districts within the great metropolitan areas of contemporary America. More and more the people of the United States, particularly the urban population of the United States, become dependent upon the services of these special-interest organizations to represent their various particular interests. An organized system of representation, unknown to the Constitution and largely unknown to the laws of the land, has grown up alongside the representative institutions established by the Constitution for the service of the people.

The pressure groups which seek to influence the course of legislation at the national and state capitals are of many kinds. Prominent among them are the "special publics," such as the League of Women Voters and the American Legion, which represent various interests of their members and seek to promote divers causes to which they may become devoted. Other organizations, such as the Anti-Saloon League and the United World Federalists, specialize in particular causes, regardless of the other interests of their members. But the most common and durable source of pressure groups, as Madison predicted, has been the development of special economic interests, above all those of capitalistic industry and of its employees. The landed and manufacturing and mercantile and moneyed interests, to say nothing of the numerous lesser interests envisaged by Madison, have multiplied and divided and subdivided, and employed legislative agents at Washington and at the state capitals, until the permanent professionalized lobby has become a veritable instrument of government. When the lobbyists at the national capital were first required to register under a provision of the Legislative Reorganization Act of 1946, almost every noteworthy special interest was represented in the original list of 842 registrants.* Though unrecognized by the written Constitution, such a lobby holds a conspicuous place in the actual system of representative government.

Special interests mean conflicting interests. The official legislators at the national capital cannot wholly satisfy one organized interest without antagonizing others. To adjust the conflicts by persuading the various organized interests to make mutual concessions is an essential function of practical politics. To fail to manage the pressures of the organized interests is to abdicate the authority of government. But the management of pressures by adjustment of conflicts through the efforts of one group of politicians, under a political system character-

* By the end of 1949 approximately 2000 individual reports had been filed under the Federal Regulation of Lobbying Act, disclosing a total compensation of more than eleven million dollars. Also, approximately 500 organizations of various kinds had reported total expenditures in excess of twenty-seven millions. The Chairman of the House Select Committee on Lobbying Activities estimated that these figures greatly understated the actual numbers of lobbyists and pressure groups operating at the national capital. See for further details the *Congressional Quarterly News Features,* March 31, 1950, pp. 381–388.

ized by freedom of enterprise for all who wish to participate in politics, is necessarily undertaken at the risk of losing business to competing groups of politicians offering more favorable terms to some of the special interests involved in a particular conflict. The struggle between the various groups of politicians to dominate, if not to monopolize, the business of adjusting the interest conflicts produces political factions, the relations between which and the larger and more durable political parties give character to the party system in national politics. The practical necessity of adjusting the conflicts between factions within the parties as well as between organized interests outside the parties and of adjusting also this informal system of representation to the formal system established by the Constitution complicates the contemporary processes of government to a degree which could not have been foreseen by the framers of the Constitution and which, if it could have been foreseen, would have been viewed by them with grave alarm. The gradual development of this problem of contemporary politics has been the first part of the ordeal of the Constitution.

THE POLITICAL EFFECTS OF
THE GROWTH OF CLASS CONSCIOUSNESS

Second in importance among the changes in the political character of the American people since the adoption of the Constitution is the growth of class consciousness. In 1787 there was a good deal of class consciousness in the Federal Convention on the part of leading members of the upper class. Gouverneur Morris and Alexander Hamilton by their speeches and Charles Pinckney by his motions were outstanding in the expression of upper-class consciousness, but consciousness of class was implied in the entire program of the Virginia planners for the establishment of a system of government in which the authority of a numerical majority of the people would be checked by institutions designed to be beyond their direct control. The Senate, the Presidency, and the Supreme Court, as originally planned, would have enabled the upper classes in town and country to balance, if not to overbalance, the rest of the people whose representatives might have been expected to dominate the House of Representatives. If Melancton Smith's argument [3] in the New York ratifying convention was sound, the upper class was likely to have a disproportionate influence even in the House of Representatives.

But the country lawyers, who chiefly represented other classes of the people in the Federal Convention, did not seem to be equally conscious of class conflicts growing out of the structure of the American economy. No delegate bothered to argue with Hamilton about his theory of social dichotomy, though Dr. Johnson intimated that few agreed with him. Charles Pinckney failed conspicuously in his effort to establish high property qualifications for office-holding on a uniform national scale and in his more speculative moods emphasized the equality of condition among the "one great body of citizens." Franklin's faith in the "common people" was certainly genuine, but it was of a sort that tended to minimize class consciousness of every kind. His vision of the common man was of a man who by the practice of industry and thrift was free to rise above his origin to a higher rank in the world. Such a man was not interested in any theoretical class struggle as long as there were attractive opportunities for individual enterprise.

Other forms of class consciousness were more evident in the course of the campaign for ratification of the new Constitution. Patrick Henry's concern for the "middling" and lower classes of people was widely shared, though not often so clearly expressed.[4] But Henry was thinking chiefly of the people in the backwoods and on the frontier. Sam Adams was the most conspicuous spokesman for the "middling sort" of people in the towns, but he was interested in the practical problems of the tradespeople and handicraftsmen whom he knew and did not indulge in the Massachusetts ratifying convention in theoretical dissertations on the class structure of the American economy. His cousin, John Adams, however, was filling his leisure in the legation at London with studies of this very kind, and it was John Adams's book[5] to which Delegate Smith referred in the New York ratifying convention, when hard pressed by Hamilton and Livingston in their controversy over the nature of an aristocracy.

John Adams had given a great deal of thought to the relations between the classes of people and the processes of government. He defined the upper class in the same way as Delegate Smith defined it in his convention speech, to which Hamilton and Livingston took vigorous exception, but he failed to make equally clear his idea of the class relationships of the rest of the people.[6] Sometimes Adams spoke of the "three natural orders in society, the high, the middle, and the low," without defining the middle and lower orders more clearly than Patrick Henry had done in the Virginia ratifying convention. On one occasion Adams mentioned a division of the people into "the very

59

rich, the very poor, and the middling sort," following the language as well as the thought of Aristotle.[7] But Adams made his idea of the "middling sort" no clearer than Richard Henry Lee had done in his letter to Governor Randolph.[8] Later in life Adams wrote of "the great and perpetual distinction in civilized societies . . . between the rich, who are few, and the poor, who are many," [9] thus relapsing into a theory of social dichotomy like that of Hamilton and Livingston and Gouverneur Morris.

Members of such great landholding families as the Schuylers, Livingstons, and Morrises came naturally by their upper-class consciousness under the social and economic conditions of New York state in 1787, but whether the rest of the population was to be distributed among two or three or some greater number of classes was less obvious. Delegate Smith's "middling sort" of people were apparently as important in the politics of most of the states as he and Richard Henry Lee claimed, but they seemed to be less class conscious than the aristocrats, whose leadership they hesitated to reject even while suspicious of their design for power. That the "middling sort" were in fact the kind of persons who composed the bulk of the delegates in the New York convention nobody would deny.

At the present time there is more accurate information concerning the distribution of property and incomes in the United States than was available in 1787, by which Hamilton's theory of social dichotomy can be tested and compared with Adams's theory of a three-class system. The National Resources Committee, better known by its later name of National Resources Planning Board, published in 1939 the first part of a projected report on the structure of the American economy. In an attempt to describe the basic characteristics of the American economy, this report included an estimate (see Table 1) of the aggregate "consumer income" of the people distributed among the successive tenths of the total number of families and individuals sharing the income of the country.[10] The "very rich" could not have been more than a small fraction of the first tenth of the families and individuals sharing the "consumer income" of the American people. How many of the groups, counting up from the bottom, constituted the "very poor" would be a matter on which opinions might well differ. Evidently, if these income statistics are to be interpreted on the assumption that there are three "natural orders" in society, there is no clear and distinct line of division between the high, the middle, and the low orders. If they are to be interpreted on the assumption that there is only one fundamental distinction between the rich and the poor, the poor outnumber the rich so greatly that the latter would seem to be helpless in a democratic state, even making the most liberal allowance for the influence of money in elections. For the

TABLE 1

Distribution of consumer income by tenths of families and individuals.

Tenths	Income Range	Percentage of aggregate (approx.)
First	Over $2600	36
Second	$1925-2600	15
Third	$1540-1925	12
Fourth	$1275-1540	9
Fifth	$1070-1275	7
Sixth	$ 880-1070	6
Seventh	$ 720-880	5
Eighth	$ 545-720	4
Ninth	$ 340-545	3
Tenth	Under $340	2

purposes of political analysis it is obvious that a system of social classification which lumps together in a single class all persons who are not very rich is inconvenient and unserviceable.

Divisions of the people into three or four classes on the basis of relative size of income have been found convenient and serviceable by contemporary political analysts. Dr. George Gallup of the American Institute of Public Opinion has employed a three-class system for the purpose of analyzing the voting preferences of the public in presidential election years. His press release of August 28, 1940, for example, divided his sample of the public into an upper income group containing families earning more than $50 a week, a middle income group containing families earning from $20 to $50 a week, and a lower income group, containing families earning less than $20 a week. He estimated that 16 per cent of the voting population fell in the upper group, 48 per cent in the middle group, and 36 per cent in the lower group. He compared the preferences of the members of these groups between President Roosevelt and his Republican opponent in August 1940 with their preferences in the campaign of 1936. This comparison showed a strikingly different distribution of preferences among the members of the three groups.

61

Another distinguished pollster, Elmo Roper, has employed a four-class system for his political analyses published in *Fortune*. He divides the public into a relatively prosperous part, consisting of those who are prosperous by the standards of the particular community in which they live; an upper-middle class, consisting of those who share the viewpoint of the owners and managers of businesses of all kinds, ranging from foremen and small shopkeepers to substantial farmers and persons on the way to becoming major executives; a lower-middle class, comprising all workers regularly employed; and a class of the poor, who work when they can get work. Roper's two middle classes prove to be considerably broader than Gallup's single middle class. In October 1937, Roper assigned 10 per cent of his public to the class of the prosperous, 27 per cent to the upper-middle class, 38 per cent to the lower-middle class, and 25 per cent to the class of the poor. Three years later, in the light of further investigation, he had modified his distribution percentages, though retaining the general scheme of classification. He then put 6 per cent of the public among the prosperous, 23 per cent in the upper-middle class, 41 per cent in the lower-middle class, and 30 per cent among the poor. He evidently had concluded that his earlier percentages were based on too sanguine a view of the economic status of the American people.

The great drive for war production in World War II increased the flow of population from the country into the cities. By the end of the war a majority of the American people were presumably residing within the limits of the metropolitan areas and most of the newcomers to the city dwellers' world appeared determined to stay there. The urban influx had been particularly marked in the great metropolitan areas on the Pacific Coast. The effect of the war on the further development of classes is more difficult to estimate. Steady wartime employment at unprecedently high wages had certainly enabled great numbers of workers to climb up from the lower class into the lower-middle, but the effect on the upper-middle and upper classes was more obscure.

A fresh attempt at a social classification of the population on the basis of postwar conditions was made by the National Opinion Research Center, one of the best-accredited of the scientific opinion-polling agencies. The status of whites and Negroes was shown separately, and the members of each group were apportioned among four classes according to their relative positions in the social scale of the particular community in which they lived, rural or urban as the case might be, North, South, East, or West. A top class of the "wealthy," under this classification, accounted for 2 per cent of the white population throughout the United States. A second class of the "prosperous" accounted for 14 per cent. A "middle class" accounted for 52 per cent. There remained 32 per cent to constitute the "poor." The striking facts about this measurement of American classes are the apparent solidarity and the large size of the middle class. None of the earlier scientific estimates had made this class seem more substantial. But more important for the study of political behavior than the size and material condition of the different classes of people is their state of mind.

The Communists have been foremost in insisting that the size of incomes is less significant in determining how people will think and act in politics than their relation to the processes of production. Bukharin, for example, in his book, *Historical Materialism*, which was highly esteemed by his Communist comrades before his liquidation, defined a social class as "the aggregate of persons playing the same part in production, standing in the same relations toward other persons in the productive process." [11] The common element of each class is its uniform source of income, regardless of the amount. According to this way of thinking there can be only two basic classes in any particular form of society, the class which commands the instruments of production, and that which works for the commanding class (or in modern capitalistic society three basic classes, if landlords be distinguished from other capitalists, as Marx suggested). Nevertheless, Bukharin could not ignore the fact that contemporary society is actually more complex. Hence, in order to give a complete description of the contemporary social order, to the three basic classes, capitalists, landlords, and proletariat, he added three intermediate, transitional and mixed classes, and one catchall category of persons defying classification upon his principles.[12]

Communist propagandists have contended that the proletariat, as defined by them, includes a majority of the total labor force of the United States. Such statistical evidence as is available suggests that this contention is correct. Lewis Corey, the author of an interesting book on class politics in the United States,[13] estimated the size of the proletariat in 1935 at 59.3 per cent of the total number of persons described by the Census Bureau as gainfully employed. Corey included in the proletariat hired farm laborers and salespeople in retail stores. He estimated the capitalists, or what he termed the big bourgeoisie, at 0.7 per cent of the total. The rest of the gainfully employed were divided between farmers, comprising 14.5 percent of the total, according to his estimate, and a residual category, which he termed the middle class, comprising members of the learned professions, shop-keepers and other little businessmen, and salaried workers except major executives. By transferring three-fourths of the salaried workers, constituting the lower-paid part of that category, from the middle class to the proletariat, Corey succeeded in raising his estimate of the size of the proletariat to 75 per cent of the total. The proletariat, as finally estimated, contained the bulk of the white-collar workers as well as all the skilled workers in capitalistic industry, regardless of the size of their incomes. But such calculations merely raise the question whether under the conditions of life and work in the United States such a classification is realistic.[14] Can the political behavior of the active part of the population be better understood by lumping the bulk of its members in a general proletarian class without regard to their actual state of mind?

The leading public-opinion pollsters have understood the impor-tance of the state of mind of the different kinds of people, as well as that of their social and economic condition, in determining the nature and size of the classes to which they should be assigned. The line between the rich or the poor and those who are neither rich nor poor may be drawn in accordance with the theories of propagandists or statisticians, or the persons concerned may be consulted in order to ascertain the classes in which they think they belong. Dr. Gallup put the question in 1939 to what he considered a fair sample of the American people: "To what social class in the country do you think you belong; the middle class, the upper, or the lower?" [15] When the persons examined by his interviewers had finally made their views clear, it appeared that 6 per cent of them regarded themselves as members of the upper class, 88 per cent regarded themselves as mem-bers of the middle class and the remaining 6 per cent put themselves in the lower class. The outstanding fact developed by this poll was the all but universal preference for a connection with the middle class by all kinds of Americans. "It made little difference," Dr. Gallup re-ported, "whether the voter was a Democrat or a Republican, whether he lived in a city or in the country, whether he worked in a factory or owned the factory himself." Along with this finding went another of equal importance. "With the sense of belonging to the middle class," Dr. Gallup added, "goes a whole pattern of thought."

Similar results were obtained by Elmo Roper from a similar in-quiry. According to his report,[16] published in *Fortune*, February 1940,

27.5 per cent of the persons, composing a fair sample of the American people, who were asked to name the class to which they belonged, said that they did not know. Of those who were able to answer, a total of 2.9 per cent put themselves in the upper class under that or an equivalent name; 47 per cent put themselves in the middle class, or in some special part of the middle class under that or an equivalent name; 14.9 per cent put themselves in the lower class, or in what they called the working or laboring class, or admitted that they were unemployed, idle, or unfortunate; 2 per cent claimed to belong to the business, executive, or white-collar class; and other miscellaneous answers accounted for the remaining 5.7 per cent of the total. When those who had not used the actual words "upper," "middle," or "lower" to describe the class to which they belonged, or professed not to know, were asked to use one of these words to designate their place in the social order, the final result was that 7.6 per cent put themselves in the upper class without further qualification, 79.2 per cent put themselves in the middle class, 7.9 per cent put themselves in the lower class, and 5.3 per cent professed still not to know where they belonged. Thus forced to choose, every class and occupation, including the lowly farmhand and the unemployed, decisively considered itself middle class. Roper noted that even those who had previously described themselves as belonging to the "working" or "laboring" classes mainly swung into the middle class rather than identify themselves with a lower-class proletariat; Negroes were the only exception to this general attitude. Of those persons whom Roper himself classified as prosperous, 68.2 per cent put themselves in the middle class; of those whom he classified as poor, 70.3 per cent put themselves in the middle class.

Roper, like Gallup, found that most of the people not only considered themselves middle class, but actually possessed middle-class attitudes when tested by suitable questions. Most of them hoped to go into business sometime for themselves, put their hopes for success ahead of their desire for security, preferred business to government as an employer, believed that employers and employees had much in common, believed that opportunity for advancement was as good as ever, and intended to send their children to college, if they had not already done so. These are attitudes which cannot be reconciled with the characteristic traits of a proletarian mentality. These people did not believe in the progressive impoverishment of all those who were not capitalists or in the inevitability of such exploitation of the toiling masses by those in control of capitalistic industry as to precipitate a struggle for existence between the exploiters and the exploited. Not even those who by objective tests belonged to the upper class thought of themselves generally as an élite. They too mostly shared the middle-class attitudes of the bulk of the population.

That the people of the United States are essentially a middle-class nation is further demonstrated by the nature of the occupations by which they earn their livelihood. These occupational statistics, collected by the census of 1940, have been skillfully arranged by one of the Census Bureau experts, Dr. Alba M. Edwards, to measure differences in general education and special training as well as differences of economic status and income.[17] Dr. Edwards's estimate of the size of the different social-economic classes, as he calls them, is based upon analysis of what the Census Bureau terms the total labor force of the United States. This force includes persons who are seeking work, though not actually employed, and persons employed on public-emergency work, but excludes newly trained workers and others who have never actually been gainfully employed. The total labor force comprised in 1940 over fifty-two millions of persons, of whom nearly forty millions were men and boys, and twelve and a half millions were women and girls. Nearly 80 per cent of all men and boys over fourteen years of age were included in the labor force, and over 25 per cent of the women and girls over fourteen were also included. The difference in the numbers of the sexes in the labor force is largely accounted for by housewives not gainfully employed outside of the home and other female members of families engaged in housekeeping.

The distribution of male employed workers by social-economic groups, exclusive of those on public-emergency work and those seeking work, for the United States as a whole and for the states of New York and Mississippi, is shown in Table 2. All the unskilled groups combined, together with the semiskilled, fall far short of a majority of the whole. Even if all those temporarily employed on public-emergency work were included with the semiskilled and unskilled, this aggregation of the underprivileged, as they have sometimes been called, would have been outnumbered by the skilled and white-collar workers, the proprietors, managers, and officials, and the members of the professions. Conditions can be imagined under which the white-collar workers, the skilled, and the semiskilled might feel that they belonged in the same class with the unskilled, constituting a proletariat, if the various groups had lost their faith in the America they had known.

66

But such conditions certainly did not exist in 1939 and 1940, when Gallup and Roper were making the investigations which led them to conclude that the United States is middle-class. In the light of those investigations it is more likely that most of the semiskilled and many of the unskilled would feel that they belonged in the middle class along with the skilled and white-collar workers. Such a middle class would contain a large majority of the labor force of the United States,

TABLE 2

Distribution of male employed workers.

Groups	Distribution by Groups (per cent)		
	U.S.A.	New York	Mississippi
1. Professional persons	5.0	7.0	2.5
2. Proprietors, managers, and officials			
a. Farmers (owners and tenants)	14.6	3.2	46.2
b. Wholesale and retail dealers	5.3	6.7	2.9
c. Other proprietors, managers and			
officials	4.9	6.1	2.2
3. Clerks and kindred workers	14.1	20.6	5.2
4. Skilled workers and foremen	15.0	17.1	5.8
5. Semiskilled workers	18.2	22.6	7.1
6. Unskilled workers			
a. Farm laborers	8.5	2.8	17.1
b. Other laborers	10.7	7.2	9.0
c. Servants and personal service laborers	3.8	6.6	2.1
Total	100.0	100.0	100.0

and the greater part of the proprietors, managers, officials, and professional persons.

Not less significant than the distribution of the total labor force among the different social-economic classes is the trend of change in the relative size of the different classes. Dr. Edwards's statistical analyses throw light upon the trend during the seventy years from 1870 to 1940. During that period the proportion of farmers in the American economy sharply decreased, and there was a relative decrease also in the unskilled. The skilled remained a constant proportion of the total. The semiskilled, the white-collar workers, the proprietors, managers, and officials, other than farmers or farm managers, and the members of the learned professions increased rapidly and formed a much larger part of the total labor force at the end of the period than at the beginning. The evidence which Dr. Edwards has extracted from the Census Bureau's occupation statistics supports the general conclusion reached by Lewis Mumford in his brilliant study of the effect of technological changes on the structure of the American economy. "The general change that characterizes all genuinely neotechnic industry," Mumford declared,[18] is "the displacement of the proletariat."

Further light on the relative strength of the middle class and of the proletariat in the American economy is furnished by the distribution of the social-economic classes in the leading capitalist and agrarian states, New York and Mississippi. In Mississippi, which is no more agrarian than most American states were a few decades ago, the farmers and farm laborers constitute a substantial majority of the total labor force. In New York, these classes combined constitute only 6 per cent of the total. All other classes in New York, with the sole exception of unskilled laborers in industry and commerce, form a larger percentage of the total than in Mississippi. The semiskilled workers are relatively three times as numerous in New York as in Mississippi, the skilled workers and foremen are also approximately three times as numerous, the white-collar workers are four times as numerous. Whereas the unskilled groups, most likely to develop proletarian sympathies and attitudes, are relatively more numerous in Mississippi, the intermediate groups, which have always tended strongly toward middle-class consciousness, are greatly superior in relative numbers and presumably also in political importance in New York. Since the country as a whole has tended to move from the agrarian type of economy toward the urban industrial type, represented by New York, the conclusion is unavoidable that the tendency has been, as pointed out by Mumford, to displace the proletarian elements in order to make room for a larger and stronger middle class.

The change in the structure of the American economy since 1787 that has the greatest political importance is not the probable increase in the size of the middle class as a whole, but the great shift in its distribution between country and city. In 1787 the predominant class in the body politic was the rural middle class. By 1940 the urban middle class had come to be both more numerous and at least potentially more influential in national politics. The rise of cities and the general predominance of the city dwellers in the modern economy have caused the social structure of the urban population to become a more important matter in national politics than it could have been in 1787. In the framing of the Constitution the urban middle class played a minor role because of its numerical insignificance and its political disadvantages in competition with the big merchants and their lawyers for places on the delegations to the Federal Convention. Franklin and Sherman were the only delegates of the first rank who understood its needs through personal experience and were qualified to voice its aspirations, and both of these statesmen were too big to be merely the spokesmen of any class. The urban middle class has now reached a stage in its development where it can essay the more important role played by the rural middle class in the earlier years of the Republic.

The political influence of any class depends less upon its numbers than upon its self-consciousness and practical capacity for political organization. Class consciousness, regarded as a political phenomenon, has always been weak in the United States. In the framing of the Constitution it was manifestly weaker than sectional feeling. It has not yet become as strong as Communist and Fascist political theorists think it should be under the social and economic conditions of the contemporary world. Class consciousness has been regarded as something un-American among members of the rural middle class, who have thought of themselves rather as average Americans than as members of any particular class. That it has not yet become much stronger among members of the urban middle class, who, according to the Communist and Fascist ideologies, should be definitely class conscious, is clearly indicated by the researches of the Lynds in their classical studies of Middletown and by Alfred Winslow Jones in his brilliant analysis of opinion among the people of Akron, Ohio.

Jones's study of social conflict in a modern industrial city culminated in an attempt to measure the impact of conflicting rights upon political ideas. This experiment in the measurement of political attitudes should have great interest for American politicians. One of his conclusions throws a strong light on the state of class consciousness in an American industrial community. "It is fairly clear," he wrote,[19] "that public opinion would, in its confusion, block a destructive attack upon corporate property, as long as such an attack appeared in any way even vaguely to be a threat to property in general, which occupies a firm position as a value. Public opinion, however, would welcome any change in, or even the abolition of, corporate property rights, if it were made obvious that corporate property is a very special form of property in general, and if the changes would make life, liberty, property, and the pursuit of happiness demonstrably more secure." This is obviously an attitude that could develop only in a modern industrial city, but it is not the attitude of a proletariat.

It seems to be one more of the middle-class traits that are characteristic of most Americans who have shared the traditional way of life.
The persistence of the idea of classlessness, particularly among the
members of the middle classes, both rural and urban, doubtless owes
a great deal, as Jones properly noted,[20] to the illusion of equality that
has permeated American society since the settlement of the country
began. That the ideas of Americans on the subject of classes are manifestly still lacking in sharpness [21] does not alter the political importance
of the gradual shift of a great part of the middle class from a rural to
an urban habitat. This shift marks the second phase in the ordeal of
the Constitution.

THE POLITICAL EFFECTS OF
THE DISLOCATION OF SECTIONALISM

The third important change in the political character of the
American people is the dislocation of sectionalism.[22] In 1787 there was
the basic division between North and South. The boundaries between
the two sections were not altogether clear, but the disposition to emphasize the differences of interest springing from the presence or
absence of Negro slaves was certainly one of the most stubborn facts
in national politics. The conflict between East and West, taking these
terms not strictly as geographical expressions but rather as symbols
of two competing ways of life, was less evident in the Federal Convention than in the state ratifying conventions, particularly those of
Massachusetts, New York, and Virginia. In the final outcome of the
process of constitution-framing the conflict between East and West,
though less conspicuous, was hardly less important than that between
North and South. But these major sectional conflicts were complicated
and obscured by the clashes between the interests of minor sections
which at times seemed to exert a greater influence upon the settlement
of the details of the new frame of government than the conflicts between North and South and between East and West.

The major and minor sections of 1787 have left an indelible mark
upon the geographical basis of national politics, but through the
years the patterns of sectional controversy have grown more complex.
The expansion of the Republic to the Pacific Ocean has moved the
West ever farther westward and the earlier Wests have successively
disintegrated under the impact of social and economic forces similar
to those which originally created the minor sections on the Atlantic

seaboard. At the present time the United States can conveniently be divided into four major sections, the Northeast, the North Central, the South, and the West, but each of these major sections breaks down into minor sections characterized by diverse social and economic conditions and corresponding political interests. If the fundamental task of national politics is to reconcile these conflicting interests, as Franklin already supposed in 1787, the modern conditions make the task more complicated than in the Federal Convention.

The boundary between North and South can most conveniently be drawn by a line separating the area in which the Negro population exceeds 10 per cent of the total from that in which Negroes are less numerous. Since the Negroes who have escaped from the South into northern and western cities are numerous enough to be an influential factor in the politics of many states and actually control two congressional districts in New York and Chicago, the political South should be more precisely defined as those contiguous congressional districts in which Negroes were reported by the census of 1940 to form more than 10 per cent of the population in a majority of the counties or more than 20 per cent in at least one county. By such a definition western Maryland, western Virginia, eastern and central Kentucky, and eastern Tennessee must be excluded from the South, and also northern Oklahoma and western Texas. A few border districts have to be dealt with arbitrarily. It is convenient to exclude Delaware from the South, notwithstanding the considerable percentage of Negroes in the rural population, on account of the affinity of the predominantly urban population of that state with Pennsylvania, and to include a few districts in western Oklahoma and central Texas, where the percentage of Negroes is low but the white population is mainly southern in origin and political outlook.

The North, considered as a political phenomenon, needs to be divided into a Northeast section and a North Central section. The most suitable line of division is one which, disregarding state boundaries, divides the watershed of the North Atlantic Coast from that of the Great Lakes and Mississippi Valley. Such a division throws Pittsburgh and Buffalo and their tributary areas into the North Central section, where politically they belong, rather than in the Northeast. The western boundary of the North Central section can also be located most conveniently without regard to state lines. The most important fact about the western border of the Central section is the declining rainfall and the growing aridity of the soil. Where agriculture becomes

71

hazardous without irrigation and field crops give way to grazing, the dominant economic interests change and political behavior tends to change also. Here the North Central section, regarded as a political entity, ends.

The modern West may be said to begin at the point where the average density of population in the rural counties falls below ten per square mile. The boundary begins at the Canadian border in eastern North Dakota, and runs through central South Dakota, Nebraska, and Kansas, and into western Oklahoma and Texas. The rest of the country, constituting the political West, comprises about half of its total area. In fact West is a term which has been used to designate so many different areas at different stages in the westward movement of population that it has lost much of its utility as the name of a section. The arid West, comprising the Great Plains, the intermountain plateaus, and the mountains themselves as far as the eastern slopes of the Sierra Nevada and Cascade ranges, contains a sparse population which offers a striking contrast in economic interests and political behavior to the denser population on the Pacific Coast. Western Washington and Oregon and most of California form a Pacific West which resembles the Northeast in respect to the growth of cities and development of industry more than the arid West or the Middle West or any of the earlier Wests.

A description of the geographical basis of political sectionalism and an analysis of the local interests which give vitality to national politics cannot stop with a definition of the major sections of the country. But the general pattern of contemporary sectionalism emerges from a statistical view of the distribution of congressional districts among the major sections, showing the numbers of urban and rural districts in each of the sections (Table 3). The wholly urban districts are located chiefly in the great metropolitan areas on the North Atlantic Coast, on the shores of the Great Lakes, and on the Pacific Coast. The predominantly rural districts are located chiefly in the cotton and tobacco belts of the South, in the corn and wheat and dairy belts of the North Central section, and in the grazing and mineral areas of the West. Smaller groups of rural districts are located in the mineral and subsistence-farming areas of the Appalachian mountain region and in the sugar and subtropical fruit belts along the South Atlantic and Gulf Coasts. The districts of mixed urban and rural population are more evenly distributed among the various sections of the country. The bare enumeration of the leading interests within these major and minor sections of the United States indicates clearly enough the complexity of the interests which are to be reconciled by national politicians.

The pattern of contemporary sectionalism is further complicated by the election of Senators and Presidents in electoral districts composed of the states as integral units, regardless of their differences of size and of the unequal manner in which the principal special interests are distributed among them. A statistical view of the distri-

TABLE 3

Sectional basis of national politics, I.
*Congressional districts under apportionment of 1941.**

Major Sections	Wholly Urban	Mixed Urban-Rural	Predominantly Rural	Total
I. Northeast	61	34	16	111
II. North Central	44	49	68	161
III. South	8	30	68	106
IV. West	17	12	28	57
Total	130	125	180	435

* Under the apportionment to follow the census of 1950 the West is expected to gain at least ten Congressmen, most, if not all, of whom will represent urban districts, while the three other sections suffer a corresponding net loss of seats, mostly in the rural areas.

bution of the states and electoral votes among the sections, showing also the numbers and character of the urban and rural states, respectively, in each of the sections, throws further light on the nature of contemporary sectionalism (Table 4). Such a view involves a somewhat arbitrary classification of those states through which run the boundary lines between the various sections, but in general the resulting classification is sufficiently realistic to be significant. In the case of the states on the border between the North and the South, an assignment to either of these major sections would be excessively arbitrary and unrealistic, and a new section of the Border States has therefore been recognized. The remainder of the South, the Solid South of popular political terminology, consists of the eleven states which formed the Southern Confederacy in 1861.[23] The Border States comprise the other states in which slavery then existed, together with the then Indian Territory and adjacent area from which the state of Oklahoma was subsequently formed. There can be no question of the enduring importance in national politics of the distinction emphasized by Madison in 1787 between the states in which Negroes were numerous and the other states.

The traces of the original groupings of delegations in the Federal Convention of 1787, which can be detected in the pattern of contemporary sectionalism, attest the durable nature of the special interests which formed the minor sections at the beginning of national politics. The mercantile interests of 1787, which controlled the dele-

TABLE 4

Sectional basis of national politics, II.

Electoral votes under apportionment of 1941.

Sections	States	Senators	Represen-tatives	Electoral Votes
I. Northeast				
1. Predominantly urban states	6	12	114	126
2. Semiurban and rural states	3	6	6	12
II. North Central				
3. Predominantly urban states	3	6	66	72
4. Semiurban and rural states	8	16	52	68
III. South				
5. Border States	6	12	43	55
6. Solid South	11	22	105	127
IV. West				
7. Mountain States	8	16	16	32
8. Pacific Coast	3	6	33	39
Total	48	96	435	531

gations from three states in the Federal Convention, have expanded into the great capitalistic industrial interests of modern times, which are most highly developed in the states in which a majority of the people live in the large cities. There are ten states in which a large majority of the people are classified as urban by the Census Bureau, and in which at least a majority of the people live in the large urban areas termed by the Census Bureau metropolitan districts. Six of these are situated on the North Atlantic Coast, extending from Massachusetts to Pennsylvania; three are situated in the region of the Great Lakes, Ohio, Michigan, and Illinois; and the tenth, California, is situated on the Pacific Coast. Altogether these ten highly industrialized, predominantly urban states possess 223 electoral votes. They lack only 43 votes of enough to elect the President of the United States. In these states organized labor as well as organized capital find their principal sources of strength. In these states also the old order of rural politics has undergone the greatest change, giving way to the new order of urban politics.

The four rural sections of 1787 have developed in various ways, but vestiges at least of their original character remain in the present pattern of sectionalism. The original Upper North has dwindled to the three states of northern New England, since the dairy belt of northern New York long ago lost the power to control the politics of that state. The North Central dairy belt forms a special interest, which might be described as upper northern, but it is located in states where the grain-growers are strong and which can more conveniently be grouped with the other grain-growing states of the upper Mississippi Valley. A new kind of upper north has developed in the Pacific Northwest, where the states of Oregon and Washington cannot be fitted satisfactorily either into the arid West with the Mountain States or with California into a new industrial Pacific Coast. These two minor sections together elect only ten Senators and possess only 26 electoral votes.

The original Middle States have disappeared as a rural section. In their place two new mainly rural sections, dominated generally, like the original Middle States, by graingrowers and cattlemen, occupy an intermediate position in the sectional pattern of the country. They are the corn- and wheat-belt states of the North Central section, and the grazing and mining states of the arid West. These new intermediate or middle sections extend from Indiana and Wisconsin in the old North West to Idaho and Arizona in the new Far West. The two sections combined elect thirty-two Senators and possess 100 electoral votes. This group of states as a whole is neither northern nor southern in the traditional senses of these political terms, and is more typically western than the states farther west on the Pacific Coast.

The original Upper South, the most important of the minor sections in the Federal Convention, was disrupted by the Civil War. Virginia, North Carolina, and Tennessee have merged with the Lower South, forming the Solid South of contemporary national politics. This section of eleven states with 127 electoral votes is the most definitely rural and the most homogeneous of all the contemporary political sections, despite growing diversification of both crops and urban industries. The six Border States, extending from Delaware and Maryland through West Virginia and Kentucky to Missouri and Oklahoma, present a mixture of manufacturing and mining, tobacco and cotton growing, and corn, hog and wheat raising, which prevents their inclusion in any of the adjacent sections. With their twelve Senators and fifty-five electoral votes, they constitute a minor section with little solidarity and not much greater resemblance to the Upper South of the early years of the Republic. But this section, like the others, is important in national politics, since social and economic interests can gain political significance only through the action of the districts and states and sections which they are able to dominate.

A comparison between the pattern of sectionalism in 1787 and that one hundred sixty years later introduces the third phase in the ordeal of the Constitution. The later pattern is not only more complex than the earlier, but also less well balanced. Washington and Franklin had five well-defined sectional interests to reconcile in the Federal Convention. The fact that these interests were nearly evenly matched proved to be a happy accident for the leadership of the Convention. No particular combination of sections enjoyed a great advantage over other possible combinations in the negotiation of settlements between the contending factions in the framing of the Constitution. This circumstance facilitated the arrangement of a series of compromises, which adjusted the conflicting interests so equitably that all could join in supporting the final product of the delegations' work. The addition of a declaration of rights, insisted upon by the representatives of the various local "Wests" in the principal state ratifying conventions, completed the process of sectional adjustment. The finished Constitution provided for a truly national government deriving its powers from the consent of the whole body of the governed. With skillful political leadership the pattern of sectionalism made for great stability in the approved instrument of government.

The original pattern of sectionalism was gradually distorted by the unequal rates of growth of the different sections. The rural middle section grew much more rapidly than the other sections. The relations between the sections eventually grew so seriously out of balance that those which were threatened with a status of permanent inferiority in the Union could be persuaded to try to withdraw and establish an independent confederacy. The failure of secession was followed by the establishment of a closer Union but not by the restoration of the original sectional equilibrium. The further growth of different sections at unequal rates has made the contemporary pattern of sectionalism more distorted than ever. Now it is the development of the highly urbanized and industrialized sections which threatens to upset the balance of the traditional system of national politics. Can the urban middle class perform the function once performed by the rural middle class, and through its control of the most influential sections maintain the harmony of the political system and the stability of the Constitution? In 1788 it was the rural middle class, particularly in the large and close states of Massachusetts and Virginia, that determined the outcome of the struggle over ratification. Now, after more than a century and a half of government under the Constitution, the great industrial states have taken over the leadership in the conflict between the sections, and the urban middle class may be expected to play the role once taken by the followers of Samuel Adams and John Hancock, of Patrick Henry and Thomas Jefferson. Can the urban middle class exploit its ascendancy in the great industrial states so as to hold the balance of power in national politics and duplicate the triumph of the middle-class farmers during the earlier years of the Republic? This is the test which completes the present ordeal of the Constitution.

CHAPTER FOUR

The Unplanned Institution of Organized Partisanship

THE UNSOLVED PROBLEM OF PARTISANSHIP AND FACTIOUSNESS

Madison's opinion concerning the nature and role of political parties in a popular government was most clearly expressed in the tenth number of *The Federalist*. In an often-quoted passage he set forth his reason for believing that under the new Constitution, despite the menace of narrow and intense party spirit, factious parties should not be expected to cause excessive confusion and political instability. "Among the numerous advantages promised by a well-constructed Union," he wrote,[1] "none deserves to be more accurately developed than its tendency to break and control the violence of faction. The friend of popular governments," he added, "never finds himself so much alarmed for their character and fate, as when he contemplates their propensity to this dangerous vice. The instability, injustice, and confusion introduced into the public councils have in truth been the mortal diseases under which popular governments have everywhere perished."

By a faction Madison understood "a number of citizens, whether amounting to a majority or minority of the whole, who are united and actuated by some common impulse of passion, or of interest, adverse to the rights of other citizens, or to the permanent and aggregate interests of the community." He traced the causes of faction to the essential nature of man, and declared that the natural propensity of mankind to fall into mutual animosities was so strong that "where no substantial occasion presents itself, the most frivolous and fanciful

78

distinctions have been sufficient to kindle their unfriendly passions and excite their most violent conflicts. But the most common and durable source of factions," he believed, "has been the various and unequal distribution of property. Those who hold and those who are without property have ever formed distinct interests in society. Those who are creditors, and those who are debtors, fall under a like discrimination. A landed interest, a manufacturing interest, a mercantile interest, a moneyed interest, with many lesser interests, grow up of necessity in civilized nations, and divide them into different classes, actuated by different sentiments and views. The regulation of these various and interfering interests forms the principal task of modern legislation, and involves the spirit of party and faction in the necessary and ordinary operations of the government."

It was to the diversification of interests in an extensive country like the United States that Madison confidently looked for the most efficacious check against the virulence of faction and the abuse of power by factious majorities. "The smaller the society," he argued, "the fewer probably will be the distinct parties and interests composing it; the fewer the distinct parties and interests, the more frequently will a majority be found of the same party; and the smaller the number of individuals composing a majority, and the smaller the compass within which they are placed, the more easily will they concert and execute their plans of oppression. Extend the sphere, and you take in a greater variety of parties and interests; you make it less probable that a majority of the whole will have a common motive to invade the rights of other citizens; or if such a common motive exists, it will be more difficult for all who feel it to discover their own strength, and to act in unison with each other . . . The influence of factious leaders," he concluded, "may kindle a flame within their particular States, but will be unable to spread a general conflagration through the other States . . . A rage for paper money, for an abolition of debts, for an equal division of property, or for any other improper or wicked project, will be less apt to pervade the whole body of the Union than a particular member of it, in the same proportion as such a malady is more likely to taint a particular county or district than an entire State."

Madison's principle of natural limits to the power of numerical majorities was the most speculative of the three principles by which he tested the merits of the new system of government for the United States. He wanted a government which would be strong enough to control all the people throughout the country and yet which would not itself get out of control and abuse its power. Such a government ought to satisfy two requirements. It must be able to govern. It must also give assurance that, while a majority of the people could protect themselves against exploitation by any minority, at the same time they could not themselves oppress any minority, particularly not in the case Madison chiefly feared, where the minority would consist of the rich.

No member of the Convention openly challenged Madison's faith that the obstacles to the formation of powerful national parties were so great that the abuse of power by partisan majorities in the national government was less likely than in popular governments within the narrower limits of the individual states. Some of the leading members, however, did not share Madison's distrust of popular majorities. Franklin, for instance, preferred a government in which a majority in the House of Representatives would possess a predominant authority. He must have been less content than Madison with the new Constitution, if he believed Madison's argument to be sound, since the alternative to powerful popular majorities would have seemed to him to be the more dangerous possibility of government by minorities of some kind, particularly minorities dominated by the rich. If Madison feared lest by the formation of strong national parties the poor would be enabled to oppress the rich, Franklin may well have feared that without strong national parties the rich would be able to oppress the poor.

Another of the more democratic delegates, the old revolutionist Roger Sherman, differed from both Madison and Franklin. Like Franklin, he had greater confidence in popular majorities than Madison, but unlike Franklin his confidence was placed primarily in the popular majorities within the several states rather than in a majority of the nation. Like Madison, he hoped for efficient checks on the power of majorities of the nation, but unlike Madison he did not count heavily on an ingenious contrivance of checks within the internal structure of the government to keep its several parts in balance. Sherman's support of the great compromise in the matter of presidential elections reveals his expectation that national parties were unlikely to gain such strong popular support as to transform the electoral colleges from nominating agencies into organs of final election. Sherman evidently did not share the fears of either of his great fellow delegates.

Other delegates, however, apparently expected that the advantages to be gained by concerted arrangements for concentrating a majority of the electoral votes upon a particular candidate would probably stimulate the development of parties capable of procuring the election of their candidates by the presidential electors. Gouverneur Morris and other leaders among the aristocratic Nationalists in the Convention were very likely of this opinion. Whether such parties would be permanent and, if not, what would be the effect of temporary combinations among the presidential electors upon the organization of parties in the Congress, the leaders of the various factions did not choose to discuss in the Convention. Whether such parties would be strong enough, not only to dictate to presidential electors how they should vote, but also to dominate the business of the Congress, was a vital question which was likewise ignored by the Convention. Franklin may well have hoped so. Madison, and presumably Washington also, must have hoped not. But to establish a constitution the satisfactory operation of which would require the organization of parties strong enough to choose presidents but not so strong as to enable partisan majorities in the House of Representatives to overpower them when in office — and the Senators also — was a delicate undertaking! Madison's principle of natural limits to the power of political parties, if sound, was likely to be an important factor in the development of government under the Constitution.

The framers of the Constitution were familiar with the manifestations of human nature in politics. There had been plenty of factiousness in the politics of the states, as of the colonies before the Revolution. The perennial struggles of the "outs" against the "ins" were spread upon the record, which most of the delegates had shared in making, and the ingenuity of politicians in forming combinations for more effective action at the polls and in the legislative bodies could cause no surprise to seasoned campaigners. Some of them may have read Edmund Burke's spirited defense of parties, in which he sought to justify them as organizations for the purpose of promoting the national interest by joint action of their members upon some particular principle in which they were all agreed. Realistic politicians, of whom there were many in the Federal Convention, would have been as skeptical as were most of the members of the British House of Commons, to whom Burke addressed his argument, concerning the predominance of the national interest in the minds of many partisans they had known. They would have been equally skeptical concerning the unanimity of partisan support for any particular principle of public policy. Whether the great variety of private and local interests throughout the Union would lead to the formation of a corresponding variety of factions in the Congress, or whether the various special interests would be able to work together permanently in a smaller number of organized national parties, and, if so, how many such parties might be operating at the same time, were questions which no delegate was prepared to answer. That there would be partisanship and factiousness in national politics they could be sure, but what form these activities might take the delegates did not venture to say.

It was clear to the framers of the Constitution that the great prize in American politics would be the presidency. Presumably the primary object of political combinations among politicians and voters would be to influence presidential elections. Secondary objects might be to influence action upon appointments and other business in the Senate and upon proposed legislation in the House of Representatives. It was possible for most of the framers to hope for some satisfactory form of organized action in national politics, which would facilitate the operations of politicians under the Constitution, either a one-party system, a two-party system, a multiple-party system, or no system of permanent parties, leaving the field open for temporary factions formed in response to the challenge of circumstances. Some of the framers, as the record shows, were not hopeful of the development of any kind of political system in which they could have faith, and surrendered themselves to gloomy forebodings of the inevitable end of their work in an oppressive oligarchy or a monarchy.

THE PERENNIAL STRUGGLE BETWEEN "INS" AND "OUTS"

The simplest of all theories designed to explain the organization of parties in connection with presidential elections was mentioned more than once during the debates in the Federal Convention. Speaking on July 19th in favor of a six-year term for presidents, Oliver Ellsworth observed [2] that "if the elections be too frequent, the Executive will not be firm enough. There must be duties which will make him unpopular for the moment. There will be *outs* as well as *ins*. His administration therefore will be attacked and misrepresented." Gouverneur Morris made substantially the same observation on September 5th during the debate on the final great compromise concerning the presidency. "If the President shall have given satisfaction," he remarked,[3] "the votes will turn on him of course . . . If he should be disliked, all disliking him would take care to unite their votes so as to ensure his being supplanted." These two sagacious politicians evidently expected the organization of administration parties and antiadministration parties, though how durable such parties might be, and what sort of party system might emerge from the conflicts between them, they did not say.

The record of forty-one presidential elections shows how right these prophets were. There was, of course, no Administration party at the first election in 1788, nor was there opposition to the election of Washington. The important "ins" at that time were the factions in control of the state governments, particularly those of the large states where the opposition to unconditional ratification of the Constitution had been formidable. In Virginia, where the governor was elected by the state legislature, Patrick Henry and his friends controlled the legislature, and they were the "ins." In Massachusetts and New York, where the governors were elected by the voters at large, Governor John Hancock and Governor George Clinton and their respective friends were the "ins." General Washington was the leader of the "outs" and the combination of factions formed under his wise leadership in the Federal Convention was the first organized national party in American politics. It triumphantly procured the adoption of the Constitution and installed its leader as first President of the United States. Thereafter Washington and his friends were the "ins" and the Administration party strove to maintain their control of the government. The absence of organized opposition to Washington's reëlection in 1792 deferred the beginning of the normal struggle of "outs" against "ins" until the choice of his successor four years later.

The choice of candidates for the presidency reveals the essential traits of the "ins" and the "outs." Twenty-two times an Administration party has renominated the president in office and fifteen times he has been reëlected. On three other occasions an Administration party has nominated the Vice-President for the presidency, and twice he has been elected. Members of the President's Cabinet have been candidates for the succession at five elections, and five such candidates have been elected. At one of these elections, that for the choice of a successor to President Monroe, two Cabinet officers sought the presidency. One, Secretary of the Treasury William H. Crawford, obtained the nomination from the Congressional Caucus, but the other, Secretary of State J. Q. Adams, was finally chosen by the House of Representatives. At one other election, that of 1880, James A. Garfield, a member of the Administration faction of the party in power, though not a member of the Cabinet, was nominated. He too was elected. Thus in thirty-one

83

of the forty elections since the original election of General Washington the candidate of the "ins" has been a member of, or a person closely connected with, the Administration. Five times the party supposedly in power has nominated a party or factional leader more or less at odds with the Administration, but has elected such a candidate only once. Twice the party in power has nominated a state governor not directly connected with any faction at Washington, of whom one was elected. Twice seeking to get away from an unpopular Administration as far as possible, it has nominated a prominent general, of whom one was elected. Thus in twenty-three of the twenty-six successful attempts by the "ins" to stay in office, the candidate has been a person connected with the Administration. Of the nine candidates of the "ins" not connected with the Administration, only three have been successful.

The "ins" have manifestly been most successful when they were able to stick closely to the Administration in the selection of a presidential candidate. The attempt to rescue an unpopular Administration by going outside of its own membership for a candidate has not generally proved to be winning strategy. General Grant was able to rescue the Radical Republicans from the unpopularity of the Johnson Administration in 1868, but General Scott failed to rescue the conservative Whigs in 1852 from the unpopularity of the Fillmore Administration. Governor R. B. Hayes of Ohio saved the day for the "ins" at the close of the Grant Administration, but Governor James M. Cox of Ohio at the close of the Wilson Administration could not rescue his party from the mistakes of its official leaders. On two other occasions, when the succession of a willful or weak Vice-President had seriously compromised the party in power, such outstanding national leaders as Henry Clay and James G. Blaine were unable to keep the party from being turned out of office. Lewis Cass likewise was unable to heal the breach in the Democratic Party at the close of the Polk Administration, and William Jennings Bryan, the "peerless" leader, despite great eloquence and extraordinary efforts on the stump, could not bring victory to the disorganized party of Grover Cleveland. Buchanan's success in 1856 was a striking exception to the general rule that prominent party leaders, not connected with a discredited Administration, cannot save their party from defeat. Twice outstanding national leaders have run independently when an unpopular Administration has refused to yield the leadership to them, but neither Stephen A. Douglas in 1860 nor Theodore Roosevelt in 1912, despite strenuous efforts and spectacular campaigns, could reach the White House.

In general the friends of an Administration have possessed a decisive advantage over independent party leaders in any contest for control of the party. When they have been unable to nominate a member of their own faction within the party, they have preferred a candidate from outside the ranks of the national party leaders to a leader of a rival faction. The record of the presidential elections clearly discloses the superior availability of "dark horses" under such circumstances. But the nomination of a "dark horse," though occasionally winning sensational victories for the "outs," as in the cases of James K. Polk and Franklin Pierce, is a highly speculative expedient for the "ins." Garfield's closely contested campaign in 1880 is the most striking exception to the general rule that nothing succeeds for the "ins" like success on the part of their official leaders.

The pattern of presidential nominations by the "outs" is very different. In only eleven out of forty campaigns — there was no opposition to Monroe's reëlection in 1820 — has their candidate been a national party leader, or at least a politician whose availability depended mainly upon his participation in national politics. Five of these candidates have been elected. In a dozen of the campaigns the "outs" have chosen for their standard bearer a state governor — generally with little actual experience in national politics — of whom five have been elected. In the same number of campaigns the candidate of the "outs" has been a military hero — also generally with little or no experience in national politics — of whom five have been elected. Five times the search for "availability" has led the "outs" further from the ranks of the active opposition party politicians. Twice their candidate has been a judge, whose official duties had kept him out of active partisan politics during the years immediately preceding his nomination. Three times the "outs" have nominated a candidate previously affiliated with the party in power. All five were residents of New York — an important element in their availability — and all five were defeated. The record suggests that it is an advantage for an opposition candidate not to be connected with the official opposition in the Congress. Systematic and persistent opposition by partisan legislators to the measures of the chief executive has not generally opened the road to the presidency.

Down to the period of the Civil War military success was the most useful asset for leadership of the opposition to the party in power. Generals Washington, Jackson, Harrison, and Taylor were successful leaders of the opposition in campaigns for the presidency, though both Jackson and Harrison were unsuccessful in their first attempts. General Charles C. Pinckney, however, who succeeded Washington as the head of the Society of the Cincinnati, though twice a candidate for the presidency, was unable to repeat Washington's performance in politics by restoring the Federalists to power. General Pierce was the last politician whose eligibility for leadership of the opposition in a campaign for the presidency rested largely on his military record to reach the White House. He defeated a much more capable and eminent military commander, General Scott, but at the next election Colonel Frémont failed to rally the full strength of the opposition to the Pierce Administration. Generals McClellan and Hancock failed to lead the opposition to victory in the campaigns of 1864 and 1880, and no military hero has been selected to lead the opposition in any subsequent presidential campaign. Since the Civil War, state governors have proved to be most eligible for leadership of the opposition in presidential campaigns. The Democrats, when out of power, have tried to get into office under the leadership of Governors Seymour, Tilden, Cleveland, Wilson, Smith, and Franklin D. Roosevelt, and the Republicans under the same circumstances have fought campaigns under the leadership of Governors McKinley, Landon, and Dewey. In general the military type of leadership seems better suited to the simpler conditions of the nineteenth century than to the more complex conditions of modern times. Under modern conditions the instructive experience of governing a great state has proved excellent preparation for governing the nation as well as for uniting the "outs" against the "ins."

The outstanding example of an opposition leader who led his forces to victory in a presidential campaign against an established national Administration without benefit of military reputation or gubernatorial independence was Thomas Jefferson. The only other opposition leader, holding a position of national eminence, who has ever succeeded in winning a presidential election and putting his followers in power was Grover Cleveland. He made a successful comeback in 1892, but was unable to hold his party together when restored to office. Clay, Calhoun, and Webster, the outstanding civilians among leaders of the opposition before the Civil War, strove in vain to reach the presidency. Even when united, as they were for a time by the formation of the Whig coalition in 1834, they could not accomplish their purpose of ejecting the Jacksonians from office, until their impatient followers drafted a military hero to head their ticket. In later years James G. Blaine and William Jennings Bryan were the most active and persistent aspirants for the presidency and were phenomenally successful in building up eager and faithful bands of partisans. But they never attained their objective. Lesser men in their own organizations, or greater men from outside the national organizations, achieved what the most conspicuous party leaders were unable to accomplish. There seems to be a natural principle of the American political order which handicaps the most eminent members of the opposition at Washington in the contest for leadership in the struggles of the "outs" against the "ins." Only Senator Harding in the present century has been chosen from the opposition in the Congress to lead a campaign against the party in power, and he was among the least of the Republican senatorial leaders.

The most important fact about the national party system is that it is a two-party system. This is not the result of any lack of candidates for the presidency. There are usually at least half a dozen tickets in the field at each election with organized support and active campaigns throughout the country. But ordinarily only two of these tickets receive much attention from the voters and the supporters of the others fail to elect any of the presidential electors. In the thirty-nine campaigns since Washington's retirement from politics there have been only nine in which more than two candidates received any electoral votes. In one campaign only one party had a ticket in the field. In the other twenty-nine campaigns the issue was clearly joined between a party which had been successful at the previous election and another party which had united the bulk of the opposition. In modern times the two major parties ordinarily have polled between them more than 95 per cent of the total popular vote. In most of the recent elections they have polled over 99 per cent of the votes. The minor parties have often conducted vigorous campaigns, but they have rarely made serious inroads upon the followings of the two major parties.

On those exceptional occasions when the presidential electors have distributed their votes among more than two candidates, the event has generally been the harbinger of some radical readjustment in the alignment of the major parties. In 1824 the "ins" were unable to unite upon a single candidate, and though one of their candidates was ultimately elected, their party broke up and was never again able to reform its ranks. In 1832 and 1836 the opponents of General Jackson were unable to unite upon any single candidate, but they did presently succeed in organizing an opposition party, which could contest the presidency against the Jacksonian Democrats with fair hopes of putting their candidates into the White House. In 1856 the Whigs broke up, as the Jeffersonian Republicans had done a generation earlier, and in 1860 the Democrats also were divided, so that in the first of these campaigns three parties, and in the second, four parties, were able to carry one or more states for their candidates. The result was a radically new alignment of parties and an early restoration of the two-party system. In 1892 the Populists carried several of the Western states for their candidate and forced a realignment of parties at the following election, as the Antislavery Republicans had done a generation earlier. The split in the Republican Party in 1912, however, was healed with little permanent effect on the partisan alignment, and the effort of the elder LaFollette in 1924 to force a realignment of parties came to nothing through his inability to get any electoral votes outside his own state of Wisconsin. Of the split in the Democratic Party in 1948 it is too early to predict the consequences.[4]

The party history of the United States falls into sharply defined periods in which one of the two major parties has on the whole dominated the political scene, while the other has maintained a practical monopoly of the opposition. The Federalists were dominant long enough to organize the government of the more perfect Union and demonstrate that the Constitution could be the basis of a serviceable political system. The Jeffersonian Republicans were masters of the scene during the first quarter of the nineteenth century, then the Jacksonian Democrats tended to predominate until 1860. The Antislavery Republicans managed to stay in power during the greater portion of the following period, despite the interruptions of the Cleveland and Wilson Administrations, until the advent of the New Deal in 1932. The parties in power made great changes in their policies through the years, but the organized opposition continued generally to maintain a united front despite the persistent diversions and occasional successes of the minor parties. The perennial struggle of the "outs" against the "ins," regardless of the ebb and flow of issues, seems to be the essence of the two-party system.

THE TECHNIQUES OF MAJOR-PARTY LEADERSHIP

The process of forming parties, by means of which ambitious politicians may hope to win the presidency, was described most realistically by a brilliant French student of politics, who visited the United States early in the age of Jackson.[5] "The pains which are taken to create parties are inconceivable," de Tocqueville wrote, "and at the present day it is no easy task. In the United States there is no religious animosity, because all religion is respected and no sect is predominant; there is no jealousy of rank, because the people are everything and none can contest their authority; lastly, there is no public misery to serve as a means of agitation, because the physical condition of the country opens so wide a field to industry, that man only needs to be let alone to be able to accomplish prodigies. Nevertheless, ambitious men will succeed in creating parties, since it is difficult to eject a person from authority upon the mere ground that his place is coveted by others. All the skill of the actors in the political world lies in the art of creating parties. A political aspirant in the United States begins by discerning his own interest, and discovering those other interests which may be collected around and amalgamated with it. He then contrives to find out some doctrine or principle which may suit the purposes of this new association, and which he adopts in order to bring forward his party and secure its popularity . . . This being done, the new party is ushered into the political world."

De Tocqueville's observations of American party politics were made at the time when Clay, Calhoun, and Webster were striving to organize the opposition to the Jacksonian Democrats. The latter had recently come into power. Its leaders were determined to stay there as long as possible. Jackson himself, while seeking to turn out J. Q. Adams and his division of the Jeffersonians, had advocated the democratic principle of rotation in office and had even declared in favor of a constitutional amendment to apply that popular doctrine to the presidency by limiting its incumbents to a single term. However, those of his political associates who cherished no hope of succeeding him, at least not immediately, persuaded him to follow the example of Jefferson and accept one reëlection in order to vindicate his conduct of the government. Those who aspired to succeed him without such delay were extraordinarily vigorous and resourceful politicians at the head of powerful factions eager for a greater voice in the determination of public policy. Clay, during the greater part of a generation, had been the most conspicuous and successful spokesman for the elements in American public life which can most conveniently be designated as the West. Calhoun was the ablest representative of the cotton planters in the Lower South, who held the view expressed by the younger Pinckney in the Convention of 1787 that the leading agricultural interests were entitled to govern the country without interference by adverse local and special interests such as the merchants and manufacturers of the Northern seaports and mill towns. Webster, on the other hand, was the most effective spokesman for these same special and local interests, who were not disposed to take a subordinate position in national politics, if skillful leadership could give them a share in the ruling power. These were the circumstances which afforded an uncommon opportunity for the organization of a political party in the manner described by de Tocqueville.

The formation of the Whig Party afforded a perfect illustration of what de Tocqueville reported as the typical technique of the American politician. Clay promised to advance the interests of the American farmer by measures designed to develop the home market for his produce. These included protection for American industries, whose increasing numbers of workers would consume greater quantities of the farmers' flour and meat, and improvements in the means of internal transportation, which would make the home market more accessible to the products of the farm. For the campaign of 1832 Clay proposed to add to this program a demand for the extension of the privileges of the Bank of the United States, a measure to which he had been sternly opposed at the beginning of his career in national politics a score of years earlier. These measures were designed to appeal also to the Eastern mercantile and manufacturing interests. Taken together they constituted Clay's celebrated "American System." Webster, who had entered national politics shortly after Clay as a stout opponent of protective tariffs, lest they interfere with the profits of foreign commerce, and had shown little interest in internal improvements at federal expense, responded to Clay's appeal to interests rapidly becoming more important in his section of the country. The two leaders joined forces against Jackson.

Calhoun, whose devotion to the doctrine of nullification betrayed his belief that the Southern planters could dominate the political scene without compromising their special interest in free trade, though more bitterly opposed to Jackson than either of the other rivals, refused to join with them in the campaign of 1832, and the organization of the opposition remained incomplete. The crushing defeat inflicted by the Jacksonian Democrats upon their opponents in the election of that year caused a change of strategy by the opposition leaders. Practical differences over the tariff were compromised for the sake of a united front against the Jacksonians, and theoretical differences over states' rights were tacitly laid aside. Thus in 1834 the great Whig coalition was formed. In 1836 the coalition ran different candidates in different sections of the country, in the hope of getting enough electoral votes to throw the final choice into the House of Representatives, but could not prevent the succession of Jackson's political heir, Vice-President Martin Van Buren. In 1840, aided by the depressing consequences of the panic of 1837 and by the selection of a romantic military hero for a candidate, the Whig coalition attained its primary objective of ejecting the Democrats from office, but failed in its ulterior purpose of winning the presidency for any one of its original chieftains.

From the viewpoint of the political strategist, described by de Tocqueville, the Whig Party must be pronounced a miserable failure. Twice it elected its candidate for the presidency, but on each occasion it evaded the conflicts of interest between its component factions by nominating a popular general, who ran without benefit of an authentic platform. Factional dissensions among its members prevented it from making any effective use of its victories, and after twenty years it broke up because it could not face the issues which had become paramount in the minds of its members. It never succeeded in putting one of its principal leaders into the White House. Calhoun was the first of its organizers to abandon the Party, when he found that he could not make it serve his purposes. Webster finally became disgusted with it also, when he failed to get its nomination in 1852. Clay could only get its nomination, as he himself lamented, when the chances of election were unfavorable. The method of uniting the "outs" against the "ins" by coördinating the special interests of different factions and finding a principle which could suit their common purposes, when employed by three of the most skillful "actors" who have ever appeared on the national political scene, brought them only frustration and disappointment.

There is more in the "art of creating parties" than was recognized by de Tocqueville. Man is doubtless a rational animal, as de Tocqueville assumed, and will pursue his special interests, particularly his economic interests, with perspicacity and determination. But he is also a creature of natural impulses and instincts, which may cause him to disregard the carefully coördinated programs of ambitious and ingenious politicians and to upset their nice calculations. Voters naturally like a leader whom they recognize as one of their own kind. They make of him a symbol of the type of leadership they crave. This consciousness of kind registers the strength of powerful inner springs of human action, and makes personality an independent force in politics. General Jackson offered no specific program of measures when he first entered the race for the succession to President Monroe. He did not set himself up as a coördinator of factional interests. He simply raised a standard to which all could repair who were weary of the familiar faces at Washington and wanted a change. The stern and resolute warrior embodied a type of political action that appealed strongly not only to the rugged frontiersman and pioneer, but also to plain folks everywhere. The sophisticated members of the Monroe Cabinet who sought to succeed their nominal chief could not stir the feelings of the new generation of Americans, responding to the challenge of national politics in unprecedented numbers, as General Jackson stirred them. Operating in the name of General Jackson, ambitious and realistic politicians, notably Martin Van Buren, were able to mobilize the opposition to the National Republicans more effectively than the leaders of the great Whig coalition were ever able to mobilize in their own names the opposition to the Jacksonians. The technique which elected General Jackson also served to elect Generals Harrison and Taylor. But this was not the technique celebrated by de Tocqueville. It was a technique which understands the role of human nature in politics, and, disregarding factional interests, exploits to the full the latent power of personality.

This is the technique which Graham Wallas had in mind when he wrote [6] that "the empirical art of politics consists largely in the formation of opinion by the deliberate exploitation of subconscious non-rational inference." It was employed more systematically and effectively by the Whig campaign managers in the "log-cabin" campaign of 1840 than ever before in American politics. It was of great assistance in the election of Generals Harrison and Taylor, but it was never helpful to Clay, Calhoun, or Webster. For the purpose of putting the "outs" in place of the "ins" it seemed more decisive in the hands of the Whig campaign managers than the technique of coördinating political factions by the deliberate exploitation of the conscious rational pursuit of economic interests. It greatly aided in holding the Whig coalition together for a score of years as the major opposition party, and in giving the dominant Jacksonian democracy lively competition for control of the federal government.

There is a third technique which has held a significant place in the organization of political parties. This is the technique of sublimating the specific economic interests of different political factions by merging them in more general interests, which can be identified with the public interest of the whole body of people. Clay's well-publicized "American

System" was an excellent specimen of this technique. It served to put his leadership on a higher plane than that of mere scheming subservience to private and local interests in different sections of the country. But as a sublimation of factious political interests it was greatly inferior to Washington's identification of the public interest with a more perfect Union or to Jefferson's identification of the public interest with Liberty as well as Union. Liberty and Union were profound public interests. Washington's and Jefferson's successful sublimation of their specific political programs by means of devotion to such transcendent interests perhaps goes further than any other parts of their general political strategy to explain the glorious success of their efforts to rally scattered oppositions and form them into effective Administration parties.

THE RECORD OF THE MAJOR PARTIES

The organization of the Federalists represented a highly successful combination of all three of these techniques. There was the powerful appeal of a masterful personality, reënforced by the skillful exploitation of the natural popular responses to the stimuli of the symbols of government. There was also the skillful coördination of rational special interests, chiefly economic, dominating important sections of the country. Finally, there was the triumphant sublimation of those broader interests in better government which could thus be identified with the general public interest. Washington's less competent political associates, particularly Hamilton and Adams, failed to hold the Federalist Party on the high plane on which Washington established it — Hamilton because he failed to see beyond the special interests of classes too narrow to dominate the government of the Union, and Adams because he relied too much on inadequate powers of personality. These failures contributed heavily to the ruin of the Federalist Party.

Jefferson was more successful in maintaining the character of his party, which as the instrument of both Liberty and Union drove the organized opposition off the field of national politics. His sympathetic personality, though lacking the glamour of the victorious general, made a powerful appeal to the independent farmers and middle-class tradespeople who composed the bulk of the American population at the end of the eighteenth century. He also was able, as Beard has convincingly demonstrated,[7] to coördinate the major economic interests of most of the sections in which these natural admirers of his were numerous and influential.

The sectional character of the Jeffersonian party is clearly revealed in the record of the national elections beginning with the contest over the vice-presidency in 1792. Since General Washington was unopposed for reëlection, the contest between the "ins" and the "outs" turned on the choice of the Vice-President, and, since Washington was a Southerner, by common consent the choice lay between the outstanding Northern leaders. Vice-President John Adams was the obvious choice of the "ins," and Governor George Clinton the equally obvious choice of the "outs." Adams carried every state north of the Potomac except New York, which went for Clinton. He also carried South Carolina, which held to its bargain with New England, originally struck in the Federal Convention. Virginia and the other Southern states cast their votes for Clinton, except Kentucky which voted for both Washington and Jefferson. The head of the Administration maintained his hold on the hearts of his countrymen everywhere, but the Administration party had not won over the elements in the population which had originally opposed the unconditional ratification of the Constitution.

In 1796, when Jefferson was free to enter the contest against Adams directly, the true nature of the Federalist Party was clearly revealed. It could carry the states in which the mercantile interests were still dominant. It could also carry the states in which the foremost Puritan in politics was naturally admired by the bulk of the population. Finally, it could carry the small states, New Jersey, Delaware, and Maryland, which had been won over to Federalism by the great political compromises in the Convention of 1787. This brought Adams to the Potomac without the loss of a Northern state except Pennsylvania, where the plain farmers and backwoodsmen repudiated the leadership of the big landowners and Philadelphia merchants. South of the Potomac he could not carry a single state. Even South Carolina, which cast her votes for Adams's running mate, Pinckney, voted also for Jefferson. With the rapid westward movement of population steadily favoring the Jeffersonians, mercantilism could not hold the great and politically decisive states of Pennsylvania and New York against agrarianism. The eventual defeat of the Federalists was certain, and would have come even without the factional dissensions between Adams and the Hamiltonians. Massachusetts, Connecticut, and Delaware remained loyal to the Federalists until the last, but no party constituted like the Federalists could have successfully withstood the challenge of the

Jeffersonians under the social and economic conditions prevailing at the beginning of the nineteenth century.

Jefferson's party was ruined by its own success. It was not possible for any political organization to function simultaneously as both the party of the "ins" and that of the "outs." A one-party system of government was incompatible with the growth of democracy under the Federal Constitution, particularly when that party permitted a Congressional Caucus to select its candidates for the presidency. A governing party which could not democratize itself could not maintain a monopoly of the opposition to itself in a country whose people were becoming deeply interested in the processes of government. When all practical politicians had become Jeffersonians, the party had no longer a function.

The great service of the Whig coalition in the development of the American political system was its contribution to the firm establishment of the two-party system. What Washington thought of partisanship in politics is revealed by his "Farewell Address." He was resolved to entrust the government of the country to the friends of the Constitution. He appeared to possess no misgivings over their monopolization of the power to govern, and he certainly did not countenance deliberate efforts to make a system of government out of organized opposition to the Administration. Jefferson's ideas on the subject of party government and its relations to constitutional government were no clearer than Washington's. He certainly intended to organize the "outs" in order to seize power, but he seemed content with his success and never advocated the organization of the opposition for the sake of opposition. Jackson was a man of action who was disposed to leave political speculation to his lieutenants. Very likely Van Buren, who was bred in the pragmatic school of New York politics, understood and believed in the two-party system. His posthumous books on politics support this view.[8] But the politicians who first made a virtue of opposition for opposition's sake were Clay and his companions in the Whig coalition. The very name was designed to dignify the function. Jackson's mastery of the political scene was to be opposed regardless of the immediate prospect of turning him and his copartisans out of office and getting themselves in. Opposition not only to such a President, but also to such a concept of the presidency as Jackson's, was to become a permanent rule of political action. Clay could be at times as imperious as Jackson himself, but his place in American history is due, not to his imperiousness, but to his services as the Great Compromiser. These services were a fruit of his conception of the proper function of party leadership, whether in or out of office. He made the opposition party a permanent instrument of government.

Regarded not as an Administration party but as an opposition party, the Whig coalition was an impressive success. It gave the dominant Jacksonian democracy formidable opposition through five presidential campaigns. It could not prevent the organization of independent antislavery parties, the Liberty Party in 1840, the Free Soilers in 1848, and the Free Democracy in 1852. But it kept them within narrow limits until antislavery feeling in the North burst out of bounds under the spur of the repeal of the Missouri Compromise. Though the Whigs broke up in 1854, the Administration party itself split in two, six years later, under the impact of similar stresses and strains.

During the period of its activity as the party of the opposition the Whig coalition found substantial support in all sections of the country and contended with the Administration on fairly equal terms. Its popular vote was never far behind that of the Democrats, and the states which it carried for its presidential candidate in a majority of its campaigns were distributed among all the major sections. There were only six states participating in all its campaigns which it never carried. They also were widely distributed: New Hampshire, Virginia, Alabama, Illinois, Missouri, and Arkansas. On the whole the Whigs developed less strength than the Democrats on the frontier and in the Lower South, but were superior to them in the Upper South and in New England. The balance of power lay in New York and Pennsylvania, and the rivalry between the two major parties for the ascendancy in these two big doubtful states produced a sense of accountability to the independent farmers and tradespeople, who dominated their politics, which made for moderation in the choice of measures as well as of men. Such an opposition formed a genuinely national party, and gave the voters at every election an alternative to the dominant party, which was always sufficiently attractive to keep the latter on its mettle. This situation represented the two-party system at its best.

The realignment of parties after the repeal of the Missouri Compromise confirms the conclusions concerning the national party system based on the experience of the Whig coalition, the Jacksonian Democrats, and their predecessors back to 1787. A short period of factious confusion ended with the restoration of the two-party system. The Antislavery Republicans and the Douglas Democrats laid the foundations for new Administration and opposition parties, which proved capable of competing for power on fairly equal terms most of the time down to the present and of generally offering the voters a choice of candidates uncomplicated by serious diversions to minor parties. The Republicans have now maintained a continuous organization for more than ninety years, and the two-party system which emerged after 1860 has persisted with only minor readjustments. Efforts to bring about a fresh realignment have been made repeatedly, but the essential features of the original partisan pattern have endured despite great vicissitudes of circumstance and fortune.

The antislavery Republican Party began its career under leadership that was manifestly inferior to that of its predecessors. Seward, Chase, and Sumner were famous men in their day, but they hardly matched Clay, Calhoun, and Webster. The party managers possessed exceptional skill in the technical aspects of campaign management, as was effectively demonstrated in both 1856 and 1860, but the official candidates made heavy demands upon their talents. The first presidential candidate, Colonel Frémont, was doubtless a romantic figure, but he could not bear comparison with such earlier leaders of newly organized oppositions as Generals Washington and Jackson. Abraham Lincoln proved to be far the greatest of dark horses, but the "rail splitter's" wisdom and magnanimity, like the "pathfinder's" deficiencies, were not fully revealed until after the campaign. In the generation of Republican leaders after the Civil War none of those of the first rank in national politics reached the presidency. Blaine could not get elected, while John Sherman and Roscoe Conkling could not even get nominated. More recent experience does not point to any different conclusion. As an instrument for gratifying the ambitions of its leading politicians, the Republican Party has been as much a failure as the Whig. The greatest Republicans were statesmen whose greatness was revealed after they reached the White House.

The prospects of the new Republican Party as an instrument for coördinating special interests were not much more impressive. The Antislavery Republicans inherited the essentials of Clay's American System from the Whig Party, to which most of its original members had formerly belonged. But the former Jacksonian Democrats who joined the new party in substantial numbers could not generally favor a protective tariff, and the need for internal improvements at government expense had been greatly reduced by the astonishing development of the railroads. From the Free Soilers the Antislavery Republicans inherited a spirit rather than a program, since the Dred Scott decision outlawed the proposal to exclude slavery from the national territories. The opening of the federal territories north of the Missouri Compromise line to slavery would have been a heavy blow to the prospects of men without land or capital, who had hoped to settle in the West, but for the Free Soilers' promise of the Homestead Act, which offered compensation in the form of new hope for supremacy in the territories. This addition to the remnants of the American System formed an economic program with a powerful appeal to farmers and workers and small businessmen throughout the North. But against these gains in the North had to be set off the special interests in the South which were alienated and even hopelessly antagonized by these same measures.

The greatest source of strength to the new party was its sublimation of the issues springing from the controversy over slavery. Douglas was as ingenious a coördinator of special interests as any of the Antislavery Republican leaders, but he could not touch "the mystic cords of memory," to which Lincoln appealed in his "First Inaugural," in order to "swell the chorus of the Union." It was Lincoln who possessed the magic to call forth "the better angels" in the nature of the American people and transmute a political campaign into a moral crusade. He gave new meaning to the vision of democracy and new purpose to Republicans of whatever extraction. The mighty force of conscience gave an impulse to the new party which swept it to heights beyond the reach of politicians who would live only by the exploitation of a leader's personality and the rationalization of their followers' interests.

As an opposition party the Antislavery Republicans could capture the presidency, but as an Administration party they were heavily handicapped. They could capture the presidency, because the concentration of Republicans in the Northern and Western states enabled a minority of the whole body of voters to carry enough states to win a majority of the presidential electors. They were heavily handicapped as an Administration party, because the limited distribution of the Republicans made it impossible for them to elect a majority of the members of Congress. During the Civil War the absence of representation from the South enabled the Republicans to control all branches of the national government, but it was painfully clear to the Republican leaders that the reconstruction of civil government in the South would bring an end to Republican supremacy at Washington. A successful Administration party needs to control the Congress as well as the presidency, and for that purpose it was essential to broaden the base of the party membership.

The first plan of the Republican leaders for preserving their control of the federal government was to give votes to the freedmen. The enfranchisement of the former slaves would presumably bring a flood of ballots from a grateful people. Several of the Southern states might be expected to go Republican, and the prospects of the Party would be correspondingly improved. But it proved impracticable to enforce Negro suffrage in the South except at the point of the bayonet, and presently it proved impracticable also to keep federal troops in the South solely for that purpose. The withdrawal of the federal troops by the Hayes Administration was a convenient solution of the dispute over the presidential election of 1876, but it also marked the end of Republican hopes for any substantial growth of the party in that section of the country which became known as the Solid South.

The second plan of the Republican leaders for preserving their control of the federal government was to admit new states into the Union from the West. Nevada had been hastily admitted in 1864, despite the smallness of its population, with an obvious eye on the presidential election of that year, and the rapid settlement of other parts of the West under the stimulus of the Homestead Act with a strong preponderance of Republicans among the voters enhanced the prospect that new Republican Congressmen from the West would swing the balance of power in favor of the party. Throughout the latter decades of the nineteenth century only Texas in the Southwest could vie with the Northwest in rate of settlement, and the admission of new Republican states confirmed the Party's superiority in the Senate and greatly improved its position in the House of Representatives. The Fifty-first Congress (1889–1891), in which the Republicans held good working majorities for the first time since 1875, admitted half a dozen new states, extending across the country from the Dakotas to Idaho and Washington, and the outlook for continued Republican supremacy was better than at any time since the Civil War. Then the rise of Populism diverted Republican voters to a new and more radical party in what had been the strongest Republican states, extending from Kansas, Nebraska, and the Dakotas to Idaho and Nevada, and the plans of the Republicans for consolidating their position in national politics were again upset.

The Republicans were finally transformed from a successful opposition party into a successful Administration party in spite of the leaders' plans. They would have preferred to evade the silver issue in 1896, as the Whigs had sought to evade the slavery issue in 1852, in the hope of retaining both Silver Republicans and Gold Republicans in the same organization. The fusion of the Populists with the Democrats in 1896 and the nomination of Bryan as the most aggressive and magnetic leader of the opposition to the Cleveland Administration compelled the Republicans to choose the other side of the currency question, or risk the fate of the equivocal Whigs. The Republican leaders knew better than to try to ignore the paramount issue in the minds of millions of voters. Making a virtue of necessity, they accepted responsibility for the defense of the gold standard and thereby became the favorite champions of those Eastern financial and business interests which had never forgotten their distrust of, nor overcome their dislike for, the Radical Republicanism of the Party's early years. What had begun as a predominantly farmer-labor party with an incidental appeal to businessmen now developed into a farmer-labor-business party with major emphasis on the political requirements of business. The unplanned evolution of Radical Republicanism into Conservative Republicanism brought unexpected accessions of strength in the urban and industrial sections of the country. This evolution gave the Grand Old Party, as it now liked to call itself, the breadth of base which it needed, and had so long sought in vain, for an effective Administration party. The "party of prosperity," of "sound money," and "the full dinner pail," was in to stay, except for the interlude of the Wilson Administration made possible by unmanageable internal dissensions, until the debacle following the great stock-market crash in 1929.

The disruption of the Jacksonian Democrats in 1860 converted their organization from an Administration into an opposition party. In the Northeast the New York State party organization with powerful support in Wall Street supplied the leadership for opposition in that section of the country to the men and measures of the dominant Republicans. In the North Central section the Douglas Democrats bequeathed a large body of partisans and a tradition of vigorous leadership to the organizers of opposition to Republicanism. The Solid South after Reconstruction supplied the largest, though not the most influential, element in the new party of opposition. The relations among these three principal factions largely explain the development of the opposition party down to the present time.

The Democratic Party, like the Republican, has been a farmer-labor-business party. In Jackson's time the farmers were the dominant element in the Party, and agrarian interests continued to be dominant in its North Central and Western and Southern sections long after the Civil War. In the Northeast the labor and business interests were beginning to challenge the leadership of the rural interests before the disruption of the Party in 1860.[9] The rapid growth of urban industrial interests thereafter gradually changed the relative influence of these different elements in the opposition to the dominant Republicanism. The dominant interests in the three major sections of the Party were opposed to one another as well as to the dominant Republicans, and the struggles between them for the control of their party greatly complicated their combined efforts to turn out the Republicans and put their own candidates in power.

First, the national leadership of the Party was seized by the Northeastern business interests. A series of New York governors, Horatio Seymour, Samuel J. Tilden, and Grover Cleveland, headed the national ticket in most of the campaigns down to 1892 and set the tone of the opposition to Republicanism. Military heroes in 1864 and 1880 did nothing to alter the general character of the Party during this period. The farmers, particularly the Western farmers, had always been restive under this leadership, particularly when, as after 1873 and 1893, business depressions reacted ruinously upon the value of farm products. But during more prosperous times the business interests were able to retain their leadership, and the accent of the presidential campaigns, after opposition to the Republican policy of reconstruction was finally abandoned, was placed upon the demand for reform — administrative reform under Tilden, and both administrative and fiscal reform under Cleveland.

A second period in the history of the Democrats as the party of opposition was inaugurated by the Bryan campaign in 1896. The leaders of the Western farmers seized control of the Party and, vigorously aided and abetted by Western mining interests, reversed the policies of the opposition. The Western agrarian interests, like the Eastern financial interests, could count upon the steady support of the Solid South, since the latter's primary interest was the maintenance of home rule in the South, a price for its support which both Northern factions were ready and eager to pay. They concentrated at first on reform of the currency, but the revival of prosperity under the McKinley Administration compelled them in the later Bryan campaigns to broaden the base of their opposition. The nomination of Judge Parker of New York in 1904, like the nomination of Wall Street lawyer

John W. Davis twenty years later, marked the temporary success of efforts by the Eastern business interests to recover control of the Party, but they could not recover control of the national government without the ungrudging coöperation of the agrarian interests in the Party. This they did not get. Woodrow Wilson in 1912 succeeded better than any of his predecessors in reconciling the conflicting factions within the Party, and the division of the Administration party made him an easy winner in the campaign of 1912. Only the obscuring of domestic issues by the European war, however, enabled him to win a reëlection in 1916.

The third period in the history of the Democrats as the party of the opposition was inaugurated by the Alfred E. Smith campaign in 1928. For the first time the industrial labor elements in the Party, led by the efficient political machines in the great cities, captured the nomination and attempted to rally the scattered opposition to the dominant Republicans. But Al Smith did not appeal to the Western farmers more strongly than John W. Davis, and he could not hold the Southern Democrats, who liked the new Northern leadership much less than the old. Four years later Governor Roosevelt accomplished what Governor Smith had failed to bring about, and the three main factions of the Party, united by enthusiasm for a sympathetic leader and further incited by the egregious failure of the Republicans to maintain their good name as the party of prosperity, turned the Administration out of office and came once more into power. The old problem, which had confronted the Federalists under Washington in 1789, the Democratic-Republicans under Jefferson in 1801, the Democrats under Jackson in 1829, and the Republicans under Lincoln in 1861, came up again. Could the New Deal transform the followers of Franklin Delano Roosevelt from a successful opposition into a successful Administration party? Or was F.D.R., like Grover Cleveland and Woodrow Wilson, to be merely an interlude between the administrations of the dominant Republicans?

Parties are more than their leaders. Leadership seems to be the most important factor in the original organization of political parties, but when a party becomes a going concern, its character is determined in some measure by its followers. They become weary of factional leaders haggling incessantly over the adjustment of conflicting private and local interests. They demand a more inspiring leadership, which can appeal to their better selves, and sublimate their tedious search for personal advantage into a demand for more principle in politics. Administration parties, which have the first opportunity to define the issues in presidential campaigns, have furnished some striking illustrations of successful sublimations. The Republicans were extraordinarily successful in 1920 in making their commonplace candidate, Warren G. Harding, seem to stand for Americanism. Coolidge's constitutionalism served well enough in the campaign of 1924. Even Hoover's individualism was a valuable asset to his party as long as it could maintain its reputation as the party of prosperity. But in adversity, when the unfortunate victims of depression clamored for relief, individualism deteriorated into official irresponsibility. Hoover's Reconstruction Finance Corporation lent substantial aid to banks and railroads and other great corporations, but did little for the individual. Coolidge's constitutionalism, in the face of unprecedented need for vigorous governmental action, broke down into judicial obstructionism, and Americanism degenerated into isolationism, The New Deal cleared a path for a new set of sublimations, until new wars again diverted the attention of the voters from domestic issues.

The opposition parties have perhaps even better opportunities than Administration parties for the advancement of political principles, but the opportunities are always conditioned by the membership of the factions from which the opposition is organized and which determine its character. It is easier for the major opposition party to leave the pioneer work on behalf of new principles to the minor parties. The latter are not embarrassed by the necessity of coördinating such a variety of special interests as the major parties and can more conveniently concentrate their energies on the educational function of political parties, while the major opposition party devotes itself to the "practical" side of politics, the selection of candidates with the best chances of success at the polls and the management of election campaigns against the party in power. The major opposition party must be alert to take over a new principle, when minor parties have cultivated the tender plant and developed it to political maturity, or risk the forfeiture of its leadership of the opposition, like the Federalists after 1815 and the Whigs after 1854. It may find itself burdened with a losing instead of a winning issue, like the Democrats in 1896, but this misfortune also is one of the risks which major opposition parties must assume. The bipartisan system in national politics is one of the native fruits of the free-enterprise system in the American way of life, and the major opposition party must carry the risks if it is to enjoy the benefits of freedom to rally to its standard as many as possible of the factions which seek to travel the road to power.

The record of presidential elections shows that the best opportunities for the leaders of opposition parties come with economic crises and depressions. There have been five major crises since the final establishment of the two-party system in the age of Jackson and Clay. The crisis of 1837 found the Jacksonian Democrats in power. The Whigs captured the House of Representatives in 1838 and the presidency in 1840. The crisis of 1857 found the Democrats again in power. The Republicans captured the House of Representatives in 1858 and the presidency in 1860. The crisis of 1873 found the Republicans in power. The Democrats captured the House of Representatives the following year, and failed to capture the presidency in 1876 only because the Republicans were barely able to recoup their heavy losses in the North and West with the aid of Negro votes in the Lower South. The crisis of 1893 found the Democrats in power. The Republicans captured the Congress the following year and the presidency two years later. The crisis of 1929 found the Republicans in power. The Democrats captured the House of Representatives the following year and the presidency two years later. These ruinous cataclysms affected different elements of the people differently, but they brought depression throughout the country and invariably marked a turn in the partisan as well as in the business cycle.

Foreign wars have likewise offered favorable opportunities to the opposition parties. The Mexican War was sponsored by a Democratic Administration. The Whigs captured the House of Representatives in 1846 and the presidency in 1848. World War I was sponsored by another Democratic Administration. The Republicans captured the Congress in 1918 and the presidency two years later. World War II was also sponsored by a Democratic Administration. The Republicans captured the Congress in 1946 and expected to capture the presidency in 1948. It seems to have been popular dissatisfaction with the record of the Republican Congress that frustrated those expectations. The Spanish War of 1898 also provided an occasion for a change of the party in power. Inept leadership by the opposition contributed to the loss of the opportunity offered by Administration errors in waging the war and making the peace. It is not possible to demonstrate that participation in war leads as directly to political defeat as involvement in economic depression, since there were other complications affecting the loss of power at the end of the Polk and Wilson Administrations, but prudent leaders of the "ins" will not expect in the light of past performances to improve their hold on power by resort to war.

Besides these postwar and economic-crisis elections, there have been six other presidential campaigns since the final establishment of the two-party system which have resulted in the "outs" ejecting the "ins" from office. The Democrats frustrated Henry Clay's last bid for power in 1844 by replacing accidental President Tyler with dark horse Polk; in 1852 they turned out another derelict Whig Administration under accidental President Fillmore with dark horse Pierce; in 1884 they turned out a derelict Republican Administration under accidental President Arthur with Grover Cleveland; and with the aid of third-party diversions they turned out Presidents Harrison and Taft in 1892 and 1912, respectively. The Republicans recovered power in 1888 by replacing President Cleveland with dark horse Benjamin Harrison, likewise without aid of war or depression. In all these elections except the last the winning of the presidency was preceded by the winning of the midterm congressional elections. It is evident that chance has played an important role in the fortunes of the parties and that the influence of personality in presidential politics has been greatly complicated by other less conspicuous factors, such as the relations between the factions composing the party, the general circumstances of the time and, in close elections, the skill of the campaign managers.

These considerations expose the unreasonableness of the opinion expressed by N. I. Stone in his book, *They Also Ran.* Having compared the successful and unsuccessful candidates at presidential elections on the basis of their personal qualifications for the office, as he appraised them, he concluded:[10] "The score is tied: not even by the meagerest margin has democracy been able to prove that it has the discernment to choose the best man available for the most important office in the land." Waiving the obvious question concerning Mr. Stone's qualifications for passing final judgment on the character of the candidates and for reviewing the verdict of the voters at all these elections, the political analyst may well inquire why the voters should base their choice exclusively on the personal qualities of the candidates, when other matters, particularly the general leadership of the party, the relations between the factions composing the party, and the nature of the paramount issues, should exert a due influence upon their judgment.

A major party is more than its candidate for a particular office and a decision concerning its claim for power must take into account all the matters which can affect the expectations of the voters concerning the use of power, if granted, by the party. There must be a realistic analysis of the components of the party and of the relations between those components before a political critic can properly say that the American people have failed to make a rational use of their power to choose presidents. The two-party system may rightly be held responsible for the quality of the men that it has furnished for the practical business of government, but to denounce it because what one may think to be the better of the two principal candidates for the presidency has not always, or even not usually, been chosen for that high office is to mistake the essential nature of party government under the Constitution. In deciding whether to support the "ins" or the "outs," the voter has more to consider than the personal qualities of the candidates. He must be mindful also of the quality of their party friends, the purposes of the factions whose interests are involved in the success of the party, and the general needs of the times. When the difference in the quality of the candidates is not great, the public interest as well as the private interest of the individual voter may well require that the character of the candidate be subordinated to the character of the party.

The most successful of the opposition parties has been the Democratic Party since the loss of its earlier supremacy in national politics in 1860. Three times it has found a candidate capable of taking advantage of the mistakes and misfortunes of the party in power and driving its leaders from office. Compared with this record, that of the Whigs is poor and that of the Federalists after 1800 is pathetic. The stresses and strains of holding power disclosed the weaknesses of the Democratic combination of factions and prevented it under the leadership of Grover Cleveland and of Woodrow Wilson from preserving its ascendancy over the Republicans. Under Franklin D. Roosevelt's leadership the Democrats made more serious inroads upon the Republican sources of strength and, despite the mutual incompatibility between the rural Southern and the urban Northern factions, offered a more formidable challenge to the "ins" than at any time since the initial rise of Andrew Jackson. The presidential election of 1948 finally demonstrated that the Democratic Party had succeeded under the New Deal in exchanging roles with their Republican opponents.

The most successful of the "ins" up to the debacle of 1932 was the present Republican Party. Despite great vicissitudes of fortune and permanent exclusion from a large part of the South it managed to elect its presidential candidate at all but four of the campaigns between 1856 and 1932. It maintained its ascendancy, despite interludes of opposition triumph, more than twice as long as the Jacksonian Democrats. It produced few great Presidents, but could find many candidates capable of uniting its various factions and successfully exploiting the possibilities in the established alignment of the major parties. Yet, when driven from power in 1932, it was unable to regain control of the government in five successive elections, a period of uninterrupted defeat exceeded only by that of the Democrats following their downfall in 1860.

THE PUZZLE OF THE IRRATIONAL BIPARTISAN SYSTEM

The unplanned institution of organized partisanship has been surprisingly successful as a means of furnishing the American people with a more democratic process for the election of Presidents than was planned by the framers of the Constitution. The two major parties have ordinarily been able to present to the voters a choice of candidates which has been at least acceptable, if not always satisfactory, to the great majority of those who have been sufficiently interested in an election to go to the polls. Not once since the final establishment of the two-party system has the partisan electoral process failed to produce a President without resort to the undemocratic process of election by the House of Representatives, in which in accordance with the arrangement hastily improvised by the framers each state delegation would cast a single vote regardless of its size. Until the election of 1948 there had been no instance under the bipartisan system when a presidential elector had insisted on exercising his constitutional right to vote according to his own judgment despite the mandate of the party to which he was supposed by the voters to belong. The abolition of the electoral colleges and of the electoral function of the House of Representatives, to make way for a more popular electoral system, had long been an academic question without interest to practical politicians. The manipulations of the Dixiecrats, however, made the abolition of the anachronistic electoral colleges an urgently needed reform.

The bipartisan system has not been equally successful as a means of organizing popular majorities and demonstrating the consent of the governed for the leadership of partisan presidents. The difficulties which have stood in the way of bringing together a numerical majority of the whole body of people throughout the Union in support of a particular party, as Madison anticipated, have proved formidable. Since the election of John Quincy Adams by the House of Representatives, when much less than a majority of the popular votes had been cast for him, there have been a dozen presidential elections at which the successful candidate has received less than a majority of the popular votes. Presidents Polk, Taylor, Buchanan, Lincoln at his first election, Garfield, Cleveland and Wilson at both of their elections, and most recently Truman received no more than a plurality of the popular votes. Two Presidents, Hayes and Benjamin Harrison, did not receive even a plurality over their nearest opponent. The closeness of these elections attests the excellence of the bipartisan system as a means of giving the voters an effective choice between candidates. But it reveals the imperfections of the system regarded as an instrument for such a coördination of special and local interests as to give an impressive show of popular consent for the measures of the victorious candidate.

The limitations of the major parties, as agencies for the coördination of political factions, are disclosed by the small size of the majorities obtained by the most successful candidates for the presidency. Neither Andrew Jackson nor Abraham Lincoln, whom history has ranked among the greatest Presidents, was ever able to poll as much as three-fifths of the popular vote. Both General Grant and Colonel Roosevelt, popular favorites who scored smashing victories when they came up for reëlection, failed to gain the distinction of a three-fifths majority of all the votes cast at the polls. Among all the victorious candidates only Warren G. Harding and Franklin D. Roosevelt were able to win by even the narrowest margin this high mark of popularity among the voters. Warren G. Harding, running for the presidency under the attractive banner of "Americanism," was a handsome and winsome candidate; Franklin D. Roosevelt, asking for a vote of confidence at the end of his first term, made what seemed an irresistible appeal to many who had never before supported his party. Why doesn't nearly everybody vote for the winner now and then as nearly everybody once did vote for James Monroe? Why should so many voters at every election support the losing candidates?

It is evident that the roots of partisanship extend far below the surface of political campaigns and are deeply embedded in the traditional interests and inveterate habits of the men and women throughout the land who compose the national electorate. An adequate understanding of the bipartisan system in national politics calls for more than analysis of the characters of the candidates and inquiry into the circumstances of the campaigns. It is necessary also to investigate the character of the factions which constitute the major parties and the conditions which make for durability in their relations with one another. A satisfactory explanation of the bipartisan system should throw light on the permanent causes of the existing alignment of parties and on the outlook for a partisan realignment which would be more pleasing to voters seeking a rational basis for partisanship. Above all, it should throw light on the conditions which govern the formation of electoral majorities and on the validity of Madison's theory of the natural limits to partisan power.

CHAPTER FIVE

The Natural Limits
to Partisan Power

THE PROBLEM OF FACTIONAL COÖRDINATION

INQUIRY into the nature and limits of partisan power begins with an analysis of partisan voting in presidential elections. Since the major parties are instruments for the coördination of factions, as well as means of promoting the political fortunes of their leaders, their character must be derived in part from that of the factions of which they are composed. The determination of the character of a particular party involves the investigation of the factional interests upon which the party is dependent for its success at the polls. These interests are measurable in terms of the electoral votes which may be won for the party in the states where they are influential. An interest may be of importance to a party, because it can dominate a state which in the past has generally supported that party, or because it can hold the balance of power in a close state. In either case the character of the interests will affect the character of the party as long as the votes of the states which they may control are essential for partisan victory in presidential elections. In the former case the factional leaders will insist on the identification of the interests of their faction with those of the party. In the latter case the factional leaders will make the best terms they can as the price of their coöperation in the elections.

The problem of factional coördination at the latest presidential election had developed through a rational evolution from that which had existed at the beginning of national partisan politics in the Federal Convention of 1787. The various special and local interests of the American people were much more diversified in 1948 than in 1787. Some of the basic social and economic forces in national politics had been completely transformed. The relative importance of the principal factions had altered greatly. But the coördination of the major sectional interests into effective political associations presented to the party leaders a problem which was essentially the same as before.

In 1948 as in 1787 there were five major political divisions of the American people. The powerful combination of interests built around the cotton and tobacco planters made the postbellum Solid South a more formidable section than the earlier Lower South ever was, though its persistent adherence to a one-party system in national politics made it less influential in the nomination and election of Presidents than in the determination of partisan policy in the Congress.[1] The contemporary Border States could not pretend to replace the original Upper South as a factor in national politics, but their special interests and peculiar position in the array of sections made them still a political force to be reckoned with. The grain-growing and stock-raising interests of the original Middle States, which had rapidly expanded into the Central and Mountain sections and had long ago become the most powerful single interest in national politics, remained despite the growth of industry and of cities in these sections the most numerous, though not the most solid, of the leading interests in the rural sections. The Northern dairy interests, the principal successors to the original farming interests of the Upper North, were relatively less powerful than in 1787 but more conscious of their special economic position and political kinship. Finally, the big merchants and urban tradespeople and shopkeepers of 1787 had expanded into the capitalists, businessmen, and wage earners of modern industrial society and had become far the most important of the major sectional interests, taking into account their powerful position on the North Atlantic Coast, in the Lake States, and on the Pacific Coast. Modern party leaders do not have to solve Washington's hard problem of uniting all these factions in support of a new constitution, but they must strive to bring together in a national party enough of them to elect Presidents and, if possible, also to control the Congress.

THE PRESIDENTIAL ELECTION OF 1948

The latest presidential election affords an extraordinarily interesting illustration of the political relations between the factions of the two major parties. The "ins" had suffered a severe defeat at the mid-term congressional elections. After the second World War, as after the First, there was grave popular discontent with the party in power and a strong desire for a change. The Republicans had successfully exploited the impatience of the voters with the failure of the Democrats to find prompt solutions for the new and perplexing problems of the postwar period. Having won control of the Eightieth Congress by the simple expedient of asking the voters if they had had enough of Democratic rule, they expected to win complete control of the political branches of the national government in 1948 by the same campaign strategy. Their only problem was to retain the support of the voters who had supported their congressional candidates in 1946. The problem of the Democrats, namely, to recover the support of those who had supported Roosevelt in 1944 and deserted the Party's candidates in 1946, seemed more difficult.

The defeat of the Democrats at the congressional elections of 1946 not only had cost them control of the legislative branch of the government but also had seriously discredited the Administration itself. One Democratic Senator even suggested after the elections that the President resign in order to make way for a Republican leader in the White House. Many Democratic politicians in 1948 would have liked to nominate a candidate as far removed as possible from the Administration. But General Eisenhower refused to enter politics and Supreme Court Justice Douglas made himself unavailable. Without a military hero or a dark horse to divert attention from the faults of the Administration the Democratic Convention was forced to make a virtue of necessity and renominate the President. Former Vice-President Wallace, who had been supplanted by Senator Truman in 1944 and dismissed from the Truman Cabinet in 1946, had already announced his candidacy for President at the head of an independent party. Heavy losses among the more progressive New Deal Democrats to the new party seemed inevitable. To outbid Wallace for their support without alienating indispensable conservative Democrats was impossible. The Democratic Party leaders found themselves in an awkward dilemma.

President Truman attacked the problem of campaign strategy boldly. In dealing with domestic issues he took his cue from Henry Wallace. He proposed to make the New Deal permanent by a suitable program of measures which he subsequently named the Fair Deal. He even proposed to push his Fair Deal beyond the point reached under Roosevelt by enforcing the civil rights of Negroes and other victims of economic and social discrimination. He also responded to the challenge of Wallace's Progressives in the field of foreign policy. He could not go as far as Wallace by accepting the support of Communists, but early in the campaign he alluded to Marshal Stalin in a seemingly friendly manner as "Old Joe," and late in the campaign he proposed

112

to stop the "cold war" by sending Chief Justice Vinson to Moscow — as President Washington had once sent Chief Justice Jay to London and President Adams had sent Chief Justice Ellsworth to Paris — on a mission of conciliation. By wooing Wallace's followers he risked costly disaffection among conservative Democrats everywhere. By seeking to appease the Negroes he alienated the Dixiecrats in the Lower South. But President Truman adhered persistently throughout a strenuous campaign to his strategy of boldness.

Governor Dewey, an experienced and smooth campaigner, whom the Republicans nominated a second time despite his defeat in 1944, attacked his problem of campaign strategy cautiously. Like Governor Hughes in 1916, he began with a comfortable majority of the votes. The combination of sectional interests, which had won elections for the Republicans from 1896 to 1908 and seemed about to do so again in 1916, had apparently been restored in 1946. Governor Dewey resolved to avoid Governor Hughes's tactical errors, which cost him the votes of California and the presidency, while adopting the basic strategy of the 1916 campaign. President Truman's boldness, which seemed in advance to be rather the recklessness of desperation, should have made the task of the "outs" less difficult than that of the Republicans under Hughes when confronted by Wilson's canny evasion of contentious issues. The tactics indicated by the slogan, "He kept us out of war," enabled Wilson to hold his party together while Hughes caused his own defeat by his unhappy treatment of California's governor, Hiram Johnson. Governor Dewey took the precaution of putting the governor of California on the ticket with himself. Rarely have the prospects of a presidential candidate seemed so bright as those of Dewey at the beginning of the campaign in July.

Governor Dewey chose his campaign strategy deliberately. He seemed not to need the support of additional sectional interests and had to face therefore no new problems of factional coördination. Moreover, the Democratic candidate possessed no such advantageous opportunity to exploit a glamorous personality as in 1944. The proper strategy for the Dewey campaign was obviously to sublimate the partisan issues. The candidate logically stressed the public interest in political harmony and administrative efficiency. National unity became the favorite Republican slogan. Governor Dewey did not "stub his toe" like Governor Hughes, but he neglected to dramatize his opposition to the "ins" and failed to hold the attention of the voters. President Truman's counterattacks on Communists and on Wall Street broke the force of the attack by Wallace's Progressives. The Republicans would not support the diversionary movement on the Democratic left and could not come to terms with the Dixiecrats on the Democratic right. Governor Dewey seemed to patronize without vigorously defending the Republican Congress, when a shrewder candidate would have aggressively claimed for his party the credit for the widespread prosperity which was making contented voters think twice before voting for further changes in the control of their national government. In the end Governor Dewey fell a victim to tactical errors, which, though different from those of Governor Hughes, were equally fatal.

The election returns prove the characters of the parties. The states in which the strongly partisan factions have their principal bases, as well as those in which the popular choice is most doubtful, are shown in Table 5.[2] At most presidential elections, states in which more than 60 per cent of the popular votes are cast for the candidates of either of the major parties may be defined as strongly partisan. At the election of 1948, however, on account of the division of Democratic voters in the Lower South between regular Democrats and Dixiecrats, the states in that section which are classified as strongly Democratic are those in which the Republican vote fell below 40 per cent. The states in which the margin of victory by either of the major parties over the other was less than 5 per cent of the total popular vote are classified as close states. These are the states in which minor political factions can hold the balance of power and exploit their position by driving hard bargains with the leaders of the major parties. If they are large states, the tactical position of such factions may be very strong. The other states, which hold an intermediate position between the strongly Democratic or strongly Republican states and the close states, are shown in their proper places in the table without special designation.

This table discloses an arrangement of states which in general possesses a superficial resemblance to the traditional partisan pattern. The Democrats, except for the diversion by the Dixiecrats, were strong in the Solid South and in some parts of the Border States. They possessed considerable strength also in the Mountain States, in some of which voters from the South have settled in large numbers, taking their partisan predilections with them. Republican strength was most conspicuous in the rural portions of the North. Altogether there were eleven strongly Democratic states, if the walkout of the Dixiecrats be disregarded, but there was only one state which was strongly Republican. Most of the predominantly urban and highly industrialized states

114

TABLE 5

A partisan classification of the states.

Presidential election of 1948.

Section	Number of States	Democratic		Republican	
		Strongly Dem.	Close States	Close States	Strongly Rep.
I. Northeast					
1. Predominantly urban states	6		Mass. R.I.	Conn. N.Y. N.J. Pa.	
2. Semiurban and rural states	3			Me. N.H.	Vt.
II. North Central					
3. Predominantly urban states	3		Ohio Ill.	Mich.	
4. Semiurban and rural states	8	Minn.	Wisc. Iowa	Ind.	Kan. Neb. S.D. N.D.
III. South					
5. Border States	6	Okla.	W.Va. Ky. Mo.	Del. Md.	
6. Solid South	11	N.C. *S.C. Ga. Fla. *Ala. *Miss. †Tenn. Ark. *La. Tex.	Va.		
IV. West					
7. Mountain States	8		Mont. Colo. Utah N.M. Ariz.	Wyo. Ida. Nev.	
8. Pacific Coast	3		Wash.	Calif. Ore.	

* Dixiecratic states.
† One electoral vote for Dixiecrats.

were close. This group included all the states of this class in the North Central section and on the Pacific Coast as well as the two most highly industrialized of the Border States. It included all but two of the industrial states in the Northeast. The remainder of the close states were semiurban states in the North Central section and three of the smaller Mountain States.

The significance of this pattern of partisanship becomes clearer in the light of the distribution of electoral votes. The total number of electoral votes cast for each party ticket in the strongly partisan and close states of each section of the country is shown in Table 6. A

TABLE 6

A partisan classification of the electoral votes.

Presidential election of 1948.

	Democratic			Republican			
Section	Strongly Dem.	Close States	Close States		Strongly Rep.	Total
I. Northeast							
1. Predominantly urban states		20		106			126
2. Semiurban and rural states					9	3	12
II. North Central							
3. Predominantly urban states			53	19			72
4. Semiurban and rural states		11	22	13	22		68
III. South							
5. Border States	10	34		11			55
6. Solid South	116*	11					127
IV. West							
7. Mountain States		22	10				32
8. Pacific Coast		8	25	6			39
Total	126*	106	110	155	31	3	531

* Including the 39 votes cast for the Dixiecrats.

striking fact about the electoral vote is the large number of votes cast by the close states. These states control almost enough votes to elect the President. The close urban states alone possess more votes than all the strongly partisan states. This fact suggests that the influential factions in these close urban states occupy a stronger strategic position in the political war between the parties than any other element of the electorate. Their specific character and their disposition and practical capacity to make their strength count must necessarily be of the utmost significance in the operations of the major parties.

Another striking fact about the 1948 election is the extreme closeness of the popular vote in several of the largest urban states. Ohio and California were carried by President Truman by pluralities of less than 0.5 per cent. Illinois would apparently have been lost by him, if the Wallace electors had not been removed from the ballot. These states, if carried by Dewey, would have given him the election. Evidently the Wallace campaign failed by the narrowest margin to throw the election to Governor Dewey. On the other hand, Dewey's margin of victory over Truman in five states — New York, Maryland, Michigan, Indiana, and Oregon — was less than the Wallace vote in these states. Only a little more success for Truman's counterattack against Wallace's Progressives would have given him a clear majority of the electorate and a wide margin of electoral votes over Dewey. The balance of the parties was delicately adjusted in 1948. Small causes could easily have produced great changes in the results of the election.

The effects of the Truman strategy are disclosed by comparing the results of the elections of 1948 and 1944. Truman's counterattack against the Wallace Progressives was not powerful enough to prevent the loss to Dewey of several leading industrial states which had been carried in 1944 by Roosevelt. New York, Pennsylvania, New Jersey, and Connecticut in the Northeast, Delaware and Maryland among the Border States, and Michigan in the North Central section went over to the Republicans in 1948. But Truman was able to hold Illinois and California and regained Ohio, which had been carried by Dewey in his first campaign. These three industrial states cast twice as many electoral votes as were lost by Truman in the Lower South to the Dixiecrats. Yet the losses to Dewey in the industrial states of the Northeast would have cost Truman the election but for his extraordinary gains in the grain-growing and stock-raising states. His ability to recapture Wisconsin, Iowa, Colorado, and Wyoming, which Dewey had carried in 1944, and to hold Minnesota and Washington, which had voted for Roosevelt at the earlier election, secured his victory.

The grain-growing and stock-raising interests, which had monopolized the balance of power in national politics during the years when agrarian interests ruled the political scene, still held the balance of power in 1948. They could not have held it if the industrial states had been united in support of either party. But with leading industrial interests so uncertain in their political allegiance that the electoral vote of the industrial states was almost evenly divided between the two major parties, agrarian interests similar to those which had finally decided the issue of the struggle for a more perfect Union in 1788 were able to decide the issue of the presidential election in 1948. The partisan pattern in this latest election was not identical with any of its predecessors. The nature of the principal factions, however, and their relative importance in the general scheme of factional coördination, were consistent with the traditional character of national politics.

Further light on the character of the major parties is furnished by the congressional election returns. The states contained on the average nearly three millions of inhabitants, but the congressional districts averaged only a little over three hundred thousand. On the smaller stage of the congressional district the special interests which require coördination by the leaders of the major parties can be more easily segregated and their political behavior more closely observed. The interests which support the major parties in the strongly partisan sections of the country can be more clearly identified. The possible combinations of interests which may give a major party control of the close states may be better understood. Above all, the nature of the interest combinations in the great urban states, which exert such a decisive influence in presidential elections, and presumably also upon the true character of the parties, should become more intelligible. For the purpose of such an interest analysis the classification of congressional districts already utilized in analyzing the growth of the sections may again be usefully employed.

The character of the major parties emerges more clearly from the patterns of partisanship in the congressional elections. The partisan distribution of the congressional districts of various kinds, urban, rural, and mixed, in the principal sections of the country is shown in Table 7. The Democrats carried all but one of the districts in the South. The exception was Maryland's Eastern Shore district, which had been Democratic for many years but was captured by the Republicans in 1946. The solidarity of the political South, as this region was defined in a previous chapter, extended to districts of all kinds, rural and urban alike. In the Northeast the Democratic strength was definitely concentrated in the districts within the large metropolitan areas. In the mixed urban-rural districts the Democrats did poorly and in the predominantly rural districts they did little better than the Republicans in the South. In the North Central section the partisan pattern was much the same. Here the better showing of the Democrats in the rural districts was due chiefly to the inclusion in this section of districts in the Border States, where tobacco planters and other farmers have retained a traditional preference for the Democratic Party despite the development of economic and social conditions which are more Mid-

TABLE 7

A partisan classification of congressional districts.
Eighty-first Congress.

Section	Democratic Districts			
	Urban	Mixed	Rural	Total
I. Northeast	*40	11	2	*53
II. North Central	35	23	20	78
III. South	8	30	67	105
IV. West	9	8	11	28
Total	*92	72	100	*264

Section	Republican Districts			
	Urban	Mixed	Rural	Total
I. Northeast	21	23	14	58
II. North Central	13	25	45	83
III. South	0	0	1	1
IV. West	8	4	17	29
Total	42	52	77	171
Grand Total	134†	124†	177†	435

* Includes one American Labor Party district in New York City, in which regular Democrats outnumbered the Republicans.
† These totals differ from those shown in Table 3 on account of the effects of a redistricting act in Illinois, shortly before the election of 1948, which increased the number of districts in the Chicago metropolitan area by four and correspondingly reduced the number of districts in the rest of the state.

western than Southern. In the West, as previously defined for purposes of political analysis, there was a slender Republican majority resulting from Republican superiority in the rural districts.

The results of the congressional elections in the rural districts confirm the identification of the special and local interests which dominate the rural wings of the major parties. The cotton and tobacco planters are solidly Democratic. The dairymen are almost as solidly Republican. The woolgrowers, who, like the dairymen, depend upon the domestic market for the sale of their products, also tend to take the opposite side in national politics to the great exporting agricultural interests. The fruitgrowers, including the growers of subtropical fruits outside of the South, and the producers of other foodstuffs which depend mainly upon the domestic market, manifest a similar tendency. The graingrowers, who are the most numerous and have been historically the most influential of the agricultural interests, together with the livestock interests, are more evenly divided between the parties. Outside of the South, however, they inclined in 1948 definitely to the Republican side.

This inclination is clearly reflected in the election results. Whereas President Truman carried several of the corn-belt and wheat-belt states, the congressional delegations from the same states remained strongly Republican. The Republicans elected all the Iowa Congressmen and nearly all the Congressmen outside of the large cities in Illinois, Wisconsin, and Minnesota, though Dewey lost these states to Truman. On the other hand, the Democratic senatorial candidates in three of these states ran ahead of President Truman. The corngrowers and also the cattlemen further west, while seeming to prefer Republicans for their immediate representatives, were manifestly more discriminating in their use of their votes than were the members of the other leading agricultural interests. This is a type of political behavior which is consistent with their historical role as holders of the balance of power between the major parties during the years when rural interests dominated the American political scene. The graingrowers and cattlemen are still the great middlemen among the rural factions.

The meaning of the congressional elections in the urban districts is not equally obvious. The Democrats were consistently stronger than the Republicans in 1948 in the large cities throughout the North and West, but the sources of their strength were concealed in the conglomerations of votes which make up the partisan majorities in the urban districts. The territorial basis of representation does not bring out the character of the dominant local interests in the great cities as it does in the country districts. The alignment of the various special interests in the cities cannot be so readily inferred from the pattern of partisanship. Democratic candidates for Congress, however, were definitely stronger than their own party candidate for the presidency, as well as stronger than the Republicans, in most of 'the large urban centers outside of the South.

The variations in the relative strengths of the presidential and congressional candidates in different sections of the country throw further light on the nature of the factions which compose the parties. President Truman ran ahead of the rest of the Democratic ticket in his own state, as would be expected, and in the adjacent Border States and also in the Far West. But he ran behind the rest of the ticket in the Lower South and in most of the Northeastern states and in the industrial North Central states. In Connecticut, New York, Pennsylvania, Indiana, and Michigan, in all of which President Truman was defeated, the Democrats made substantial gains in the congressional districts. In three of these states the Democrats also elected their candidates for governor. If the alignment of parties be gauged by the presidential vote, the Democrats appeared relatively stronger in the corn belt and in the rural North Central and Mountain sections and weaker in the industrial East. If the partisan alignment be gauged by the congressional vote, the reverse appears to be the lesson of the 1948 elections.

THE NORMAL ALIGNMENT OF PARTIES

The nature of the established partisan alignment becomes clearer when the results of the latest elections are compared with those of previous elections.[3] The Democrats carried twenty-eight states in 1948 and in 1944 thirty-six states. Roosevelt polled 53.3 per cent of the total popular vote in 1944, while Truman in 1948 polled only 49.5 per cent of the popular vote. In the latter election Truman could not hold the Dixiecrats and the Wallace Progressives, both of whom had supported Roosevelt in the previous election. Each of these factions polled a little over 2 per cent of the total popular vote. The Republicans also failed to hold all of their previous support. In 1948 Dewey's share of the total was 45.1 per cent, while four years earlier it had been 45.8 per cent. Votes for the presidential candidates of all the minor parties increased from 0.9 per cent in 1944 to 5.4 per cent of the total in 1948. The Democrats lost their popular majority at the elections of 1948 and the Republicans lost their previous monopoly of the opposition. But the two-party system retained its mastery of the political scene.

There were only seven states which the Democrats were unable to carry at either of the most recent elections. Two, Maine and Vermont, were in the rural Northeast. One, Indiana, was a semiurban state in the North Central section. Four, Kansas, Nebraska, and the two Dakotas, were rural states on the western edge of the North Central section, where the fertile grain-growing region merges into the more arid cattle country. In addition to these states, the Republicans also carried in 1944 three other states in the North Central section, Ohio, Wisconsin, and Iowa, and two of the Mountain States, Colorado and

Wyoming. In 1948 they lost these states but won from the Democrats New Hampshire in the rural Northeast, four urban states in the same section, Connecticut, New York, New Jersey, and Pennsylvania, the eastern Border States, Delaware and Maryland, Michigan in the industrial North Central section, and Oregon on the Pacific Coast. The partisan pattern seemed to have undergone a radical change. But there were two factors tending to obscure the true nature of the electoral trend. One was the difference between the distribution of partisan strength in the presidential and congressional elections of 1948. The other was the difference in the size of the popular votes cast for the successful presidential candidates in the two elections.

The most important fact concerning the alignment of the major parties is not the magnitude of the popular or electoral victory at a particular election, but the relations of the factions within the parties. The Democratic Party, since the great realignment of parties in the course of the struggle over slavery, has consisted of three principal factions: the cotton and tobacco planters and associated interests in the South, a substantial part of the graingrowers and cattlemen and associated interests in the North and West, and a diversified group of urban interests in the same sections, in which since the Al Smith campaign of 1928 labor interests have been growing more important. The fluctuations in the size of the popular votes of the parties are deceptive. When in 1936 Roosevelt polled over 60 per cent of the popular vote and carried forty-six of the forty-eight states, the partisan pattern looked very different from that of 1928, when Smith polled barely 40 per cent of the popular vote and carried only eight states. It was different, but the most significant differences do not stand out on the face of the returns. The character of the Democratic Party or of the Republican Party does not appear from a comparison of Democratic with Republican states in either one of these interesting battles between the parties. It appears from a comparison of the relative positions of the different factions in the same party at different elections.

Such a comparison may be most conveniently made by calculating the percentage of the popular vote cast for the presidential ticket in the country as a whole, and the corresponding percentages of the popular vote cast for the same ticket in the individual states, and noting the deviation from the nationwide norm in each state. These deviations produce a pattern for each election in which the factional composition of the party is closely reflected. These partisan patterns for different elections can be compared, and the outstanding differences reveal the real changes which take place in the nature of the parties. In 1948 Truman's percentage of the total popular vote was so close to 50 per cent that the partisan pattern shown in the table of electoral votes at that election is a satisfactory approximation to a standard pattern of partisanship. The standard pattern for 1944, when Roosevelt's percentage of the total popular vote was 53.3 per cent,[4] is shown in Table 8.

TABLE 8

Standard pattern of partisanship.
Election of 1944.

Section	Democratic Deviations			Republican Deviations			Total
	Over 10%	10%–2½%	Under 2½%	Under 2½%	2½%–10%	Over 10%	
I. Northeast							
1. Predominantly urban states		4		98	24		126
2. Semiurban and rural states				4	5	3	12
II. North Central							
3. Predominantly urban states				28	44		72
4. Semiurban and rural states				11	39	18	68
III. South							
5. Border States			32	23			55
6. Solid South	104	23					127
IV. West							
7. Mountain States		8	11	4	9		32
8. Pacific Coast		33		6			39
Total	104	68	43	174	121	21	531

A study of the deviations from the norm in the standard pattern of partisanship for 1944 shows that the Democrats carried all the states with a Republican deviation of less than 2.5 per cent together with three others, Connecticut, New Jersey, and Michigan, in the next group of Republican states. It is evident that if the partisan pattern had remained unchanged and the Democratic percentage of the total popular vote had fallen by a very little, these last three states would have gone Republican. It would not have been necessary for the Democratic percentage of the total to have fallen as low as 50 per cent to have thrown the election to the Republicans. But it could have fallen so low as to have overturned the result almost everywhere without disturbing the supremacy of the Democratic Party in the Solid South. Every state in that section showed a marked Democratic deviation from the national average, and most of them were strongly Democratic. Altogether nearly one-half of the 266 electoral votes needed for a Democratic victory were furnished by the eleven states which formed the Southern Confederacy in 1861. Other states with a definite Democratic deviation were widely scattered. One, Rhode Island, was in the Northeast. Two, Arizona and Utah, were among the Mountain States. Two others, California and Washington, were on the Pacific Coast. Rhode Island had inclined toward the Democratic side ever since Governor Smith's campaign for the presidency. Arizona had generally been more strongly Democratic than other Western states. The Pacific Coast had responded more favorably to the challenge of the New Deal than any other section of the country. But these states with definite Democratic deviations altogether supplied less than two-thirds of the votes needed for success in the election. To win the victory the Democrats needed at least ninety-four votes from the close states.

The Republican Party found its principal sources of strength in the rural and semiurban states of the Northeast and North Central sections. Vermont in the rural Northeast and Kansas, Nebraska, and South Dakota in the rural North Central section were the strongest Republican states. The only other states actually carried by the Republican presidential candidate in 1944 besides Ohio, which was carried by a very narrow margin, were situated in these same sections and in the Rocky Mountain section. But other states in these same sections with a definite Republican deviation brought the total electoral vote of the states which were comparatively favorable to the Republicans to a little more than half of the number needed for the election of their candidate. The states in the predominantly urban sections of the North furnished nearly as many of these electoral votes as the semiurban and rural states, though the latter generally showed the stronger Republican deviations. The West was a minor source of Republican strength, since only Colorado and Wyoming showed definite Republican deviations. The South made no contribution to the sources of Republicanism.

The close states are easily identified. All the Border States were close in 1944, and also half of the Mountain States together with Oregon. In the Northeast, New Hampshire, Massachusetts, New York, and Pennsylvania showed slight Republican deviations, likewise Illinois and Minnesota in the North Central section. Most of the other close states showed Democratic deviations. Altogether these seventeen states accounted for 217 electoral votes, of which more than half were cast by the three great industrial states, New York, Pennsylvania, and Illinois. It is evident that the standard pattern of partisanship for 1944 is not the same as for 1948. In the latter year the Democrats were torn by dissensions in the Solid South, but the Democratic factions in the rural portions of the North Central section and of the West had gained strength, while those in the urban portions of the North and West seemed to have retained their relative positions in the party with little change. In the Republican Party also there had been a shift in the relative positions of the principal factions. The agrarian wing, particularly in the North Central section, was relatively weaker in 1948 than four years earlier. The industrial wing, particularly in the Northeast, was relatively stronger.

The standard patterns of partisanship for the four New Deal elections under Roosevelt's leadership throw further light on the factional relationships within the major parties. In 1932 Roosevelt had been relatively stronger in the semiurban and rural states of the North Central section than in 1944 and relatively weaker in the Northeast, but none of the states which were close in 1944 had been strongly Republican in 1932 except New Hampshire, Pennsylvania, and Delaware, and none of the 1944 close states had been strongly Democratic at the first victory for the New Deal except Oklahoma and Nevada. The greatest change in the partisan pattern took place in the "dust-bowl" states of the Middle West. Already in 1936 the Democrats had lost the favorable deviations in these states, which they had carried by large majorities in 1932. They could raise the price of wheat by crop-production control and other measures, but they could not make the rain fall on the wheatgrowers' parched fields. In the Northeast, Pennsylvania registered the greatest relative gain for the party of the New Deal. Its addition to the list of close states by the conversion of coal miners and other wage earners was one of the most significant results of the Roosevelt leadership.

The standard pattern of partisanship for 1944 preserves the leading features of most of its predecessors. The greatest changes in the partisan pattern since the foundation of the Republican Party had occurred in the close states. The Border States, which had become the closest section of the country by 1944, reported only a few more Republicans in 1856 than the Lower South. The closest states at that time were

Pennsylvania and California. In 1944 the parties were closely matched also in most of the Mountain States, but the close states in the Border section and the West together did not possess enough electoral votes to give the election to the Democrats, even if their candidate could carry them all in addition to the states with a stronger Democratic deviation. To win a presidential election the Democratic Party had to get some electoral voters in the North from close states with a slight Republican deviation. The Republicans could win, assuming that they could hold all the states with a definite Republican deviation, by keeping the Democrats from making serious inroads into this class of close states.

Under these circumstances the battleground of the major parties lay in the great urban states of the Northeast and North Central section. If the Democrats could carry two or three of these states, and hold their lines in the close states with a Democratic deviation, they would not need to carry any of the smaller urban states in the North and could safely leave the semiurban and rural Northern states entirely to the Republicans. If the Democrats could carry most of the great urban states, they could afford substantial losses among the close states in the Border section and in the West. But they could not afford to disregard the problem of holding their lines in the states with a more definite Democratic deviation. The Border States, where the partisan pattern seemed comparatively rigid, were likely to go Democratic if New York and Ohio and Illinois went Democratic, but the greater flexibility of the partisan pattern in the West made for greater uncertainty in national elections. Since California had become one of the great urban states, it was no less important in the battle of the parties than Ohio or Illinois. New York, however, remained, and apparently would long continue to be, the most important part of the battleground.

The political importance of these great states is reflected in the frequency with which their electoral votes appear on the winning side in presidential elections. New York has cast its electoral vote on the losing side only six times in the history of national politics, and one of these, the election of 1876, loses significance because of special circumstances. Only twice since then, in the close election of 1916 and again in 1948, has New York cast its vote on the losing side. Ohio and Illinois have been on the winning side almost as regularly as New York, but Pennsylvania, until Roosevelt offered its laboring population an attractive share in the New Deal, was generally more strongly Republican than the other great states. California has been recorded on the side of the winner in every election for sixty years, except in 1912, when it supported the Progressive candidate, Theodore Roosevelt.

The selection of candidates attests the recognition by the party leaders of the importance of these pivotal states. New York has furnished at least one of the principal presidential candidates at sixteen elections since the Civil War. On three occasions it has furnished both major-party candidates. Most of the other major-party candidates since the foundation of the Republican Party have come from Ohio, Illinois, or California. When a major party has not taken its presidential candidate from one of these close states, it has almost invariably selected its candidate for the vice-presidency from one of them.

The presidential election of 1948 upset the calculations of the party leaders. Truman was able to lose four states in the Solid South and still win the election. The partisan pattern of that year closely resembled, except for the diversion of the Dixiecrats, the standard partisan pattern for 1916. The patterns for 1932 and for 1896 were similar, though the actual result in the earlier instance was an epoch-making victory for the Republicans and in the later instance a disastrous defeat. All alike showed relative Democratic weakness and Republican strength in the Northeast and the reverse in the North Central and Western sections. The standard pattern for 1944, however, more closely resembled the standard patterns for 1940, 1920, and 1904. The Democrats won two of these four elections and the Republicans two, but the distribution of partisan strength and weakness was similar in all four. The principal Democratic factions in the Northeast were relatively stronger, while the principal Republican factions in the North Central and Western sections were relatively stronger, than in the elections of 1896, 1916, and 1932. Always the relative positions of the factions in the close states seemed to vary less than the relative positions of the factions in the strongly partisan sections outside of the South. But in 1948 these long-established factional relations were profoundly disturbed. It was the factions in the close states and in the South which seemed most changeable. Could this portend a basic change in the traditional partisan alignment? [5]

This question calls for further analysis of the congressional election returns. Two patterns of partisanship in the congressional districts are shown in Tables 9 and 10. The first of these tables shows the

127

partisan distribution of districts at the election of 1946. The classification, it should be noted, is one of districts and not of Congressmen.

TABLE 9

A partisan classification of congressional districts.

Eighteth Congress.

	Democratic Districts			
Section	Urban	Mixed	Rural	Total
I. Northeast	24	5	1	30
II. North Central	17	7	8	32
III. South	8	30	67	105
IV. West	6	5	11	22
Total	55	47	87	189

	Republican Districts			
	Urban	Mixed	Rural	Total
I. Northeast	37	29	15	81
II. North Central	27	42	60	129
III. South	0	0	1	1
IV. West	11	7	17	35
Total	75	78	93	246

Districts represented in the Eightieth Congress by a member elected with the endorsement of both major parties, or by a member of a minor party, are classified in accordance with the vote of the district in state elections. Where Congressmen are elected in a state at large, the state is treated like a district. A comparison of the partisan patterns in the congressional districts at the elections of 1946 and 1948 reveals more clearly the location of the battleground between the parties. The Republican districts outnumbered the Democratic at the elections for the Eightieth Congress 246 to 189. But at the elections for the Eighty-first Congress the position of the parties was reversed, the Democratic districts outnumbering the Republican 264 to 171 (see Table 7). The districts which changed sides in these elections mark the location of the battleground between the parties. The districts which were carried by the same party in both elections mark the location of the interests which were the principal sources of partisan strength. Because of exceptional cases, in which partisan control of a district shifted in the direction opposite to the general trend, the totals for each class of districts within the same general region indicate the net result of the elections in the districts of that class.

The principal sources of partisan strength stand out clearly from the election returns. The Democrats counted sixty-seven dependable rural districts in the South, thirty mixed rural-urban districts in the same region, twenty-four urban districts in the Northeast, seventeen urban districts in the North Central region, eleven rural districts in the West, and smaller numbers of districts of each kind in all four regions. The Democratic districts of all kinds in the South formed a substantial majority of all the districts which they carried at both elections. The Republicans counted forty-five dependable rural districts in the North Central section, twenty-six mixed rural-urban districts in the same section, twenty-three districts of the same class in the Northeast, twenty-one urban districts in the Northeast, seventeen rural districts in the West, fourteen rural districts in the Northeast, and a few scattered districts of various kinds. The Republican districts of all kinds in the North Central section formed little short of a majority of all the districts which they carried at both elections. In both parties the rural districts were more numerous than either the urban or the mixed urban-rural districts. The Democrats could count more dependable districts than the Republicans in both the rural and the urban classes, but not so many in the mixed urban-rural classes.

The location of the close districts may be readily determined by the same returns from these congressional elections. At the elections to the Eighty-first Congress the Democrats gained eighteen seats in the urban districts of the North Central section (partly owing to a redistricting in Illinois which gave Chicago fair representation for the first time in many years), sixteen in the urban districts of the Northeast, fifteen in the North Central mixed urban-rural districts, a dozen in the North Central rural districts, half a dozen in the mixed urban-rural districts of the Northeast, three each in the urban and mixed districts of the West, and one in the rural districts of the Northeast. Half of all the gains were made in the urban districts. The fewest gains were made in the rural districts. There can be no doubt concerning the location of the battleground between the parties in congressional elections. It lies in the metropolitan areas on the North Atlantic Coast, in the North Central section, and on the Pacific Coast. The Democrats could have taken away from the Republicans the majority which the latter held in the Eightieth Congress without capturing a single district in the mixed or rural classes. In striking contrast to its location in the presidential election of 1948, the balance of power in the congressional elections was located definitely in the great cities of the North and West.

That the battleground between the parties is located in the great cities of the North and West is confirmed by a comparison of the elections for the Eightieth and Seventy-ninth Congresses. The congressional election returns for 1944 (Table 10) show a distribution of partisan strength similar to that shown by the returns for 1948. The

TABLE 10

A partisan classification of congressional districts.
Seventy-ninth Congress.

	Democratic Districts			
Section	Urban	Mixed	Rural	Total
I. Northeast	40	9	2	51
II. North Central	29	13	13	55
III. South	8	30	68	106
IV. West	12	9	15	36
Total	89	61	98	248

	Republican Districts			
	Urban	Mixed	Rural	Total
I. Northeast	21	25	14	60
II. North Central	15	36	55	106
III. South	0	0	0	0
IV. West	5	3	13	21
Total	41	64	82	187

Democrats won control of the popular branch of the Seventy-ninth Congress in 1944, and lost it in the Eightieth Congress only to regain it with a greater majority than before in the Eighty-first. The pattern of Democratic losses at the election of 1946 corresponds closely to the pattern of gains in 1948. A clear majority of the losses in 1946 were suffered in the urban districts of the same sections as those in which the gains of 1948 were made. The Democrats lost more districts in the West in 1946 than they regained in 1948 and they gained more in the North Central section in 1948 than they had lost in 1946. In the Northeast the gains and losses were more nearly in balance. But the important fact is clear. The balance of power between the parties in the congressional elections was definitely located in the great cities on the North Atlantic Coast, in the North Central section, and on the Pacific Coast.

Though the relative positions of the parties in the Eighty-first Congress correspond generally to those in the Seventy-ninth, there are some noteworthy differences. The Democrats won a bigger congressional majority in 1948 than in 1944. But the Republicans nearly held their own in the Northeast and made substantial gains in the West. The Democratic gains in 1948 over 1944 were made almost entirely in the North Central section. They gained six urban districts in the big cities of this section, partly in consequence of the redistricting in Illinois, nine mixed urban-rural districts, and seven rural districts. The gain of rural districts is considerable but not as striking as the gain of states over 1944 in the presidential election of 1948. On the other hand, the gain of urban districts in this section and the ability of the Democrats to hold their own in the urban districts of the Northeast, despite the loss of states in this section in 1948 to Dewey, are significant. The Democrats evidently held many urban voters in the congressional elections of 1948 whom they lost in the presidential election. The efforts of the C.I.O. and other labor organizations to elect Democratic Congressmen brought impressive results. In the congressional elections organized labor seems to have exerted extraordinary influence, like that of the grain-growing and stock-raising interests in the presidential election. Whether it was as significant as that of these important rural interests in the working of the American party system is a question which demands further investigation.

THE SHIFTING AND INCIDENCE OF THE BALANCE OF POWER

Recent congressional elections demonstrate that the people of the urban areas in the leading industrial states have gained a share of the balance of power in national politics originally held by the "middling sort" of people in the rural areas. The Constitution was not adopted until enough of the followers of Governor John Hancock, Governor George Clinton, and ex-Governor Patrick Henry in the state ratifying conventions were won over to give a majority to the advocates of a strong general government. Those delegates who were won over in the states which held the balance of power in 1787 were farmers, and lawyers representing mainly farmers, belonging to the middle class.

The rural middle class continued to hold the balance of power in national politics until recent times. In the states which chiefly held the power to decide presidential elections down to the middle of the last century, particularly New York and Pennsylvania, these middle-class farmers were predominantly graingrowers and stock raisers. The progress of westward settlement enhanced the importance of the largest states west of the Appalachian Mountains which were closely divided in national politics. These states in the latter part of the nineteenth century were Ohio, Indiana, and Illinois. The graingrowers, particularly those in the corn belt, continued to hold the principal share in the balance of power. The Republican practice of selecting presidential candidates mainly from these corn-belt states, which persisted from Lincoln's time to that of Taft and Harding, attests the importance for that party of nominations with a strong appeal to the middle-class farmer. The Republicans during that period usually went to New York for their vice-presidential candidate, thus reversing the practice of the Democrats, who favored New York for presidential candidates and the corn belt for candidates for the vice-presidency. For many years the Republicans recognized the superiority of the rural middle class over the urban in the struggle for supremacy in the close districts and states. But in recent years the behavior of the party leaders in the selection of candidates affords convincing evidence that the old order in their opinion is changing and giving place to a new.[6]

Woodrow Wilson in some of his political speeches during the campaign of 1912 claimed that the Democratic Party, regarded as an instrument for the coördination of political factions, was superior to the Republican. Wilson viewed the political scene with a more philosophical eye than most candidates for elective office and his reason for preferring his own party as an instrument of factional coördination as well as a means of furthering his own political ambitions remains of exceptional interest. The Democratic Party, he argued, had its roots firmly planted in all the major sections of the country, while the Republicans were practically excluded from the South. The Democratic Party therefore, he concluded, was better qualified to represent the interests of the whole body of the people and more likely to promote the national interest than its opponent. This is an argument which possesses obvious merit in so far as it relates to the representative character of the two major parties. Whether the more representative party is likely also to be more successful in promoting the national interest depends upon how effective the party proves to be in the

132

actual performance of its function as a coördinator of factions. The evidence of practical capacity to perform this function must be found in the legislative proceedings of the Congress as well as in the nomination and election of presidential candidates.

In general, the task of factional coördination in the Congress seems to have been more difficult for the Democrats than for the Republicans. A comparison of the strong Democratic and Republican districts shows why this is ordinarily to be expected. The cotton and tobacco planters and the Democratic interests in the great Northern cities together have possessed a clear majority of the Democratic districts. If their representatives could agree, they could easily control the action of the party in the House of Representatives. If they could not readily agree — and the grounds for dissension have been many — the Western districts and the rural districts in the North, though widely scattered, might acquire a considerable influence in the party. Evidently the most important partisan interests in the Democratic Party have been radically different and the task of factional coördination could not be easy. The leading Republican districts in the Northeast and North Central sections on the other hand have seemed to possess better natural ground for harmony. The Republican Party likewise has surpassed the Democrats in the extent of its support in the mixed urban-rural districts of the North, that is, districts not definitely dominated either by graingrowers and dairymen and other farmers or by the industrial populations of the cities. Representatives in Congress from such districts must be responsive to a greater variety of interests than representatives from the cotton and tobacco belts or from the congested areas of the great cities.

The greater proportion of mixed districts in the Republican Party and the greater concentration of its support in the North make for greater solidarity in its congressional representation than in that of the Democratic Party. These characteristic differences between the two major parties make the Democrats, when in control of the Congress, more dependent on vigorous executive leadership than is necessary for the Republicans. It may be more than coincidence that the most vigorous Presidents in modern times have been Democrats. The Republicans have only Theodore Roosevelt to match against F. D. Roosevelt, Woodrow Wilson, and Grover Cleveland. The Republicans, however, should ordinarily be better able than the Democrats to coördinate the various factions of their party in the Congress without strong executive leadership.

The growing ascendancy of the urban population in the great doubtful states makes it important to ascertain what kinds of urban voters are most likely to hold the balance of power under the new political order. If the greatest influence is exerted by what Madison tactfully termed the "opulent" and Hamilton more bluntly called the "rich," the new order would be not only more urban than the old but also more plutocratic. Under such circumstances it would be possible to speak, as Communists do, of a fascist trend in national politics. If, on the other hand, it is the "indigent" who are gaining power by the passing of the old order, the way would seem to be opening for the development of parties of a communist type. But the rise of an urban middle class to a position comparable to that of the farmers in the corn belt would point to an indigenous political phenomenon incompatible with either Communism or Fascism. Its significance would depend upon the nature of urban middle-class traits and the practical capacity of an urban middle class to maintain the traditional American middle-class political attitudes.

There is no measure of the social character of the populations of urban congressional districts which is as satisfactory to the political analyst as the simple classification of rural districts according to the dominant type of agriculture. It is easy in most cases to determine whether a rural district lies mainly in the corn or cotton belt or in one of the other broad agricultural regions. Having determined that the typical voter of a rural district is a corngrower and not a cotton planter, fruitgrower, or other type of farmer, it is possible to identify his economic interests and consider intelligently what sort of appeal may be made for his support by party leaders bent on forming a combination of factions which can win presidential and congressional elections. But the diversification of industry in the large cities is great, and the ordinary classifications of economic interests divide the urban voters into groups which are too numerous and generally too small to dominate congressional districts as certain types of agriculture dominate many rural districts. Even a rough classification of urban voters as upper, middle, or lower class is dependent upon the crude statistical devices which are applicable to voters distributed into congressional districts.

The most interesting census data which throw any light on the class character of congressional districts in the great cities are the figures which show the range of residential rents by city blocks. These have been compiled for the largest cities and published in books of maps which make it possible to determine the distribution of residential property, classified in accordance with its rental value, by congressional districts.[7] On the basis of these urban rental maps the congressional districts themselves may be divided into those with relatively high rents, those with relatively low rents, and those with residential property mainly of an intermediate rental value. Where an urban area is populous enough to contain a considerable number of congressional districts, such a classification of districts according to the rental value of residential property gives a rough measure of the class character of the voters in the districts. The Port of New York, with a total of thirty-nine districts wholly or mainly in the metropolitan area (including eleven in New Jersey and one in Connecticut), is the political region to which such a classification is most applicable. Other metropolitan areas containing a sufficient number of congressional districts to make such a classification useful are Chicago, Los Angeles, Philadelphia, Boston, and Detroit. The results are so uniform in all these cities as to support some rough generalizations concerning the social character of the major parties in Northern and Western cities and the influence of the urban middle class upon the balance of power in national politics.

In all these cities the partisan pattern is the same. The only districts which have been consistently Republican for a considerable period of time are those with the highest rents. These have been generally suburban districts. The most striking exception is the Fifth Avenue district in New York City. The districts which have been most consistently Democratic are those with the lowest rents. Formerly some districts with a large Negro population were an exception to this rule, but since the beginning of the New Deal these districts too have generally become Democratic. Two of them, one in New York and one in Chicago, have sent Negro Congressmen to Washington. The districts with a preponderance of intermediate rents are the districts which have been most doubtful from the viewpoint of the major parties. These are the districts in which the Republicans made the greatest gains from the Democrats at the election of 1946, and in which the Democrats in turn made the greatest gains from the Republicans in 1948. They are the districts to which the party leaders must give the most attention in making their plans for the coördination of factions in national elections.

These close districts with a preponderance of residences at moderate rentals contain the same categories of people in all the metropolitan areas. They are small businessmen, white-collar workers on modest salaries, and skilled or semiskilled wage earners. They are regularly employed in all but the worst times. Such people commonly regard themselves as members of the middle class, if class conscious, and if not class conscious would so regard themselves if pressed to classify themselves by agents of the pollsters. They believe in the future of their country and in themselves as heirs to a great tradition which they should be able to maintain. They ordinarily distrust extremists of any kind and favor moderate measures and middle-of-the-road leadership. They differ more or less among themselves according to their natures and circumstances, and thereby offer a fertile field for competition among politicians for their support. But they are unlikely to recognize any social or economic divisions among themselves as wide or deep as those which separate the city-dwellers' world in which they live from the rural areas upon which they depend for food and the raw materials of industry.

The political attitudes of these middle-class city dwellers are facts of the utmost importance in the calculations of party leaders bent on the coördination of factions capable of bringing victory to a major party. To form a winning combination of urban factions in the great industrial states it is necessary to include at least a majority of these middle-class city dwellers. The logical alternative — a combination of the very rich and the very poor against the urban middle class — is most unpromising under the existing conditions in the great cities, particularly the wide distribution of middle-class incomes. It is always possible, of course, for practical politicians to direct special appeals at self-conscious social groups, such as the various immigrant racial and nationalistic groups and the Negroes.[8] It is even possible to show by the election returns that at particular elections some one of these groups actually held the balance of power in the decisive states. At the presidential election of 1948 the Negroes possessed more than enough votes, if they had wished to give them to a single party, to have turned the election to the Republicans in the decisive states of Ohio, Illinois, and California. The same, however, can be said for several other groups. The partisan exploitation of racial interests and prejudices can become very complicated and uncertain. An appeal to middle-class interests and attitudes, however, can cut across racial and even religious barriers. Particularly under modern conditions of campaigning, when the radio compels party leaders to speak the same language and use the same arguments in every kind of home, the identification of the public interest with that of the middle class becomes the first principle of practical politics.

The middle-class character of the urban districts which form the battleground of the parties in the great cities has other important political consequences. First, it insures that political principles will continue to play their traditional role in national politics. Superficial critics have often complained of what they call the lack of principle in the major parties. This of course is a great mistake. The major parties do not lack principles. Both have principles, but their principles are the same. They are necessarily the same, since in order to win national elections the party leaders must secure the support of the same classes of people. In the beginning the balance of power lay mainly in rural areas and now it has shifted in large measure to urban areas, but the basic political principles cherished by those whose support must be retained by the "ins" in order to remain in power, or must be obtained by the "outs" in order to replace the "ins," have not changed. They have never been systematically and comprehensively formulated in any single public document, but may be collected from the state papers which have gained the greatest popularity, the Declaration of Independence, the federal and state Bills of Rights, Washington's "Farewell Address," Jefferson's "First Inaugural," Lincoln's Inaugurals and "Gettysburg Address," Wilson's and Roosevelt's war messages, and sundry Supreme Court opinions. These principles have always commanded the approval of middle-class Americans regardless of residence in town or country. They may be expected to continue to command such approval, wherever such people may establish their homes.

The average man, as American politicians have generally preferred to call the kind of voter who has always held the balance of power in national politics, regards these principles as beyond partisanship. The parties have not always interpreted these principles alike, and when principles have conflicted, as must sometimes happen since they do not form a comprehensive and consistent logical system, different parties have assigned different weights to the same principles. But the perennial necessity of retaining the confidence of the average man, because of the difficulty of carrying the districts and states holding the balance of power without it, has compelled major party politicians to respect these principles. There have been elections at which shrewd campaign management has enabled a particular candidate to get more than his share of the credit for loyalty to Americanism or constitutionalism or some other attractive symbol of the fundamental principles which lie behind the American way of political life. But no major party has ever attacked these principles or admitted a better claim to their defense by their opponents.

Secondly, the decisive importance of the average man furnishes a powerful incentive to opportunism in national politics. Since the major parties cannot profitably make issues of basic principles, they must be governed in their contentiousness by expediency. Aggressive and pugnacious leadership may offer an attractive appeal to the average man for a time, but in the long run promises must be followed by action of some kind, and party leaders whose ability to perform their promises depends upon the coördination of factions with different interests must tread the path of compromise. The adjustment of the conflicts of interest between the factions whose collaboration is essential to effective government by any of the major parties is impossible without mutual concessions. No matter how selfish the factions may be which constitute the firmest elements in the party which is supposed to be in power, they cannot use their influence within the party exclusively in their own interest. They must come to terms with other factional interests, preferably in ordinary cases with the interests which share in the balance of power and without whose collaboration power is a mockery and illusion. If the combinations of factions which constitute the major parties are to be sufficiently stable to serve as useful instruments in gratifying the ambitions of their leaders, a reasonable disposition to give and take in the adjustment of conflicts within a party is indispensable for successful leadership. The average man understands this elementary truth of democratic politics better than abnormal men, whether abnormally rich or abnormally poor. Hence, the middle classes form the soundest basis for prudent government by discussion and compromise. The increasing importance of the urban middle class, as that of the rural middle class declines, favors the continuation of moderate measures in national politics and leadership capable of self-restraint in the practice of party government.

A third consequence of the increasing importance of the urban middle class in national politics is the progressive development of a demand on the part of special interests for special representation independent of the major parties. Since the essential interests of the middle class tend to be general public interests, special interests find inadequate opportunity for expression through partisan representatives. Major-party representatives from most districts as large as the modern congressional district are responsible for the representation of a great variety of local and special interests. In so far as these interests conflict with one another, it is impossible to represent them all equally well and discrimination among them creates discontent on the part of those who feel neglected. The diversification of interests is likely to be greatest in the great urban areas where the balance of power tends to be located, and the demand for more specialized representation than can ordinarily be offered by the major parties tends therefore to grow with the growth of cities and of urban industry.

The need for more specialized representation than that offered by ordinary political representatives was not great at the framing of the Constitution. Great merchants and planters could attend the Convention in person and had a fair opportunity to see that their special interests were duly considered. A common criticism indeed of the work of the framers is that these special interests were too well represented in the Convention and secured more consideration than they deserved. The common man, it is charged, was represented only by middle-class lawyers who were unable or unwilling to challenge with sufficient boldness the pretensions of the big planters and merchants. The small farmers and tradesmen generally had better representation in the state ratifying conventions and eventually obtained the promise of a bill of rights which could give them a sense of security against oppression. The special interests of particular kinds of small farmers were well enough represented, as long as rural interests remained predominant in national politics, by the representatives of their respective sections. Cotton planters, big or little, were protected by the representatives from the cotton belt. But in the great cities of modern times the diversification of interests has gone too far for effective representation of more than a few of the most important of them by the ordinary political representative, regardless of partisan affiliation. The special interests must organize their own representation in order to exert a satisfactory influence upon the making and enforcing of the laws.

One method of representing special interests, not satisfactorily represented by major parties with their notorious disposition to equivocate as well as to compromise, is the organization of third parties. Why recognize a right of a second major party to monopolize the opposition to the party in power, when the opposition leaders fail to give what is deemed due consideration to the interests of an important faction which feels strong enough to stand by itself, alone if necessary, in national politics? Why not organize an independent party which will be responsive to the interests of a faction which might at least control the representation from its own section of the country?

This method of procedure is difficult to distinguish in practice from that in which the initiative is taken by a disaffected leader of one of the established major parties rather than by the members of a faction dissatisfied with its prospects under the established partisan alignment. What was really back of Wallace's Progressives and of the Dixiecrats in 1948? Did the elder Senator La Follette or organized labor take the initiative in organizing the Independent Party in 1924? Did Theodore Roosevelt or the "progressive" interests lead the way in forming the Bull Moose Party in 1912? The Populists in the early eighteen-nineties and the Greenbackers in the eighteen-seventies were more clearly the product of popular uprisings among the farmers in depressed areas of the West and South, which demanded and obtained leadership from available politicians in the sections in which their strength chiefly lay. The long series of independent labor, Socialist, and Communist parties, beginning with the Labor Reform Party in 1872, have sprung up without the benefit of assistance from influential politicians in the major parties. They have been responsive to special interests so remote from those of the average man as to have little prospect of satisfactory collaboration with major party leaders. The Prohibitionists likewise have always preferred to travel alone rather than to make the compromises necessary for association with other special interests under leadership capable of bringing together a majority of the voters.

The record of the third parties discloses their limitations as instruments for the effective representation of special interests. Either they promptly develop sufficient strength to cause major party leaders to make room in their own organizations for the interest groups which the third parties represent or they maintain their independence without the capacity to influence appreciably the measures of the major parties. Thus the Populists fused with the Democrats in 1896 and ultimately were absorbed by them. They were destroyed by their own success. The Free Soilers were even more successful. They fused with dissident Whigs and Democrats in 1854 and ultimately supplanted the former with a new major party. But the various independent labor parties have had little success in national politics. They have elected Congressmen from time to time, but they have gained little influence at Washington. Their principal function has been not political, but educational. They have emphasized problems, to which major party leaders have been eventually compelled to give attention, and they

140

have advocated solutions from which major party leaders borrowed such ideas as seemed to them practical, generally without acknowledgment of their source. The Bull Moose Progressives, on the other hand, and the La Follette Independents, to say nothing of more recent third parties, were interested in immediate political results. Their objective was to seize control of a major party or, by winning the balance of power, to bring about an altogether new partisan alignment. The Prohibitionists, who have been most consistently devoted to the educational function which a minor party can perform, were content to leave practical politics to the Anti-Saloon League. The record points to the conclusion that special interests cannot hope to get satisfactory results in national politics by means of third parties, if they remain minor parties. They must seek other ways to influence politicians, or be content to operate really, if not ostensibly, in the field of political education.

The alternative to the organization of a third party for special interests not satisfied with their influence in the major parties is the method so conspicuously illustrated by the Anti-Saloon League.[9] Few pressure groups would undertake to generate the immense power needed to amend the Constitution of the United States, and none other except the advocates of political equality for women has been successful. To influence the ordinary course of legislation and administration at Washington less effort is required. The minimum is the employment of a spokesman who can appear before congressional committees and talk to individual Congressmen about measures in which a particular group is specially interested, when such measures are under consideration. Greater influence is within reach of those interests which can maintain permanent offices at the national capital and keep in close and constant touch with members of both major parties, particularly those representing districts or states in which the organized pressure group possesses substantial voting strength or other means of influencing elections.[10] Powerful special interests, such as the great farm organizations, organized labor, and the leading trade associations and industrial institutes, support well-disciplined bodies of highly skilled retainers, some of whom may be paid much more than Congressmen or Cabinet officers and may enjoy equal security of tenure. Thus arises an informal system of representation, unknown to the Constitution and little affected by the laws, which supplements both the official system of representation under the Constitution and the semiofficial organizations of the major parties.

141

The representation of organized special interests at the national capital has developed to an extent which challenges the practical capacity of the major party leaders to manage the official system of representation under the Constitution. The proliferation of code authorities under the National Industrial Recovery Act in the early years of the New Deal, and of business advisory committees under the War Production Board, the War Food Administration, and the Office of Price Administration during World War II, suggests the possibilities of such a representative system. There were nearly six hundred code authorities under the N.R.A. and a greater number of wartime advisory committees. The total number of business organizations which might share in the representation of special interests in national politics, reported by the Directory of Trade Associations published by the Department of Commerce, is much greater. The addition of the representatives of organized agriculture and organized labor, to say nothing of powerful special interests such as the organized veterans, the great professional associations, and even the League of Women Voters, emphasizes the complexity of the representative function in contemporary national politics. The system of special-interest representation tends to become a rival and competitor of the major parties in the process of adjusting the conflicts of interest which naturally arise among the people of the United States. If, as Madison argued persuasively in the famous tenth number of *The Federalist*, the adjustment of conflicting economic interests is the principal task of modern legislation, the organized special interests as well as the political parties must play an important role in the legislative process.

The relations between the major parties and the special-interest organizations are not easily disentangled. Since the major parties are founded on combinations of special interests, it is not surprising that the party leaders should strive to coördinate all such interests that promise to be helpful in national elections. Those that are so concentrated in particular localities as to exert a strong influence in local politics are most likely to establish close relations with a major party. Some of these interests, notably the silver producers, the sugar and wool growers, and the coal miners, are so favorably situated that their relations with their official representatives may become intimate and influential. Others are so dispersed that they are necessarily more dependent upon their unofficial representatives. Contemporary Congressmen, particularly those representing urban districts, cannot hope to satisfy all the special interests in their districts and may give the greatest satisfaction by avoiding intimate relations with any of them. This is most likely to be the wisest course for representatives of the urban middle-class districts. Hence the tendency for such a representative to regard himself rather as an adjuster of conflicting interests than as a special representative of any portion of them. This tendency leaves the function of representing the more contentious interests as well as the less important ones to the appropriate special-interest organizations. It makes for further moderation in the use of power by the leaders of the major parties. It strengthens the general influence of middle-class attitudes in partisan politics.

The growth of the organized special interests in numbers and influence creates new problems for the major-party leaders. The new extraconstitutional system of representation must be put in its proper place in the general system of representative government. The political parties, which have already made an important place for themselves in the actual government under the Constitution, though having no explicit part in the original plan, must come to terms with the interest groups. Working arrangements of some kind between the party leaders and the interest-group managers must be improvised in order that the major parties may maintain their practical monopoly of the business of organizing popular majorities and thereby perform their mission of reconciling the requirements of constitutional government with the general demand for popular government. The major-party leaders cannot afford to ignore the demands pressed upon them by the organized special interests. To fail to adjust the conflicts of interest among the pressure groups means to abdicate the power to govern. Neither can the major-party leaders afford to yield too much to the pressure groups. To do no more than maintain an equilibrium of pressures would mean to lose the confidence of the general public, that is, above all of the middle classes. The test of success for party leaders is to convince the middle classes that they are making such adjustments of conflicting special interests as will best promote, or least impair, the common interests of the whole body of people. The problem of coördinating political factions is more complex than de Tocqueville made it appear in his account of party strategy in the age of Andrew Jackson and Henry Clay. It involves finding a proper place for organized interest groups as well as for political parties in the legislative process. Under the conditions of contemporary national politics it is soluble because of the political strength and good sense of the middle classes, both rural and urban.

THE STRATEGIC POSITION
OF THE URBAN MIDDLE CLASS

The shifting of the dominant influence in national politics from the rural to the urban middle class is unlikely to change radically the general character of the national party system. The leaders of the major parties will continue to seek support from special interests which can be coördinated into manageable organizations with attractive prospects in presidential elections. The major parties themselves will remain combinations of factions capable of dominating important sections of the country and of making effective contests in the close states and districts. The "ins" should be able to rely with reasonable confidence on the support of the sections where their principal strength lies. Under favorable circumstances they should have a better chance than the "outs" of winning the close districts and states. The "outs" should be able to monopolize the bulk of the opposition, and, if they do not become more closely identified with special interests than is essential to their control of the districts and states in which they find their principal sources of strength, should expect to be returned to power whenever the circumstances of the times and the mood of the public call for a change in the conduct of public affairs. Experience shows that changes will be called for often enough to maintain the unity and coherence of the organization of the "outs" and to reward the patience and moderation of its leaders.

The growth of class consciousness among the American people does not mean a radical change in the place of sectionalism in national politics. Candidates for the presidency can still be elected only by carrying states casting a majority of the electoral votes or congressional districts controlling a majority of the states in the House of Representatives. The territorial basis of elections insures that class consciousness can do no more than infuse a new spirit into sectionalism. Originally there was a tobacco planters' interest and a rice planters' interest, a graingrowers' interest and a hay-and-pasture farmers' interest, a frontiersmen's interest and a mercantilists' interest, which struggled for power at the national capital. The rise of urban industrial interests produces new cleavages but creates no better opportunities for interests incapable of carrying districts and states. Definite urban middle-class consciousness, like the indefinite and almost unconscious rural middle-class sentiment which set the general tone of national politics throughout the earlier history of the United States, favors a certain kind of leadership, which has generally held sway in the major parties. This kind of leadership has made the American way 'what it has generally been in the conduct of national affairs. It has encouraged moderation of temper, respect for the rights of individuals, and a disposition to abide by the decisions of majorities until they can be changed by methods sanctioned by the Constitution. The new spirit will resolutely dicountenance ill-considered and unbalanced appeals to the interests of the very rich or the very poor. It will make the way hard for Communist or Fascist parties in the future as for excessively narrow sectional parties in the past.

There will always be ambitious politicians and discontented factions watchfully waiting for opportunities to break up the established factional combinations and bring about a new alignment of the major parties in which their own prospects of influence would be greater. They will deplore the lack of principle in ordinary partisan contests and demand a more rational party system. Under normal circumstances experienced major-party leaders will be able to hold their lines against such attacks. Such party leaders know that no new party alignment is possible which is not based on the coördination of existing special interests in the different sections of the country. Nor could a new pair of major parties easily be formed on a more rational basis than the old. The differences of interest are too great and the force of tradition and habit too compelling. Perhaps the best party system would be one in which each of the major parties was as nearly as possible a fair sample of all the important factional interests in the country.[11] Under such a party system the voters would possess the greatest freedom of choice between the candidates for important offices on grounds of merit and fitness. Under the existing system such freedom of choice is restricted by the necessity of choosing between the parties as well as between the candidates. Perhaps under a new party alignment each of the major parties might be a truer sample of the whole body of people than is either of the present major parties. The possibility of such improvement in the major parties is a useful check upon the operations of the major-party leaders. The threat of party disintegration is a perpetual safeguard against the abuse of factious power.

A two-party system, based upon the ascendancy of the middle classes, is a happy development under the American Constitution.[12] It is a development which was partially foreseen by the most far-sighted of the framers. Madison anticipated the organization of at least one great national party, able to elect presidents and carry on the government of the country, and expected that the diversity of interests would help to prevent such a party government from abusing its power. Madison's theory of natural limits to the power of numerical majorities has been supported by the history of parties under the Constitution. It has taken the practical form of natural limitations upon the power of the major political parties. The variety of interests among the American people has been, as he predicted, a limitation upon the practical capacity of party leaders, when in a position to speak for popular majorities under the Constitution, to pervert their great powers for private and factious ends. As the country has grown and the diversification of interests proceeded to unanticipated lengths, the importance of this limitation upon the power of partisan leaders has been enhanced. It has greatly contributed, as Madison hoped that it would, to the serviceability of the Constitution and the stability of the Union.

The most convincing evidence that Madison was right in believing that a great variety of interests would afford the best security against the abuse of power by organized majorities in a popular government, is the unwillingness of the special interests to be content with representation through the major parties. Their insistence on organizing their own voluntary associations and keeping them under their own private control attests their craving for a more complex system of representation than that established by the Constitution. The multifarious businessmen's and farmers' and workers' organizations, which maintain permanent national headquarters, supply an extraconstitutional system of representation, which is closer to the work, if not to the lives, of the people than are their elected political representatives. The major political parties are eager to serve various special interests and gain their support, but they find it practically impossible to satisfy them with the quality of their service. They can cater with greater hopes of success to the more general interests, which different special interests share in common, but the more general the interests to which the party politicians cater the less content are those who share these interests to rely exclusively on the party for the more specialized services which they require from their government. Thus the contemporary development of organized pressure groups, representing these special interests and also the special "causes" which the people of the country support and the special "publics" into which the people are divided, seems to fulfill the requirements of Madison's argument.

But Madison did not foresee the present application of his favorite political principle. He was seriously concerned over the effects of the future growth of cities and the concomitant development of an urban working class. He had little faith in the political capacity of what we now call the masses and dreaded their future influence in national politics. He hoped that agrarian interests, together with the "opulent" in the cities, would be able to protect themselves against the abuse of power by the urban masses through the natural divisions which might develop between sections of the urban as well as of the rural population. The latter divisions he foresaw clearly, the former but darkly. The moderating role of the urban middle class he did not foresee at all. The record shows that the beneficent effect of the natural limits to partisan power is magnified and fortified by the moderating and stabilizing influence of the middle classes. The effectiveness of these natural limits has been enhanced by the development of a two-party instead of a one-party or a multiparty system in national politics. It has been further enhanced by the spectacular success of the middle classes, rural and urban, in holding the balance between the parties and setting the tone of national politics.[13]

A two-party system, dominated by the middle classes, was beyond the range of vision of most of the framers. It was far beyond the vision of those aristocratic Nationalists who based their plans of government upon a belief in the division of the people into two main classes of the rich and the poor. Hamilton and Gouverneur Morris would be amazed by the present operation of the system of government devised by their fellow delegates for the more perfect Union. Washington possessed a better understanding of the political qualities of the American people. His constant example of moderation in the use of power and his persistent preference for rational compromises between the conflicting interests of the different factions in the Federal Convention reveal a sturdy confidence in the practical capacity of the different elements in the body politic to adjust their differences in such a manner as to promote the best interests of the whole body of people.

The framer who seems to have had the clearest understanding of the political character of his fellow Americans was Franklin. He never propounded a systematic theory of American politics. He was naturally more interested in practical politics. But he seemed to anticipate the role which the middle classes might play in the actual government under the Constitution. At the close of the Convention, when delegates like George Mason, with whose views on the desirability of a more popular form of government Franklin deeply sympathized, were stricken with passionate discontent, Franklin's serenity attested his faith in the ability of the people to form effective electoral majorities and at the same time to use their power in national politics with moderation. Madison's principle of natural limits to the power of numerical majorities seems indeed to have been supplemented by another principle of politics which might well have been fathered by Franklin. This is the principle of the political mean. It is a principle with many manifestations in American politics. As manifested in the operations of the political parties it means the natural tendency of the major parties under a two-party system to reflect the reasonable requirements and moderate tempers of middle-class Americans.

CHAPTER SIX

Majority Rule in the House of Representatives

THE INFLUENCE OF PARTISANSHIP IN THE HOUSE OF REPRESENTATIVES

WHEN the framers of the Constitution divided the Congress into two branches, the principle of the independence of the states, to borrow de Tocqueville's expressive phrase, triumphed in the formation of the Senate, and that of the sovereignty of the nation in the composition of the House of Representatives. In the debates over the organization and powers of the House, as a matter of fact, the framers did not talk much about the sovereignty of the nation. Neither that expression nor the related expression, popular sovereignty, was much used in American politics until the French Revolution and neither became popular until the age of Jackson. But the framers were perhaps better agreed upon the function of the House of Representatives than upon any other leading feature of their new political system. It was the branch of the Congress that was designed to reflect the interests and wants of the whole body of the American people and to serve as the instrument by means of which popular majorities could influence the processes of government.

There are three main divisions of the task assigned to the House by the framers. In the first place, the House is to study the state of the Union and determine the need for legislation. In order that the House might be better prepared for the performance of this part of its task, the framers imposed on the President the duty of giving to the Congress from time to time information concerning the state of the Union and of recommending to its consideration such measures as he might deem necessary and expedient. Secondly, the House is to deliberate on proposed legislation and put approved measures into the form of law. To this end the House was authorized to compel the attendance of absent

149

members, to determine its rules of procedure and to punish its members for disorderly behavior, and was required to keep and publish a journal of its proceedings and to enter the results of roll calls therein, and to recognize sundry other obligations deemed likely to promote a greater sense of responsibility on its part to the people. Thirdly, the House is to watch over the execution of the laws and supervise the general administration of public affairs. The power of impeachment, vested solely in the House, was supposed to provide a potent sanction for the effective performance of this portion of its task. The framers disagreed radically over the amount of influence they wished the House to exert in the legislative process. But there was little disagreement over the final decision that the House should be the instrument for giving to the opinions of popular majorities some weight in the government of the more perfect Union.

The natural limits to the power of numerical majorities of the people might be expected to operate most efficiently through the institution which was originally designed to express the popular will. But the practical application of Madison's third principle of politics was profoundly affected by the unpredictable growth of organized partisanship. The people express their will, not only through their representatives, but also by means of their parties. There are many issues in national politics and the likelihood that the same majority of the whole body of the people will agree on more than a few of them at a time is small. Party organization in the House of Representatives may facilitate the enactment of popular measures into law, if endorsed by the party in power, but the greater the influence of the majority party, the greater the uncertainty concerning the practical capacity of other majorities in the House, not identical with the particular majority composing the majority party, to give effect to the wishes of those various popular majorities which they rather than the majority party represent.

The question arises, what are in fact the relations between the majority party and the other majorities which may exist in the House, and the problem develops, how should the power to act for the House be divided between the majority party and the other nonpartisan and bipartisan majorities by which the various popular majorities may be represented. In short, the House may be an instrument of popular government or it may be an instrument of party government, but what assurance can there be that it will be the instrument of both kinds of government at the same time? In any representative body there is always the problem of making a proper adjustment between the conflicting interests of the majority and of the minority of the body. In a representative body in which a party system flourishes there is the further problem of adjusting the relations between the majority party and the other majorities which would like to join together in the support of measures not supported by the majority party, particularly when these measures seem to be favored by a majority of the people.

The solution of these problems has been made difficult in the House of Representatives by a great and unwanted increase in its size and in the volume of its business. Since the apportionment of Representatives following the census of 1910 the House has been more than four times as large as in the age of the Federalists and has contained two hundred more members than in the ages of Jackson and Lincoln. Under recent apportionments the policy has been to fix the maximum membership at 435 and the latest reapportionment act makes this policy permanent. Congressmen clearly recognize the danger of letting the House grow too large, but they avoid this danger at the risk of making congressional districts so large that Representatives can no longer keep in close touch with their constituents. The popular branch of the Congress finds itself caught on the horns of a real dilemma.

The growth of business has been even more spectacular than that of the House. The Eightieth Congress, the first to be elected after the drastic limitation of private and local bills by the Legislative Reorganization Act of 1946 (better known as the La Follette-Monroney Act in honor of its two principal sponsors), was not called upon to consider as great a volume of proposed legislation as its predecessors for many years. Nevertheless the load was too heavy to permit really free deliberation by the whole House. A simple calculation shows how necessary it still is to impose a rigid discipline upon the members. During the two regular sessions of this Congress the House sat on 245 days and the total time devoted to its proceedings amounted to 1,101 hours. Altogether 8,385 measures were introduced for consideration.[1] If each had received an equal amount of consideration by the whole House it would have been necessary to dispose of these measures at the rate of more than seven and a half per hour. If each member had received an equal amount of time for their consideration, he would have had a little over one second for each measure. The burden on the House is greatly reduced by the use of committees. Only 2,174 measures were reported out of committee and placed on the calendars of the House. If all these measures had received equal consideration by the House and each member had shared equally in the time, he would have had four seconds in which to speak on each measure. It is obvious that there can be no equality of opportunity for members of the House in the conduct of its deliberations.

In fact, during the regular sessions of the Eightieth Congress the House passed 2,196 measures, including those originating in the Senate, and 1,258 were finally enacted into law. Actually, of course, not all the time that the House is sitting is available for the consideration of proposed legislation. Quorum calls, of which there were 120, and roll calls on measures before the House, of which there were 159, consumed a half hour or more each. It is evident that the House cannot get through its business without giving priority to the more important proposals for legislation. Any serviceable priority system necessarily involves the apportionment of the time of the House among different classes of business and the granting of special privileges to leading members of the House in order to keep the business moving. Rigid rules of procedure and strict discipline are essential.[2] Ordinary unprivileged Congressmen have more freedom of action on the floor of the House than members of a petty jury in a court of common law, but in the nature of things they cannot be as free as the framers expected them to be or as they were in the earlier years when the members of the House were less numerous and the business of the Congress was lighter.

The party system furnishes a basis for the organization of the House, but, as will be shown later, it does not provide an effective method for the enactment of legislation. The majority party can elect the officers and control the committees, but it cannot produce the votes that are needed to pass all controversial measures of general public interest through their several stages. What then, it is in order to ask, is the relationship between party government and popular government in the House of Representatives?

The limitations of partisanship in the House of Representatives appear plainly in the record of action by the House in the First Session of the Eighty-first Congress.[3] This was a session particularly favorable to action by partisan majorities. The members of the House had been elected at the same time as the President of the United States and a majority of them stood on the same platform during the campaign. Their disposition to follow their party leaders must be presumed to have been as high as it is likely to be under the American party system. Under these circumstances the composition of the actual majori-

152

ties on important controversial legislation, as disclosed by the official roll calls, of which there were 121 during this session, is significant. Forty-four roll calls showed a straight party vote, in which at least a majority of the majority party, that is, the Democrats, were recorded on the winning side and a majority of the minority party, that is, the Republicans, were recorded in opposition. (In two of these votes the Democrats actually failed to reap the fruits of their victory because they failed to get a needed two-thirds majority.) Fifty-six roll calls showed a bipartisan vote, in which a majority of each party was recorded on the winning side. Twenty-one roll calls showed a majority of the majority party on the losing side, in consequence of their desertion by enough of their party associates to give the victory to the opposition.

Further analysis of these roll calls discloses the full extent of the confusion in the alignment of partisans on these measures. Of the forty-four straight party votes, in which the Democrats were on the winning side, eleven would have resulted in defeat for the Democrats if they had not been supported by Republicans who did not go along with the majority of their party associates. If these roll calls are added to those in which the majority of the Democrats were on the losing side, the number of the remaining votes in which the majority party can claim exclusive credit for the result is reduced to thirty-three. Much the largest group of votes is that in which majorities of both parties support the same side of the question. Most majorities in the voting on important controversial measures during this session were bipartisan and the so-called majority party could not be held solely responsible for the action on most measures of this kind.

Majority rule in the House of Representatives at this session was far from identical with rule by a majority party. The organization of the House is consistent with a theory of responsible party government, but the legislative process is one in which the responsibility for action must be divided between the party nominally in power and the party nominally in opposition. This is not necessarily incompatible with what might be called popular government,[4] but it must be unsatisfactory from the viewpoint of those who hold that the best security for popular government is effective control of the action of the House by the party under whose auspices a majority of its members have been elected.[5] A question is bound to arise: Should there be more party government as a means to more complete popular government, or should the proponents of legislation in the House be as free as possible to find majorities for their measures wherever they can, regardless of party?

The lack of effective party discipline in the House is further disclosed by analysis of the voting records of the individual members.[6] In the First Session of the Eighty-first Congress only 27.7 per cent of the Democratic members voted with a majority of their party associates on 90 per cent or more of the roll calls resulting in straight party votes on controversial measures. The full extent of party disunity may be measured by the distribution of partisans into groups according to their records for voting with their party associates on roll calls of this kind. Those Democrats who voted with their party in straight party votes on at least 80 per cent but less than 90 per cent of the roll calls formed 32.3 per cent of the total party membership. In the group of at least 70 per cent but under 80 per cent participation in straight party votes there were 17.7 per cent of the Democrats. There were 10.4 per cent and 9.6 per cent in the next two groups, respectively, and 2.3 per cent of the Democrats voted with their party in less than half of the straight party votes. The corresponding figures for the Republicans were 26.3 per cent, 33.9 per cent, 16.9 per cent, 12.9 per cent, 7.0 per cent, and 3.0 per cent, respectively. The differences between the two parties with respect to the support of the party line by their members seem unimportant. The important fact is the striking absence of party unity on both sides in the voting on measures where partisanship should exert its greatest influence. It is not surprising that comparatively few of the straight party votes showed large majorities of the two parties on opposite sides. As many as 90 per cent of each party were recorded on opposite sides on very few roll calls except those of a perfunctory nature. Partisanship in the House of Representatives, judged solely by the record of roll calls on controversial measures in the First Session of the Eighty-first Congress, would seem to be a precarious institution.

The imperfect state of party discipline in the House of Representatives makes the legislative process in that branch of the Congress depend heavily on the chances of effective collaboration between the major-party leaders, or between substantial numbers of their followers, or both. The result is that the ability of the House to legislate seems itself to be too largely a matter of chance. Party government breaks down into a struggle of factions in which casual majorities are found for particular projects, while responsibility for the results cannot be clearly fixed either upon the majority party or upon any other majority which the voters can call to account. Individual members, regardless of party, look to their several districts for the sanction of their course of action. Local and special interests seem too likely to prevail over the general public interest.

The stoutest defender of the legislative process, as conducted in the House of Representatives, is Robert Luce, author of a voluminous treatise on the science of legislation and a legislator of exceptionally long experience. He was a member of a state legislature for nine terms and of Congress for an equal number of terms. He rose to the chairmanship of his party caucus in the House of Representatives and spoke with the authority of his practical experience in lawmaking as well as with the aid of immense learning on the subject. Writing near the end of his long public career,[7] he confessed: "After serving in both Legislature and Congress, my own conviction is that the work of a Legislature brings the more of personal satisfactions." His further comment throws a hard light on the legislative process at Washington from the viewpoint of a sympathetic and discriminating insider. "The most serious loss felt by the man who goes to the national House from the Legislature [of a state] is that of the opportunity to share in the treatment of the important questions that reach the floor from other than his own committees. The House is so large and the volume of its business so great that inevitably its members become specialists, with work confined to the problems of their respective committees. On the floor of the House itself they rarely get the chance to take influential part in discussion of the more important bills reported by committees other than their own." He concluded, however, on a more sanguine and positive note. "I end my task with strengthened conviction that in its frame and in its working our government is the best that man has yet devised. It can be bettered. Its machinery should be adjusted to new conditions."

External observers of the legislative process in the House of Representatives are generally more critical than Luce. Among recent writers Young, Galloway, Burns, and Bailey have examined the record with special care and have agreed upon the urgency of further improvements in the organization and procedure of the House in order that its machinery may be better adjusted to present conditions.[8] There can be no doubt that the natural limits to partisan power tend to restrain the majority party from abusing its power. But what about the artificial limitations, imposed by the majority party upon the practical capacity of other possible majorities of the House to operate under the rules so as to give effect to the wishes of popular majorities other than that represented by the majority party? Does the system of party government in the House make genuine majority rule there excessively difficult and thus prevent the House from performing with due efficiency its proper role in the government of the Nation?

An opinion has long been growing, and appears to be widespread, that in fact the House of Representatives does not play well the part assigned to it in the process of government by the framers. This opinion was most emphatically expressed by a recent foreign critic of the American political system. "The House of Representatives," Professor Laski wrote,[9] "has always been the least successful of federal institutions, and it retains that unenviable characteristic." Professor Laski's condemnation extends beyond the period of enlarged membership and swollen volume of business. He believed that the House had never fulfilled the expectations of the framers.

THE LEGISLATIVE PROCESS
UNDER THE CONGRESSIONAL CAUCUS SYSTEM

Differences of opinion concerning the role of the House of Representatives in the legislative process cannot be settled by argument, but only by investigation. The record shows that the influence of the House has varied greatly at different stages in the development of the system of party government. In the first stage, extending from the beginning of the First Congress in 1789 to the end of the Eighteenth in 1825, the House was the most successful of federal institutions. Its members took a principal part in the original organization of the government under the Constitution. They continued to exert a major influence in the legislative process throughout the Federalist and Jeffersonian Republican eras. The Congressional Caucus, in which the members of the House played the leading part, was a powerful factor in the whole conduct of public affairs. The House was clearly the predominant partner in the business of Congress.

The Senate in the early years met in secret, and its leaders had little opportunity to win the confidence of the people. Senators might be instructed by the state legislatures and despite their longer terms could not feel the same independence of action enjoyed by members of the House, whose constituents could not dictate to them between elections. John Quincy Adams resigned his seat in the Senate rather than oppose Jefferson's embargo in obedience to the instructions of the Massachusetts legislature, and a generation later John Tyler manifested a similar deference to the legislature of Virginia. Henry Clay was elected to the Senate before his first election to the House, but for many years preferred the leadership of the House to a place in the Senate and made the office of Speaker one of the foremost in the land. Under his leadership the House elected the President of the United States in 1825 and reached the climax of its power. John Quincy Adams, after his expulsion from the presidency by Andrew Jackson, was happy to accept an election to the House of Representatives and crowned his political career by his years of service in that body. De Tocqueville, writing after the authority of the House had already begun to wane, was still under the impression that the popular branch of the Congress exerted the greatest influence in the process of legislation. "There is so irresistible an authority in the legal expression of the will of a people," he declared, "that the Senate could offer but a feeble opposition to the vote of the majority expressed by the House of Representatives." [10]

By the end of the first period in the development of party government in the House of Representatives the organization of the House had attained essentially its present form. The Speaker was the principal spokesman for the majority of the members, the standing committees were the principal agents in the determination of policies and the preparation of bills, and the committee chairmen were the principal actors in the process of legislation. The membership of the House was still small enough to permit genuine freedom of speech on the floor, and the practical supremacy of a single party assured ample liberty to the individual member to vote in accordance with his own view of the public interest and the needs of his district. The most powerful instrument of majority rule was the Congressional Caucus, in which the House by the weight of superior numbers exerted a preponderant influence. But the failure of the Caucus to bring about concerted action in support of a single candidate in the scrub race for the presidency in 1824 portended the development of a more popular and efficient system of party organization and a concomitant decline in the prestige and influence of the House of Representatives.

Neither the aristocratic Nationalists nor their more democratic opponents could have been altogether satisfied with the performance of the House of Representatives during this first period in the development of the system of party government. The former sought to reduce their theories of government to practice through the instrumentality of the Federalist Party, but the Party leaders depended too greatly upon their personal influence in the branches of the government designed to check the authority of the popular branch. The Senate was not yet the popular institution which it later became, and its veto over the measures of the House lacked authority. Nor could much be made in the brief period of Federalist supremacy out of either the executive or the judicial veto. To the surviving aristocratic Nationalists the influence of the House, especially after the development of the Congressional Caucus by the Jeffersonian Republicans, must have seemed dangerously excessive. Gouverneur Morris, Rufus King, and the other impotent Federalist chieftains, observing President Madison accept a renomination to the presidency in 1812 by the Congressional Caucus apparently at the price of submission to the war policy of the leaders of the House, could not have regarded that branch as the least successful of federal institutions. Madison himself would probably not have disagreed with them.

But the Jeffersonians were by no means pleased with the House. According to their theories it ought to have been the most important factor in the government. Jefferson himself, by taking an invisible hand in the business of the House through his influence with the Party leaders and committee chairmen, made it seem more important than it really was. Under his less politic successors the House leaders were really as important as they seemed to be, but the lack of unity in their ranks, resulting in part doubtless from their very success in crushing the party of the opposition, prevented the ascendancy of the House from becoming as complete as it should have been in the opinion of Jeffersonian theorists. Majority rule in the House of Representatives meant the actual rule of casual majorities in response to the challenge of transitory circumstances. The greatest legislative act of the period was the Missouri Compromise. This was primarily the act of the House of Representatives under the leadership of its Speaker. The concurrence of the Senate was obtained without the aid of the Congressional Caucus or the intervention of the President. Never perhaps was a majority of the House more free to speak for a majority of the·people or more effective in dominating the legislative process. But the majorities in both House and Senate, which supported the policy of Speaker Clay, were majorities improvised for the occasion. The system of majority rule was not based on the operations of a responsible majority party.

Such a system of majority rule was too casual to endure. A Speaker who was at the same time both popular and imperious, like Henry Clay, could dominate the House and furnish effective leadership in the legislative process. The effectiveness of such leadership was enhanced by filling the presidency with creatures of the Congressional Caucus, like Madison and Monroe, of exceptionally coöperative dispositions. But the people, when their attention was sufficiently attracted to national politics and their interest aroused in the selection of Presidents, would not consent to the nomination of candidates by the Caucus, and a supply of Speakers of the caliber of Henry Clay was bound to be uncertain. Congressional government, as developed in the period of the ascendancy of the House, was a matter of comparatively simple processes and unfettered majority rule, but the majority was excessively irresponsible. The factions of which it might be composed were accountable only to the localities and sections from which they drew their support, and the Speaker could not speak for the House as a whole or for any permanent majority within the House but in the last analysis only for himself. He was certain, when the opportunity arose, to prefer a more powerful or at least a more secure position either in the Executive or in the Senate. In the nature of things there could be only one Speaker Clay.

THE LEGISLATIVE PROCESS
UNDER THE DELEGATE CONVENTION SYSTEM

The second period in the development of party government in the House of Representatives was marked by a gradual decline in the influence and prestige of the House. This period corresponded roughly with the ascendancy of the delegate convention system in the organization of the major parties. It began in 1825 with the refusal of most Democratic-Republican Congressmen to acknowledge the President, elected by the House, as the Leader of the Party, and it ended in 1910 with the refusal of a majority of the House to acknowledge the Speaker, elected by the majority party within the House, as the Housemaster. During the earlier part of the period the organization and procedure of the House remained much the same as under Speaker Clay, but thereafter there was a progressive and toward the end of the period a prodigious concentration of power in the hands of the Speaker. The result was the consolidation of the control of the House in the leadership of the majority party, but the impairment of the authority of the House in its relations with the Senate and the President. How these changes in the operation of the system of checks and balances came about is easy to understand. To explain their effects upon the power of numerical majorities in the process of government is more difficult.

The delegate convention system of party organization greatly altered the operation of the system of checks and balances. In the first place, by taking the control of presidential nominations away from the Congress it made the President more independent and hence a more important factor in the legislative process. Secondly, in conjunction with the spoils system of filling subordinate executive offices, it produced a more independent and a more powerful Senate. The constitutional system of checks and balances was transformed from a system in which the House of Representatives was the most popular and on the whole the most influential branch of the government into one in which its members were forced to compete for public attention and support under increasingly disadvantageous conditions with Senators and Presidents. Party government became immediately more important as the most suitable means of making the separate branches of the constitutional government work together. At the same time the House of Representatives lost its leading position in the organization of national parties. The age of Jackson meant more than resolute leadership in the determination of legislative policy by a masterful chief executive, supported by the confidence of an admiring public and sustained by the vigorous use of the executive veto and the executive patronage. It meant also that the leaders of the dominant political factions in the states tended more and more to gather together in the Senate where they could better secure their positions in the party organizations and thereby more effectively assert their authority against that of the President and of the House of Representatives.

It is easy at the present day to underestimate the force of the democratic movement in the ideas and manners of the people which produced the age of Jackson in American politics. It was by no means a mere personal triumph for an extraordinary popular hero. Besides Old Hickory there were Old Tippecanoe, Old Rough and Ready, Young Hickory, and, it may be added, Honest Abe. This hero worship, both natural and synthetic, expressed a popular craving produced by the march of democracy itself. Senators as well as Presidents shared in the wave of popularity. Presidents might come and go, but the Senate always remained. Strong men like Jackson were the exception in the White House. But the leaders of the strongest factions in national politics could always be found in the Senate.

The original idea that property should have special representation in the process of government, cherished by the aristocratic Nationalists but never approved by all the framers of the Constitution, was lost from view. De Tocqueville, who rightly understood this aspect of the age of Jackson, was led to observe in his chapter on the "Remains of the Aristocratic Party in the United States" [11] with no more than a pardonable touch of exaggeration: "At the present day, the more affluent classes of society have no influence in political affairs." Doubtless the political operations of Nicholas Biddle and other big bankers, as well as those of big merchants and big planters, should not have been dismissed so lightly, but certainly the less affluent classes did not regard Senators or Presidents as special representatives of the "opulent," to use the forgotten expression of the aristocratic Nationalists. When Clay and Webster and Calhoun chose the Senate as the principal scene for organizing the opposition to the Jacksonians and staged the great debates which defined the policies of the age, they diverted public attention from the House without giving the people any feeling that the process of government at Washington had thereby become less democratic. The Senate became a more popular at the same time that it became a more powerful institution.

In the latter part of the nineteenth century the number of very rich men in the Senate markedly increased. The use of money by some of them in procuring their elections from corrupt state legislatures became a national scandal. The feeling grew that the Senate was more subservient to the influence of wealth than the House.[12] Yet so discerning a writer as James Bryce, discussing the relations between the two branches of the Congress at the very time when the influence of wealthy Senators was most conspicuous, was not much impressed by the argument that the differences in the composition of the two branches were matters of great importance in the process of government. "The respective characters of the two bodies," he wrote,[13] "are wholly unlike those of the so-called upper and lower chambers of Europe. In Europe there is always a difference of political complexion generally resting on a difference in personal composition. There the upper chamber represents the aristocracy of the country, or the men of wealth, or the high officials, or the influence of the Crown and Court; while the lower chamber represents the multitude. Between the Senate and the House there is no such difference. Both equally represent the people, the whole people, and nothing but the people . . . Both are possessed by the same ideas, governed by the same sentiments, equally conscious of their dependence on public opinion. The one has never been, like the English House of Commons, a popular pet, the other never, like the English House of Lords, a popular bugbear."

It would be absurd, of course, to deny the influence of wealth in the process of legislation. As campaigns for election, whether to the Senate or to the House, became more expensive, candidates who possessed wealth of their own, or could command the resources of others, gained an advantage over their more impecunious competitors. Special interests that were well organized likewise gained an advantage over unorganized interests. The invention of the electric telegraph and the development of the steam railroad promoted greater centralization in the organization of special interests of all kinds, by no means excluding the major political parties. Technological changes produced similar effects in the management of political campaigns. Wealth as well as persons influenced all the processes of representative government. But their influence was not greatly unequal in the operations of the two branches of the Congress. Most members of both branches were lawyers by profession and tended to reflect in much the same way the wishes of their constituents, particularly of their organized constituents, or that portion of them on whom they chiefly depended for reëlection, as if they were private clients rather than sectors of the general public. The more expensive the electoral and legislative processes became, the more plutocratic the political institutions seemed to be. Whether the Congress as a whole, toward the end of this second period in its history, should be described as a democratic or as a plutocratic institution, is difficult to determine. The "opulent" were prone to regard it as excessively subject to popular impulses. Unorganized voters, and most of those whose principal organization was their political party, were easily persuaded in times of excitement over political issues that their representatives were excessively subject to the influence of wealth. But there was little ground for distinguishing between the House and the Senate with respect to the power of money in politics.

The tendency of the principal party leaders to congregate in the Senate reënforced the other tendencies of the age, which were working against the influence and prestige of the House of Representatives. Foremost among these was the growth of the size of the House. A body of 106 members, as in the time of the Federalist supremacy, or even of 213 members, as at the climax of Clay's speakership, could be an efficient deliberative assembly. But a body of 435 members, which has been the size of the House since the reapportionment following the census of 1910, is no longer capable of free and easy debate on all the public measures which may come before it, or even upon the smaller number of measures of general public interest upon which it may be required to act. In such a large assemblage, before the coming of electric amplification, members had to shout in order to make themselves heard, and shouting is not conducive to rational deliberation. Under the most favorable circumstances for debate the pressure of numbers precludes an equal distribution of the time among all the members. If the champions of the various factions and the members most interested in particular measures are to have sufficient time for thorough discussion, the bulk of their colleagues must content themselves with brief remarks or remain completely silent. Masterful speakers toward the end of this period, like "Czar" Reed and "Uncle Joe" Cannon, often seemed to dominate the debates in an arbitrary and dictatorial manner, but for each member of a multitude to talk as long as he pleases is plainly impossible.

The immense growth of the volume of business was a second condition unfavorable to the influence and prestige of the House. The number of bills introduced into the popular branch of the Seventy-eighth Congress was forty times as great as the number introduced into the same branch of the First Congress. The number of committee reports increased in the same proportion. Since the number of days that these two Congresses were in session increased only from 519 to 695, and could not have increased much more, the pressure of the increased volume of business upon the time of the House was much more intense.[14] If each member of the House were to take an equal part in the discussion of each bill, the time available for each speech would be only a few seconds. In the Senate, where both the number of members and the volume of business is smaller than in the House, the burden of business is lighter and the need is less for restrictions upon the liberty of the individual member to speak when and as long as he pleases. But in the House, acceptance of an order of business in which (1) the length of speeches is strictly limited, (2) more important kinds of business receive priority of consideration over other business, and (3) leading members are privileged to speak more frequently than others, is a necessary condition of any effective system of public debate, to say nothing of reaching a vote and getting final action on those measures approved by a majority of the members. The acceptance of such an order of business, however, creates a serious problem

163

of management, if the rights of the individual member to speak, of the majority of all the members regardless of party to act, and of the official leaders of the majority party to perform its pledges to the people, are to be equitably adjusted.

The House of Representatives postponed a radical solution of this problem of management as long as it could. From 1830 to 1870 it set itself resolutely against any increase in the number of members. Then the expectation of an extraordinary increase in the size of the electorate in consequence of the adoption of the Fourteenth and Fifteenth Amendments caused a change of policy. The rapid growth in the size of the House as well as in the volume of its business thereafter compelled the House to put itself in bondage to its leaders. Early in its history it sought to find time for participation in debate by as many members as possible by limiting the length of speeches, and for the consideration of as many measures as possible by authorizing a motion to end debate at any time by a vote of a majority of its members. In the eighteen-seventies and eighties further efforts to relieve the growing pressure on the time of the House were made by distributing jurisdiction over important business more widely among its committees. Responsibility for the management of the business of the House was dispersed among the committee chairmen.

It was at this time that Woodrow Wilson wrote his sensational book on *Congressional Government*. Congressional government, he declared,[15] was committee government. "Nobody stands sponsor for the policy of the government. A dozen men originate it, a dozen compromises twist and alter it." Taking the Congress as the center of authority in the governmental system, he deplored the lack of centralized leadership and the debilitating diffusion of power. The legislative process, he asserted, should be "a straightforward thing of simple method, single unstinted power, and clear responsibility." It was in fact, he declared, none of these things. The most promising remedy, he concluded, was to strengthen the executive and give it a more active position in the business of lawmaking. Something like the British system of cabinet government, he urged, should be introduced into the United States. The established system of checks and balances, he thought, had outlived its usefulness.

The House of Representatives recognized the nature of the disease but preferred a different remedy. If the House needed a master, it would find him among its own members rather than seek salvation from another branch of the government. The elections of 1888 gave one

164

of the major parties effective control of all the political branches for the first time since the panic of 1873, but the Republican majority in the House was small and more efficient legislative methods were indispensable, if the victors were to perform their campaign promises. Under the dynamic leadership of Speaker Reed the House gave its answer to the critics. The nature of the answer is revealed in the sobriquet by which the Speaker is known in history, "Czar" Reed.

The foundation of the Speaker's power was the right of recognition. No member of the House could make a speech, or even offer the simplest motion, unless the Speaker recognized his right to the floor. A resolute determination to use this power to favor those who supported his leadership and to discriminate against those who opposed it, especially those members of his own party who in his judgment should support him, though they might not wish to do so, would enable the Speaker to control the course of business. He might not be able to force the passage of measures which were unacceptable to some of the members of his party without help from the opposition, but he could ordinarily prevent the passage of measures to which he was opposed. Ruthless exercise of the right of recognition could give the Speaker a virtual veto against measures disapproved by his supporters. Speaker Reed possessed the resolute determination to use his veto ruthlessly. Commanding the confidence and unfaltering support of a majority of his party in the House, he could force recalcitrant partisans into line and consistently overpower the opposition.

Later Speakers further developed the power of recognition. At the climax of the system under "Czar" Cannon the Speaker would inquire of a member, seeking recognition, for what purpose he desired to obtain the floor, and, if the answer was unsatisfactory, would refuse to recognize him for that purpose. To avoid such refusals members desiring to get ahead with their business would visit the Speaker in advance and solicit a place on a list of those to be recognized by him. Such a practice presented to the Speaker opportunities to consolidate his position and maintain the discipline of his party which masterful politicians could exploit in the interest of a more centralized and better integrated leadership than the House had ever known before. The system was well designed to strengthen the authority of the majority party, but jeopardized the practical capacity of the minority party to maintain an effective opposition and threatened to destroy the independence of the private member.

A second source of the Speaker's power was the right to interpret the rules. The decision of points of order should presumably be governed by the precedents, but the raising of novel points or of familiar points under new circumstances gave the Speaker further opportunity to control the order of business in the interest of the majority party and of its regular leadership. The possibilities of this power were illustrated by Speaker Reed's claim of authority to count as present for purposes of a quorum members of the opposition who had actually left the chamber, when the count of a quorum was about to begin, in the hope of preventing the transaction of business. His success in defeating the dilatory tactics of the opposition and other efforts at obstruction contributed to the improved efficiency of the House as a legislative body. But he could not escape the charge that his use of discretionary power to interpret the rules was arbitrary and might be oppressive.

A third source of the Speaker's power in the latter part of this period was his chairmanship of the Committee on Rules. This committee, which in the beginning had been a select committee, not ordinarily employed in the current management of the business of the House, became a standing committee in 1880, composed of five members; three places were assigned to the majority party and two to the minority. Since the Speaker was chairman, he virtually was the Committee for all partisan purposes. Under an earlier ruling of the Speaker, the House could adopt by an ordinary plurality vote a special rule reported by the Committee of Rules for the purpose of setting aside the regular order of business. Since the rules could not otherwise be suspended except by a two-thirds vote, this ruling made the Committee on Rules the most effective agent of the majority party for the purpose of regulating debate on partisan measures. In the eighteen-eighties the power to report special rules was employed chiefly to prevent obstruction but in the nineties it became the practice to adopt special rules for the purpose of limiting the length of debate on controversial measures when obstruction was not apprehended. Thus the Speaker, who could recognize one of his colleagues on the Committee on Rules whenever he wished, gained effective control over the order of business and could regulate the whole process of legislation in the interest of the measures approved by the majority party or by its principal leaders.

A further source of power for the Speaker was the right to appoint the members of the standing committees at the beginning of each Congress. Since the numerous committees were by no means of equal importance, the power of appointment gave the Speaker a commanding influence over the individual member. The best appointments were reserved for his most faithful followers or were so distributed as to strengthen as much as possible the ascendancy of the established leaders within the majority party. Since the work of the important committees was the best part of the work of the House, committee appointments came to be a kind of patronage the control of which secured the position of the Speaker in the system of lawmaking. The choice of committee chairmen by seniority of service increased the importance of the Speaker's control of committee appointments and made harder the way of the individual member who might venture to challenge the established leadership of his party and resist the new system of business management in the House.

Finally, among the factors tending to confirm the supremacy of the Speaker in the legislative process, there was the power to control the reference of bills to committees. Ordinarily the committee which should take jurisdiction over a bill, and thereby largely determine the character and fate of proposed legislation, at least in the House, was indicated clearly enough by the nature of the bill. The reference of such bills could be safely left to the Clerk of the House. But important controversial measures might receive friendly treatment in one committee and hostile treatment in another. A bill to remove discriminatory taxes from margarine would fare badly in a Committee on Agriculture dominated by the dairy interests, but might have brighter prospects in a Committee on Interstate and Foreign Commerce dominated by manufacturing interests, or in a Committee on Ways and Means dominated by urban interests. A strong Speaker could use this power to insure that the measures favored or opposed by the party leaders would go to the committees where the desired action would be most likely to follow. By appropriate use of the power of reference, moreover, such a Speaker could increase the importance of the authority of the Committee on Rules over bills for which a special rule might be needed in order to secure timely consideration and action. This power, unimportant in appearance, completed the arsenal of weapons by means of which Speaker Reed and his successors established their mastery over the House and made the legislative process in that branch of the Congress the "straightforward thing of simple method, single, unstinted power, and clear responsibility," the lack of which had been so recently deplored by Woodrow Wilson.

In later editions of Wilson's *Congressional Government* the perspicacious author recognized the trend of the times and acknowledged the obsolescence of his criticism of that part of the system for which the House of Representatives was responsible. In the preface to the fifteenth edition, published in 1900, he candidly confessed [16] that his description of the system was "not as accurate now as I believe it to have been at the time I wrote it." Among the causes of change he specified the "gradual integration of the organization of the House," which he ascribed to the growth of the power of the Speaker and of the Committee on Rules. There can be no doubt that, toward the end of the second period in the history of the House of Representatives, the House had found a radical solution for its problem of legislative management. It was a solution which made the speakership, as Speaker Reed once remarked, an office with "but one superior and no peer." [17]

This radical solution of the problem of legislative management in the House of Representatives had consequences which were probably unforeseen and certainly unintended. It made Speaker Cannon at the end of the second period in the history of the House a greater power in the proceedings of the House than Speaker Clay had been at the end of the first period, but it made the House itself less influential in the legislative process as a whole. George W. Norris of Nebraska, then an inconspicuous member of the House, who had learned by hard personal experience how impotent the ordinary member had become and what frustration he must suffer if he ventured upon an independent course of action, read the signs of the times aright. "So far as the enactment of legislation is concerned," he wrote in La Follette's *Weekly*,[18] "the House of Representatives bears about the same relation to the National Government as the appendix does to the human body. It has no well-recognized function. For all practical purposes our National Government, like Gaul of old, is divided into three parts: the Senate, the President, and the Speaker. This perversion of the real intent and object of the Constitution has been brought about so gradually and quietly that until recently the people have not understood the method of its accomplishment." Norris understood, and he deplored the result more vehemently than Wilson had deplored the evil for which the dictatorship of the Speaker was a remedy. The exaltation of the speakership might be pleasing to the leaders of the majority party, but it could not fail to be distasteful to the minority party and to private members of independent temper regardless of party.

In practice the new system of management could not be entirely satisfactory even to the Speaker. The very extent of his power over the House subverted his influence in dealing with the Senate over problems of legislative policy. In the conference committees, which finally settled the details of important controversial legislation, the representatives of the House were at a disadvantage in the adjustment of differences between the two branches of the Congress. Since the House possessed rules under which the reports of conference committees could be speedily adopted, no matter how objectionable might be the concessions yielded to the Senate, whereas under the rules of the Senate the approval of conference-committee reports over the objections of recalcitrant Senators was more uncertain, the compromises reached in conference between the two bodies were likely to be more favorable to the Senate than to the House. Because the proceedings of the conference committees had become decisive in the final stages of the legislative process, the more centralized leadership and better integrated organization of the House were leading factors tending to lower its influence over the business of Congress. Speaker Cannon himself lamented the galling situation into which his official success helped to bring the House over which he presided. Never before had its authority in the actual operation of the constitutional system of checks and balances sunk so low.

The effect upon the power of numerical majorities of the people to influence the process of legislation was depressing. The Speaker possessed a virtual veto upon the acts of the Congress, which made him a more powerful factor in the legislative process than the President — except in those extraordinary instances, such as Theodore Roosevelt's railroad rate regulation and pure food bills, where public opinion could be forcefully aroused — but did not make him a more effective spokesman for the general public. He was in fact only the spokesman for a majority of the majority party. On matters concerning which the majority party was united he might be the spokesman for a majority of the people as well, but, since the major parties were essentially leagues of sectional and local factions, there were few such matters. The Speaker, though he certainly represented more than his own district, generally spoke only for a minority of the people. The various possible majorities of the House, which might have been found for particular measures, were without leadership. Their efforts under the system of party government in the House were doomed to futility. It was not only the minority party, but the potential majorities, composed of members of both parties, which were threatened with constant frustration under the established system of party government in the House. It was not only individual members with their private bills, who might be oppressed with a sense of futility if they ventured upon an independent course of action, but majorities of the whole House, seeking an opportunity to act in what they believed to be the public interest, who were condemned to subjection under the heavy yoke of the Speaker. The aristocratic Nationalists of 1787 would doubtless have smiled with satisfaction, if they could have viewed the political scene under "Czar" Cannon, but Benjamin Franklin would have shaken his head sadly.

Woodrow Wilson, with his usual perspicacity, reached more quickly than most critics of congressional government a correct estimate of the effect of the changed position of the Speaker on the operation of the system of checks and balances. The Senate, he noted in the Preface to the later editions of his *Congressional Government*,[19] had also undergone "a noticeable change" in its political character. Since the "vested interests have now got a much more formidable hold upon the Senate than they seemed to have" when he first wrote his book, that branch of the Congress now seemed to him less representative than formerly of "the several elements of the nation's make-up." By this he apparently meant that the Senate had come more manifestly under the influence of men of wealth than before, that is, it was more like what the aristocratic Nationalists of 1787 had hoped that it might be. There was a further tendency which would doubtless have been equally gratifying to this faction among the framers of the Constitution. "The tendency seems to be," Wilson continued, "to make the Senate, instead of merely a smaller and more deliberate House of Representatives, a body of successful party managers." Moreover, "the congressional caucus has fallen a little into the background." In short, instead of the traditional system of checks and balances, there was now a system of party government, which produced a new system of checks and balances, resembling more closely what the aristocratic Nationalists had originally planned than anything that had previously existed in the actual government under the Constitution. It was a two-party instead of a one-party system, which the aristocratic Nationalists would have liked best, but by exalting the Speaker over the House it cleared the way for a more powerful Senate and President than would have been conceivable in the time of Speaker Clay.

THE LEGISLATIVE PROCESS
UNDER THE DIRECT-PRIMARY SYSTEM

The third period in the development of party government in the House of Representatives has brought some improvement in the legislative position of the House. This period corresponds roughly with the ascendancy of the system of direct nominations of Congressmen by the major parties at the primary elections. The direct-primary system made many Representatives more independent of local party managers and "bosses," but increased their dependence upon influential interests within their districts. The direct primary did not destroy the influence of special interests in politics or diminish the advantage possessed by organized interests over those which are unorganized. The important change brought about by the new system of party nomination was the shifting of power from local party organizations to more specialized forms of interest organization, business organizations, trade unions, organized veterans, and others. The influence of money in politics was not ended, but the monopoly of power once possessed by party managers in many localities was broken and the way was cleared for greater influence by other organized interests.

Three important reforms in the organization and procedure of the House of Representatives have contributed to the improvement in the position of the House during this latest period in its history. The first was the reform of the rules brought about by the "Insurgent" Republicans in 1910. The second was the abolition of lame-duck sessions by the Twentieth Amendment to the Constitution in 1933. The third was the increase of the efficiency of the House by the Legislative Reorganization Act of 1946. None of these reforms destroyed the system by which the majority party controls the business of the House, but each of them tended in different ways to improve the position of the individual member, regardless of party, and thereby to improve the position also of majorities other than strictly partisan majorities in the process of legislation.

The "Insurgent" Republican revolt against the dictatorship of Speaker Cannon had for its prime objective the limitation of the arbitrary power of the speakership. "Czar" Cannon was not personally unpopular, but the system which he personified had become intolerably oppressive to the ordinary private member. The ordinary member of the majority party, forced by the new system of direct primaries to pay more attention to the opinions and sentiments of his district than was generally necessary under the delegate convention system of nominations, became more critical of the official party leadership. The direct-primary system rendered ordinary members more independent of the regular party organizations and made it safer for discontented members of the majority party to repudiate the regular leadership.

171

The members of the minority party, particularly the minority-party leaders, resented their dependence upon the majority-party leaders for any adequate opportunity to bring forward their own measures and to publicize their party program. The combination of the minority party with a minority of the majority party under the leadership of Representative George W. Norris of Nebraska broke the power of the majority-party organization. "Uncle Joe" Cannon managed to retain his office, but the monopoly of the leadership which had been vested in the Speaker was effectively dissolved.

There were two important changes in the speakership. The first was the loss of the power of appointing the members of the regular standing committees. The second was the loss of the chairmanship of the Committee on Rules. The effect was a wider distribution of the control of the majority party and of the House itself among the party leaders. The Speaker remained the foremost leader of his party in the House, but he could act effectively only in coöperation with others, particularly the Floor Leader and the chairmen of the important committees, above all the Chairman of the Committee on Rules. A narrow oligarchy succeeded to the former monarchy in the government of the House. The nature of the system, however, was not essentially changed by the redistribution of the powers of the speakership.

The operation of the new system of party leadership has gradually raised the Floor Leader to a position of authority second only to that of the Speaker. Originally he had been designated by the Speaker himself, and had generally been at the same time the chairman of one of the most important committees, usually the Committee on Ways and Means but sometimes the Committee on Appropriations. After 1910 the Floor Leader was elected by the party caucus and, beginning in 1919, when the Republicans recovered the control of the House, he held the positions simultaneously of Chairman of the Committee on Committees and of the Steering Committee. The former committee was elected by the party caucus and exercised the powers formerly possessed by the Speaker of selecting the Republican members of the committees of the House. It was authorized also to appoint the Steering Committee, which was a committee of the party. The Steering Committee was responsible for determining the order in which party measures should be brought before the House and in general for arranging the program of business for the majority party. A similar practice was followed by the Democrats, when they controlled the House, though the details of their system of organization were not precisely the same.

172

The Floor Leader, like the Speaker, was excluded from the regular standing committees of the House, and the two men were expected to devote themselves to the management of the business of the House in the interest of the majority party.

Under the new system of party leadership in the House, as under the old, the collaboration of the Chairman of the Committee on Rules is indispensable in handling all important measures of a controversial character. In recent years the Committee on Rules has assumed an increasing authority to pass on the merits of the measures which are scheduled for consideration on the floor of the House under a special rule. A Rules Committee which is determined not to report a special rule, fixing an hour and limiting the time for the consideration of proposed legislation, unless it approves the policies of the measures, can exercise a decisive influence over the fortunes of bills. Since it now possesses the power to report either an open rule, under which amendments to a bill can be proposed on the floor by any member, or a closed or "gag" rule, under which no amendment will be in order unless approved by the committee in charge of the bill, it has acquired an unprecedented influence over the other committees of the House. It can hold hearings on measures, like the committees to which they were originally referred, and reach its own decisions independently of the other committees. Thus the Speaker, the Floor Leader, and the Chairman of the Committee on Rules became a triumvirate whose power to dominate the proceedings of the House must have seemed to the ordinary private member in the Eightieth Congress as formidable and as ominous as that of "Czar" Cannon did to Representative Norris at the end of the second period in the development of party government in the House.

The chairmen of important standing committees, under the new system of party government as under the old, are in a much better position than the ordinary private member. They cannot get controversial measures through the House without the assistance of the ruling triumvirate, but on the other hand, if supported by a majority of their committeemen, they can ordinarily prevent the consideration of measures which have been referred to their committees, except in a form which they approve. Thus they possess a kind of veto over legislation within the jurisdiction of their committees, which they can use for the purpose of controlling the policy of the majority party in such matters, or at least dictating the terms on which action may be undertaken.

The most powerful of these committee chairmen is the Chairman of the Committee on Appropriations. As long as he is supported by a majority of his committee, he can influence any policy of the party which requires for its execution the expenditure of money. If he is determined to press his power to the limit, he can assert his authority over the measures of other committees, like the Chairman of the Committee on Rules, by reducing or withholding appropriations until those in charge of proposed legislation meet his views concerning the policies embodied in their bills. In the Eightieth Congress Chairman Taber of the Appropriations Committee exerted an influence over many important measures not inferior to that of Chairman Allen of the Rules Committee. It could not be said, as Woodrow Wilson did say with no more than a pardonable touch of exaggeration in his classic indictment of congressional government as it existed before the time of Speaker Reed, that "nobody stands sponsor for the policy of the government." But the legislative process in the House was not the "straightforward thing of simple method, single, unstinted power, and clear responsibility" that it had become in the time of Speaker Cannon. The majority party was a team whose play could be marred by confused leadership and faulty discipline. Uneasy and uncertain was the rule of the House triumvirate.

The authors of the reforms of 1910 were interested in improving the opportunities for majority rule in the House of Representatives, but they did not intend to establish a monopoly of legislative power for that particular majority of the House constituting the majority party. They planned to clear the way for action by any majority, regardless of party affiliations, which might wish to join in promoting a particular measure. To this end they proposed three important changes in the rules. One was designed to free the individual member from undue dependence upon the favor of the majority-party leaders for the consideration of private and local bills. A second was designed to enable any majority of the House, whatever might be its partisan composition, to consider and adopt a measure upon which that particular majority was agreed. The third proposal was to reorganize the Committee on Rules so that its members would fairly represent all the various factions within the two major parties. Evidently the "Insurgents" against the rule of "Czar" Cannon wished to restore to the House what they believed to be constitutional government instead of government by what was at best the majority faction, or combination of factions, within the majority party.

The Republican "Insurgents" of 1910 failed to reorganize the

Committee on Rules in accordance with their plan. Their Democratic allies, although favorable to the proposal to remove the Speaker from the Committee on Rules, were unwilling to join in carrying out the rest of the program for reforming that committee. The reason for this desertion of the "Insurgent" Republicans by the Democrats is clear. They were eager to take the balance of power in this highly privileged committee away from the Speaker, but they did not wish to transfer the balance to a minority faction in the majority party. Such a shift of power would be ruinous to party discipline, and would threaten the legislative program of the minority party with disaster whenever it should become the majority party in the House. The minority-party leaders, like those of the majority party, wished to preserve the system of responsible party government as nearly intact as was compatible with better protection against the abuse of power by an autocrat in the Speaker's chair. The minority party was ready to redistribute power more widely among the party leaders, but would not join in over-throwing the system of majority-party rule in the House. The majority of the majority party was left in complete control of the Committee on Rules.

The "Insurgents" were more successful in their other attempts to reform the rules. First, the reformers set apart one day in each week for the consideration of bills in their regular order, and prohibited the use of time for other purposes on such days except by a two-thirds vote of the House. The object of this reform was to enable a majority of the House to pass bills which were pending for action on the regular calendars, but which were not brought up under special rules in pursuance of the legislative program of the majority-party leaders. Furthermore, two new legislative calendars were established. One was a so-called unanimous-consent calendar. The other was a calendar of motions to discharge a committee from further consideration of a bill. The object of the former was to facilitate the passage through the House of private members' bills, reported favorably out of the proper committees and not of a controversial nature. The object of the latter was to enable any majority of the House, regardless of party, to bring a bill before the House for action. The intent of the reformers was clear. They would clear the way for action in the House by majorities of any kind, even at the cost of some impairment of the system of party government. They wanted popular government, they declared, rather than government by political bosses operating in the name of synthetic and often misrepresentative parties.

The "Insurgents'" plan to secure the right of any majority of the House, regardless of party, to pass the measures on the regular calendars in which they may be interested has met with only limited success. The reservation of one day a week for this purpose has not provided sufficient time for free debate on any considerable number of controversial bills of general public interest. There are too many such bills for the House to act on those which majorities of its members are most eager to adopt without the aid of a special rule or of an agreement of some kind to arrange for the necessary time. The day reserved for the consideration of bills in their regular order has been generally consumed in discussing measures of little public interest, which happened to stand first on the calendars. The business which has been transacted by the House under this procedure has generally consisted of routine legislation which the House leaders would have managed to get through the House somehow under the unreformed rules. The power of unorganized majorities to adopt measures not sponsored by the leaders of the majority party has not been perceptibly increased by this reform.

The plan to enable a majority of the House to take a bill from a committee which has been obstructing action by refusing to make a report on it of any kind has proved practically unworkable. Under the latest form of the rule for discharging committees from further consideration of such bills a petition must be signed by a majority of the members of the House and the time reserved for the consideration of such petitions, and of the bills to which they relate, is so limited that favorable action is excessively difficult. A telling illustration of the use of this rule to end a conflict between popular government and party government in the House was the discharge of the House Committee on Agriculture in the Eightieth Congress from further consideration of a bill to repeal certain statutory discriminations against margarine in favor of butter. The dairy interests controlled the Committee on Agriculture, but the producers of cottonseed oil and other vegetable oils contained in margarine, as well as the consumers of the product, were strong enough in the House to pass the bill, if they could bring it to a vote. This was not accomplished, however, until too late in the session to get action on the bill also in the Senate. In general, coalitions of factions from both major parties to bring forward measures which the majority party leaders, or those in control of the Committee on Rules and other important standing committees, refuse to sponsor have been unable to accomplish their purpose by the use of the discharge rule. The organization and procedure of the House, despite the reforms of 1910, remain more favorable to party government than to popular government.

A special problem arises when the power of a House majority to act is blocked by the refusal of the Committee on Rules to report a special rule under which the desired action can be taken. Ordinarily the Committee on Rules can defeat any controversial measure to which it is opposed by simply refusing to make time available for its consideration. A spectacular victory for a majority of the House was the discharge of the Committee on Rules in the Seventy-fifth Congress from further consideration of a special rule in order to bring the wages and hours bill before the House. This was a leading measure of the Roosevelt Administration and was supported by a majority of the House, including a majority of the Committee on Labor. But there was strong opposition within the Democratic Party, particularly from the Southern wing of the Party, and the opposition dominated the Committee on Rules. By means of the rule for discharging committees the Committee on Labor prevailed over the Committee on Rules, and the Administration, supported by a bipartisan coalition of Democrats and Republicans, was able to get the bill through the House. It was a triumph for the principle of majority rule in the popular branch of the Congress, but also it was a triumph for the Administration. In general this process for enabling a majority of the House to have its way was too difficult. At the beginning of the Eighty-first Congress the rule was amended so that the Committee on Rules might be discharged from further consideration of a special rule by a vote of the House on a motion by the chairman of any one of the standing committees. This change transferred back to the Speaker and committee chairmen some of the power monopolized by the Committee on Rules since 1910, but could not greatly improve the position of ordinary members of the House.

The results obtained by the establishment of the unanimous-consent calendar have been more substantial. The bulk of the non-controversial legislation which passes through the House is adopted by this process of tacit consent to what are in fact the decisions of the standing committees. Private members no longer need to go to the Speaker, or any other majority-party leader, seeking a promise of recognition or other favors in order to get unobjectionable bills through the House. Power which could too easily be abused to put pressure on private members to follow their party leaders has been effectively taken away. The effect on the legislative process has been to make the standing committees the final deliberative bodies in the adoption of measures to which there is no organized opposition. Since these measures are not ordinarily of general public interest, this success on the part of the reformers of 1910 is a triumph less for popular government than for the freedom of the individual member to serve his own district. This reform has put an end to a serious abuse of the party system without impairing too much the practical capacity of the party leaders to control the legislative process in matters of general public interest.

The Twentieth Amendment to the Constitution, in the adoption of which George W. Norris also took the lead, likewise tended to liberate the individual member from undue bondage to the party leaders without seriously impairing the system of party government in the House. By advancing the date for convening a new Congress almost a year, the amendment enabled the members to begin their work while the issues of the campaign were still alive and each member could speak with the greatest confidence for the voters of his district. By abolishing the lame-duck session, with its early dead line for the enactment of legislation and its pitiful spectacle of legislators repudiated by their constituents and dependent for uninterrupted continuance in public life upon the favors of party leaders, the amendment enabled Congressmen to finish their work under conditions more favorable to freedom of action. The members of the House gained more independence by this amendment than the Senators, since their numbers were greater and the pressure of business upon their time more intense. It is not surprising that the amendment should have passed the Senate six times before the leaders of the House could be persuaded to give it their sanction, or at least to give the members of the House an opportunity to act freely upon it. It was certainly clear to them that the power of the party leaders to control the proceedings of the House, and hence to dominate its action upon matters in which they were interested, was fortified by the shortage of time for transacting its business as well as by the dependent position of many members in a lame-duck session. The gain to popular government by the adoption of this amendment in the House is incalculable, but none the less real. The impairment of authority of the party leaders to conduct the business of the House is also incalculable, but their anticipatory fears seem to have been largely imaginary.

Senator Norris would have carried his efforts to establish free majority rule instead of party government in the Congress further, if he could. In his own state he led the successful campaign for the consolidation of the two branches of the legislature. The Nebraskan system, improved by electric voting and other devices to economize the time of the lawmakers and make the legislative process more efficient, demonstrated that representative government on the limited scale of a Midwestern agricultural state could be made less partisan and more popular. Despite his restlessness and that of other independent-minded Congressmen under the restraints of the bipartisan legislative system, as developed in response to the challenge of the varieties of opinion and pressure of work at Washington, Norris was never able to devise an acceptable substitute for the domination of the majority-party leaders in that part of the business of the House in which the general public was most interested. He wrote his name large in the history of representative government at Washington, but he could not find a better way to overcome the natural limitations to the formation of majorities on the great scale of the lawmaking process at the national capital than the system of permanently organized bipartisan politics. His lifelong struggle to break the chains of that system showed how right Madison was in his analysis of the difficulties tending to prevent effective majority rule in a national house of representatives. No politician in American history tried harder than Norris to bring about that which the aristocratic Nationalists most dreaded. His career showed more clearly than that of any contemporary both the possibilities and the limitations of the free-enterprise system in national politics.

The reforms initiated by the "Insurgent" Republicans afford the most tangible evidence of the effect of the direct-primary system of nominating Congressmen upon the legislative process at Washington. The system increased the exposure of a Congressman to the pressure of local interests. The reforms restored to the individual Representative much of his original freedom of action in handling the private and local business of his district. But they did not destroy the necessity for party government in the House of Representatives. Special interests of many kinds, like politicians themselves, were constrained by the march of time to organize on a national scale. Individual Representatives, like the general public, needed protection against the power of the organized interests. The party leaders found increasing difficulty in maintaining the discipline of their own organizations. Adequate protection for the public interest called for more powerful leadership than could be established within the House itself by any improvement in its own organization or procedure. The reform of the rules could not restore to the House the primacy which had been enjoyed under the speakership of Henry Clay. But it could make the House a more active partner in the business of Congress than under the dictatorship of Speakers Reed and Cannon.

The Legislative Reorganization Act of 1946 increased the efficiency of the House of Representatives. It relieved the members of much of the heavy burden of private business by transferring jurisdiction over the settlement of private claims and the adjustment of pensions, the building of bridges over navigable waters, and other private and local legislation to executive agencies or to the courts. It provided more numerous and more competent clerical and technical assistance both to private members and to committee chairmen. It strengthened both the office of the Legislative Counsel in the House and the Legislative Reference Service of the Library of Congress. It improved the procedure of the committees and reduced their number from forty-eight to nineteen. It restricted each member to service on a single committee and insured that each committee would have jurisdiction over a substantial volume of important business. It required the registration of lobbyists and quarterly reports on the use of money by pressure groups of all kinds. Better organization, improved procedures, and a lighter work load, to say nothing of increased compensation and better protection against undue influence by special interests, insured a better opportunity for all members to perform their principal duties: the study of the needs of the public, the consideration of proposed legislation, and the supervision of administration.

The increase of efficiency did not alter the position of the House in its dealings with the Senate, since the Act applied to both branches of the Congress alike, but it improved the position of the Congress as a whole in its dealings with the executive department of the government. Whatever increased the efficiency of the Congress diminished its dependence upon outside aid, whether from the Executive or from the lobby and other organized "pressure groups." The Eightieth Congress, the first to operate under the new act, was one of the exceptional Congresses in which each branch was under the control of the political party in opposition to the President. Partisan legislation was impossible except for measures, such as the Taft-Hartley and tax-reduction acts, receiving enough support from members of the minority party for passage over the presidential veto. Some observers predicted a paralysis of all legislative business on account of the political differences between the Chief Executive and the party in power in the Congress. Despite these differences the Congress demonstrated surprising capacity for the transaction of nonpartisan business. The immediate results of the Legislative Reorganization Act would have strengthened popular confidence in the soundness of representative government, as conducted at Washington, but for the emphasis in the presidential campaign upon partisan conflicts.

The Legislative Reorganization Act of 1946 made the House more efficient without making it more democratic. No change was made in the organization or in the high privileges of the Committee on Rules, and the power of the party leaders to control the course of business remained unimpaired. The continued appointment of committees by the party leaders and selection of committee chairmen by the rule of seniority insured the continuation also of the established system of legislative management in the House. The distribution of power between the party leaders and the ordinary members was preserved intact. The relationship between party government and popular government remained what it had become in consequence of the reforms initiated by the "Insurgent" Republicans in 1910.

The position of the House of Representatives in the legislative process during this period of its history was further influenced by the great development of lobbying on the part of representatives of local and special interests from all sections of the country. The organized "interests" and "causes" and "publics" formed the habit of looking to their own spokesmen, rather than to party leaders or the representatives of particular districts, for action on the measures which they wished to promote or oppose.[20] The pressure of these organizations on the members of Congress to give consideration to the measures which they originated tended to relieve Congressmen of responsibility for planning legislative programs and preparing the measures to carry the programs into effect. It made them less dependent on party leadership for the coördination of their efforts in the legislative process. Like the new system of direct nominations of Congressmen at the primaries, the development of "pressure politics" tended to undermine party discipline and subvert the system of party government. The special interests looked more and more to their own special organizations for representation at Washington and ever less to the major political parties. The role of the parties in the legislative process in the latter part of this period was definitely inferior to what it had been in the days of Speakers Reed and Cannon.

PARTY GOVERNMENT
VERSUS POPULAR GOVERNMENT

The ability of the congressional leaders in the Eightieth Congress to get together majorities for their measures, even two-thirds majorities to pass measures over presidential vetoes, brought fresh evidence of the true nature of representative government under the Constitution of the United States. Party government, as developed in the House of Representatives, does not mean that legislative action is dependent upon the support of a well-disciplined and coherent partisan majority for the measures of the majority-party leaders. It means a legislative process in which action depends upon the practical capacity of the majority-party leaders to find majorities for their measures wherever they may exist regardless of party. Unorganized numerical majorities of the House are ordinarily incapable of action to which the majority-party leaders are opposed. Even a majority of the majority party is incapable of action to which the party leaders are opposed. Only the regular leaders of the majority party can make the law-making machinery work. They need the support of at least a majority of their partisans in the House in order to keep control of the machinery, but a majority of the majority party is not ordinarily a sufficient force to insure the success of their leadership.

Numerical majorities of the representatives of all the various sections and classes of the people in a country as wide as the United States, as Madison predicted, are not easily brought together. Only the leaders of the House, who control the course of business, under normal conditions can organize such majorities for effective action. They rely upon their own party followers for the needed majorities when they can accomplish their purposes by such means. They utilize available elements of the opposition party when they must in order to get a majority together. Action in the House in all matters not disposed of by unanimous consent is partisan action, in the sense that it is not ordinarily accomplished except under the direction, or at least with the consent, of the majority-party leaders. But it is not partisan in the sense that it is accomplished by the united efforts of the majority party against the united opposition of the minority party. On the contrary, the record shows that much important controversial legislation of general public interest is passed through the House by bipartisan majorities against the opposition of many members of the majority party and even in some cases against the opposition of a majority of the majority party.

A vote as recorded on a roll call is not always self-explanatory, and more than an analysis of roll calls is necessary for a proper understanding of the action of Congressmen. Nevertheless a knowledge of the votes of the people's representatives is the beginning of political wisdom in a modern democracy. Figures based upon analysis of the roll calls in the First Session of the Eighty-first Congress have already been cited to show the lack of party unity following the elections of 1948. The figures for the Eightieth Congress show a similar situation.[21] The Republicans being in a majority, and feeling presumably a greater sense of partisan responsibility than in the Eighty-first Congress, showed a higher degree of party unity. The Democrats showed considerably less party unity in the Eightieth Congress than the Republicans. Party government is only one of the forms of majority rule. In the House of Representatives majority rule takes other forms than that of strict party government to such an extent as to render unrealistic those descriptions of the legislative process which represent it as a process in which the party system has superseded the system originally planned by the framers of the Constitution.

It is clear that the degree of party unity disclosed by the roll calls in the House of Representatives furnishes an inadequate basis for effective party government. With such uncertain support for the party line from members of the majority party, many of their measures — even a considerable number of their leading measures according to the analyses in the *Congressional Quarterly* — would fail to pass without support from substantial numbers of the minority party. In fact a large part of the important controversial measures which passed the House in the Eightieth Congress were supported by a majority of the members of each of the major parties. The Republicans voted almost as generally in support of these bipartisan measures as in support of the party line. The Democrats also showed almost as much solidarity in support of the bipartisan measures as in following the party line. More than half of the important votes, according to the *Congressional Quarterly's* analyses of the roll calls, were supported by majorities of both parties in both sessions of the Eightieth Congress. In short, partisanship was not the major factor in the formation of majorities for the controversial measures which passed the House.

The importance of majorities other than strictly partisan majorities is even greater than these figures would suggest. In several cases where a majority of each party did not join in supporting one of these measures, and where the members of the majority party favoring the measure did not constitute a majority of the whole House, a majority of one party was assisted by a minority of the other large enough to make a majority of the House. Moreover, some of the measures on which the final roll call showed majorities of the two parties on opposite sides were actually measures of which the most controversial features were settled by preliminary bipartisan votes. Partisanship is an important matter at congressional elections and in the initial organization of the House itself. But in the ordinary process of law-making, bipartisanship is more important. It is a legislative system which could not operate satisfactorily — in the long run it could not operate at all — without moderate tempers and a generous spirit of mutual accommodation on the part of the leaders on both sides. It involves the continuous compromise of the sectional differences within the country. It involves also the conciliation of class differences and in general the predominance of middle-class points of view in the process of legislation.

Majority rule in the House of Representatives is a system of government involving action by majorities of various kinds besides partisan majorities. The leadership is partisan, while the actual majorities are unstable combinations of local and special interests with a casual and fitful regard for party. Each measure must stand on its individual merits. The majority-party leaders appraise the need for legislation in the various fields of interest and get together a majority as best they can for such measures as they deem expedient from the sections of the country and the classes of people which favor action of the kind the party leaders are willing to sponsor. The House is a legislative assembly plant in which the majority-party leaders plan the order and determine the general character of production. The components of the needful majorities are taken where they can be found. The details of the measures become what they may. It is a difficult process — as Madison foresaw — requiring a high order of skill in the management of men and a wide knowledge of the needs and desires of the many different elements which make up the people of the United States.

The efficiency of the legislative process in the House is contingent upon the solidarity of the majority-party leadership rather than upon that of the majority party itself. From this point of view the organization of the House leaves still much to be desired. The gravest defect is the excessive influence of seniority in the appointment of committee chairmen and the assignment of places upon the more important committees. The result is that chance plays too big a part in the selection of the real leaders of the House. The members of the factions from the sections of the country where the party finds its greatest strength, who happen to represent the safest districts and thereby to enjoy the longest unbroken periods of service in the House, become the party leaders. They are not necessarily the ablest members of the party. They may even be grotesquely unsuited for the chairmanship of the important committees on which they happen to serve. They may be out of sympathy with, or even bitterly opposed to, the measures favored by the majority of their fellow partisans. They may be suffering grievously from the infirmities of old age. But they cannot be displaced from their positions in the organization.

The seniority system is the cause of numerous ills. It prevents the rapid rise of the ablest members to positions of influence. It discourages the spirit of enterprise on the part of junior members of the important committees. It divides the authority of the party leaders and impairs their practical capacity to carry out consistently a general program of party legislation. It may even defeat the projects to which the majority of a party have been publicly pledged. It introduces a demoralizing element of speculation into the councils of a party. It makes the party system a less effective instrument than it might and should be in organizing majorities within the House for serving the manifest needs of the people of the country.

Another grave defect in the present organization of the House of Representatives is the unrepresentative character of the highly privileged Committee on Rules. This Committee, rather than the unofficial Steering Committee of the majority party, is the real policy committee of the House. The influence of seniority in its appointment makes it the natural agent of the "Old Guard," the elements in the majority party which are least affected by the march of time, and insures a dilatory response to the tides of popular opinion as reflected in the congressional elections. This, of course, is such a limitation on the power of numerical majorities of the people as was hoped for by the aristocratic Nationalists in the Convention of 1787. It would seem to be a salutary development to the spirits of Gouverneur Morris and Alexander Hamilton. But democratic Nationalist Ben Franklin would again shake his head sadly at the egregious failure of the popular branch of the Congress to provide as fair and responsible a system of majority rule as is clearly within its power.

The test of good representative government is not, of course, its quick and unreflecting responsiveness to every demand that may be expressed by the most articulate part of the public in the name of the people. The people's representatives should have better information than the public at large; they should be able to look further ahead and be less perturbed by transient events or the mood of the moment; they should be persons of greater natural intelligence than would be obtained if the selection, as in the choice of a jury, were made by lot; their judgment should be strengthened by their longer experience in public life; they should possess a better understanding of the permanent interests of those whom they represent. In a democratic age it is reasonable to demand that the popular branch of the Congress should execute promptly the mandates of the people expressed at a general election. But in the nature of things such mandates cannot be numerous. There cannot easily be a single issue which all the voters throughout the whole of a great and diversified country such as the United States will regard at the same time as of paramount importance. It is unlikely that there will be more than a very few issues on which a majority of all the voters express clear opinions at a single election.

One of the functions of the major political parties is to define the major issues in a campaign and to frame the questions to be decided so that the public can express its opinion concerning them. However, even if the parties perform this function efficiently, the public cannot indicate its judgment on more than one such question at a time, unless by chance the public happens to divide on two or more such questions in precisely the same way. Otherwise the members of the public have to determine which is the most important question, and unless they all reach the same conclusion the meaning of the election will be uncertain and the mandate of their representatives will be unclear. When the popular mandate is clear, the obligation of representatives belonging to the victorious party should be clear also, but obviously that part of the business of the Congress which can be transacted in accordance with a clear mandate of the majority party must be very small. The prompt execution of the known will of the people, as expressed at the polls, cannot be the greatest of the duties of the House of Representatives.

More numerous doubtless are the matters in which politicians are professional experts because of the nature of their occupation. Their opinions on such matters carry weight because of their technical competence. This competence, however, in the case of legislators as a class, is necessarily limited to the fields of legislation in which their political experience makes them genuine experts. These are the waging of election campaigns, the conduct of elections, and the operation of the machinery of government. In these fields a Congressman may act on the basis of his own knowledge and beliefs, but they are narrowly limited fields and cover but a small part of the business of the Congress. Unhappily these are matters also in which the legislators are apt to be personally interested. An example is the process of voting in the House of Representatives. The adoption of electric voting, as in many state legislatures, would save the equivalent of several weeks of tedious work in every regular session of the House and free the overburdened members for more important business. But by reducing the pressure of business upon the time of the House it would weaken the grip of the party leaders upon the machinery of lawmaking. The interest of the party leaders and perhaps even of the majority party is opposed to that of the greater number of private members, regardless of party, and to that of the general public. It is in this part of its business that the House appears at its worst. A Congressman is also personally interested in the maintenance of the bipartisan system, under which he has triumphed over his opponents, and is strongly biased in favor of the political methods which he associates with his own success. This is well understood by the voters. They expect to look elsewhere for leadership in reforming the machinery of government. As a technical expert, therefore, the Congressman enjoys little popular prestige, and in this role he performs the least of his services to the public.

The bulk of the business of the House of Representatives consists of matters on which legislators must act, not as technical experts nor as political agents with a clear popular mandate, but as a sample of the public. In a country as extensive as the United States the public cannot form opinions concerning the bulk of the business which comes before their representatives. They are too preoccupied with their private affairs to have either the time or the inclination to inquire into the need for legislation, except on a few subjects with which they may be personally concerned, or to examine the evidence and weigh the arguments which can support an intelligent opinion concerning the bulk of the measures which may be proposed for enactment into law. Congressmen occupy an excellent position for the performance of this function. They are paid to devote their time to the business of legislation, they possess superior facilities for becoming acquainted with the needs of the public, and they have the strongest incentives to make laws which will meet with public approval. They should be able to reach the decisions which the people themselves would reach, if they enjoyed the same opportunities as their representatives for participation in the legislative process. This portion of the business of the Congress accounts for most of the strictly legislative work of the Congressmen.

In dealing with this part of its business the test of a good representative body is its willingness and ability to act as the public itself would act, if its members were aware of the necessity of choosing between different courses of action, were in a position to get the facts essential for a rational choice, and were able to reach a decision by an effective process of deliberation. The party system, as developed in the House of Representatives, certainly increases the practical capacity of the House for action of some sort in matters of this kind. But it does not insure more representative action. In so far as Representatives support their party contrary to their own better judgment, the action of the House on matters constituting the bulk of its business is presumably less representative than it should be. The importance of bipartisanship in the business of the House is from this point of view a sign of better representative government than could be expected under a system of strict party government.

The passage of bills through the House of Representatives with the support of a majority of both major parties, or with that of a majority of one of them and a substantial minority of the other, affords the best security for the triumph of reason in the legislative process. It is the process which best reflects the spirit of moderation, acclaimed and practiced by the two greatest leaders in the Convention of 1787, Washington the aristocratic Nationalist and Franklin the democratic Nationalist. Differing as they did on many important details of the Constitution, they agreed in extolling the merits and setting the example of an even temper and a conciliatory disposition in the business of the legislator. The conduct of business in the House could easily be better than the current practice. This practice, however, is certainly better than that in the earlier stages of party organization in national politics.

The system of majority rule in the House of Representatives has often been compared unfavorably with the parliamentary system as practiced in the best-governed European countries. Such comparisons are beside the point. Cabinet government in countries with parliaments involves a peculiar relation between the legislative and executive departments. The different relation between these two departments in the United States is a vital feature of the American Constitution which calls for special consideration. In Great Britain, party government is the essence of constitutional government. In the United States, there is both party government and constitutional government. The connection between the two is complex and obscure. Their interrelations are not to be ignored. Meanwhile, it can be observed that the House, when it functions as a sample of the various interests which constitute the general public, appears to better advantage than when functioning as a party machine or as a body of technical experts. The adjustment between the liberty of the individual member and the authority of the House as a whole is intricate, and wholly satisfactory to neither. The adjustment of the relations between partisan majorities and bipartisan majorities is even less satisfactory. Nevertheless, the processes of majority rule in the House are surprisingly efficient. That there are many critics of its performance is evidence primarily that there is much difference of opinion among the people of the United States concerning both the need for legislation and the kind of legislation needed. The legislative output, or lack of output, of the House will always be the subject of criticism, as long as public opinion itself is free and vigorous. No system of majority rule in a representative government can function normally without systematic and persistent criticism of its fruits.

Further criticism of the particular system of majority rule developed in the House of Representatives must be deferred until the whole system of checks and balances, planned by the framers of the Constitution, has been examined. Some of the framers feared that the majority of the House would exercise too much power, and that its power would be too much abused. Others, on the contrary, feared that it would not be able to exercise enough power, and that its lack of power would threaten the preservation of popular government. Such fears still exist. Their continued existence is perhaps the best evidence that the particular adjustment between the rights of the individual member and the authority of the House, which has been worked out in the present stage in the development of the party system, is by and large well suited to the requirements of the times. The party system is an indispensable expedient for facilitating majority rule under the Constitution. It is indispensable for working the legislative process in the House. But it is not capable of getting to-

189

gether the necessary majorities for putting through the House all the legislation needed and desired by the people of the United States. The system of majority rule in the House is more than an incident of party government. In this branch of the business of Congress constitutional government is far from having been supplanted by party government.

The record of legislative action in the House of Representatives down to the present time supports the view that Madison was right in believing that the natural limits to the power of numerical majorities in a country as large as the United States would afford some protection against the abuse of power under any system of majority rule in the popular branch of the Congress. The actual system of organized partisanship tends to overcome the natural obstacles to majority rule within the restricted area of effective party government, but creates additional obstacles to the action of majorities other than partisan majorities. This is all to the good, in so far as it checks irresponsible logrolling by casual combinations of local and other special interests. It is not so good, when it frustrates action desired by majorities of the Representatives, forming an obviously fair sample of a majority of the whole body of people. These artificial obstacles to bipartisan and nonpartisan systems of majority rule hamper the development of popular government, based on the free enterprise of the individual Representative, without apparently improving the quality of party government within the area for which it possesses a clear popular mandate. What seems to be most needed in the popular branch of the Congress is not stricter discipline in the majority party, but better facilities for majorities, regardless of party, which fairly represent a majority of the people. Yet no final judgment on the system of checks and balances, as it has been applied to the legislative process at the national capital, can be reached without examining the roles of the Senate and the President in the exercise of legislative power.

CHAPTER SEVEN

The Role of the Senate in the Legislative Process

GUARDIAN OF MINORITY INTERESTS

THE Senate was designed to play a dual role in the government of the more perfect Union. According to the original plan of the aristocratic Nationalist leaders in the Convention of 1787, the role of the Senate was to check the power of the majority in the House of Representatives and maintain a proper balance between the interests of the "opulent" and of the "indigent." The original Federalists, on the other hand, insisted that the Senate should be utilized as an agency of the states to protect their rights under the Constitution and guard their independence in their own sphere of authority. The first of the great compromises sought to reconcile these two objectives. The primary function of the Senate was recognized to be the guardianship of the rights of the states, but hope was not abandoned by the aristocratic Nationalists that Senators would also be found serviceable as guardians of the interests of the "opulent."

The principle of federalism was accepted reluctantly by Madison and the other aristocratic Nationalists in the Convention of 1787. They wished to establish a national government which could operate directly upon the people of the United States without any checks interposed by the governments of the states. They would have made no provision for a balance of any kind between the state governments, which they proposed to transform into local governments, and the government of the Union. They would have preferred to treat questions of conflict between national and state governments as political questions, to be decided by the political departments of the national government. The more moderate of these Nationalists would have been content to rely, for preserving the supremacy of the national government, upon a veto by the Congress of state legislation in conflict with the Constitution. The ultra-Nationalists would have gone further and provided for a congressional veto of state legislation conflicting with any policy of the national government. In order to enforce the supremacy of policies deemed by national leaders to be in the national interest, Hamilton and Charles Pinckney would even have favored the appointment by the President of state governors with a power of veto over state legislation, like royal colonial governors before the Revolution.

In accepting the principle of federalism as an essential principle of the American Constitution, the various kinds of Nationalists in the Convention of 1787 by no means accepted the original Federalists' view of its function in the general scheme of constitutional government. In the fifty-first number of *The Federalist* Madison made a virtue of necessity and admitted the principle of federalism into his political philosophy. From the federal principle he derived one of his three main reasons for believing in the stability and durability of the new system of government, but his reasoning was radically different from that of the original Federalists. He was interested in the principle of federalism primarily because of its effect on the government of the more perfect Union, whereas the original Federalists were more interested in its effect on the governments of the states. They still put their trust chiefly in the state governments, which they regarded as their principal hope for good government.

The original Federalists recognized the need for a stronger general government to supplement the governments of the states, but they could not believe that it would be a better government in its field of action than the state governments in theirs. The more democratic middle-class Federalists were particularly insistent upon preserving the rights of the states as the best security for the rights of the people themselves. Under a federal system of government, the people of each state would possess a government of their own to serve their particular interests. They would also share in the government of the Union for the better service of their more general interests. Federalism was regarded by the originators of the Connecticut compromise as something more than a means of reconciling the conflicting interests of large and small states. It seemed to them a political invention capable of raising popular government to higher potentialities of public service. It should be of benefit to all the states regardless of their size.

Madison and the other aristocratic Nationalists adopted the name of their Federalist opponents, when they accepted the federalist principle, without accepting the Federalists' faith in the state governments. The authors of the Virginia plan could not put their trust to the same extent in governments, particularly in legislatures, which seemed to them excessively devoted to local interests and incapable of taking a state-wide view of state interests, to say nothing of taking a national view of national interests. They regarded the abuse of power by the state legislatures, even in matters within their own proper field of action, as one of the chief evils to be curbed by a well-constructed national government. They might accept the principle of federalism, but they could not approve the Federalists' reasons for supporting the rights of the states. The great advantage of the federal system, from Madison's point of view, was that it afforded an additional means of checking the abuse of power by a numerical majority of the whole body of people without unduly limiting the practical capacity of the national government to promote the general welfare. Like the natural limits to the power of numerical majorities, it should tend to protect the interests of minorities against the tyranny of selfish majorities. If it could give better protection to that particular minority which Madison regarded as most exposed to danger of oppression by popular majorities, namely, the "opulent," a well-devised federal system with a suitable distribution of authority between national and state governments would be a justifiable departure from the aristocratic scheme of centralized national government originally advocated by the authors of the Virginia plan.

The advantages of a federal system of government were better understood by the delegates who could not be as confident as the Virginia and Pennsylvania Nationalists that the states from which they came would dominate the government of the new and more powerful Union. The most important of these states were located in New England and the Lower South. John Rutledge of South Carolina and Nathaniel Gorham of Massachusetts, the leaders of the delegations from these two sections, were eager to preserve the rights of the states within their proper sphere. They did not approve the demand of the original Federalists for equal representation of the states in the Senate of the new Union, but they could join the original Federalists in treating questions concerning the rights of the states and of the Union, respectively, under the Constitution as justiciable rather than political questions, to be settled by the Supreme Court, and in excluding questions touching the policies of the states within their proper sphere from consideration by the political departments of the national government. The unwillingness of these Unionists, as it is convenient to call them, to support the aristocratic Nationalists in attacking the independence of the states in the field of local government prevented the Nationalists and Unionists of various kinds from opposing a united front to the original Federalists and contributed to the eventual victory of the latter on the bitterly contested point of equal representation of the states in the Senate. The influence of these Unionists, however, was decisive in the struggle over the essential issue of the Federalist program: the limitation of the national government to the legislative powers plainly expressed or clearly implied in the Constitution and the reservation of all other legislative powers to the governments of the states.

There were two features of the Federalist program which were particularly repugnant to Madison. One was the insistence that questions of conflicting jurisdiction be treated as justiciable rather than political questions and be reserved for final adjudication in the Supreme Court of the United States. He felt that judicial review would be too narrow for adequate protection of national interests against injury by the action of the states. The second was the equal representation of the states in the Senate of the United States. He felt that such unequal representation of the special interests of different parts of the whole body of people, combined with the Senate's dependence upon the state legislatures, would impair too much its practical capacity to protect the particular special interest which he regarded as most in need of protection under a system of government as popular as that provided by the Constitution of 1787. Madison's disappointment with these fruits of the great constitutional compromises was deep. They threatened to frustrate one of the principal purposes of the Nationalists in promoting the Constitutional Convention.

Despite the repugnance with which Madison contemplated these features of the federal system, he reconciled himself to their incorporation into the Constitution. The principle of federalism, by subdividing powers already divided between separate departments of government, certainly increased the checks against the abuse of power, which Madison considered the prime safeguard of the liberties of all kinds of people. These additional checks, he evidently concluded, might bring about a better balance between the various parts of the constitutional system than that originally proposed by the authors of the Virginia plan. A Senate representing states instead of the class of the "opulent" might not be as capable of safeguarding the interests of the "opulent" as he would have liked, but if wealthy men were more likely to be elected to the Senate by the state legislatures than by the people, as some of the more aristocratic framers believed, it should interpose substantial barriers against the abuse of power by the representatives of popular majorities in the House of Representatives. The proposed Senate, imperfect as it appeared to the aristocratic Nationalists, might still be from their point of view a useful institution.

GUARDIAN OF THE INTERESTS OF THE RICH

The performance of the Senate in its dual role under the Constitution, like that of the House of Representatives, has been profoundly affected by the development of the party system. The transitions between the three main periods in the evolution of the unplanned institution of organized partisanship have been even more sharply defined in the case of the Senate than in that of the House. The rise of the delegate convention system of party organization, culminating in the age of Jackson and Clay, brought greater changes in the position of Senators than in that of Representatives. The introduction of the system of direct nominations at primary elections, culminating in the adoption of the Seventeenth Amendment, also brought greater changes in the position of Senators than of Representatives. The Senate has become a different factor in the general process of government at Washington from what was anticipated by either the original Federalists or the aristocratic Nationalists. The high hopes of the authors of the Connecticut compromise have not been altogether fulfilled. But compensation has been found in unexpected ways to justify the sanguine view set forth by Franklin in his famous valedictory at the close of the Federal Convention.

The first period in the adjustment of the Senate to a system of party government began under favorable auspices for the successful performance of the role for which it had been cast by the aristocratic Nationalists. At the elections to the First Congress, among the successful candidates for the Senate were big planters and merchants, and lawyers with aristocratic connections, in impressive numbers. Eleven of the original Senators — half of the total membership of the Senate at the time — had been members of the Federal Convention. Though adherents of various factions in the Convention, they were all loyal friends of the new Constitution and likely, at least at the beginning, to

195

be devoted followers of the Washington Administration. Among them were several of the ablest of the framers, notably Ellsworth and King, Dr. Johnson and William Paterson. The big merchants were competently represented by Robert Morris and John Langdon, the big planters by Butler of South Carolina and William Few of Georgia. From outside the ranks of the framers came General Schuyler of New York, a warm friend of General Washington's, and Richard Henry Lee of Virginia, no friend of Washington's but an outstanding member of the big planter class. These Senators were well qualified to vindicate the claims of their body to superiority over the House of Representatives, in which there were only eight of the original framers, of whom Madison and Sherman alone could challenge comparison with the Senate leaders. In the House also were many more country lawyers and other representatives of the rural middle class than in the Senate. The composition of the two branches of the first Congress seemed to fulfill the hopes of the authors of the original Virginia plan.

The record of the Federalist Senate did not justify its early promise. Its members were unwilling to accept the role of privy councillors, which Washington ventured to offer them,[1] but were unable to contend successfully with the House for the confidence of the general public in the role of popular lawmakers. The initial insistence of the Senate on preserving the secrecy of its debates gave the House an advantage at the bar of public opinion, and its persistence in asserting its right to be an independent legislative body rather than a privy council frustrated all efforts to lord it over the more popular branch of the Congress. The senatorial voice in the distribution of patronage gave Senators no ascendancy over Representatives in the primitive state of party organization in the 1790's, and their inferior numbers in the Congressional Caucus condemned them to a subordinate position in the councils of the parties. The struggle over the Jay Treaty demonstrated the superior power of the House of Representatives. It was easier for the Administration to get the two-thirds majority in the Senate necessary for ratification than to get the bare plurality of votes in the House for the legislation which was indispensable for carrying the treaty into effect. Senators were forced to abandon their practice of secrecy in the discussion of proposed legislation, and Representatives made good their pretensions to recognition as the chosen spokesmen of the people.

The Senate never did succeed in establishing itself as the peer of the House until its members freed themselves from the bondage of the

Congressional Caucus and discovered in the convention system of party organization a more favorable terrain for their operations in the struggle for power. The Senate improved its political position in the age of Jackson, not because Clay and Webster and Calhoun chose to sit there and deliver eloquent orations, but because the leaders of the party organizations in the states went there and, fortified by their practical control of a more abundant patronage, made the Senate the principal scene for the management of the national parties. State leaders might manipulate the delegates in national conventions and dictate the nominations of presidential candidates, but they could not maintain their organizations satisfactorily without good working relations with Senators. The famous team of William H. Seward and Thurlow Weed was a sign of the times no less significant than the even more famous association of Daniel Webster and Henry Clay at the head of the Whig coalition. Power tended to slip through the fingers of the most conspicuous national party leaders and into the hands of cliques of Senators in closer alliance with the party leaders in the states. Martin Van Buren, William L. Marcy, and Silas Wright, James Buchanan, Lewis Cass, and Stephen A. Douglas, were no less characteristic products of the age of Jackson than Daniel Webster or Henry Clay. Presidential timber grew in the Senate with unprecedented profusion, though the state leaders might occasionally bring forward rank outsiders like James K. Polk and Franklin Pierce in the interest of party harmony and a united front against the political foe. The Senate, chosen by all the most ambitious politicians as their favorite field of action, definitely moved ahead of the House of Representatives in the government of the more perfect Union.

The new ascendancy of the Senate in partisan politics and in the legislative process alike was far from a fulfillment of the hopes of the aristocratic factions among the framers of the Constitution. Senators had become more influential than members of the House but represented substantially the same bodies of people. All the great Jacksonian chieftains hailed from small towns or the open country and stood primarily for agrarian interests. Big planters, with the backing of the cotton or tobacco interests, might hope to reach the Senate along with the country lawyers generally favored by the ordinary planters, but big merchants or manufacturers could not easily get elected to Congress except in a few urban districts on the North Atlantic seaboard. The explanation was correctly understood by the observant de Tocqueville. "At the present day," he wrote,[2] "the more affluent classes of society have no influence in political affairs; and wealth, far from conferring a right, is rather a cause of unpopularity than a means of attaining power. The rich abandon the lists, through unwillingness to contend, and frequently to contend in vain, against the poorer classes of their fellow-citizens. As they cannot occupy in public a position equivalent to what they hold in private life, they abandon the former, and give themselves up to the latter; they constitute a private society in the state."

De Tocqueville was stimulated by this observation to some interesting reflections. "They submit to this state of things as an irremediable evil, but they are careful not to show that they are galled by its continuance; one often hears them laud the advantages of a republican government and democratic institutions when they are in public . . . But beneath this artificial enthusiasm, and these obsequious attentions to the preponderating power, it is easy to perceive that the rich have a hearty dislike of the democratic institutions of their country." Whether Senators in the age of Jackson were more considerate of the rights of the states than members of the House of Representatives does not appear clearly from the records of congressional legislation. All members of the dominant party were equally pledged to the defense of states' rights by the official party creed. But neither branch of the Congress interposed a formidable barrier against the power of popular majorities in the special interest of the rich. Obviously de Tocqueville did not look to the Senate for protagonists of the political theories of Alexander Hamilton or Gouverneur Morris. What Webster and Clay may have thought of Hamilton's economic doctrines is of course another matter.

Tradition has settled upon the era of Clay, Webster, and Calhoun as that in which the power and prestige of the American Senate reached its zenith. This era was approximately coterminous with the life of the Whig Party. The great political achievements of this era were the compromises which held the Union together in the face of the increasing hostility between Northern and Southern interests in general and between Abolitionists, Free Soilers, and the Slave Power in particular. It is interesting to compare the Senate of the Twenty-third Congress, which upheld the Compromise Tariff of 1833 and created the Whig Party, with that of the Thirty-third Congress, which in 1854 repealed the Missouri Compromise and destroyed the Whig Party. The earlier Senate possessed the three great Senators, but the names of their associates make little impression on the modern mind.

Thomas Hart Benton, John M. Clayton, Thomas Ewing, Felix Grundy, William R. King, William C. Rives, John Tyler, Hugh L. White, and Silas Wright, to mention the most notable of them, were prominent men in their day, but not a constellation of stars to defy comparison with Senators of later times. The later Senate was led by David R. Atchison, the president pro tempore, James A. Bayard, Jesse D. Bright, Lewis Cass, Stephen A. Douglas, Hannibal Hamlin, Sam Houston, R. M. T. Hunter, James M. Mason, and John Slidell for the Democratic majority, and on the Whig side by John Bell, Judah P. Benjamin, John M. Clayton, Edward Everett, William H. Seward, Robert Toombs, and Benjamin F. Wade. The Free Soilers were represented by Salmon P. Chase and Charles Sumner. The Senate of the Thirty-third Congress was perhaps a somewhat more aristocratic body than its predecessor by twenty years, and in repealing the Missouri Compromise showed a solicitude for property in slaves which would have been gratifying to a few of the aristocrats in the Federal Convention of 1787. John Rutledge and the Pinckneys would have rejoiced, but Gouverneur Morris and Rufus King would have shaken their heads sadly. A majority of the Senators in both Congresses were members of the middle class, and their function was rather to protect the interests of their several sections of the country than those of property owners as a class. The Senate was behaving as the original Federalists hoped that it would rather than according to the hopes of the aristocratic Nationalists.

President Truman's deliberate charge in the campaign of 1948 that the Eightieth Congress was the second worst in history touched off a discussion of the character of its predecessors. Judged by the action of the voters, the worst Congresses were some of those which had the misfortune to face the electorate on the morrow of an economic crisis at a time of deepening business depression. Such Congresses, however, clearly were the victims of circumstances and were presumably not what the President had in mind when he gave the Eightieth Congress a low rating. More than one president would doubtless have considered the Fortieth Congress, the Congress which impeached President Andrew Johnson, as the worst. A strong case can be made for the view that the worst for the country was the Thirty-third, since it set in motion the train of events which led directly to the Civil War. But this was not a greatly changed Congress from the Thirty-first, in which Clay and Webster, opposed this time by Calhoun, led the battle for the Compromise of 1850. The repeal of the Missouri Compromise was a sorry service to the people of the United States, but the loss of Clay and Webster and Calhoun was not enough to convert one of the best Senates in American history, if the quality of its personnel entitled the Thirty-first to that distinction, into one of the worst. The intellectual and political superiority of the Senates in these two Congresses to the House of Representatives is incontestable, but there seems to be no ground for the view that either branch of the Congress was more or less fairly representative of the people than the other.

The character of the Senate in the latter part of the nineteenth century reflected the changes in the American way of life and in the relations between organized partisanship and the conduct of public affairs. The Civil War marked a turning point in the American economy. The accelerated growth of urban industry offered a sharper challenge to the predominance of agrarian interests in national politics than in the age of Jackson. The further development of the party system, with its insubordinate local organizations, its potent state leaders and "bosses," its swollen patronage, and its intimate relations with protected manufacturers, subsidized railroads, and business corporations generally — all great favorites of the law in a period of rapidly expanding capitalistic enterprise — created new sources of influence for politicians and enhanced the advantages of Senators over Representatives. It also raised the question whether the Senate might not at last have become such a guardian of the interests of the "opulent" as had been hoped for by the aristocratic Nationalists in 1787.

Evidence of the greater wealth of Senators was chiefly circumstantial, but it was convincing. In the period after the Civil War, when journalists began to write familiarly of the Senate as a rich man's club, the great wealth of many Senators was conspicuous. Rich men whose wealth was an obvious element in their availability for public office openly sought election from approachable legislatures. The most impressive evidence of the influence of wealth in senatorial elections was the ability of such men, unable to procure their own elections, to prevent other candidates from being elected. Senatorial seats sometimes remained unfilled for long periods. Delaware for a time was deprived of all representation in the Senate through the stubbornness of a rich man who could not get himself elected and would not permit the election of anybody else. Despite occasional scandals success in business was not generally considered a disqualification for service in the Senate. Under the circumstances of the time, the character of the Senate was certain to be more favorable to the interests of the "opulent" than in the age of Jackson.

Writers who emphasize the importance of economic interests in politics have magnified the influence of the capitalist system over the institution of organized partisanship, and of the party leaders and "bosses" over the conduct of public affairs, in the period following the war. Matthew Josephson, one of the most recent and best informed of these writers, has furnished a vivid picture of the legislative process at Washington in the age when General Grant, James G. Blaine, and Grover Cleveland were outstanding actors on the political scene and excellent specimens of the leading species in the new order of public men. "The true style-character of the historical period pictured here," Josephson wrote,[3] "arises from forces stronger than, and overlying, the party institution itself. It is fixed by the absolute triumph of a single group or class, the industrial capitalists, over the landholders and proletarians . . . The party institution, which originated in response to popular democratic needs and independent of capitalism, is gradually absorbed and turned to account, so that its immense resources might serve as a bulwark in days of crisis."

This view of the unplanned institution of organized partisanship as a means of transforming an agrarian democracy into a capitalistic democracy led logically to a consistent, if unrealistic, conclusion concerning the evolution of the framers' system of checks and balances. "Where the Founding Fathers had trusted fondly that the ingenious compromises of our Federal Charter and the arts of statesmen would with 'wise regulation' achieve an equilibrium between the different classes," Josephson opined, "the configuration of events in the last third of the nineteenth century forbade the realization of such hope." Josephson seems to be saying that the plan of the aristocratic Nationalists for a Senate which would protect the "opulent" against the "indigent" had come to naught for the reason that the "opulent," that is, the capitalists, had gained control of all branches of the government of the more perfect Union through the agency of the party system. Dominating all branches of the government, the capitalists had no need of a special position in any one of the branches. Senators and Representatives alike would serve the interests of their capitalistic masters. The interests of farmers and workers would be lost from view in the sham battle of the parties, while the politicians in the Congress dedicated themselves to the advancement of business. Instead of an equilibrium of classes, there would be a dictatorship of the bourgeoisie.

How unrealistic this view is appears from the census reports showing the proportions of urban and rural population in the United States during this period. The returns for 1870 showed only three states in which a majority of the population lived in cities or towns of more than 2500 inhabitants. These were, in order of density of urban population, Rhode Island, Massachusetts, and New York. The other thirty-four states then in the Union were predominantly rural. In many of them less than 10 per cent of the inhabitants lived in towns or cities. As late as 1900 there were only eight urban states, counting all the places with as few as 2500 inhabitants as urban. Since 1870 only New Jersey, Connecticut, Pennsylvania, Illinois, and California had joined the ranks of the urban states. By that time forty-five states were represented in the Senate. It is impossible to explain the influence of capitalists over the legislative process at Washington as the result of an "absolute triumph" over the "landowners and proletarians," that is, over the farmers, artisans and craftsmen, mechanics, small merchants, and others making up the bulk of the American people. If capitalists obtained an influence in national politics disproportionate to their numbers through the manipulation of the party system — as doubtless they did — the use of money in legitimate and illegitimate ways can give no more than a partial explanation of their success. In a period of rapidly expanding capitalistic industry, capitalists gained much of their new political influence because new railroads, steel plants, textile and flour mills, packing houses, and factories of many kinds seemed to the farmers and workers, who supplied most of the votes at national elections, to be valuable public improvements.

The testimony of a competent foreign observer in the age of James G. Blaine and Grover Cleveland is as illuminating concerning the influence of wealth in the legislative process at Washington as in the age of Jackson and Clay. Bryce had formed the opinion that both the Senate and the House equally represented the people. "The individual members," he pointed out, "come from the same classes of the community; though in the Senate, as it has more rich men (in proportion to numbers) than has the House, the influence of capital has latterly been more marked." [4] Bryce did not underestimate the influence of rich men in public affairs. But it seemed to him to be a personal rather than a class interest. He would not have understood what Josephson meant by an "absolute triumph" of "the capitalist class" over "landlords and proletarians." He felt no need for such categories in analyzing late nineteenth-century American politics.

Bryce was deeply impressed by the vigor and enterprise of American businessmen. Above all other captains of industry, the managers of American railroads made a profound impression on him for their "splendid boldness" and "autocratic character." No talents of a practical kind, he thought, could be too high for such a position as that of railroad president. He dwelt with manifest respect upon the concentration of power in their hands and their "almost uncontrolled" discretion. "These railway kings," he declared in a final burst of enthusiasm, "are among the greatest men, perhaps I may say, are the greatest men in America." [5] He proceeded to marvel at their wealth, their fame, and their power. They traveled in "palace" cars; their journeys were like "royal" progresses. They yielded in prestige only to the greatest authorities in the land. He recognized that such vast power created special problems in a democratic republic. He doubted whether it would ever be brought under effective governmental control.[6] But he did not regard the spectacular phenomenon of "railway kings" in a democratic republic as a harbinger of political domination by a capitalist class through partisan manipulation of Representatives and Senators.

Bryce was even more deeply impressed by the general diffusion of wealth among the farmers and workers of America. Immense numbers of little men were consequently interested in the defense of property. Bryce was familiar with conditions in Europe, where class consciousness was strongly developed and jealousy, even hatred, of the rich was widespread. He found little evidence of such feelings in America. The common man might hate particular politicians, when he suspected them of undue subservience to special interests. He might even hate the great corporations in an abstract sort of way. But he could not hate the capitalists as a class. In America, Bryce observed, class distinctions were comparatively obscure and lightly regarded.[7] "I do not think," he declared, "that the ruling magnates are themselves generally disliked. On the contrary, they receive that tribute of admiration which the American gladly pays to whoever has done best what everyone desires to do." [8]

Bryce, a natural aristocrat by John Adams's classification of mankind, was perhaps incapable of appreciating the character of an institution in which the artificial aristocracy, to employ the expression favored by Adams and Jefferson, exerted as great an influence as it appeared to exert in both branches of the Congress in the latter part of the period, when the delegate convention system was in full flower. Bryce was not favorably impressed by the pretensions of plutocratic politicians in either branch of the Congress. Of the Senate he said [9] that it had "lost as much in the intellectual authority of its members as it [had] gained in their wealth." The House, he found, "suffers from the want of internal organization." This was on the eve of Thomas B. Reed's exaltation of the speakership. Bryce's poor opinion of the House may be recalled by the present generation without surprise. His unflattering description of the Senate gives a greater shock to present-day Americans, particularly those who have believed that the quality of the Senate was lowered by the direct election of Senators under the Seventeenth Amendment.

The adoption of the Seventeenth Amendment inaugurated the third major period in the evolution of the Senate. There has been much difference of opinion concerning the effect of this change in the method of electing Senators. George H. Haynes, the leading historian of the Senate, expressed an opinion widely held by conservative critics. "There can be no question," he wrote,[10] "that in the years since the ratification of the Seventeenth Amendment the prestige of the Senate has suffered serious decline." This adverse judgment has been endorsed also by one of the more radical of recent writers on congressional history. Ernest Sutherland Bates, like Professor Haynes, was writing after the collapse of Republican supremacy in the Congress during the Great Depression, and, unlike Haynes, under the influence of the more critical attitude prevalent in the early years of the New Deal. "Just as the overthrow of the slavocracy," he declared,[11] "was preceded by a marked decline in the intellectual calibre of the Southern leaders,[12] so the Republicans of the 'twenties proved hopelessly inferior to their fathers in the 'nineties." These two writers agree concerning the fact of a decline in the quality of Senators, though the more conservative of the two attributed the decline to the change in the method of election and the more radical to an unexplained deterioration in the quality of the artificial aristocracy.

As growing distance in point of time adds greater objectivity to the view of the political scene, it becomes more practicable to compare the quality of the Republican leadership in the Senate at various stages during the Party's long ascendancy on Capitol Hill. In the Fortieth Congress (1867–69) there were Cameron of Pennsylvania and Conkling of New York, Sherman and Wade of Ohio, and Sumner and Wilson of Massachusetts, to mention a few of the leaders; in the Fifty-fifth Congress (1897–99) there were Aldrich of Rhode Island and Allison of Iowa, Cullom of Illinois and Hanna of Ohio, Platt of

New York and Quay of Pennsylvania; in the Seventieth Congress (1927–29) there were Borah of Idaho and Curtis of Kansas, Moses of New Hampshire and Reed of Pennsylvania, Smoot of Utah and Watson of Indiana. The last list does seem inferior to its predecessors in glamour and political prestige, though not in parliamentary skill and standards of political ethics. Whether the explanation lies in the method of election or in the decline of the capitalist spirit is a more difficult question, though the capitalist spirit did not seem to have declined when Calvin Coolidge was living in the White House. But neither of the quoted writers claimed that the Senate had been at any time a notably stouter "bulwark" of the capitalist class than the House of Representatives. The investigations of Robert Luce, a leading American authority on the science of legislation, though more favorable to the quality of recent Senators and Representatives, pointed toward the same conclusion.[13] There seemed to him no noteworthy difference between the class basis of the House and that of the Senate. Whatever may have been the class character of the Senate, it could not have been a check upon the action of the House of Representatives, as hoped for by the aristocratic Nationalists. The Senate, it seemed, possessed a class character not notably different from that of the House itself.

Now ten more Congresses have passed into history. The Eightieth Congress was elected at a time when the new electoral system had had a long enough trial to make evident the significant consequences of the direct election of Senators. The election came after fourteen years of Democratic supremacy on Capitol Hill, when the effects of the New Deal upon the capitalist system, though complicated by the additional impact of a second World War, could be taken into account. What, it is time to ask, is the character of the Senate? And what is the significance of accumulating experience with the legislative process at Washington concerning the actual operation of the framers' system of checks and balances?

The nature of the contemporary Senate appears most clearly from the record of its members' previous political experience.[14] Of the ninety-six Senators in the Eightieth Congress, twenty-eight had served as governors of their states before their election to the Senate. Most of these were actually so serving at the time of their first senatorial election. One of them had also served previously in the national House of Representatives. Nineteen other Senators had served in the popular branch of the Congress before their election to the Senate. Seventeen

Senators had had previous experience in state legislatures or other elective state offices, but had held no previous federal office. Fifteen were businessmen who had been actively interested in politics without holding any elective public office. Some of them, however, had had significant experience in special-interest organizations of various kinds. One had been president of the Chamber of Commerce of the United States and vice-president of the National Association of Manufacturers, another had been president of the National Grain Dealers Association, and a third had been active in the American National Livestock Association and in the National Woolgrowers Association. Nine of the Senators were lawyers with similar records in public affairs. Eight were members of other professions or otherwise occupied before their election to the Senate, though none had been prominent in the affairs of organized labor. Several of these had held appointive offices which gave them valuable political experience, but a few broke into the Senate without previous experience in partisan or public offices.

The size of a Senator's fortune was certainly less important in explaining his political behavior than the nature of his previous political and professional or business experience. One of the wealthiest of the Senators was one of the most devoted to political projects generally opposed by men of wealth, and some of the most impecunious were conspicuously unresponsive to the appeals of supporters of such projects. The motivation of all men, and particularly of politicians, is complex and obscure. That of Senators, however, seems unlikely to be different from that of members of the House of Representatives. Most of the Senators had sprung from the middle class, resided in places of moderate size, and, judging from their official biographies in the Congressional Directory, had associated during most of their earlier lives chiefly with those who were neither very rich nor very poor. A Senator's salary, even before the increase under the Legislative Reorganization Act of 1946, was sufficient to qualify him for a statistical classification in the upper class of the national economy, but the extraordinary expenses of political life, including the maintenance of a home in two places and, in many states, the high cost of campaigning, together with the long sessions of the Congress, which interfered with gainful pursuits once a ready source of additional income to Congressmen, kept the average Senator in much the same frame of mind as the average Representative and the average voter, struggling to maintain a higher standard of living than his circumstances really warranted.

In short, the direct popular election of Senators has definitely ended any lingering hope that the Senate might eventually play the role planned for it by the aristocratic Nationalists. In the large states the great size of the senatorial electorates compels a greater dependence of Senators on party organization than in the election of members of the House. This has the same effect in senatorial elections as in presidential elections. It tends to enhance the influence of the middle classes, especially the urban middle classes. In the small states there is little difference in the conditions under which Senators and Representatives are elected. The longer terms and greater authority of Senators make election to the Senate more attractive, but Senators and Representatives alike tend to represent the same kinds of people in the same way. Above all they tend to represent the "middling sort" of people. If the Senate is more powerful than the House, then it is a more influential guardian of the interests of the middle classes. It is a role not anticipated by the aristocratic Nationalists in the Federal Convention. It is a role which makes the division of the Congress into two branches less objectionable to democratic Nationalists like Franklin than could have been expected in 1787. It gives the bicameral system unforeseen significance in the practical operation of the system of checks and balances.

GUARDIAN OF THE INTERESTS OF THE STATES

The character of the Senate is manifestly more favorable to its performance of the role envisaged by the original Federalists than that planned by the aristocratic Nationalists. The most striking fact about the previous experience of the Senators in the Eightieth Congress was the large number who had been governors of their states or had held other state elective officers compared with the number who had previously served in the national House of Representatives or had held appointive federal offices. No politician is in a better position to understand the interests of a state than its governor and a substantial number of states in all sections of the country were represented in the Senate by former governors. More than a quarter of all the Senators had been governors of their states and nearly half of them had held positions in state government which gave them a special insight into the conduct of state affairs. The membership of the Senate was evidently well qualified by experience to appreciate the problems of the states and to protect them against the trespasses of national majorities as represented by the more popular branch of the Congress. If senatorial review of popular legislative projects, like judicial review of questions of constitutional law, is regarded as a political device for maintaining the balance of the federal system, the Senate would seem to be equipped for the efficient performance of this function.

States, however, are political entities which derive their vitality from the purposes of their citizens. When Senators speak of the interests of the states which they represent in the Congress, they may be thinking of such general interests as are expressed in the preamble to the Constitution. They are more likely to be thinking in most cases of the particular interests which contend for influence in the process of lawmaking. A Senator represents his state, to be sure, but he also represents those particular interests within the state which are or may be influential in the legislative process. A private citizen may be associated with more than one of these special interests and may exert an influence on legislation through more than one of their organizations. A Senator must be mindful of the requirements of enough of these special interests to prevent defeat by a combination of them against him at the polls, if he would continue to represent his state in the Congress. The support of a political party which can command a majority at the polls simplifies the task of the Senator at general elections, but he still has the problem of getting the party's nomination. A Senator must be mindful of realities as well as of abstractions.

Senators, like other representatives of the people in modern legislative bodies, do not like to pose as the spokesmen of special interests, and rightly, since the proper test of a good legislator is first, his skill in adjusting the conflicts between special interests in such a manner as to promote the general public interest, and second, his disposition to make such adjustments to the best of his ability. But it is easy to confuse the general public interest with the more powerful of the special interests. Since large numbers of voters are associated in one way or another with such special interests, the task of the voter in passing judgment upon the legislator or would-be legislator at the polls is difficult. If the candidate does not consciously deceive the voter concerning the nature of his intentions, the voter may unconsciously deceive himself. It is for this reason that voters do well to base their choice among candidates largely upon their appraisal of the candidates' characters rather than upon a comparison of campaign promises or party platforms. Happily this is the kind of judgment which the average voter is most competent to make.

The equal representation of the states in the Senate results in the unequal representation of the dominant interests in the states. Those interests which are most powerful in a number of small states carry a weight in the legislative process at Washington which exceeds their importance in the economy of the country. The leading agricultural interests are able to exert a disproportionate influence on national legislation, because the rural states are still in a majority despite the relative decline of the rural population. Those interests which are most influential in the small states of the arid West are particularly favored by the constitution of the Senate. Whether differences in wealth between the membership of the Senate and of the House of Representatives are now significant in the legislative process at Washington is a matter of dubious speculation in the light of the available evidence. What is clear is, that the vesting of special powers and privileges in those representatives of the American people who are chosen in the special electoral districts called states must make the adjustment of conflicting interests in the process of lawmaking at Washington more favorable than it would otherwise be to the special interests which are overrepresented in the Senate. That this is of any advantage in maintaining the balance of the federal system is unlikely. Whether it is of consequence in protecting minorities of any kind against the abuse of power by partisan or other majorities in the House of Representatives is another matter.

The development of the party system in national politics has made the relations between the two branches of the Congress different from what was planned by the framers of the Constitution. During sixty-four of the eighty-one Congresses the party which has possessed the greatest number of votes in the House of Representatives has also possessed a majority of the Senators. The influence of partisanship upon legislation may often be obscure and uncertain, but at least during these sixty-four Congresses the influence of the party system in both branches of the Congress should have tended to make each branch less critical of the other than in the other seventeen. During the Federalist and Jeffersonian Republican Administrations, however, the two-party system was not yet solidly established in national politics. Partisanship was not as well defined or as permanent as in later times. The prime function of the Senate came to be the equal representation of the Free States and the Slave States in the legislative process.

The period of Jacksonian Democratic ascendancy in national politics was characterized by increasing conflict between the House and the Senate. The House tended at first to follow the leadership of the

President, and the Senate became the stronghold of the opposition to presidential leadership. Later the rise of antislavery sentiment was reflected more promptly in the House than in the Senate and it became increasingly difficult for any major party to gain control of both branches of the Congress at the same time. Altogether there were eight Congresses between 1830 and 1860 in which the two chambers were controlled by opposite parties. In these Congresses the political differences between the House and the Senate made all constructive legislation difficult and partisan legislation impossible. The greater part of the period was consumed in factious controversy, while the people of the country were trying to make up their minds concerning the policies they wished to prevail. Each chamber was an effective check upon the other, but the relation was very different from that contemplated by the framers of the Constitution.

The relations between the Senate and the House of Representatives from the Republican victory in 1860 to the adoption of the Seventeenth Amendment in 1913 were not greatly changed. During these twenty-six Congresses there were eight in which the Senate and the House were controlled by opposite parties. Seven of these Congresses fell within the twenty years from 1875 to 1895. That again was a period in which the people of the country were closely divided between the two major parties and found it hard to make up their minds which party they wished to entrust with power. Their failure to choose decisively meant again extraordinary difficulty in enacting constructive legislation upon the controversial issues of the day. Only two Congresses, the Fifty-first (1889–1891), which was Republican, and the Fifty-third (1893–1895), which was Democratic, were able to execute comprehensive party programs. Both of these programs the voters promptly repudiated at the polls. Constructive legislation dealing with important problems could be enacted in other Congresses only by means of bipartisan combinations in each branch of the Congress. Party control of the legislative process was more effective during the two portions of this period, 1861 to 1875 and 1897 to 1911, when the Radical and the Conservative Republicans, respectively, were strongly entrenched in office. Clashes between the Senate and the House were comparatively rare, and the volume of constructive legislation was greater. During the Congresses in which opposite parties controlled the two branches, partisanship was a more important factor than any constitutional difference between the House and the Senate in checking the output of legislation. During the Congresses which were controlled by a single party the great obstacle to legislation dealing with major issues was not the division of the Congress into two branches but the division of the major party into inharmonious factions. In these Congresses the natural limits to partisan power, as Madison would have called them, were more effective than the artificial limitations resulting from the existence of two separate legislative bodies.

The latest period in the history of the bicameral system includes the Congresses since the adoption of the Seventeenth Amendment. In only one of them has the control of the two chambers been divided between the two major parties. It is easy to denounce the incapacity of the Congress during the last two years of the Hoover Administration to deal effectively with the emergency created by the Great Depression, but it is also easy to recognize the incapacity of public opinion at the same time to give a clear mandate to the Congress for a legislative program. The public needed time to determine to what extent it wished the national government to assume responsibility for measures of relief, recovery, and reform. The failure of the Congress to agree promptly upon a systematic or comprehensive program, to say nothing of an effective program, must be explained by less superficial causes than senatorial obstruction of policies favored by the House and the jockeying by the parties for a favorable position in the next presidential campaign. The public knew by November of 1930 that it wanted a change of policy in the national government, but it needed two more years to be ready to consent to as radical a change of policy as circumstances required. The delay in bringing the majority of the Senate into line with the majority of the House could not have interfered greatly with constructive legislation by the Congress. It was the uncertainty concerning the kind of action which should be taken that was the major cause of delay. There is little reason to suppose that the legislative record of the Seventy-second Congress would have disclosed more vigor and effectiveness if partisan control of the two chambers had been as complete as in all the other Congresses since the direct election of Senators began or if, following Franklin's suggestion, there had been no Senate at all.

The real effect of the party system on the relations between the two branches of the Congress and on the congressional phase of the whole legislative process is a disputed question. The influence of partisanship on legislation has always been complicated and obscure, and doubt has always existed concerning its exact nature and extent.

211

The congressional caucuses and conferences are not open to the public and they keep no public records. Disclosure of the proceedings in these formal meetings of partisans, as in the more informal meetings of their leaders, is casual and inconclusive. Official roll calls in the Senate and House show how the members of the parties have voted, but they do not reveal the true reasons for votes. Pressure groups and other interested persons analyze the voting records of members of Congress, but the public pays little attention. The members of the public, as the public-opinion polls have revealed, generally think well of their own particular representatives in the Congress, but toward the Congress as a whole their attitude is one of respect for the institution mingled with skepticism and distrust concerning the unknown individuals of which it is composed. There is a general disposition to blame the majority party, if the public is dissatisfied with the course of events, whether or not that party alone is blameworthy. If affairs seem to go well enough, the party in power may get credit which should go to intelligent and industrious Congressmen, regardless of party.

It is not surprising, therefore, that the Congress should lean heavily upon the leadership of the President and should show an impaired capacity for its legislative work when such leadership is not available or is ineffective. The Eightieth Congress supplied an excellent example of the difficulties which the Congress encounters when dependent upon its own resources for the formulation of a legislative program. The Republican Congressmen controlled both branches of the Congress, and in default of executive leadership furnished by their own party were responsible for the management of its business. There were only three issues on which the Republicans claimed a mandate from the people at the November elections of 1946: the reduction of public expenditures, the reduction of taxes, and the regulation of labor unions. In transacting the rest of the voluminous legislative business of the Congress, they were forced to choose between accepting the leadership of a President belonging to the opposite party, and taking the initiative themselves. Thus the leadership of the President, whether or not the presidency and both branches of the Congress are controlled by the same party, becomes an important factor in the legislative process, and the relations between the two branches are profoundly affected by the relations between each of them and the executive department of the government. In other words, the party system tends to make the legislative process dependent upon the relations between the Congress and the President, but it also should foster a tendency toward better relations under normal conditions between the two branches of the Congress than would be expected if the Senate had become, as the aristocratic Nationalists in the Convention of 1787 hoped, a special organ for defending the interests of the "opulent" against the "indigent."

How effective the party system is in making for greater harmony between the two branches of the Congress is difficult to measure. The majority party always takes for itself a majority of the places on all important committees in both branches and controls a majority of the representatives of each branch on the conference committees which determine the final form of all controversial legislation. The parties also possess caucuses and conferences, steering committees and policy committees, which are designed to enable the members of a party to work together as effectively as possible. But the caucuses and conferences of partisans in the two chambers are held separately, and the steering committees and policy committees are severally responsible to their party associates in the particular chamber to which they belong. The majority-party leaders of both chambers may get together occasionally behind the scenes, but there are rarely, if ever, joint meetings of the party caucuses and conferences, and the House and Senate rules make no provision for joint sessions of the regular standing committees, or for joint hearings in the regular course of legislative business. There are a few joint committees for the better handling of certain special administrative services such as printing and the library, in which both chambers are equally interested, but joint committees for the consideration of proposed legislation, or for the supervison of the executive departments and other agencies of public administration, have been rare. There has been for some years a Joint Committee on Internal Revenue Taxation, which has been provided with a more competent technical staff than most committees. The Joint Committee on the Economic Report, established by the Employment Act of 1946, and the Joint Committee on Atomic Energy, established the same year, are recent exceptions to the general practice which may signify the beginning of closer relations between the two chambers in the future.

The majority party in each chamber may be theoretically responsible for the action of that chamber on important matters, but its responsibility under the existing form of the party system is actually divided between the party members in the chamber as a whole and

213

the party members of the committees in which proposed legislation receives its first real consideration. Experience over a long period of years shows that the proceedings in the committee constitute much the most important stage in the course of a bill through the chamber, but these proceedings are secret. There are no records to show the attitude of the different factions within the committee. The majority-party members may exclude the minority from any share in the framing of a bill, or the action of the committee may be the result of a combination of factions belonging to both parties in which even a majority of the majority party may find themselves in a minority within the committee. Committee chairmen, deriving their authority from the irrational rule of seniority, possess special privileges in determining the action of committees, which give to the faction of the majority party that are able to keep their seats in the Congress for the greatest number of consecutive terms a disproportionate influence over the adjustment of interest conflicts within the committees. These are the factions which are located in the sections of the country where the party is strongest. The result is that, when the Democrats are in control of the Congress, the agricultural interests of the rural South and the labor interests of the Northern and Western cities struggle for the right to speak for their party, and when the Republicans are in control, the business interests of the Northern and Western cities and the farming, dairy, and ranching interests of the rural areas in the North and West struggle for the right to speak for their party. Party responsibility disintegrates in the clash of the contending factions.

The majority party, when in power in both chambers, may be theoretically responsible for the action of the Congress as a whole on important legislative matters, but its responsibility under the existing form of the party sytem is actually divided between the majority party in the Senate and the majority party in the House of Representatives. Controversial legislation, involving the adjustment of conflicts between important interests, is almost certain to pass the two chambers in different forms, and no instrument is provided for the reconciliation of these differences except a conference committee. The conference committees have gradually developed extraordinary powers. Originally authorized to make no changes in the bills referred to them except where necessary to bring about agreement between the two chambers, they have assumed a right to make any changes in a bill which a majority of their members may deem desirable. They may even introduce provisions into a bill not previously approved by either chamber.

They have thus become an instrument for the revision and improvement of legislation by means of which the adjustments of interest conflicts, already made in the two chambers, may be further revised and the final decisions of the party leaders in matters of legislative policy may be carried into effect. These conference committees have to get their reports approved by both chambers, but they are not responsible to the general body of their fellow partisans. The minority party in each chamber is represented on these conference committees, and, since their deliberations are secret, there is no record of the influence of the various factions of the majority and minority parties on the final product of the legislative process. Party responsibility under these conditions necessarily tends to disintegrate. It cannot easily be reintegrated under a party system which permits each of these conference committees to become the master in its own field of legislation.

The record of the roll calls on legislative questions in the Senate throws further light on the process of legislation and the relative influence of the two branches of the Congress. Roll calls must of course be interpreted with care. Congressmen may vote on the same side of a question for different, or indeed for opposite, reasons. The influence of partisanship upon their votes may differ widely and be difficult to estimate accurately. The true reasons for particular votes may not appear at all in the published record. The most significant votes may not be the final roll calls on the passage of bills. Earlier votes on critical amendments, or even on questions of procedure, may give more useful information concerning the real attitudes of Congressmen on the issues of the day, and such votes are not always easy to identify from the printed record. Nor are they always recorded by a roll call. Nevertheless, the analysis of the roll calls in recent years reveals some interesting facts concerning the operation of the party system in the two chambers.

The most striking fact about party government in the Senate is the almost complete absence of straight party voting on important controversial matters. There is much disagreement among political analysts concerning what constitutes a party vote, and no experienced observer would expect to find all the members of a major party voting together on a controversial matter of any importance. The major parties at best are no more than loose federations of state and local factions which are held together by the desire to win presidential elections rather than by any expectation that they will be able to unite in the Congress for the promotion of legislation in support of which they will all agree. A leading political analyst has defined a party vote as one in which at least nine-tenths of the members of one party vote on the same side of a question, while at least the same proportion of the other party vote on the opposite side.[15] By this test there are few party votes in either branch of the Congress, except votes of the most perfunctory kind. On controversial matters of public importance the diversification of opinion within the major parties is such that both parties are likely to be divided and the majority to be composed of substantial numbers from each party.

The roll calls on controversial measures in the Senate may be analyzed in the same way as in the House of Representatives.[16] The extent of party unity among the members of both major parties is disclosed by the figures which show how many times each Senator voted with a majority of his party associates on roll calls where at least a majority of each party was recorded on opposite sides of the question. The figures for the First Session of the Eighty-first Congress are given in Table 11. Such extensive party irregularity as is shown by these

TABLE 11

Voting in roll calls on controversial measures in the Senate.

Participation in Party Votes: Percentage of Total Number of Roll Calls	Number and Percentage of Senators			
	Democratic		Republican	
100	0	0.0	0	0.0
90–99	18	35.3	15	35.7
80–89	12	23.5	9	21.4
70–79	9	17.6	5	11.9
60–69	9	17.6	7	16.7
50–59	0	0.0	3	7.1
40–49	2	4.0	2	4.8
30–39	1	2.0	0	0.0
20–29	0	0.0	1	2.4
Total	51	100.0	42	100.0

figures is obviously incompatible with any high degree of straight party voting on controversial measures. In fact, out of 225 roll calls in this session there were eighty-three on which a majority of each party voted on the same side. Of the other roll calls the number on which the majority party, without help from the minority, cast enough votes to prevail over the opposition of the minority party together with dissident members of the majority party itself, was only forty-four. On sixty roll calls the majority party could not have prevailed over the opposition without help from members of the minority party. On thirty-eight roll calls the majority of the majority party were recorded on the losing side, losing enough of their members to the opposition to give the victory to the minority party. The figures for the Eightieth Congress showed for the Senate, as for the House, a higher rate of party voting by the Republicans, but a lower rate by the Democrats.

The record of the roll calls in recent years shows on the whole less party solidarity in the Senate than in the House on controversial questions of general public interest. This doubtless is to be expected from the differences in the position of the party leaders under the rules of procedure in the two chambers. The greater freedom from party ties in the Senate on important controversial measures is but a portion of the greater freedom enjoyed by the individual Senator in the whole conduct of this office. Strict party votes may be found in the Senate on matters of party interest rather than of general public interest, but ordinarily party leaders in the upper chamber drive with a loose rein. Their followers are governed by the interests of their states, that is, by sectional and local interests, rather than by the interests of their parties.

Party government in the Senate tends even more than in the House to dissolve under the impact of sectional conflicts. Under the actual conditions of American politics the Senators are the most powerful representatives of the dominant interests within the states and hence the most responsible for the enactment of legislation which can command the consent of the major interests in the different sections of the country. The final answer, therefore, to the question concerning the real function of the Senate in the legislative process at Washington must be sought in an investigation of the interests which may be expected to exert the greatest influence upon Senators. The role of the Senate in the federal system emerges from the character of the states regarded as electoral districts. This role has manifestly been altered by the adoption of the Seventeenth Amendment and the shifting of the scene of senatorial elections from the state legislatures to the voters of the states. The election of Senators by the legislatures under the methods of representation in most of the states insured the predominance of rural members in the choice of most Senators. The direct election of Senators gave to the urban voters for the first time an opportunity to develop a proportionate influence in the choice of Senators. The manner, however, in which the states themselves, regarded as election districts for the choice of Senators, are laid out still insures to rural voters a disproportionate representation in the Senate.

It is evident how right Madison and Hamilton were when they contended in the Convention of 1787 that the delegates from the middle-sized and smaller states exaggerated the danger of a combination against them by the larger states. The largest states in 1787 were Virginia, Massachusetts, and Pennsylvania. These three states were united with all the others in supporting Washington for the presidency twice and they were agreed in the last three New Deal campaigns in supporting Franklin D. Roosevelt. But in the thirty-five intervening presidential elections all three were on the same side only three times. Twelve times Pennsylvania joined Virginia against Massachusetts and eighteen times it joined Massachusetts against Virginia. Twice, in 1912 and in 1932, it was opposed to both of them. This was the result also in 1948.

Pennsylvania is the only one of these states which is among the largest today, but the lack of any stable relation between the size of the largest states and their interests in national politics is clear. It is because the largest states are generally the most highly industrialized and the small states are preponderantly rural that the equal representation of the states in the Senate is now an important political factor. As the conflict between urban and rural interests becomes more acute, the role of the Senate under the federal system tends to become more unlike what was originally planned by the framers of the Constitution. Doubtless those who possess today the same distrust of the urban masses as was felt by many of the aristocratic members of the Convention of 1787 will feel that the framers, in designing the Senate, built better than they knew. Modern believers in popular government, preserving the spirit of Franklin, will feel that the great compromise has turned out no better in this respect than he feared.

The Senate, regarded as an organ for the review of legislative measures initiated by the House of Representatives in order to protect the rights of the states, has not fulfilled the purposes of the framers of the Constitution. The presence in the Senate of many former state governors and legislators adds to its practical capacity to deal intelligently with legislative problems in which the state governments may claim an interest. Their presence in the Senate adds also to its disposition to respect the state governments as instruments of the popular will in their proper spheres of action. But there is no evidence to support the view that the equal representation of the states in the Senate adds anything to its practical utility in maintaining the balance of the federal system. The original Federalists were surely right in believing that the state governments were capable of rendering services to their respective peoples which could not be as well rendered by a general government operating from a single center. But when they insisted upon an equal voice in the Senate for each state, regardless of its population or contribution to the general welfare, they exacted a high price for this solid advantage. There is no reason to suppose that the state governments would now occupy a less honorable or useful place in the general scheme of constitutional government, if the views of the original Federalists had not prevailed and the larger states had been allowed to possess a representation in the Senate more nearly proportionate to their size and political importance, while the smallest states rested content each with a single Senator.

Nevertheless the abandonment of the Nationalists' plan for a Senate specially designed to represent the "opulent" as a separate "estate" within the nation was a great gain in the struggle for a durable constitution. While the American people remained predominantly rural and the country as a whole predominantly agrarian, the large states and the small states were dominated by similar interests and their equal representation in the Senate was a matter of little practical consequence. The Connecticut compromise cleared the way for the easy advance of democracy in the government of the United States, as the state governments became more democratic, and for many years the price paid for this inestimable advantage seemed cheap. At the present time the overrepresentation of rural sections, particularly the arid West, and the concomitant excessive influence of certain special interests, notably silver-mining, cattle-raising, wool-growing, and beet-sugar production, make the bargain seem more questionable. The equal representation of the small states, particularly of the small rural states, can be justified, if at all, only as a counterweight to the exaggerated influence of the big industrial states in presidential elections.

The Senate was designed to give greater influence in the legislative process to minority interests. It does afford greater opportunities for influence than exist in the House of Representatives to special interests in small states. Moreover, since the adoption of the Seventeenth Amendment the participation of the Senate in the legislative process has confirmed and strengthened the influence of the middle classes, particularly the urban middle class. In consequence of the structure of the national economy this does not mean special representation for another minority interest. It means under the established system of bipartisan politics an improvement in the position of a majority of the people. The interest of the middle classes is not identical with that of the whole general public. Nevertheless, under the existing circumstances the interest of the middle classes tends to approximate the public interest. A system of government characterized by a deliberate preference for the interests of the middle classes is not an ideal political system. But it is the next best to the ideal and may well be the best practicable system of constitutional government in a modern agrarian-industrial society. Under this system the Senate has definitely stepped into a new role. It has become one of the main bulwarks of the ascendancy of the middle classes in the government of the more perfect Union.

SENATORIAL ARROGATION OF LEGISLATIVE POWER

The American Senate can be best understood as a continuation of the Continental Congress. Under the Articles of Confederation the Congress possessed almost all the powers, legislative, executive, and judicial, which were conferred upon the government of the United States. Under the new Articles of Union, as the delegates to the Convention of 1787 were at first disposed to call their proposed constitution, the judicial powers of the Senate were restricted to judging the elections and qualifications of their own members and to the trial of impeachments; their executive powers were restricted to giving their advice and consent to the appointment of public officers by the President; and their legislative powers were restricted by the necessity of getting the approval of both the House of Representatives and the President for their acts, except in the case of treaties, for which a special procedure was arranged. From the viewpoint of the original Federalists the Senate was still the most important organ of the general government. As the official plan for the government of the more perfect Union first came from the Convention's Committee of Detail, the Senate would have been even more important than under the final form of the Constitution, as reported by the Committee of Style. The sagacious compromises effected in the Committee on Postponed Matters and Unfinished Business produced a more promising system of checks and balances and greatly improved the prospects of the proposed Constitution. The Senate, however, remained the principal successor to the authority of the Continental Congress.

220

Whatever may be the effect of the party system in promoting agreement between the two branches of the Congress — with or without the aid of the President — it has not equalized their authority. On the contrary, the development of the system seems to have strengthened and confirmed the superiority of the Senate over the House in the management of legislative business which was first definitely established in the age of Jackson and Clay. There are three principal causes of the superiority of the Senate in the legislative business of the Congress under the present system of party government. The first cause is the method of procedure in the House of Representatives. The Senate leaders' knowledge that the House leaders have effective control over the machinery of legislation in their branch of the Congress puts the House at a great disadvantage, as has already been shown in the previous chapter, in the struggle for power which goes on between the two chambers in the conference committees.

The second cause of the superiority of the Senate in the legislative business of the Congress is the method of procedure in the Senate. In the upper chamber the rules do-not permit the majority party to limit debate on controversial measures and to fix the time for voting, as in the House. There are no limitations which can be imposed by a majority vote on the length of speeches at any of the stages in the consideration of bills; there is no provision for moving the previous question in order to force a vote against the opposition of the minority party; and there is the greatest laxity in enforcing the rule that Senators shall speak to the pending question, when recognized and in possession of the floor. A method of closing debate was adopted in 1917, which permits each Senator to speak only once and for not more than one hour after a vote by the Senate on a motion seconded by sixteen Senators, but this motion requires a two-thirds majority of the Senate for its adoption. This requirement means that under normal conditions the closure cannot be employed by the majority party to end dilatory action and obstruction by the minority. A two-thirds majority is ordinarily unobtainable without substantial support from both parties. Since the adoption of the rule there have been many filibusters, and only a few of them have been broken up by means of its use.

Legislative business is generally conducted in the Senate with great informality. Private understandings between the party leaders take the place of regular rules, and without objection by any Senator almost anything can be done. The ability to get the bulk of the business done by unanimous consent is a great convenience to the party leaders, but the right to object gives great power to the individual member. The small membership of the Senate makes legislation by unanimous consent practicable under ordinary circumstances, but it also compels the party leaders to give greater consideration to the opinions of individual Senators than would be necessary under a more formal method of procedure. In the conference committees, where the final decisions on the form of controversial measures are made, the weakness of the Senate closure rule gives the Senate conferees a great advantage over those from the House in negotiating compromises between the contending interests and getting agreement upon the definitive text of a law. All the committee members know that it will be easier to obtain the approval of the House for concessions to the Senate than to obtain the approval of the Senate for concessions to the House. This knowledge strengthens the Senate members and weakens the House members of these powerful committees. Thus the privileged position of the individual Senator under the Senate rules of procedure strengthens the position of the Senate in the process of legislation. This is the direct contrary of the situation in the House of Representatives, where the privileged position of the leaders weakens its position in the legislative process.

The third important cause of senatorial superiority over the House is the practice of senatorial courtesy. The success of the informal system of senatorial procedure is dependent upon one kind of senatorial courtesy, since frequent abuse by Senators of their privileges in debate would make the system impracticable. But there is another kind of senatorial courtesy which adds much in a different way to the power of the Senate as a legislative body. This is the practice of refusing consent to appointments to public offices, in cases in which the consent of the Senate is necessary, when the proposed appointment is objectionable to a Senator from the state in which the candidate nominated by the President resides. Effective party government requires the existence of some systematic method by means of which the availability of candidates for appointive offices can be determined, and the existing practice of senatorial courtesy supplies a method which is logical under a federal system of constitutional government.

That the practice of senatorial courtesy tends to strengthen the executive power of the Senate is obvious. This system of distributing party patronage compels the President to secure the approval, not only of a majority of the Senate, as required by the Constitution, for an appointment, but also of the Senators from a particular state, whether or not their votes are needed to make a majority. The necessity of such a system, when the Senators belong to the same party as the President, is clear, if harmony is to exist within the party, but its propriety is less clear, when the Senators from the state in which a candidate for an appointment resides happen to belong to the opposition party. That senatorial courtesy may apply to appointments in such cases also attests the strength which the system has acquired under the conditions of party government in the Senate. In all cases it makes the President more dependent upon the advice and consent of the Senate in the exercise of his power of appointment than the framers of the Constitution could have intended.

The effect of the practice of senatorial courtesy upon the legislative power of the Senate is less obvious. The individual Senator's influence over appointments makes him a more important member of the party organization in his state. The President may consult the national committeeman of the majority party or other competent party officers in the state before submitting an appointment to the Senate, and such clearance of appointments will of course strengthen the state party organizations. He may even consult the party leader in a large city before submitting the nomination of a person residing in that city. But in any case this system of distributing party patronage requires for its smooth operation good working relations between the Senators and the competent party officers in the states. The influence of the Senators in the state party organizations increases their influence in all political matters, including legislation pending in the Congress, in which their states are specially interested. Many Senators become the most influential party leaders in their states. Even state governors may carry less weight in their party's councils. The framers of the Constitution wisely provided two Senators for each state and gave each a separate vote. This provident arrangement insures some competition between the Senators for power in their state organizations, but does not prevent the ascendancy of the Senators over the members of the House of Representatives in party affairs, particularly in the larger states. Senatorial courtesy, by making Senators more important party leaders, was designed to enhance their authority in their dealings with the President, but it manifestly has the effect also of strengthening their hands in dealing with the members of the House of Representatives.

The ascendancy of the Senate in the legislative business of the Congress has been little affected by the Franklin proviso, as adopted by the final great compromise in the Convention of 1787. Whether this proviso in its original form would have made the House of Representatives the predominant partner in the legislative process may well be doubted. Certainly the privilege of originating revenue bills, which the Senate can amend like other bills, has added little, if anything, to the authority of the House. The history of tariff legislation over a long period of years offers the most convincing proof of the practical capacity of the Senate to alter such measures by amendment as greatly as measures of any other kind. The Senate Committee on Finance has been able to hold its own hearings and write its own bill, which the Senate then can substitute for the bill prepared by the Committee on Ways and Means and adopted by the House. This procedure frustrates the plan to exalt the authority of the latter, as predicted by the aristocratic Nationalist leaders in the Federal Convention. The House has been more successful in asserting its authority in the proceedings on the appropriation bills, in which it was not guaranteed precedence by the Franklin proviso in its final form. The Senate Committee on Appropriations has not usually wished to take the trouble necessary to write appropriation bills, based on laborious investigation of expenditures by the executive departments and independent establishments, and the Senate has consequently been less effective in reviewing the appropriation bills of the House than its revenue bills. But the Senate can always make a fight for any amendment to an appropriation bill deemed desirable by Senators, as in the case of other bills. The special privileges of the House relating to money bills, whether prescribed by the Constitution or derived from the rules and practices of the two chambers, have not materially changed their relative influence in the process of lawmaking. The subordination of the House to the Senate is clearly established.

The superiority of the Senate over the House of Representatives in the process of lawmaking is greatest in dealing with partisan measures. When there is strong leadership from the White House, the party leaders in both branches of the Congress may be expected to agree in support of the party program. Since the procedure of the House is designed expressly for the purpose of passing measures in pursuance of a partisan program, whereas the Senate procedure is designed to give great freedom of action to the individual member regardless of party, the House leaders will ordinarily concede to the Senate leaders also greater freedom of action. Concessions by the House to the Senate concerning the details of a bill are necessary and proper under the circumstances in order to get the support of a Senate majority for its essential provisions. This type of relationship between the two branches of the Congress was well illustrated during Franklin D. Roosevelt's first term, when executive influence in the legislative process was at its peak in modern times. Administration measures passed through the House in rapid succession without long debates or radical amendments. In the Senate, debate was extended and amendments were sometimes important. The influence of the Senate over the details of the Administration's measures was manifestly superior.

The influence of the House of Representatives on party legislation is likely to be greater when negative than when positive. The House leaders can kill proposed legislation by denying facilities for its consideration, and the rank and file can kill it by voting against it. The negative influence of the House on a partisan program was clearly revealed during Franklin D. Roosevelt's second term. The court-reform proposal was considered first in the Senate, because the House leaders advised the Administration that it would be impossible to pass any bill on that subject in a form acceptable to the Administration, unless it was first approved by the Senate. The House defeated the Administration's reorganization bill after it had first passed the Senate, and prevented the passage of the Administration's wages and hours bill until the grip of the House leaders on the machinery of legislation had been broken by a bipartisan combination of private members. The reluctance of the House leaders to go along with the Administration diminished the importance of partisanship in the enactment of constructive measures. The volume of party legislation during Roosevelt's second term was comparatively small.

The impairment of party solidarity deprives the causes of senatorial superiority in the legislative process of some of their potency, but does not alter the general character of the relation between the two branches of the Congress. This was well illustrated during Franklin D. Roosevelt's third term. Party leaders in both chambers and on both sides understood the wisdom of stopping partisanship at the water's edge in time of war and the President's preoccupation with military and international problems caused him to give less attention to ordinary domestic affairs. The struggles in the Congress over revenue bills, price-fixing, and the regulation of labor and industry produced divisions of the members running across party lines and brought new and heavy responsibilities to the party leaders in each branch. It proved more difficult to get the needed majorities for essential legislation in the Senate than in the House, and the influence of the Senate on the form and substance of controversial legislation remained therefore greater than that of the House. The influence of partisanship was most manifest in matters of particular interest to politicians, such as the arrangements for voting in the presidential election by soldiers overseas. The bulk of the legislation was of the kind with which the members of Congress deal as a sample of the public rather than as political experts or as members of a party with a mandate from the people.

The relation between the two chambers, when dealing with legislation without a popular mandate, is illustrated by the proceedings in the Seventy-ninth and Eightieth Congresses. In the former, majority-party leadership by the executive was weak and in the latter it no longer existed. The Democratic leaders in the House and Senate during the Seventy-ninth Congress and the Republican leaders in the Eightieth were free to act on their own initiative. There was in fact a considerable body of important legislation on controversial subjects. The Seventy-ninth Congress passed several outstanding constructive measures, notably the (Administrative) Reorganization Act, the Administrative Procedure Act, the Legislative Reorganization Act, the Employment Act, and the Atomic Energy Act, and took the necessary steps for adherence to and participation in the United Nations. The Eightieth Congress passed the National Security Act, the Greek-Turkish Aid Act, the Foreign Assistance Act, and a Housing and Rent Act. It also passed a Tax Reduction Act and the new Labor-Management Relations Act over the President's veto. Most of this legislation was prepared by congressional committees in the House and Senate. The latter took the lead in preparing the extraordinarily important Atomic Energy Act in the Seventy-ninth Congress and imposed its views of policy upon the former also in the Eightieth Congress in connection with the labor-management relations legislation. The House imposed its views upon the Senate in the final passage of the Employment Act of 1946 and of the Legislative Reorganization Act of 1946, and in the struggle over the reduction of taxes in 1947. In all three instances the results of the assertion of authority by the House leaders were negative. In general, the record shows that, when left to their own devices by the default of effective party leadership in the legislative process as a whole, the Senate was more productive of constructive leadership than the House.

The greater freedom of debate in the Senate is undoubtedly a major factor in its legislative superiority over the House. But the importance of the lack of an effective form of closure in the upper chamber is not easy to appraise accurately. Lindsay Rogers puts the case for unlimited debate in the Senate in its most extreme form. "My view," he wrote in 1926,[17] "is this: The undemocratic, usurping Senate is the indispensable check and balance in the American system, and only complete freedom of debate permits it to play this role." At that time the closure had been used twice to bring debate on an important measure to an end. In 1919 it was used to force a vote on the proposal to join the League of Nations and in 1926 on the proposal to join the World Court. Both measures, when brought to a vote, were defeated, because of the constitutional requirement of a two-thirds majority for the ratification of a treaty. If there had been rules in the Senate for closing debate as strict as those in the House of Representatives the result would have been the same in these two cases. Whether treaties, like other laws, should be passed by ordinary majorities in both chambers, instead of passing only by a two-thirds majority in the Senate, is the real issue raised by these two episodes.

Since 1926 the closure has been used successfully to end debate only twice. Two measures of minor importance were adopted more quickly by this means than would otherwise have been possible.[18] Both instances occurred in 1927. Down to the end of the Seventy-ninth Congress, on the other hand, the closure was invoked in vain twenty-five times. How many times the threat to invoke closure caused a voluntary agreement by unanimous consent to end a debate and vote without further delay is uncertain. Doubtless this has occurred sometimes. On the other hand, the mere threat of a filibuster may force concessions to the opposition, which would never be granted on their merits, in order to get action on a bill. Senators understand the power which freedom of debate brings to them both as individuals and as a body. They also understand the objection which lies against the abuse of this freedom in order to make the wishes of a minority prevail over those of a majority. It has been forcefully expressed by W. F. Willoughby.[19] "While a majority can use its powers in an illegitimate way, the same is true of the minority, and as between the two, the former [is] the lesser evil."

Investigation of the measures which have failed to come to a vote on account of endless discussion by opponents on the floor of the Senate throws some light on the practical force of this objection. Many of the measures which have been the victims of dilatory debate and obstruction were eventually passed in some acceptable form, or now

227

seem trivial. Momentarily hot passions were aroused by the filibusters, but the lapse of time makes possible the conclusion that it did not matter much whether these measures were adopted promptly, if ever, in their original forms. Migratory-bird refuges are doubtless desirable features of the landscape in a great country, and Boulder Dam was certainly a valuable public improvement, but migratory birds have not been too much neglected and Boulder Dam was built without undue delay and without abridgment of the freedom of debate. Occasionally filibusters, or the threat of filibusters, have been utilized to extort concessions of a private or local nature from the managers of bills which were expected to pass, and the smallness of the business may explain the success of the maneuver.

The most sensational filibusters in recent years have been directed against measures designed to interfere with the treatment of Negroes in the South. The antilynching and anti-poll-tax bills were definitely of this character, and the fair employment practices bill encountered the most obstinate opposition in that section of the country. These bills were defeated by filibusters, which could not be broken up by the closure. The filibuster against the F.E.P.C. bill of 1946, which lasted from January 17 to February 9, was the most impressive demonstration of the opportunities for obstruction under the Senate rules.[20] A minority of some sort may have been protected by this abuse of unlimited debate, but it certainly was not the minority most in need of protection, namely, the Negro.

The latest of the filibusters against legislation designed to prevent discrimination against Negroes broke out early in the Eighty-first Congress. The Democratic Party had pledged itself in its 1948 platform to promote legislation for the better protection of the rights of Negroes and its candidate for President had made the enforcement of civil rights a leading issue in the campaign. The Republican Party also was committed to such legislation and in particular to the prompt enactment of laws to end the "disgrace" of lynching. Despite these platform pledges by the two major parties, a combination of Dixiecrats and Republicans was able to prevent even the consideration of civil-rights legislation by the Senate. Instead of adopting better protection for the rights of Negroes the Senate actually made the procedure for closing debate more difficult than before. The majority required for invoking closure was raised from two-thirds of a quorum present and voting to two-thirds of all the members of the Senate. This episode afforded a striking illustration both of the unreliability of platform promises and of the lack of solidarity and discipline in the major parties.

The importance of an effective rule for closure in the Senate springs not only from the abuse of the present system of practically unlimited debate in such cases as that of the proposed civil-rights legislation but also from the effects of senatorial courtesy on the relations between the two branches of the Congress and its influence on the legislative process as a whole. Since the normal operation of free discussion tends to increase the superiority of the Senate over the House of Representatives, the practice must be judged in the light of its impact on the relations between the special interests which gain or lose most from the system of unequal representation in the Senate. In general it is the rural interests which gain and the urban interests which lose, and in particular it is the dominant interests in the Solid South, in rural New England, and in the arid West which gain the most. Since the method of electing Presidents overrepresents the urban interests in the great industrial states, there is something to be said under the existing circumstances of the economic and social order for such a balance of power as results from the unrepresentative character of the Senate. This is certainly not the kind of balance planned by the aristocratic Nationalists in 1787. Nor is it what was advocated by the original Federalists. It makes the Senate a guardian of special regional interests rather than of the interests of states as political entities. This may be what the Unionists in the Convention of 1787 expected and desired. But no final judgment can be reached without further investigation of the role of the President in the legislative process.

Meanwhile one important conclusion concerning the practice of senatorial courtesy can be noted. It tends to make the Senate a legislative body which is likely to be more favorable to moderate measures than to those based on the extremes of opinion. It was unfortunate that the closure was made more difficult by the recent amendment to the rule. It would have been better to have made the rule more rather than less effective for stopping undue obstruction. For senatorial courtesy, if not too much abused, is well suited to the middle-class character of the Congress.

PARTY GOVERNMENT
VERSUS CONSTITUTIONAL GOVERNMENT

The actual operation of the bicameral legislative system in recent years has been different from what was planned by the framers. The special interests of the states as political entities are better served by other aspects of the system of federalism than by their equal representation in the Senate. The special interests of the rich are best served by the general costliness of contemporary electioneering, and by the influence of money in the formation of opinion, in the maintenance of party organizations and of organized group representation before the Congress, and in pressure politics generally. The division of the Congress into two branches gives Senators greater opportunities than members of the House to influence legislation. But it makes the legislative process as a whole dependent upon the functioning of the bipartisan system in national politics.

Since the President by well-established custom is a leader of his party as well as a leader in the legislative process by virtue of the provisions of the Constitution, it is not possible to appraise the work of the Congress without analyzing the relations between Presidents and Congresses. These relations cause the legislative process to become involved in the general relationship between party government and constitutional government. No estimate can be made of the usefulness of the bicameral system in its present form without surveying the effect of the party system upon the constitutional position of the chief executive. No definite conclusion can be reached concerning the value of the American principle of the separation of powers without an examination of additional evidence on the working of the actual system of checks and balances. But some preliminary observations are in order.

In the first place, the bicameral system makes for greater deliberation in the legislative process. Deliberation, if not carried to an excess, should strengthen the Congress as a whole in its dealings with the President. On the other hand, the division of power between the two branches of the Congress can play into the hands of the chief executive. It creates opportunities for skillful executives to play one branch against the other, supporting the weaker against the stronger. Under favorable circumstances a policy of divide and rule would strengthen the position of the President. Some of the framers, notably Washington and the other aristocratic Nationalists, wanted a stronger chief executive than was finally established. The original Federalists would have preferred a weaker executive. Both factions wanted a strong Senate. The record of the debates in the Federal Convention shows that these two factions had different reasons for desiring a strong Senate. The experience of eighty Congresses shows that the Senate has in fact become strong

230

regardless of the reasons of the framers, and that the Senate's superior capacity for deliberation has been an important factor in the development of its power.

Experience shows, too, that the natural jealousy between two independent and competitive bodies tends to prevent the party system from realizing its full potentialities. There are no joint meetings of the party caucuses to bring the party members of the two houses together to arrange a legislative program. Ordinarily the party leaders do not even permit the creation of joint committees for the determination of a consistent party policy on a particular issue. They prefer to leave the committees of each house free to act separately, relying upon conference committees at the final stage of the proceedings to reconcile differences between the majorities in the two houses. Such arrangements may strengthen the authority of the party leaders, who are able to keep the final decisions more closely in their own hands. But they are fatal to a united front toward the executive.

The mutual jealousy of the two branches of the Congress doubtless tends to protect their independence. Not even President Washington could break down the Senate's corporate exclusiveness. Its members refused to deliberate in his presence on the business he laid before them. But this corporate exclusiveness, by causing friction between the two branches of the Congress, diminishes the influence of the Congress as a whole in its relations with the President. The development of more effective party organization could give the Congress a greater advantage in the determination of public policy. But party discipline has not been equal to the opportunity afforded by the strong disposition of the public to support the two-party system.

The practical incapacity of the Senate, as of the House, to make the most of its opportunities to influence the conduct of the government is increased by its methods of organization and procedure. One of the most serious defects is the practice of selecting the chairmen of the standing committees by seniority. The chairmen of the important committees exert extraordinary influence upon the course of business. The seniority system insures that they shall be legislative veterans without insuring exceptional mental qualities or even physical fitness. A system which placed a man of the caliber of Senator Reynolds at the head of the Senate Committee on Military Affairs at the beginning of World War II, like that which placed a man of the character of Representative May at the head of the corresponding committee in the House of Representatives, stands self-convicted. It prevents the ablest members of the Senate from exerting their proper influence and discriminates against the sections of the country in which the parties are closely matched and long periods of uninterrupted service in either branch of the Congress are exceptional. The Senate may devise practical expedients for diminishing the evils of the seniority system, as by appointing select committees like the Truman Committee for special occasions, but no remedy short of the abolition of the system itself can put the Senate in a position to make the most of its opportunities under the constitutional distribution of power.

Another serious defect in the methods of conducting the business of the Senate is the extravagant waste of time. The volume of business, which is great and rapidly growing, and the general pressure on the members' time, which is excessively severe, should encourage the adoption of the most businesslike methods. The need for improvement has been recognized by thoughtful members and considerable relief was secured by various reforms under the Legislative Reorganization Act of 1946. But much remains to be done in the Senate as in the House. Unlimited debate, regardless of its relevancy to the topic under discussion, is an unnecessary evil. Its cure requires no limitation of the opportunity of Senators to discuss the questions of the day. It merely requires a stricter use of the presiding officer's authority to keep a Senator speaking to the particular question under discussion. The needless waste of the Senate's time in frivolous speechmaking may strengthen the position of its leaders in their relations with the House of Representatives, but hinders efforts to achieve a more influential position for the Congress as a whole in the legislative process.

The Legislative Reorganization Act of 1946 brought about substantial improvements in the organization of both branches of the Congress. It also improved the technical services available for the use of members of both houses. But legislative procedures were not improved. The Senate would have adopted, but the House rejected, the proposals for joint committee hearings and for a joint legislative-executive council. The Senate put into effect for its own use the plan for a Policy Committee to provide more efficient leadership in the legislative process at its end of the Capitol, but it could not alone give effect to the proposals for establishing a united front on the part of the Congress in its dealings with the President in matters of legislative policy. The constructive proposals of the La Follette-Monroney Committee for more effective participation by the congressional leaders in the determination of public policy seem sound. Their realization would be an important contribution to the effectiveness of the legislative process at Washington.

The unwillingness of both branches of the Congress in 1945 to permit the Joint Committee on the Organization of Congress to make recommendations for changes in the rules of procedure of either house is easy to understand. Neither house wanted members of the other to tell it how to regulate its own proceedings. The Senate preferred to decide for itself how to reconcile the individual Senator's freedom to speak and the authority of the whole Senate to act. The House of Representatives was determined to keep in its own hands the power to readjust the relations between its dictatorial Committee on Rules and the majority, partisan or bipartisan, of the whole House. But these considerations do not justify either house in making the preservation of its prerogative a pretext for the neglect of its duty to adopt a reasonably efficient as well as democratic system of transacting legislative business. The Senate will lose influence as well as prestige, if it fails to find a suitable means of protecting itself against the abuse of the filibuster. The House will suffer a further decline in its legislative authority as well as in the confidence of the public, if it is unable to make its Committee on Rules a servant instead of a master. Both houses need to find a better way to choose committee chairmen than the rule of seniority. Both need to improve the methods of conducting committee hearings and of recruiting the staffs of the committees.

It is more difficult to give a rational explanation for the refusal of the House leaders in 1946 to accept the La Follette-Monroney Committee's recommendations for joint committee hearings and a Joint Council. These recommendations may have seemed subversive to leaders bent on maintaining their established control over the business of the House, but they could hardly have failed to improve the position of the Congress as a whole in its relations with the chief executive. The strengthening of the authority of the Congress should have brought some improvement also in the position of the House as well as in that of the Senate. In the management of that part of the legislative business, for which the majority party has received a mandate from the people at the previous election, better provision for joint action by the two branches would make the power of the majority party to act more nearly equal to its responsibility under the partisan system. More efficient performance of its proper duty under a responsible system of party government should facilitate the improvement of the work of the Congress in that wider field of legislation in which it functions as

233

a sample of the public with an obligation to enable majorities of any kind, partisan, bipartisan, or nonpartisan, in either branch of the Congress to act as the majority of the public would like them to act. There is an important place for constitutional government as well as for party government in the legislative process. Both branches of the Congress, and particularly the House, need to recognize more clearly this distinction in the business of lawmaking and to readjust their methods of doing business accordingly.

The change in the role of the Senate in the legislative process is one of the most significant that has occurred in the practical operation of the system of checks and balances. No one can pretend that the Senate has become an agency of majority rule. A legislative body in which a third of the members represent small constituencies less than half as populous as the average state, and in which a majority of the people, residing in the largest states, possess less than a quarter of the total representation, cannot be deemed democratic. A legislative body which by means particularly of the brilliant improvisation known as senatorial courtesy has successfully arrogated more than its intended share of the legislative and executive powers must nevertheless be recognized as constitutional. This undemocratic arrogating Senate is evidently not what was planned either by the aristocratic Nationalists or by the original Federalists. It is not the guardian of the special interests of the "opulent"; neither is it the guardian of the special interests of "sovereign" states. At its worst it may appear to be the branch of the Congress that is most responsive to the pressures from the organized minorities which compete with the major political parties as agencies for the representation of special interests in the legislative process.

At its best, however, the Senate gives to the ablest personalities among its members, regardless of party, a matchless opportunity to influence the processes of government. The greater freedom of speech, as compared with that in the House of Representatives, and the more effective limitations on the authority of parties enhance the influence of personality in the legislative process and facilitate the operations of majorities other than that particular majority represented by the majority party. The Senate introduces an element into the process of government under the Constitution that is aristocratic in the true sense of the word and makes constitutional government, as practiced by the Congress, something more and better than mere party government. The Senate could not function well — it could hardly function at all —

if many politicians of extreme opinions and uncompromising tempers were elected to its membership. While most Senators continue, however, to possess the middle-class virtues appropriate to the American way in politics and essential for the successful operation of senatorial courtesy, the Senate will continue to make the major contribution to that unique blend of democracy, oligarchy, and aristocracy which is the American Congress.

CHAPTER EIGHT

Presidents and Congresses

THE CONSTITUTIONAL THEORY OF THE PRESIDENCY

THE framers of the Constitution agreed to vest the executive power in a single President of the United States, but they did not try to explain precisely what they meant by the executive power. The old revolutionists, Franklin and Sherman, wanted a weak executive, but the aristocratic Nationalist leaders in the Convention of 1787 were determined to make the chief executive as strong as possible. By the final great compromise it was settled that the chief executive should be strong enough to protect himself under ordinary circumstances against the abuse of power by the legislative branch of the government and to that extent prevent it from destroying the equilibrium among the three branches. To this end a limited veto over the acts of Congress was granted to the President, who thus became an accomplice of the Congressmen in the process of lawmaking. To prevent intolerable abuse of presidential powers, the Congress was authorized to remove the President from office upon impeachment and conviction of a high crime or misdemeanor, but it was not authorized to remove him because of loss of confidence in his policies or upon any purely political ground. In the interest of further safety against the abuse of presidential power, the President's power to appoint public officers, which had been greatly extended by the final compromise, was conditioned upon the advice and consent of the Senate, and the Senators thereby became partners of the President in the execution of the laws. The framers were obviously more interested in devising a serviceable system of checks and balances than in adhering to any logical theory of the separation of powers.

The use of the executive veto power affords the clearest test of the constitutional theory of the presidency. It is evident that the framers intended at least that this power should be used, when necessary, to protect the chief executive against unconstitutional encroachments upon his authority by the Congress. In discussing the distribution of power among the three branches of the government in number forty-eight of *The Federalist*, Madison declared: "After discriminating in theory the several classes of power, as they may in their nature be legislative, executive, or judiciary, the next and most difficult task is to provide some practical security for each against the invasion of the others." Most of the Nationalist leaders believed that due security for the President against the invasion of his constitutional authority by the Congress required a stronger form of executive veto than that finally granted in the Constitution; some would have preferred an absolute to any kind of conditional veto. The opposition of Franklin and Sherman and others forced the adoption of the limited veto in a more moderate form. But to what extent should the President feel free to invoke his power of veto against acts of the Congress on grounds of pure expediency regardless of their constitutionality? On this point the evidence afforded by the debates in the Convention is not conclusive. The authors of the Virginia plan certainly desired that the veto power should serve to strengthen the influence of the chief executive in the legislative process. Others among the framers preferred that the function of determining legislative policy should be reserved for Congressmen. By tacit consent the problem was left to be worked out by future Presidents and Congresses in the give-and-take of actual government under the Constitution.

The answer to the unspoken question concerning the nature of the veto power is a by-product of the two-party system in American politics. The essential function of the major parties, as Lowell observed years ago,[1] lies not so much in presenting alternative sides of public questions as in presenting alternative candidates for public office. The heart of national politics is the presidential campaign. The only common point about which the leadership of a durable major party can be effectively organized is the presidency. The natural limits to the power of numerical majorities among the American people are too formidable for permanent partisan majorities, capable of effective initiative in the legislative process, to develop in the Congress without external aid. The President is authorized by the Constitution to recommend measures to the Congress. He alone can furnish the necessary leadership, and public opinion has come to expect him to do so. But responsibility calls for corresponding power. The experience of the generations under the Constitution has taught that only Presidents, and candidates for the presidency, can conveniently produce plans for the effective use of the legislative powers of Congress. In the nature of things, the planners of legislative programs will use the powers of their office, when in office, to promote the execution of their plans. It was inevitable, therefore, as contemplated by the Nationalist leaders in 1787, that the veto power should become an instrument of legislative policy in the hands of the chief executive. To what extent the chief executive would make himself chief legislator also would depend partly, of course, upon the character of the man in the office.

The Nationalist leaders believed in 1787 that General Washington would be the first President of the United States and certainly expected him to try to carry into effect the general policies which they had supported in the Convention. They certainly hoped, too, even if they could not be sure, that the executive power, as embodied in the system of checks and balances designed by the Convention, would furnish an adequate basis for effective leadership by the presumptive first chief executive under the Constitution. They did not foresee that the President would eventually become a spokesman for the people and an agency of majority rule in competition with the House of Representatives. They did not anticipate that the natural limits to the power of numerical majorities would apply also to the authority of the President in his character of chief legislator. Least of all did they look forward to the rise of the middle classes and the establishment of a more complex class basis for their check-and-balance system of constitutional government than the simple dichotomy of the body politic into the "opulent" and the "indigent" envisaged by the most aristocratic of the Nationalist leaders.

The principle of the separation of powers, unlike that of the natural limits to partisan power, was one which Madison did not need to justify to most of his fellow countrymen. Their own political observations and the general temper of the times conspired to give widespread, if not universal, credence to Montesquieu's great generalization, which Blackstone had made familiar to American lawyers.[2] The experience of the American people since the beginning of the Revolution corresponded to that of the ages as reported by Montesquieu. Men in power would press forward until they found their limits. The nature of things, as understood by a generation still under the spell of the Newtonian cosmology, showed that power could be effectively limited. Systems of government, as well as planetary systems, could be kept in order by the nice contrivance of suitable checks and balances. How successful a government based upon this principle might be, the example of England in what then seemed the good old days of the elder Pitt made manifest.

Experience, not logic, had governed the framers in their application of the venerable principle to the task before them. In the Federal Convention not even the most fervent admirers of the English Constitution contended that an indiscriminate copy would be practicable in the United States. John Dickinson conceded that Americans would have to make shift with something intrinsically inferior, but, it might be hoped, better adapted to their circumstances.[3] James Wilson explained clearly enough why a written description of the government of a foreign country, even one with such an excellent constitution as that of Great Britain was supposed to be, could not serve the purposes and needs of Americans.[4] It was evident too that logic had not governed the English in the development of their nicely balanced institutions. The nature and extent of the royal prerogative were beyond rational explanation. The confusion of powers in the House of Lords certainly defied logic. The House of Commons fell far short of being a mirror of the common people of England. But the various checks to the exercise of power by king, lords, and commons seemed to establish a happy balance between them. The equilibrium of the parts augured the stability of the whole. By giving due thought to the contrivance of a similar equilibrium with the available materials, a similar stability might be attained in America. Madison took great pains in his explanation of the theory in the fifty-first number of *The Federalist* to make clear the grounds of his belief that the separation of powers had received a realistic application in the Constitution of the United States.

THE ACTUAL RELATIONS
BETWEEN PRESIDENTS AND CONGRESSES

Analysis of the American system of checks and balances begins with the relations between the President and the Congress. First, there is what may be called the ideal constitutional relation, in accordance with which the President deals with Congressmen as individuals and spokesmen for their districts or states and attempts to conduct public affairs without benefit of organized partisan support. He chooses his executive advisers for their administrative fitness regardless of their followings or lack of followings in the legislative branch of the government or among the factions which have joined in his election. He seeks support among the legislators for each of his policies and measures

239

on its particular merits regardless of the previous or prospective affiliations of legislators with the factions which can give his administration consistent support and bring about his reëlection. In short, he acts as if he were not only a separate officer of the government but also independent of the members of Congress and free to conduct public affairs according to his own will as long as majorities of any kind can be found in the Congress, when needed for the support of his administration.

The President who seemed most determined to maintain the ideal constitutional relationship with the Congress was John Adams. President Adams believed in as rational an application as possible of the theory of the separation of powers. His *Defense of the Constitutions of Government of the United States* contained the most systematic and elaborate exposition of the theory to be found in American political literature. He contended strenuously that the best constitution was that of what he called a monarchical republic. The essence of a republic, according to his understanding of constitutional history, was the division of legislative power. It was not the absence of a king which, according to Adams, made a republic, but the absence of a concentration of legislative power in the hands of a single person. If the power to make the laws were distributed among the members of a legislative body, the republic would be an aristocratic or a democratic one according to the nature of the body. Better than a simple aristocratic or democratic republic, Adams thought, because less likely to suffer the abuse of the legislative power, would be one in which the power was divided between two representative bodies, one representing the rich and the other the poor. In a republic with such a distribution of legislative power, the concurrence of the rich and the poor would be required for all legislative acts and the likelihood of the oppression of either class by the other would be greatly reduced. Best of all republican constitutions, Adams concluded, would be one in which the legislative power was distributed between an aristocratic and a democratic legislative branch and an independent chief executive who should be, he argued, above the class interests of either rich or poor. In such a republic, which he called a monarchical republic, the chief executive would stand for the general public interests, while the bicameral legislature would represent the separate and partial interests of the rich and the poor, and the concurrence of all three in legislative acts would give the best possible assurance that the best interests of the whole commonwealth would prevail. Great Britain was such a monarchical republic, according to John Adams, and so too was the American Federal Union under the Constitution of 1787.

John Adams was generally pleased with the Federal Constitution but he could not be wholly satisfied with the distribution of the legislative power. According to his interpretation of the theory of the separation of powers, the President should have been entrusted with an absolute veto over the acts of the Congress instead of a limited veto which might be overridden by a two-thirds vote in each of the two houses. His vigorous and persistent criticism of this arrangement provoked the Jeffersonians into dubbing him a monocrat and disparaging his fitness for the presidency under the Constitution. Despite his disappointment that the government of the more perfect Union could not have been what he would have considered a more perfect specimen of a well-balanced republican form, he was eager for the presidency with its limited veto and happy to assure his countrymen at his inauguration that he had no intention of seeking greater authority for himself as long as the people wished for a further trial of the constitutional distribution of power. He would be a true constitutionalist in his relations with the Congress. He would have liked the government of the Union better if the President had possessed an absolute veto. But he was content to hold the office as it was. He was confident of his practical ability to make the public interest prevail over that of any particular class.

John Adams's disappointment with the reality of power was even greater than with the theory of the Constitution. It was not the lack of a more decisive veto over legislation that caused his disappointment, since he had no occasion to exercise his veto. It was the failure of his countrymen to recognize him as the official representative of the whole body of people that brought him to grief and his Administration to what he deemed an untimely end. They insisted on regarding him as a party leader despite his claim to recognition as nothing less than the head of the nation. To the public it seemed that he had come into office as the successor of Washington at the head of a Federalist Administration. But he refused to act as the mere agent of the Federalists and thereby incurred the displeasure of those who claimed the leadership of the party. His practical incapacity, if he had not been unwilling on principle, to lead the Federalists rendered him unable to deal effectively with those who were resolved to oppose his Administration on partisan grounds. Disliked and in part repudiated by the aristocratic faction among the Federalists, he could not make good their defection by gaining converts from the democratic Republicans among Jefferson's followers. Upon his own principles, he was an excellent President, independent, steadfast, and public-spirited. His conduct of foreign affairs, in which he had a relatively free hand under the Constitution, was courageous and wise. But in his relations with the Congress, where his theory of the executive power was put to a severer test, he was impolitic and ineffective. His insistence on peace with France as well as with England was a great public service, but his indulgence of partisan prosecutions under the Sedition Act left an ineffaceable blot on his good name. The definitive fact about his Administration, in his own eyes and in those of contemporary American politicians, was that he could not get himself reëlected. The organization of parties might be ignored by the framers of the Constitution, but it could not be ignored by the chief executive in his relations either with the Congress or with the public.

The only later President who deliberately tried to act upon John Adams's principles of constitutional government was his son. John Quincy Adams also believed that the chief executive should always be the leader of the whole body of people and never that of any part thereof, whether rich or poor, North, South, East, or West, or any combination of geographical sections or political factions. He had been a leading member of an Administration to which there was no organized partisan opposition. During the "era of good feeling" under Monroe, all Americans, or at least all those actively engaged in national politics, seemed to have become Democratic-Republicans and partisanship therefore ceased to have its traditional significance. The younger Adams failed to receive the nomination of the Congressional Caucus, but in the light of his constitutional principles that failure seemed to him unimportant. It was the presidential electors, or ultimately the state delegations in the House of Representatives, not the Congressional Caucus, who under the Constitution were to elect the President, and that was decisive for John Quincy Adams. Under the circumstances he seemed to have an extraordinarily favorable opportunity for practising the original constitutional theory of the executive power.

The experience of the son in the presidency was as disappointing as that of the father. Despite his disclaimers the followers of all the losers in the presidential "scrub race" of 1824, especially the followers of the popular favorite, Andrew Jackson, and of the Caucus favorite, William H. Crawford, persisted in stigmatizing the younger Adams as a factional leader with a tainted title to his high office. He could not gain support for his measures from those who were determined not to recognize his right to lead their party, and he would not try to form an administration party from those who had nothing to hope from the triumph of the opposition. He did attempt to raise a standard to which the wise and honest, regardless of party, could repair, but John Quincy Adams, though one of the most scholarly and gentlemanly of Presidents, was not another Washington. Neither was Andrew Jackson, but a large majority of the people outside of New England, including doubtless a goodly share of the wise and honest, rallied to his standard. The younger Adams, like the elder, carried all the New England states in both his campaigns for the presidency. Each of them could carry New York once, but not twice. The rest of their support was scattered and ineffective except for the perennially Federalist states of New Jersey and Delaware. It was evident that the two Adamses were in fact, despite their theories, New England sectional leaders, whom fortune rather than popular favor brought to the highest office in the land, only to desert them when they were attacked by political opponents with radically different notions of the proper relationship between the President and the Congress. They were both vigorous and intelligent chief executives, but their conspicuous failures as chief legislators caused their Administrations to be remembered by practical politicians as warnings against unsound political theories rather than as examples of good government.

Subsequent Presidents who attempted to govern without benefit of organized partisan support were constrained by adverse circumstances rather than impelled by adherence to a constitutional theory. General Zachary Taylor liked to think of himself in 1848 as the People's candidate, but in fact it was Whigs chiefly who voted for him, while Democrats divided their votes between their regular candidate, Lewis Cass, and their former leader, Martin Van Buren, running on the Free Soil ticket. In office President Taylor showed unusual independence of party, but the Whigs were in a minority in both branches of the Congress and under the circumstances a partisan Administration could not have been successful. He died before his management of the relations between the Presidency and the Congress could be put to the test of a mid-term election. Rutherford B. Hayes was confronted by an adverse majority in the House of Representatives, following the disputed election of 1876, and during the latter half of his term had to govern without the support of a partisan majority in either branch of the Congress. President Cleveland faced a hostile partisan majority in the

Senate throughout his first term and in both branches during the latter half of his second term. These three Presidents were forced to govern upon the principles of John Adams, whether they wished to do so or not. They could distinguish themselves by their vetoes, but could not take the lead in any constructive legislation. They could make extraordinarily good records as chief executives, but as chief legislators they were doomed to frustration.

Two other Presidents, who might have governed with the support of partisan majorities in the Congress, chose to break with their parties. John Tyler and Andrew Johnson were factional leaders who had received the second place on the presidential ticket in order to gratify minor components in national partisan coalitions. Conspicuously unlike in many respects, they were both politicians with strong convictions and stubborn dispositions. The accidents which brought them into the White House disclosed the conflicts of opinion which had been concealed by the ambiguities of emotional campaigns. Deserted by the leaders of the dominant elements in their parties and by most of their followers in the Congress, these unfortunate chief executives were forced to choose between organizing new parties of their own and going over to the party of the opposition. Neither course proved practicable for either Tyler or Johnson. They ended their terms as independent chief executives in spite of themselves, frustrated and politically impotent. They could veto the measures of the congressional leaders, but they could not procure the enactment of measures of their own. As chief legislators their role was purely negative.

Only a lingering trace of the original constitutional theory among a few of the Radical Republicans in the Senate protected Johnson against removal from office by impeachment. His real offense was his refusal to submit to dictation in matters of policy by nominal party associates in the Congress who were unwilling to acquiesce in policies dictated by the chief executive. The differences between them were too deep for settlement by the kind of compromises which are the life of major national parties. Similar differences did not lead to an impeachment of Tyler, since the Whigs lacked the necessary two-thirds majority in the Senate for removal from office, but he had the mortification of watching helplessly while factional associates followed Calhoun into the opposition party. His active political career ended with his exit from an office to which he had not been elected by the people and which he sought to administer in opposition to the wishes of a majority of his party associates. Under such circumstances the Adams theory of the proper relationship between the President and the Congress could not but work badly.

All other Presidents have depended upon political parties for the success of their Administrations. Strong Presidents were able to put themselves at the head of their parties and through their partisan connections to hold an effective leadership in their relations with the Congress. Weaker Presidents accepted the leadership of their partisan associates in the Congress and joined in the execution of policies and measures which the congressional leaders could agree to support. Several of these Presidents were unfortunate in their partisan affiliations. The party leaders in the Congress, upon whom the President depended for the management of his legislative business, lost their control of the Congress at the mid-term elections, and the chief executive was forced to content himself thereafter with the exercise of the executive power but with no more than a negative influence over the course of legislation. The relations between the parties, as well as the personality of the President, determined the relations between the President and the Congress. The original constitutional theory of the relations between these two branches of the government had to yield to the authority of a new theory of party government.

Among the most successful Presidents were the founders of parties. President Washington has often been credited with a superiority to partisanship which is indeed suggested by his two unanimous elections. In his "Farewell Address" he issued a solemn warning against the evils of purely sectional parties and of intemperate party spirit. But he conceded that parties were a natural development in a free country and that within due limits their operations might be salutary. In the conduct of his own Administration he studiously rewarded at first those whom he regarded as friends of the new Constitution and at last those who were loyal to him as chief legislator as well as chief executive. The foundation of the Federalist party was laid in the Federal Convention, where Washington's original followers appropriated their opponents' name and as much of their program as was necessary to procure the unanimous consent of the delegations present for the establishment of a government which might be at least partly national. When Washington became President, he appointed to executive or judicial offices all the regular Nationalists who had taken a helpful part in the framing and adoption of the new Constitution and who had not been elected to the Congress. In his second term, support for the Jay treaty became the acid test of Federalism. For opposing its ratification John Rutledge failed of confirmation to the office of Chief Justice of the United States. Efficient service as a party leader in the Senate rendered Oliver Ellsworth eligible for appointment to the same high office.

President Washington's relations with the Congress reflected a practical attitude toward partisanship. He did not like what he considered to be factious opposition, and resented keenly the partisan criticism with which his Administration was eventually assailed. But he understood the necessity of coördinating a sufficient variety of interests to give him control of legislative majorities and of consolidating his leadership by suitable rewards to loyal political associates. The concept of a permanent two-party system with a disciplined administration party and an equally disciplined opposition, loyal to the Constitution if not to the leadership of the executive in office, was beyond the range of his political vision. But he would have been well content with a system of government by a successful administration party, such as Jefferson presently established. In preferring Hamilton to Jefferson as a political adviser, he disclosed his preference for an aristocratic administration party rather than for a system of government without party.

Jefferson's attitude toward the problem of party government was not essentially different from Washington's. He too deplored the excesses of party spirit and preferred a party system which would facilitate rather than obstruct the leadership of the chief executive. A well-conducted administration party, by enabling the chief executive to function effectively also as a chief legislator, could maintain harmony between the President and the Congress without jeopardizing the independence of the two political departments of government under the Constitution. But the administration party must support the leadership of a party chieftain who could simultaneously qualify as the leader of the nation. "We are all Federalists, we are all Republicans," he hopefully declared in his "First Inaugural." Time proved that his hopes were well founded, but the opposition was reconciled to his leadership on terms which were acceptable to his original followers. Henry Adams has shown in his *History of the United States* how much the Jeffersonians eventually borrowed from the Federalist program in order to consolidate their position as an administration party without effective organized opposition. But they maintained their basic principle that the leader of the party should also be the nation's leader.

Jefferson's technique of leadership was simple and direct. He strove to maintain personal relations with the officers and influential members

246

of the Congress which would insure a concert of opinion among the party leaders as the essential condition of legislative action. In this he was sufficiently successful to procure the adoption of most of the measures requisite for the pursuance of his policies. The Congressional Caucus became the principal instrument for the control of the legislative process as well as for the choice of presidential candidates. The development of party government transformed the system of government under the Constitution into a more popular type of representative government than the framers had originally planned.

Under Jefferson's less masterful successors the leadership in the legislative process passed from the President to the Congress. Madison and Monroe, as the designated political heirs of their great chieftain, were too well recommended to the people to be lightly set aside by the congressional leaders of the governing party. But they were too dependent upon the support of their congressional associates to determine the legislative policies of their Administrations. A reluctant Madison was forced to yield in 1812 to the advocates of a war with England as the price of continuance at the head of the government. A complaisant Monroe could be reëlected in 1820 without public opposition, although his opinion on the leading issue of the day, the exclusion of slavery from the western territories, was unknown. These two eminently respectable but not very forceful Presidents maintained their standing as heads of the nation, but they lost control of their parties and of the legislative process. Monroe's resort to the executive veto against the appropriation of money for the construction of a national road was designed to establish the policy that internal improvements should be made only at the expense of the state and local governments, but positive national leadership in matters of policy remained largely the possession of the congressional leaders. Henry Clay, the brilliant and popular Speaker of the House, was a more influential party chieftain than either of the nominal chiefs of state.

Andrew Jackson restored the legislative leadership to the chief executive. This achievement required more heroic-measures than had been needed or deemed proper by his most illustrious predecessors. To put an end to the dependency of the President upon the Congress he attacked the authority of the Congressional Caucus, and insisted upon a complete separation of the nomination of Presidents from the business of the Congress. He also declared that Presidents should serve no more than a single term, lest a President lose his independence in the process of getting himself reëlected. The introduction of the delegate convention system established representative government in the major parties on a firm basis, but shifted the menace to the independence of the chief executive from the congressional leaders to the party leaders in the several states. Jackson was able to force a reluctant Senate to expunge its resolution of censure from its official journal, but he could not procure the nomination of Vice-President Van Buren as his successor without the coöperation of the state and local party leaders. The result was to make the presidency a more popular institution but to render the independence of Presidents more precarious. The popular vote at presidential elections grew by the proverbial leaps and bounds, but presidential influence in the legislative process depended more than ever upon the personalities of the Presidents and the operation of the party system. A bold and vigorous use of the veto power and of the power over the patronage could help a popular President like Jackson to dominate both his party and the Congress. But neither of these political practices could help John Tyler. The expedients of the Jacksonians enabled Jackson at the end of his Administration to recover the legislative leadership from the Congress. In the long run, however, they did not assure the ascendancy of the chief executive, but merely sharpened the struggle for power between the President and the Congress.

There have been no more founders of parties in the presidency. The subsequent Presidents, who have been most successful in asserting their authority as chief executives and chief legislators, have been those who have made the most of their opportunities to appeal directly to the voters over the heads of their representatives in the Congress and of the local politicians. To the Jeffersonian and Jacksonian techniques they have added others in response to the challenge of the changing circumstances of modern times. But they have had to contend with the increased power of state and local party organizers and workers. The growth of popular interest in national elections and of popular attendance at the polls has meant greater power for the politicians who have been willing and able to do the unspectacular but essential work of keeping up the party organizations and getting out the vote.

Both chief executives and legislative leaders would have become excessively dependent upon the local politicians for their nominations and elections but for the growth also of modern methods of mass communication. The development of a cheap press and of cheaper and faster postal service and communication by telegraph, telephone, and radio, have fostered conditions favorable to the creation of public opinion by direct appeals from a single center. The telegraph encouraged a more centralized management of the major parties, the railroad facilitated greater activity by the candidates during the campaigns, the radio made possible immediate access to the voters of the whole country by the most conspicuous public men. Douglas, Blaine, and Bryan were the pioneers among presidential candidates in more active methods of campaigning. Their efforts did not bring personal success, but they helped to concentrate popular attention upon the presidential candidates and to create conditions more favorable to the exercise of centralized leadership in all phases of the process of government.

Lincoln was the first President to appreciate the possibilities of the new methods of cultivating public opinion. Theodore Roosevelt and Woodrow Wilson also shrewdly exploited the new opportunities afforded by the development of modern journalism. They pioneered in the development of the press conference, as Lincoln had pioneered in the development of relations with the great metropolitan editors.[5] Franklin D. Roosevelt made the most of the possibility of speaking directly to the people at large over the radio. These are the Presidents who have been most successful in their efforts to guide public opinion and thereby to obtain congressional support for their measures and policies. No one of them was a party leader of the first rank at the time of his nomination. All were able to make effective use of their superior access to the minds of the people in gaining the leadership of their parties and influencing the activities of the Congress.

The other occupants of the White House have been unable to dominate their parties. A few of them served parties whose congressional leaders were able to control both branches of the Congress throughout their presidential terms, thereby making possible a system of government in which the party might be held responsible for the conduct of national affairs. Presidents McKinley and Coolidge were the fortunate beneficiaries of this happy state of affairs. A greater number came into office under circumstances apparently favorable to responsible party government, but were unable with the available congressional leadership to hold the confidence of the people to the end of their terms. The loss of control of one or both of the branches of Congress at the mid-term elections put an end to the possibility of effective party government. This has been the unhappy lot of nine Presidents and of three Vice-Presidents who succeeded by accident to the presidency. Under such circumstances they were forced to choose

249

between the acceptance of such terms for a working relation with the opposition party as its leaders might be willing to grant and reverting to something like the original constitutional relation between the President and the Congress.

The Presidents who served parties possessing effective control of the Congress and who were unable to establish their personal leadership were forced, like Madison and Monroe, to submit to the leadership of their fellow partisans in the Congress or to depend on the state and local party leaders in the hope of bettering their position. When state party leaders procured their own election to the federal Senate, which became a widespread practice after the Civil War, the power of the President tended to disintegrate. This happened most conspicuously during the presidency of General Grant. The result was to deprive him of most of his authority as a chief legislator and to weaken excessively his position as chief executive. The most successful of the Presidents who have tried responsible party government was William McKinley. McKinley, like Madison, yielded reluctantly to the insistence of his congressional leaders upon a war policy, but was better pleased with their leadership on the tariff and monetary issues. He retained their confidence, and that of the people as head of the nation, and won his reëlection to a second term. Other Presidents, who were manifestly disposed to try party government, were less fortunate. The elder Harrison, Garfield, and Harding died before the consequences of their choice could become fully apparent, and Coolidge, though his party retained control of the Congress, was not rewarded with the final reëlection which, though publicly declined, he apparently would gladly have received.

Most of the Presidents who have tried party government without being able to make themselves the leaders of their party in the Congress have suffered the misfortune of seeing their party lose control of the Congress in mid-term. This was the experience of Van Buren, Polk, Fillmore, Pierce, Buchanan, Grant in his second term, Arthur, the younger Harrison, Cleveland in his second term, Taft, Hoover, and Truman in his first term. The same misfortune befell one of the Presidents who had made himself the party's leader, Woodrow Wilson, who lost his partisan majority in Congress midway in his second term. Van Buren through his influence over the state and local leaders was able to win one renomination and almost won a second, but he was not able to retain the confidence of the people as head of the nation. Polk was the most successful of these party Presidents. During the first part of his term he carried out an ambitious legislative program and pursued energetically an aggressive foreign policy, which gained much valuable territory for the nation, but did not win for himself popular confidence as the nation's head. Neither was he able to depend upon the support of the state and local party leaders, and was forced to retire at the end of his term. Pierce and Buchanan were too weak to control their parties, while their congressional leaders were too deeply interested in sectional and factional projects to gain the confidence of the nation. Thus Administrations which had seemed to start auspiciously came to bad ends. The younger Harrison, Taft, and Hoover were as coöperative with the congressional leaders as the theory of responsible party government requires, but the congressional leaders could not retain the confidence of the country and the possibility of effective party government ended in mid-term. What Grant and Cleveland might have accomplished in their second terms but for grave business panics and economic depressions it is idle to speculate. Vice-Presidents Fillmore, Arthur, and Truman came into office with their party's congressional leadership divided and the prospects for effective party government poor. Only the last was able to win a renomination and pull the bulk of his party together again.

The lack of party control of the Congress means the frustration of presidential efforts at positive leadership in the process of legislation. Hayes and Cleveland could block partisan legislation by their political opponents in the Congress and bring distinction to their Administrations by the independent use of their patronage. The former came into office with a clouded title and despite an economical and efficient Administration never established himself firmly as the head of the nation. The latter seemed to rise above partisanship to an extent that enabled him to appeal to the people over the heads of the party leaders, both congressional and state, and win two renominations and one reëlection. It was a personal triumph that could not withstand the ravages of a business crisis and factional dissension in the Congress. Both these Presidents pressed their executive authority to the limit to maintain order during great railroad strikes. Their action was particularly pleasing to capitalists but was deemed oppressive by organized labor. To the general public it seemed that the head of the nation should anticipate such troubles and seek methods of preventing what could not be happily cured. Chief executives without the support of organized parties which can share the responsibility for the conduct of public affairs bear a heavy burden. They cannot carry through positive legislative programs and the public will not be content for long with Presidents who are merely chief executives, no matter how independent and public-spirited they may be. The theory of John Adams cannot be successfully revived by Presidents whose parties meet defeat in the middle of their terms.

THE PRINCIPAL TYPES OF PARTY GOVERNMENT

The place of responsible party government in national politics is an unsettled problem of the American constitutional system. It is not even possible to say that party government expresses the normal relationship between the President and the Congress. There have been thirty complete presidential terms since the definitive establishment of the two-party system in the age of Jackson. Twelve of these terms were filled by Administrations which possessed the support of the majority parties in both branches of the Congress. During the other eighteen terms the Administrations were confronted with opposition parties in control of at least one of the branches of the Congress for at least two of the four years. From the age of Jackson to the end of the nineteenth century, effective party government was frequently impossible. Between 1829 and 1861 there was only one term in which the President and the congressional majorities were continuously of the same party. Between 1861 and 1897 there were only two such terms. In the present century stronger executive leadership has brought better opportunities for effective government by responsible parties. Nine of the thirteen terms since 1896 have seen the same party in full control of both the Presidency and the Congress.

The effectiveness of party government has depended greatly upon the character of the party leadership. When Clay, Calhoun and Webster were organizing the Whig coalition in opposition to the dominant Jacksonians, they formulated a logical theory of congressional party government. It was not the intention of the framers of the Constitution, they declared, that the President should dictate the policies of the government. His function was merely to execute the measures adopted by the representatives of the states and of the people. He might properly call to their attention the needs of the country, but it was for the legislative department of the government to agree upon the appropriate action. The executive veto was for the defense of the executive department against legislative encroachments, or in exceptional cases, as in that of Washington's veto of the first congressional apportionment bill, to protect the Constitution itself against violation. But when Jackson

252

put forth a systematic legislative program in the form of a theory of constitutional interpretation, the Whig leaders declared such a program to be an executive usurpation of legislative power. A strict construction of legislative powers by executive fiat was proclaimed an act of tyranny such as had caused the original Whigs to resist King James II and King George III. It was primarily for the congressional leaders, the great Whig Senators asserted, to define the policies of the nation and choose the measures for carrying them into effect. It would be enough for the President to take care that they be faithfully executed. Under such a theory it would have made no great difference perhaps whether the President was a member of the same party as the majority of the Congress, or of a different party, or of no party at all.

There were several objections to Clay's theory of congressional government. First, there was the theoretical objection that the Nationalist leaders in the Federal Convention were certainly not of Clay's opinion. Washington and Madison, Gouverneur Morris, Hamilton, and King, would not have been interested in securing the independence of the President and in strengthening the executive veto, if they had supposed that it would be the duty of the chief executive to submit to the wishes of the Congress in matters of policy. On the relations between the President and the Congress they would have agreed more nearly with John Adams than with Henry Clay. Secondly, there was the practical objection that Clay's theory failed to take account of the nature of Presidents. Some of them might readily submit to congressional leadership, as Madison and Monroe had generally done when Clay himself was leading the Congress from the vantage point of the speakership. But executives of Jackson's temper in dealing with opposition to his leadership, or of Lincoln's skill in reading the mind of the public, were not likely to yield authority which the Constitution, as they understood it, placed in their hands. Finally, there was the real difficulty of getting agreement among the congressional leaders on a legislative program, even when they acknowledged allegiance to the same political party, without the aid of executive influence. The diversity of interests throughout a great country, on which Madison had relied to check the abuse of power by partisan majorities in the Congress, could make sectional and factional rather than national leaders out of the most influential Congressmen and frustrate their efforts to take a national view of national problems.

There was also the point of view of the public to be considered. Congressional ascendancy would naturally be the aim of Congress-

253

men, but would the public be pleased with figureheads as heads of the nation? Dictatorial and tyrannical behavior by a President might be expected to cause a reaction in favor of more power for the Congress, but would partisans who took the trouble to put their chosen candidate at the head of the government be satisfied with an administration without influence on the determination of policies? Party government is a device which must be justified by its works. If a national party is in fact an effective instrument for making the government under the Constitution more popular than the framers planned it to be, partisans doubtless will not be greatly concerned how power is actually distributed between the President and the Congress. But circumstances prevent a decision at a general election on much more than the personalities of the candidates and the general character of the competing bodies of partisans. An election cannot register a clear decision on more than one issue, unless the voters happen to divide in the same way on different issues in all sections of the country. In a country with such diversified interests as the United States, that is unlikely.

Party leaders have difficulty in defining a paramount issue so clearly that the victorious candidates receive an unmistakable mandate from the voters to adopt particular measures. The internal conflicts within parties may even cause the party leaders to evade the issues that are uppermost in the voters' minds and most hotly controversial. The platforms of major parties are apt to be characterized by the deliberate obfuscation of major issues, while declaring their positions plainly on local and trivial matters. Even if a general election seems to settle an important public issue, new issues not considered during the campaign may quickly arise after the election. They may even dominate the political scene at the national capital throughout the following presidential term. The voters must trust their President and Congress with a wide and indeterminate discretion. The President, as the only important public officer for whom all the enfranchised people may vote, holds the most favorable position for taking the lead in the determination of public policy.

It is not surprising that party government has been more popular under presidential leadership than under that of the congressional party chieftains. The Whig coalition leaders had their great opportunity after the election of Harrison and Tyler in 1840. Calhoun, however, had abandoned the coalition before the election, and Tyler abandoned it after his succession to the presidency. Clay and his fellow Whigs in the Congress were able to carry through their tariff policy, but failed miserably through the accident of Harrison's death to carry through their money and banking measures. The variety of interests in the Whig coalition made the party, as originally organized, unmanageable. United in opposition, in office divided, it proved an ineffective instrument for the execution of a program which the people would support at the mid-term election. The Whigs never found a second opportunity to try their theory of party government under congressional leadership.

The Jacksonian Democrats of course could not approve the Whig theory, but circumstances constrained them to act upon it. Of the successors to Jackson, only Polk manifested anything like his initiative and determination. Under Pierce and Buchanan the party leaders in the Congress took charge of the legislative program and quickly discovered, like the Whigs before them, the difficulty of coördinating the factions within the party without the aid of skillful executive leadership. Ambitious and influential Senators, of whom Jefferson Davis and Stephen A. Douglas achieved the greatest prominence, could not put an acceptable program together. They could only tear their party apart. At the election of 1860 its two major factions went their separate ways. To hold the party, and the country, together something more was required than the Whig theory of responsible party government.

The Antislavery Republicans came into office with a strong infusion of the Whig spirit. But they inherited also enough of the spirit of the Jacksonian Democrats to insure a struggle for the leadership, if the party was to govern. Circumstances threw upon the young party a heavier responsibility for governing than any of its predecessors had been called upon to bear. Lincoln's readiness to assume the burden of leadership is clearly reflected in his annual messages to the Congress. The determination of the congressional leaders to assert their authority was disclosed by the establishment of the Joint Committee on the Conduct of the War and the passage of the bill to control the reconstruction of the seceded states. Lincoln killed the reconstruction bill with a pocket veto, and exerted his executive powers to the utmost to keep the process of reconstruction as well as the conduct of the war in his own hands. The exigencies of war favored the ascendancy of the chief executive, and Lincoln's tragic death prevented an extension of the contest into the period of reconstruction. Neither Johnson nor Grant was a match for the congressional leaders, and party government under congressional leadership won its greatest triumphs for the Radical Republicans. But they could not prevent the business panic of 1873 nor the ensuing loss of control of the Congress.

The Republicans had another opportunity to try party government after the election of 1888. The congressional leaders were veterans at party management. Speaker Reed and Ways and Means Committee Chairman McKinley stood out in the House of Representatives, and in the upper chamber there was a galaxy of experienced Senators. A compliant Administration concurred in raising the tariff, inflating the currency, attacking "trusts" and other combinations in restraint of trade, admitting small Western states most of whose voters might be expected to support the Republican Party, handing out bigger pensions to members of the Grand Army of the Republic, and renewing the effort to get out the Negro vote in the South. These measures were agreeable to the principal factions of what was becoming known as the Grand Old Party, but displeasing to the public as a whole. The congressional leadership was repudiated at the polls in the mid-term election by unprecedented majorities and two years later the President was defeated for reëlection.

The Democrats, who in 1892 won simultaneous control of the Presidency and the Congress for the first time in thirty-six years, demonstrated, like the Whigs under Clay, Webster, and Calhoun, how much easier it is for a national party to coördinate its component factions in opposition than in power. President Cleveland was able by an extraordinary effort to procure the repeal of the inflationary Sherman Silver Purchase Act, but he could not procure the enactment of a satisfactory tariff-reform law. Protectionist Democrats contended with free-trade Democrats, Gold Democrats with Silver Democrats, Administration Democrats with anti-Administration Democrats, and at the mid-term elections the country turned violently against the party's candidates for Congress. The Southern wing of the party had been gratified by the repeal of legislation authorizing federal intervention in elections in the South, but the Northern capitalistic and Western agrarian wings were profoundly disgusted with one another. The political situation was ripe for a realignment of parties in the next campaign.

The Conservative Republicans came into power in 1897 after a superheated campaign in which no legislative issue was decided except that a majority of the people did not want free coinage of silver dollars at the ratio of sixteen ounces of silver to one of gold. Another compliant Administration concurred again promptly in raising the tariff and eventually in establishing the single gold standard of currency value. It also concurred in a war against Spain and in the acquisition of dependent territory overseas. The congressional leaders held control of the Party until Theodore Roosevelt, after popular endorsement of his Administration at the polls in 1904, was able to challenge their unprogressive leadership and, with some aid from the opposition, to set the Party on a new course with the Employers Liability, Railroad Rate Regulation, and Pure Food and Drug Acts. The new division between Progressive and Conservative Republicans culminated in the disruption of the Party before the end of the Taft Administration. The most important portions of the Party's legislative measures were enacted during the period of presidential leadership. With the renewal of congressional leadership in the Taft Administration the coördination of the capitalistic and agrarian wings of the party proved increasingly difficult. Speaker Cannon, Ways and Means Committee Chairman Payne, and Senators Aldrich, Platt, Penrose, and associates understood well enough how to look after the interests of their sections of the country and of their factions within the Party, but they were less successful in keeping the various components of the Party in balance and maintaining the ascendancy of the Party as a whole.

Under Woodrow Wilson the Democratic congressional leaders were content to follow the confident and vigorous leadership of the President. By a skillfully planned series of measures the chief executive, acting as chief legislator, gratified the reasonable expectations of the various interests within the Party. The tariff was reduced, the banking system reformed, fair competition in industry encouraged, agriculture fostered, the hours of labor on the railroads limited, and a valiant attempt was made to improve the conditions of child labor. The Northern, Southern, and Western sections of the Party were better coördinated than at any time since the age of Jackson. The opportunity for a trial of party government seemed extraordinarily favorable.

Since the Democratic Party at the beginning of the Wilson Administration did not comprise a clear majority of the nation, it could not remain in power solely by the successful coördination of the Democratic factions. Its candidate had received little more than 40 per cent of the popular vote in 1912 and had been elected because the Republican Party was divided against itself. If the opposition to the Wilson Administration should be reunited under either Conservative or Progressive Republican leadership, the Democrats would be turned out again. Wilson's problem as head of a party government was not only to hold together the various factions of his own party but also to win over a portion of the opposition. His exclusively partisan Administration,

257

however, made no room for the leaders of any disaffected Republican faction. Unpredictable events prevented the opposition from reuniting under Republican leadership in 1916, and the suspension of partisan politics when the President led the country into war postponed the definitive test of Wilson's theory of party government until the close of hostilities. The resumption of a policy of strict partisanship by direction of the President himself at the mid-term elections of 1918, together with his stubborn attempt to make a partisan issue out of the terms of peace, discredited his leadership and opened the road for the return of the Republicans to power. The Democratic National Convention of 1920 rebuked the President by refusing to nominate any member of his Administration as his successor, and an unprecedented majority of the voters brought the reaction against Democratic Party government to a climax by electing an unknown Republican Senator to the presidency.

Woodrow Wilson's career offers an interesting study in the relations between the President and the Congress under the Constitution. As a young political theorist he had been deeply impressed by the inability of the contemporary Presidents to assert their authority against the pretensions of the congressional leaders. The need for responsible party government seemed to be great at a time when there was little of it, and the record seemed to show that the congressional leaders were more capable of filling the need than the kind of partisans who might be able to reach the presidency through the support of state and local politicians. When in the early eighteen-eighties he wrote his brilliant book on *Congressional Government*, he was convinced that an effort should be made to clear the path for more effective party government by the congressional leaders. By the time he himself was ready to seek the presidency a quarter century later, he had changed his mind. Theodore Roosevelt had already discovered the possibility of establishing the presidential independence of both congressional leaders and local politicians by appealing directly to the rank and file of the party in the country.

Wilson sketched this new theory of the presidency and of party government in his book, *Constitutional Government in the United States*,[6] written shortly before his entrance into active politics. At that time "progressive" politicians, regardless of party, expected that the new direct-primary laws and the direct election of Senators would subvert the foundations of political machines, particularly those operated by state leaders who were also United States Senators, and strengthen the chief executive by putting him in more direct contact

258

with the sources of partisan power. In Wilson's campaigns for the presidency and in his exercise of his official powers he attempted to reduce to practice the theory of party government under presidential leadership. Indeed, he practiced it too deliberately and systematically. His party associates followed him as long as he was successful, but too many of the people of the country resented what seemed to them an excess of partisanship. They wanted as head of the nation a statesman who would be more than a head of a party.

The congressional leaders of the Republican Party had another opportunity to try party government under congressional leadership during the next decade of Republican supremacy at Washington. They were successful in holding the factions of the Party together, until the great business depression dispelled the myth that the Republicans were the party of prosperity, but their record of achievement in the field of legislation was meager. They raised the tariff twice, lowered other taxes, and reduced the public debt, but they permitted an unprecedented inflation of credit currency. The former policy was gratifying to the producing interests which had traditionally supported protective-tariff legislation, but the latter should have disturbed those who had accepted the Republican claim to be the party of sound money. These policies stimulated speculation, but subverted the foundations of permanent prosperity. The most influential party leaders, representing factions which appeared to profit by this so-called return to normalcy, were unwilling to take effective action to keep the economy in balance. The establishment of the Federal Farm Board, in order that the Administration itself might apply the techniques of speculative capitalistic business enterprise to the stabilization of the market for agricultural products, was a feeble harbinger of a policy of national planning in the public interest. In general, the party leaders disparaged the capacity of government agencies, even when directed by their own Administration, to compensate by official action for the deficiencies of private business enterprise.

The nature of the emergency after the election of 1932 and the character of the new President conspired to discourage further experimentation with the theory of party government under congressional leadership. The Democratic congressional leaders were more hospitable than their Republican predecessors to vigorous governmental action and the new Administration was full of enterprise and self-confidence. The congressional leaders had learned the theory of party government under presidential leadership from Woodrow Wilson. Franklin D.

259

Roosevelt could profit by the experience of his precursors in putting the theory into practice. He enjoyed better technical facilities than Woodrow Wilson for explaining his policies to the people and securing their confidence and support. He established better working relations with the state, and especially the big city, leaders. He could be more tactful than his former chief, whose technique he had had an excellent opportunity of observing from close range, in dealing with the congressional leaders.

Franklin D. Roosevelt also understood better than Wilson the lessons of the experiment in party government under presidential leadership conducted by Theodore Roosevelt. The first Roosevelt had been determined to carry the case for his legislative program over the heads of congressional and state party leaders to the people and, like Wilson, he had visualized the great abstraction called The People in the image of the average man. But Wilson's average man tended also to be an abstraction, whereas Theodore Roosevelt thought of the average man in more concrete terms, a small businessman, an independent farmer working his own quarter section of land, a skilled mechanic, miner, or railroad trainman. Wilson always spoke to his average man in formal addresses full of elegant but impersonal diction; the two Roosevelts spoke to the various kinds of real people in more familiar terms. The second Roosevelt, equipped with radio, even spoke to them personally in their own homes. Thus the Roosevelts could make more of their roles as heads of the nation and not merely heads of a party governing the nation.

Franklin D. Roosevelt moreover possessed a clearer sense than Woodrow Wilson of the limitations of party government. He sedulously avoided a repetition of Wilson's mistake in making a party issue out of an international policy. There is an excellent practical as well as the obvious patriotic reason for stopping partisanship at the water's edge. Foreign policies often require ratification in the form of treaties and the treaty-making power cannot be exercised without the consent of at least two-thirds of the Senate. Since political parties ordinarily do not possess two-thirds majorities in the Senate, and cannot expect to gain such majorities by ordinary partisan victories at the polls, it is unwise to make a partisan issue out of a policy which can be defeated by an ordinary partisan opposition in the Congress. When in 1940 President Roosevelt recognized the existence of a national emergency, caused by the war in Europe, he brought eminent Republicans into important positions in his Cabinet and put his foreign policy, both for war and for peace, on a bipartisan basis. Party government continued in matters of domestic policy, but its importance was overshadowed by that of government in international affairs upon the original constitutional model.

During the war there was a tendency to revert towards party government under congressional leadership in matters not closely related to the conduct of the war or the planning of the peace. The President delegated a portion of his authority to a Director of Economic Stabilization and later a larger portion to a Director of War Mobilization. This officer, whose authority was further enlarged by act of Congress establishing the Office of War Mobilization and Reconversion, not only adjusted conflicts of authority between executive agencies but also functioned as chief legislator in matters not brought to the personal attention of the President. Former Senator and Supreme Court Justice Byrnes was disposed both by temperament and by experience to share his power with the congressional leaders. The difficulty of coördinating the Democratic factions without vigorous executive leadership was again discovered, and Director Byrnes's resignation on the eve of the President's death attested once more the limitations of party government under congressional leadership. The disposition to press the claims of the congressional leaders, however, naturally prevails whenever the circumstances appear to be favorable, and the succession of a Vice-President without experience in the field of international politics facilitated a transfer of the leadership in the peacemaking to the congressional leaders of both parties. The defeat of the Democrats at the mid-term elections in 1946 encouraged the Republican congressional leaders to assert their authority more confidently, and by the summer of 1947 Republican Senators were denouncing a threat of a presidential veto of a tax-reduction bill as an "impropriety." The trend was distinctly toward a revival of the early Whig theory of party government under congressional leadership.

The Jacksonian and Whig theories of party government clashed head-on in the Eightieth Congress. The Republican congressional leaders in House and Senate pursued their legislative program with vigorous, if not always well-coördinated, energy. The President retaliated with an uncompromising use of his executive veto. The congressional leaders held their party lines intact and, aided by conservative Democrats, chiefly from the South, reënacted their principal measures over the veto. The Republican National Convention of 1948, apparently uncertain about public reaction to the practical expression

261

of the Whig theory, passed over the congressional leaders for the presidential nomination, and selected a candidate who held aloof from the struggle at Washington. The Democratic National Convention, apparently distrustful of popular approval for a revival of the Jacksonian-Rooseveltian theory of party government, sought a candidate not closely connected with the Administration. Unable to find an acceptable candidate other than the man in the White House, who had forced the issue between the two kinds of party government, the Convention made a virtue of necessity and renominated President Truman. The Democratic candidate took his case to the people with all the vigor of an Andrew Johnson and with far more tact and finesse. The Republican candidate seemed to patronize the Republican Congress without effectively defending it. The people preferred the Jacksonian-Rooseveltian type of party government to that of Henry Clay, Daniel Webster, and John C. Calhoun. Thus history repeated itself and a new phase was reached in the cycle of party government.

Since the final establishment of the two-party system in national politics there has been a recurrent cycle of change in the relations between the President and the Congress. Periods of party government under presidential leadership have alternated with periods of party government under congressional leadership, separated from each other by periods of government without effective party leadership of any kind. It is not possible to say that any of these types of government is more normal than others.[7] What is normal is the ebb and flow of the leadership from the White House to Capitol Hill and back again. Sometimes one is in the ascendant, sometimes the other, and often neither. Since the beginning of the present century the periods of party government have been longer than before and presidential leadership has been more impressive than congressional leadership. But government without clear and effective partisan responsibility has occurred often enough to qualify it for a regular place in the political cycle. Under the Constitution there may be both responsible party government and government without benefit of any partisan responsibility. At times the opposition in the Congress is free to oppose the party in power as factiously as it pleases, and at other times it has to share the responsibility for the conduct of the government. At such times party politicians may not be sure which are the "ins" and which are the "outs." But it is clear enough what the framers of the Constitution originally intended. They intended that the chief executive should be primarily responsible for the conduct of public affairs, but that he was not to govern without the consent of the governed expressed by appropriate majorities in the two branches of the Congress.

THE SUPERIORITY OF PRESIDENTIAL OVER CONGRESSIONAL LEADERSHIP

There are several reasons why party government should be more successful under presidential leadership than under congressional leadership. First, the President is in a better position than the congressional leaders to take the initiative in the determination of policy. The Congress has to do its thinking, so to speak, out loud. While engaged in the process of making up its mind it seems to be suffering an agony of indecision. These protracted and at times interminable debates impair public confidence in the legislative capacity of the responsible party.

The congressional party leaders can secure greater privacy for their preliminary discussions of policy by resort to party caucuses or, as Republican Senators prefer to say, party conferences. But the obligations of participation in congressional caucuses are debatable and the guarantee of privacy imperfect. Dissatisfied partisans are quick to disclose the nature of the proceedings to the public and may even repudiate party leadership which cracks the party whip too harshly. The Senate Democrats recognize the right of any Democratic Senator to vote against the decision of the caucus, if he has made contrary pledges to his constituents during his campaign for election, or has received contrary instructions from his state government, or believes the proposed party action to be in conflict with the Constitution. Members of both parties recognize the right of a Congressman to stay away from a caucus and thereby reserve a greater freedom of action for himself. Caucuses have been used for the purpose of determining a partisan policy more frequently in the House than in the Senate, perhaps because the rules of the House make it easier for the leaders to carry out its decisions, but there seems to be no disposition to strengthen its authority and make it a more effective instrument of party leadership. In the Senate the party conferences seem to be held in the hope of reaching a general agreement by free discussion rather than by imposing the decision of a majority of a party upon a minority. They are as likely to be called for the purpose of supporting presidential leadership as of imposing a decision of the congressional leaders upon the President. The congressional caucus has made no headway in recent years as a device for strengthening the position of the congressional leaders in the leadership of the parties.[8]

The President, on the other hand, does his thinking in private, and need not disclose the trend of his thoughts until he is ready to announce a decision. Then a vigorous message to the Congress or a thoughtful answer to a question at a press conference can create an impression of deliberation and decisiveness which gives him an advantage over the members of Congress in their public appearances. The President possesses also more solid advantages over the Congressmen. He has direct access to the immense resources of the executive departments, particularly their sources of information, and enjoys the privilege of utilizing this information before it becomes available to Congressmen. The latter of course may collect information through their committee hearings, but this information is ordinarily received in public and gives the committeemen no priority in use over the executive.

The President possesses the further advantage of private consultation with an official Cabinet. Its members, inexperienced as they may be when they first receive their appointments, direct permanent establishments officered by experts and technicians of many kinds and may be aided by professional staffs of high competence. They are in a position to become valuable advisers on problems of administration and may also become useful adjuncts to the President in the exercise of his functions as chief legislator. There were deep differences of opinion in the Federal Convention concerning the functions of presidential advisers. Some members wanted to establish an executive council, which should keep a record of its advice to the President and serve as a check upon his activities. Such a council would have caused a serious division of the executive authority and might have tipped the balance heavily toward congressional supremacy over the President. But in the end those delegates who wanted an independent and powerful chief executive prevailed. The members of the Cabinet were placed under an obligation to render opinions, when requested by the President, but were excluded from any effective participation in his authority. They may obtain such influence over him as their talents permit, but they hold their offices at his pleasure. They are presidential assistants, not colleagues.

The effect of a Cabinet upon the relations between the President and the Congress depends upon the policy of the President and the character of the Cabinet. Some Presidents have brought into their Cabinets the most influential party leaders that were available, including their own rivals for the presidential nomination. Lincoln's Cabinet is the outstanding example of such an arrangement.[9] Seward and Chase had been leading candidates for the nomination; Cameron and Bates were also in the running at the nominating convention. Contemporary observers expected a struggle within the Cabinet to dominate the Administration. If any one of its members had gained the ascendancy, he would have sought to consolidate his power by intrigue with his followers in the Congress, and the authority of the presidency would have suffered. When Lincoln succeeded in establishing his own leadership in the Cabinet, his success immensely strengthened him in his relations with the Congress. It was a long time before new congressional leaders could gain the prestige previously enjoyed by Seward and Chase. Meanwhile, Lincoln's leadership of the party and of the government had been secured. His Administration had to contend with a sea of troubles, but he remained master of the ship of state.

No President has ventured as far as Lincoln in surrounding himself with his chief rivals for the party leadership, but several, weaker and less confident of themselves than Lincoln, have brought into their Cabinets some one of the principal party leaders with an evident purpose of making him the leader of the Administration. Garfield and the younger Harrison brought James G. Blaine into their Cabinets under such circumstances. The results were unhappy. Garfield's appointment of Blaine precipitated a bitter feud among the party leaders and Harrison's resulted eventually in such a sense of frustration on Blaine's part that he challenged his chief's leadership at the next national convention of their party. Woodrow Wilson was a stronger personality than either Garfield or Harrison, but he felt constrained to give William Jennings Bryan the first place in his Cabinet. Bryan became discontented with Wilson's leadership even more quickly than Blaine with Harrison's, but neither's resignation greatly affected the fortunes of the Administration. Wilson's leadership was too vigorous to be subverted by Bryan's defection and Harrison's was so ineffective that Blaine's defection could not make its prospects worse. Harding also put outstanding party leaders into his Cabinet. One of them eventually reached the presidency on his own merits, but none could save Harding from himself. There is no clear evidence that any of these party leaders, who entered a presidential Cabinet in order to strengthen the Administration in its relations with the Congress, contributed greatly to that result except by the efficient management of the affairs of his own department.

Most Presidents have included in their Cabinets one or more members or former members of the Congress in order to get the benefit of their knowledge of congressional methods of business and of their personal acquaintance with influential Congressmen. Such appointments, though not strictly speaking a part of a presidential design for power, have often been helpful in facilitating good working relations with the congressional leaders and have thereby contributed to the political success of the Administration. Franklin D. Roosevelt was particularly happy in his original selections from the Congress for his Cabinet. His attitude toward the Congress materially aided him in establishing his leadership at the beginning of his Administration. But Presidents have to consider also, in selecting the members of their Cabinets, the claims of the various elements within the party and of the various sections of the country. The Presidents have done most badly who, like General Grant, filled their Cabinets with personal friends, regardless of political or administrative considerations, and have done best when, like Governor Hayes and Theodore Roosevelt, they chose as their advisers men with exceptional qualifications for the work of the particular offices which they were to fill. Few Presidents, however, find themselves free to make many Cabinet appointments primarily on grounds of personal merit and administrative fitness. In general the most useful Cabinets have been those with the most administrative competence and the most useful Cabinet members have been those who could handle most effectively their own particular legislative problems with the appropriate congressional committees.

To what extent the Presidents' Cabinets have functioned effectively as presidential advisers does not appear from any official records. Though the Constitution authorizes the Presidents to require the opinions of Cabinet officers in writing, and President Washington adopted that practice in several important instances, later Presidents have preferred greater informality in their consultations with Cabinet officers. The proceedings at Cabinet meetings are supposed to be confidential, and the tendency for Cabinet secrets to leak out with impressive promptitude must discourage Presidents from discussing the most controversial topics in the presence of full meetings of their Cabinets. The published memoirs of former Cabinet officers suggest that different Presidents have utilized their Cabinets in different ways. Miss Perkins's disclosures concerning the Roosevelt Cabinets reveal the gradual disillusionment of the "chief" with that body as a general

266

political council and a growing disposition to utilize its meetings as a convenient opportunity to consider the particular problems of individual members. For advice concerning legislative policy the President turned more and more to private conferences at the White House with the party leaders in the Congress.

The framers of the Constitution, particularly the Nationalist leaders, did not expect much from the Cabinet as a body of councilors, and the results appear to be consistent with their expectations. If a Cabinet is reasonably harmonious, its existence should strengthen rather than weaken the President in his relation with the Congress. If not harmonious, a strong President will get rid of it and, like Jackson, get himself a new one capable of greater helpfulness. John Adams was slow in reconstructing his Cabinet, and his relations with the Congress were impaired thereby. James Buchanan was much too slow, and his place in history has suffered accordingly. Cabinet officers possessing special skill in utilizing their congressional contacts have been of material aid to strong Presidents in the development of their legislative problems. Most Presidents have been best served when they have had as members of their Cabinets men who could handle efficiently the business of their own departments.

In modern times there has been a growing tendency toward the establishment of more systematic and intimate arrangements for the exchange of political information and advice between the Presidents and the congressional leaders. Calvin Coolidge's White House breakfasts with the party leaders of the House and Senate marked a stage in the development of a relationship which might easily be institutionalized. Franklin D. Roosevelt carried further the practice of frequent consultations at the White House between himself and the party leaders in the House and Senate. The La Follette-Monroney Committee, which prepared the way for the Legislative Reorganization Act of 1946, suggested in its report the formation of a joint legislative-executive council by means of which better working relations between the legislative and executive branches of the government might be fostered. This scheme was thwarted by the opposition of the party leaders in the House of Representatives. Whether such a scheme, if adopted, would strengthen the chief executive or the congressional leaders is not clear. The result would probably depend largely upon personal factors. But such a planned institution for the better management of party government would be an improvement over the Cabinet, regarded as a council for the President in his role as chief legislator, and could hardly fail under ordinary circumstances to improve the legislative process at Washington.

A third reason why party government under presidential leadership should be more successful than under congressional leadership lies in the nature of the presidential and congressional electoral systems. The President is elected by a process which compels him to pay particular attention to the state of opinion in the big doubtful states. These are states with predominantly urban and industrial populations. Their interests are more limited than those of the country as a whole and the class structure of their populations is more typical of the modern neotechnical age. The middle classes dominate the political scene, as nearly always and everywhere in the United States, but the urban middle class is more highly developed and the rural middle class relatively less important than in most of the smaller and less doubtful states. These conditions tend to influence the political thinking and partisan planning of the President. They facilitate the development of clear and consistent legislative programs by enterprising chief executives.

The congressional leaders, on the other hand, represent every kind of state, large and small, urban and rural, doubtful and close or strongly partisan, and reflect the greater variety of interests and political attitudes in the forty-eight states of the Union. The natural limits to the power of numerical majorities on the great stage of national politics limit the practical capacity of the congressional leaders to get together on a party program as clearly defined and logically consistent as that of the President. Party programs are designed more particularly for presidential than for congressional elections and serve better to help candidates for the presidency to get into office than to guide the action of the Congress between campaigns. They have a substantial, even though imponderable, effect in putting the power of public opinion behind successful presidential candidates and sustaining his authority in contests with congressional leaders for influence over the legislative process. Party government will naturally tend to work better under presidential than under-congressional leadership, as long as Presidents continue to be elected by presidential electors chosen in each state on a general ticket by a plurality of the popular votes. While the principle of natural limits to partisan power tends to impair the authority of partisan majorities in the Congress, the principle of the political mean tends to enhance the authority of Presidents.

Despite the superior advantages of the President over his fellow partisans in the Congress in a struggle for leadership in a system of party government there will be times when congressional leadership prevails. Presidents differ in natural aptitude for leadership and up to now those with the capacity to dominate their parties have been the exception rather than the rule. The method of nominating candidates for the presidency favors the selection of a standard-bearer, both for the "ins" and for the "outs," from outside the ranks of the congressional leaders. If elected, he must be strong enough to force his leadership upon Senators and Representatives who, except for members of the party in power under a strong President, have been accustomed to look elsewhere than to the White House for the direction of the party. Standard-bearers who seem bent on asserting their personal authority if raised to the presidency, like Wendell Willkie, are thrust aside at the first opportunity. More accommodating personalities, when available, are preferred. The public, too, after a period of submission to strong leadership, seems to crave a change to leadership which, if less spectacular, is also less exacting.

Some critics of the American system of party government have argued in favor of changes designed to foster more continuous and more powerful presidential leadership. Harold J. Laski, in his widely read book on *The American Presidency*, put the case for these critics most persuasively. He concluded that, in order to make presidential leadership as effective as he thought it should be, there must be a realignment of the major parties on a more logical basis. Specifically, he deemed essential a reconstruction of parties which would result in a socialistic labor party confronting a Tory conservative party, as in Great Britain.[10] The answer to this argument is obvious. In the nature of things the alignment of parties in the United States cannot be so logical as Professor Laski desired. The soundness of Madison's third principle of government, as modified in response to the development of a two-party system in a middle-class body politic, insures that any practicable division of the whole body of people into two major parties will exhibit the dominant traits of the existing partisan alignment.[11]

A more realistic criticism of the American system of party government emphasizes the evils which attend the conduct of public affairs by a President who is confronted with hostile majorities in the Congress. Laski himself has described these evils with impressive lucidity. The President's position, he wrote, "will, naturally, be immensely more difficult when the opposition party controls one or both of the houses. Then, the whole interest of the opposition is to paralyze the presidential office in order to have the best possible chance of victory at the next election. How devastating that situation can be was decisively shown in the last two years of President Wilson's second Administration." [12] This kind of criticism does not necessarily call for stronger executive leadership. It does call for the establishment of greater harmony between the executive and legislative branches of the government under some suitable arrangement of their mutual relations.

It is not the structure of the major parties that requires improvement so much as the legislative processes and the management of the relations between the President and the Congress. Walter Lippmann has discussed this persistent problem of party government at Washington with luminous insight.[13] "Once again," he wrote, apropos of the question of presidential power versus congressional control raised by President Roosevelt's proposal of the lend-lease bill in 1941, "in dealing with the lease-lend bill, we are confronted with the perennial difficulty of the American government. It is how to relate the Presidency and the Congress so that the Executive may have adequate power and the Legislature may have adequate control . . . No one can read the record of the unending conflict between the President and the Congress without realizing, it seems to me, that the lack of a working arrangement between them exposes our government to continual trouble. We have not found a way to give the President his necessary powers without impairing the control of Congress. And we have not found a way to give Congress control without depriving the President of essential power . . . A sound relation will exist only when Congress takes the view that the way to exercise its functions is not to deprive the President of power but to increase the power of Congress to hold him accountable. Congress will never grow strong by weakening the President but only by strengthening itself." There is no adequate reply to this criticism except to improve the organization and procedure of the Congress and to strengthen its contacts with the President.

From the point of view of the general public those contentious and apparently unproductive periods, when a hostile Congress faces a frustrated President, are not a total loss. Such periods of dissension and obstruction generally mark an interval between periods of effective party government, during which many of the less resolutely partisan members of the public are trying to make up their minds whether to continue to support the "ins" or to switch their votes to the "outs" in the battle of the parties. Time so occupied may be usefully employed. If the public makes up its mind promptly, as in the latter part of the

Hoover Administration, the delay may well be justified by the event. Had the Roosevelt Administration come into power in 1930 instead of in 1932, its mandate for vigorous action would have been less clear and popular support for its policy of bold experimentation more uncertain. When the people are unable to make a decisive choice between the parties for a long time, as happened during the last quarter of the nineteenth century, party government seems excessively unstable and unsatisfactory. But under ordinary circumstances two years is not an excessively long time for a deliberate change of mind by fifty million voters.

Actually such periods of partisan deadlock during the last half-century have been neither numerous nor long protracted. The most significant fact about these periods is their infrequency under strong Presidents and their regularity under Presidents who have been unable to secure the leadership of their parties. Woodrow Wilson was the only President who successfully asserted his authority as party leader and whose party lost control of the Congress while he remained in office. Under the Presidents who were unable to establish their primacy among the party leaders in the Congress, party government broke down in almost every case before the end of their terms. Among such Presidents since the time of Madison and Monroe — except for those who died in office — only Calvin Coolidge was able to finish his period of service as chief executive without his party's losing control of the Congress. Congressional party leadership left a dozen of the weaker chief executives without effective party support before their final retirement from office.

Apparently the public distrusts, or at least dislikes, party government under congressional leadership.[14] Despite the tendency of the public to turn after a time for relief from strong presidential leadership, it cannot long endure weakness in the presidential office. The traditional system of checks and balances may offend the taste of political critics who admire the smooth flow of concentrated and unchecked power. But systems of concentrated and unchecked power, as modern history makes painfully clear, are dangerous. By centralizing the machinery for the nomination of party candidates for the Congress monolithic parties might be produced, but such parties would be inhospitable to the free enterprise system in politics. The American system of legislative-executive relations is well suited to the needs of a people who wish to keep the political branches of their government from getting out of popular control.

THE SEPARATION OF POWERS UNDER THE PARTY SYSTEM

It is easy to exaggerate the importance of party government under the American constitutional system. Party government is a convenient kind of government, when it is working smoothly, but it is not indispensable. Under party government the Congress may act as the agent of a partisan program, and by so doing may give a more popular cast to the government than was planned by the framers. But the Congress also acts as a more or less fair sample of the public, reaching its decisions as the public itself might do, if capable of direct action, without much regard for the partisan affiliations of its members. Thus during periods when party government is impossible legislation of general public interest may nevertheless be enacted. Indeed, such legislation is constantly being enacted at all times with the support of majorities of both parties in both branches of the Congress. The careful reports published in the *Congressional Quarterly* since the beginning of the Seventy-ninth Congress show separately for all members of Congress their participation both in party votes and in votes where the prevailing majorities included majorities of both parties. During the Seventy-ninth Congress (1945–46) important bipartisan votes were more numerous than important partisan votes. The United Nations Participation Act, the Employment Act, the Administrative Procedure Act, the Legislative Reorganization Act, and the Atomic Energy Act, to mention only some of the most important, were bipartisan measures which stood out in the flow of legislation. In the Eightieth Congress (1947–48) the relations between the parties were reversed, and the important bipartisan votes occurred chiefly in the field of foreign affairs. The most important controversial measures in the field of domestic policy were carried by partisan votes. The Tax Reduction and Labor-Management Relations Acts, however, through partisan measures, were carried over the presidential veto by bipartisan combinations in both branches of the Congress. The legislative process was one in which partisan responsibility and congressional responsibility for action as a fair sample of the public seemed to be inextricably mixed.

Political analysts have tried to estimate by statistical methods the relative importance of partisanship and of other factors in the legislative process. Several painstaking investigations have thrown fresh light on the forces which produce majorities for the acts of Congress.[15] It is clear that, as would be expected, the relative influence of Presidents and of congressional majorities on the legislative product has

272

fluctuated along with the changes in the character of Presidents, the partisan composition of Congresses, and the temper of the times. There is much evidence tending to show that the role of organized special interests and other pressure groups in the legislative process is more important than that of the political parties. The latter exert a decisive influence on the fortunes of the comparatively few measures for which the majority party has received a clear mandate from the voters. The former are more influential in the deliberations on the numerous controversial measures in dealing with which the Congress acts as a sample of the whole public rather than as a mandatary of a political party. In modern times the lobby has definitely surpassed the party caucus and conference as a factor in the determination of legislative policy.

Statistical investigations cannot solve problems so imponderable as the assignment of weight to all the various factors bearing upon the action of the lawmakers. The influence of public opinion, of bureaucratic planners, of pressures from organized special interests, of the peculiarities of House and Senate procedure, and of the personalities of the lawmakers themselves, all have an effect which varies from case to case. Detailed study of the enactment of any highly controversial public general legislation discloses the infinite variety of circumstances among which the lawmakers operate. No more difficult task than the making of wise laws confronts the human intellect. There is no standard pattern for the legislative process whether under presidential or congressional leadership.

The record shows that party government works unevenly in different fields of legislative policy. It works best in the field of economic policy. Measures designed to promote, or at least to protect, the economic interests of the particular sectional, regional, or local bodies of people, which furnish the leading contingents to the alliance of interests comprising the economic basis of a major party, are well suited for use in its legislative program. Party government does not work so well in other fields of legislative policy. The people of the country divide in various ways upon the issues which affect them otherwise than in their pocketbooks. There is little probability that a partisan alignment of interests on the tariff will hold fast on aid to veterans or the regulation of the liquor traffic. Even economic issues are unsuitable for use as party issues, if they divide the particular bodies of people who ordinarily are united in support of the same party. A tax which discriminates in favor of butter and against margarine may be pleasing to Republican dairymen in the hay-and-pasture belt, but it offends Re-

273

publican breadwinners in the cities. A wages-and-hours law may please Democratic wage earners everywhere, but it will not be so well received by Democratic farmers and businessmen.

There is general agreement on the superiority of bipartisanship over government by the majority party alone in the field of foreign policy. The national interest is prior to the interest of any combination of sectional or local pressure groups operating under the banner of a major political party. The national interest is also better served in many areas of domestic policy by a legislative process which permits the determination of policy by temporary combinations of organized special interests instead of the permanent combinations which form the economic foundations of major parties. The only interests which can count for much in national politics are organized interests. But there are other useful forms of organization besides the partisan. The farm bloc of the nineteen-twenties and nineteen-thirties illustrated a form of organization, cutting across regular party lines, which could play a legitimate part in the practical business of lawmaking.[16] "Pressure politics" is generally nonpartisan, and "pressures" can be managed better by the lawmakers if kept out of partisan politics. A government which does not manage "pressures" effectively has to that extent abdicated its legislative function. They can be managed more effectively by Congress as a whole than by any part of Congress, even that part operating as the majority party.

The evidence accumulated during a century and a half of partisan conflict supports the warnings against intemperate party spirit and excessive partisanship uttered by President Washington in his "Farewell Address." The organization of parties on a geographical basis, which he deplored, was inevitable under a system of representative government based on territorial units of representation, and party spirit was certain to be intense under a system of two major parties in free competition with one another for control of the government. But the utility of partisanship in the field of legislative policy is so narrowly limited that the strengthening of party government seems less important than the improvement of the action of the lawmakers in the fields of policy in which they must function either as technical experts or as a sample of the public rather than as partisans with a clearly expressed popular mandate. Under the American political system there is constitutional government as well as party government. The original theory of constitutional government still holds an important place in the legislative process.

The development of the party system has affected the importance of the principal factors in the practical operation of the system of checks and balances in ways that could not have been foreseen by the framers. Many of the leading delegates, especially the aristocratic Nationalists, set a high value on the executive veto as an instrument of political leadership, and were disappointed that it was not established in a more potent form. They feared that the President would not venture to use it vigorously against measures supported by majorities of the Congress, lest he be overwhelmed in a contest for popularity by the chosen representatives of the people. They did not foresee the time when the President, even more than the Congress, would be recognized as the people's representative and vetoes, such as Jackson's veto of the bank bill, would be immensely popular. Since the age of Jackson strong Presidents have not hesitated to use their veto as an instrument of Administration policy regardless of protests from factional leaders in the Congress.

The veto power has become an important weapon in the arsenal of the President for protecting the public interest, as he sees it, against measures promoted by casual majorities in the Congress. This weapon has been particularly effective against measures promoted by powerful pressure groups seeking special privileges for themselves, and may also be used effectively to define the issues for a presidential campaign, especially when the President and the majority of the Congress belong to different parties. But it has been of less value in dealing with important public measures, when the President and the majority of the Congress have belonged to the same party. The President cannot combat the measures which his party associates make leading issues in the Congress without damaging the prestige of the Administration itself and jeopardizing its control of the government. In the hands of a masterful President the threat of a veto can be a potent instrument for keeping restless factions within the party from joining the opposition for the purpose of enacting measures which the party leaders do not wish to support. But its action is negative. It does not enable a President to get positive action from his party associates, if party discipline is weak and factions within the party threaten to become unmanageable. A few of the strong Presidents, notably Jackson and Lincoln, have used their veto power in order to keep a free hand for the development of important public policies by executive authority. Usually the strong Presidents have found other means for procuring the enactment of their legislative programs by the Congress.

In recent years the executive veto has been developed into an effective instrument for the improvement of private and local legislation and the revision of minor public measures not in harmony with the general policy of the Administration. President Cleveland showed most impressively how it could be used to protect the public treasury against indefensible appropriations by private and local bills, and President Franklin D. Roosevelt with the aid of the Bureau of the Budget organized an efficient system of reviewing minor public bills for the purpose of protecting the treasury and the general consistency of legislative policy. Though the early Presidents were reluctant to use the veto power and resorted to it rarely, if at all, recent Presidents have vetoed large numbers of bills at or after each regular session of the Congress, to the advantage of the public and the enhancement of their own prestige. President Roosevelt during his several terms vetoed over six hundred bills, of which only nine were reënacted by the Congress. But even he suffered some humiliating defeats, as in the cases of his veto of the veterans' bonus bill and of the revenue bill of 1943–44.

The development of the party system has effected the use of other portions of the executive power in various ways. The power of appointment, for instance, under the impact of the party system, has generally been a source of weakness rather than of strength in the President's relations with the Congress. Outstanding exceptions were Franklin Pierce's use of patronage to overcome opposition to the repeal of the Missouri Compromise in 1854 and Grover Cleveland's use of patronage to effect the repeal of the Sherman Silver Purchase Act in 1893. Such use of patronage is difficult except near the beginning of a presidential term. The growth of the spoils system practically transferred the power of appointment to the Senators and Representatives belonging to the President's party and seriously impaired the President's practical capacity to take care that the laws be faithfully executed. The gradual development of a professional civil service has tended to redress the balance between the President and the Congress in respect to appointments, but the practice of senatorial courtesy still operates adversely to the authority of the chief executive. On the other hand, the power of impeachment has been of little practical importance in the operation of the system of checks and balances. Since the failure of the attempt to remove President Johnson on charges which were essentially political, the task of holding the chief executive responsible for his official acts, in so far as he is not held in check by the congressional power of the purse, has been left to the voters and to the judiciary. These developments were not foreseen by the framers. Nevertheless, though they have shaken the original system of checks and balances, they have not upset the equilibrium between Presidents and Congresses.

The influence of the President in the legislative process can be increased by the adoption of improvements in the organization of the executive.[17] The nature of many such improvements was suggested as long ago as 1937 in the report of President Roosevelt's Committee on Administrative Management. The adoption of the Reorganization Act of 1939, the establishment of the Executive Office of the President, and the expansion of the staff services of the Bureau of the Budget opened the way toward substantial gains in the efficiency of the executive and in the strengthening of its position vis-à-vis the Congress. The establishment of more adequate planning agencies under executive control, particularly the creation of the Council of Economic Advisers by the Employment Act of 1946 and of the National Security Resources Board by the National Security Act of 1947, marked a further step in the development of a more competent and more effective chief executive. Experience during World War II with the planning of war production and the reconversion of industry showed the usefulness of other administrative techniques to a modern high-powered President. The report of the Hoover Commission in 1949 gave fresh impetus to the quest for greater administrative efficiency and more vigorous executive leadership. Meanwhile the Congress was gaining ground in its perennial struggle to maintain the balance of the system of legislative-executive relations by the resolute and at times even reckless development of its investigatory powers. Through the agency of its regular committees and special investigating committees it invoked the power of public opinion to supplement that of the purse. Despite the expansion of executive authority in the emergency of war, the balance of the system was maintained.

Improvements in the organization and procedure of the Congress would doubtless improve the prospects of party government under congressional leadership.[18] It is clear that both the Congress and the Executive can be made more efficient and potentially more effective in the performance of their legislative functions. The challenge of the future may stimulate responses of various kinds by the two great political departments of the government. The record of the past does not indicate clearly what course future changes will take, or what would be the precise effect upon their mutual relations if both legis-

277

lative and executive departments were as well organized and as efficiently operated as may be possible, and if the organization and discipline of the major parties were developed to the utmost. What the record does show is that Madison's confidence in the constitutional arrangements for distributing power between the Congress and the President has been justified by the experience of more than a century and a half in national politics. The cycle of the presidential-congressional relationship runs its course. The public endures the interregnums, when neither of the major parties is in a position to govern, confident of its ability to put one of the parties in power whenever it can make up its own mind what general policy it wishes the governing party to pursue. Neither the President nor the Congress gets too much the better of the other in the constitutional struggle for power. The theory of the separation of powers has been reduced to practice in this field of government in the form of a workable and serviceable system of checks and balances.

The actual working of the theory of the separation of powers has on the whole been better than the framers could have foreseen. The system of checks and balances, as originally planned, has been greatly modified by the activities of the major parties. The congressional leaders feel a special responsibility to the voters, particularly the voters belonging to their own party or to their own faction of the party, in the states and districts in which the strength of the party chiefly lies, whereas the President must be more mindful of the interests which may control elections in the great doubtful states where presidential elections are decided. This means that at the present time the President must be more mindful of the powerful interests in the great urban and industrial states than the congressional leaders of either party are likely to be under the existing circumstances, and that the interests of other sections and especially of the rural population are likely to exert a greater influence on Capitol Hill than at the White House. This difference in viewpoint between the President and the party leadership in the Congress insures controversy and conflict between them concerning legislative policies, whichever party may be in power. It creates a strong probability also that the legislative policies upon which they agree, regardless of the particular party that may be in power, will command the approval of more than a bare majority of the people of the country. The prospect for such agreements is improved by the harmonizing influence of the middle classes. The normal operation of such a legislative process should give the leaders of the "ins" a reasonable assurance that they are governing with the consent of the governed, and the latter a due sense of ultimate authority.

The relations between Presidents and Congresses have developed differently from what the framers could have anticipated. The President has become an instrument of majority rule in competition with the House of Representatives. The party system helps to reconcile the divergent views of Presidents, Senators, and Representatives on questions which become paramount issues in popular elections. But on most controversial questions the organized special interests exert a greater influence than the parties and much remains to be done by casual majorities formed by Senators and Representatives regardless of party. In the formation of such majorities efficient presidential leadership may be of great help. Thus the character of the President becomes an important factor in the legislative process. A President who, in dealing with nonpartisan issues, can function effectively as a constitutional chief executive according to the original plan can add much to the power and the glory of his office, whether he is or is not an influential party leader. If he is also an influential party leader, he can still further improve his position by a judicious mixture of partisanship and bipartisanship or nonpartisanship. The superiority of Franklin D. Roosevelt's technique of leadership over that of Woodrow Wilson is on this point conclusive.

The development of the party system has modified the working of the system of checks and balances without changing its essential character. Party government has brought advantages both to the President and to the Senate in the struggle for legislative power, but has proved disadvantageous to the House of Representatives. It has weakened the House in two ways. It has diminished the influence of partisan majorities in the House, because they cannot claim an exclusive privilege of speaking for a majority of the people. It has created artificial difficulties for majorities other than partisan majorities, since the party leaders control the organization and procedure of the House. The operations of the major parties, however, have made the legislative process as a whole more democratic than it would have been under the original plan of constitutional government. They have also tended strongly to favor the influence of leaders who possess the moderate temper and accommodating spirit which Washington and Franklin and the other principal framers regarded as the essential conditions of a stable and durable system of constitutional government.

When toward the end of the Convention of 1787 George Mason

cried out in a moment of exasperation that the government under the proposed Constitution would eventually come to a bad end either as a monarchy or as an oligarchy — which of the two he was not sure — he unwittingly testified to the soundness of the system of checks and balances which the framers were planning. If the checks against the abuse of the executive power had proved seriously inadequate, the legislative process would have been thrown out of balance, and the system would have deteriorated into a dictatorship. If the checks against the abuse of power by the Senate had proved inadequate, the system would have ended in some evil form of oligarchy. But Mason could not forecast which way the scale would tip. Now, after more than a century and a half of actual government under the Constitution, it is still not possible to make such a forecast. No evidence could be more convincing that the system of checks and balances was well designed to accomplish its purpose. The forms of government against which Mason warned his fellow framers now seem, in the light of more recent experience, even more objectionable than they did to him. The plans of the framers, however, as applied to the legislative process, have proved better than any of them could have anticipated. Both the Senate and the President have gained power at the expense of the House of Representatives, but neither has yet gained an undue advantage over the other. Nor has the House been so weakened by its losses of power and prestige as to be incapable of recovering a fair portion of its original position in the scheme of the framers.[19] The system of checks and balances, as applied to the legislative process, still possesses reassuring vitality.

THE SPECIAL PROBLEM OF
PRESIDENTIAL POWER OVER FOREIGN RELATIONS

Nevertheless, there is a cloud on the horizon. In the field of foreign affairs the Congress is being constrained by the logic of events to delegate extraordinary amounts of discretionary authority to the President. The harbinger of the new era of broad executive discretion in this field was the Joint Resolution of May 28, 1934. This emergency measure, authorizing the President to prohibit the sale of arms and munitions of war to certain South American Republics, if he should find such action desirable in the interest of peace, offered a marked contrast to the contemporary Neutrality Act with its strict prescription of standards for the guidance of the President in the practical exercise of his delegated authority. The expansion of presidential authority in recent years by similar legislation has been portentous. The Lend-Lease Act of March 11, 1941, authorized the President to extend financial aid to any country whose defense the President might deem vital to the defense of the United States. That put the determination of policy squarely in the President's hands. It meant, as Sherwood has pointed out,[20] that, if the President should so decide (as he eventually did), aid could be rendered even to the Soviet Union, though the Congress might not have approved such a policy at that time.

Since World War II this precedent has been followed far and wide in a series of important measures. The China Aid Act of 1948, for instance, authorized the President to grant "additional," that is, military, aid "on such terms as the President may determine and without regard to the provisions of the Economic Coöperation Act of 1948." The only effective limitation on the discretionary authority of the executive was the appropriation of the necessary funds for only a single year at a time and the power of the Congress, whenever it should be in session, to repeal the act. Such legislation gave to the executive power in this field an extent hardly distinguishable from that of the royal prerogative under the British Constitution.[21] But in practice the royal prerogative is exercised only with the advice and consent of the King's Ministers. Under the American Constitution there is no equivalent check on the discretionary authority of the President in the field of foreign affairs. The increasing importance of foreign affairs in the regular business of government makes this tendency toward more arbitrary executive power a growing threat to the constitutional balance of power.

The discretionary authority of the President in the field of foreign affairs is further enhanced by the modern practice of embodying foreign policy in executive agreements instead of treaties. The distribution of the control of foreign policy between the President and the Congress was not clearly defined in the Constitution, though there seems to have been an expectation in the Federal Convention that important relations with foreign powers would be regulated by formal treaties, to which the advice and consent of two-thirds of the Senators would be necessary, or, if money were needed, by suitable acts of Congress. In practice it does not seem to be necessary to embody the policies of the President in treaties, subject to ratification by the Senate, unless their satisfactory execution is dependent upon judicial proceedings in the federal courts. In all other cases, not involving the appropriation of money, the President can apparently act at his own discretion. An extreme case was the famous exchange of the fifty American destroyers for the right to build naval and air bases on British islands off the American coast. Executive agreements may have no greater force than successive chief executives choose to give them, but in cases where prompt action is desired they are likely to be more attractive to foreign powers than treaties, which cannot be concluded quickly or secretly. Moreover the President's power to enter into executive agreements with foreign states is greatly extended by his practical capacity to grant or withhold recognition of foreign governments at discretion, and his power to carry them into effect is immeasurably strengthened by his constitutional authority as Commander-in-Chief.

This unprecedented development of the power of the President to determine foreign policy under the strenuous conditions of modern times plainly threatens the balance of power under the Constitution. It tends to put the President in his relations with the Congress more nearly in the position accorded him under Hamilton's original plan for a constitution.[22] The Hamiltonian conception of the presidency was rejected by the Convention of 1787. It was not defended even by Hamilton himself in his discussion of the structure and functions of the executive in *The Federalist*.[23] It is a conception of the office which can be neither defended upon the Madisonian principles nor reconciled with the spirit of the political system which has gradually developed under the Constitution. It exposes the people to the danger that the most important decisions affecting the foreign policy of the country will be made on the basis of facts not disclosed to the public and by methods so secret as to impair the practical capacity of the Senate and House to insure due deliberation. In a democratic age the process of determining public policy in the field of foreign relations tends to become less rather than more democratic.

It is not necessary to agree with all that Emery Reves has written in his *Anatomy of Peace* [24] to recognize that the traditional arrangements for the conduct of international relations by the governments of sovereign national states create a standing menace to the rights of the peoples of democratic republics. In every field of executive action there must be an adequate guarantee that the choice of policy will always represent a widespread opinion that it is necessary and proper, and that measures which lack the support of such opinion will not be taken. In the field of domestic affairs the consent of the Congress to the measures of the President has been required for this purpose. It has been a satisfactory arrangement because of a general belief that the interests of those concerned in a particular public affair are duly represented in the Congress. But these interests are not well enough represented in the developing process for the conduct of foreign affairs.

It is clear in what direction the search for a solution to this problem should proceed. It is in the direction indicated by the United Nations Participation Act of 1945. As far as possible under the provisions of the United Nations Charter the President should act through agreement with the United Nations Security Council subject to the approval of the Congress. Better security for American interests, as for the interests of peoples everywhere, can be found only by forming a more perfect Union of the Nations. But this is an aspect of the development of the theory of the separation of powers consideration of which must await an inquiry into the role of the judiciary in the practical operation of the system of checks and balances.

CHAPTER NINE

Judges and Legislators

THE JEFFERSONIAN THEORY OF JUDICIAL POWER

THE framers of the Constitution readily agreed to vest the judicial power in a Supreme Court, and in such inferior courts as the Congress might establish, but they could not so easily agree concerning the nature of this kind of power. There was much discussion of the proper functions of judges, particularly of Supreme Court judges. Many of the framers thought that such judges should not only be the heads of the judicial establishment, but also have a share in the legislative power. There was sharp difference of opinion, however, concerning what that share should be. The principle of the separation of powers seemed to call for a clean-cut division of labor between judges and legislators, but the requirements of an effective system of checks and balances tended to bring confusion into any logical distribution of governmental functions.

The original Virginia plan called for active and vigorous participation by the judges of the Supreme Court in the process of lawmaking. The judges were to join with the chief executive in reviewing and, if deemed politic, vetoing the acts of the Congress. They were to share likewise in the revision of state legislation by the Congress and the chief executive. The power of joint executive-judicial review was to be exercised in all cases where the Congress proposed to act in a manner which the chief executive and the judges could not approve. In cases where the Congress proposed to disallow state legislation on the ground of unconstitutionality, the chief executive and judges could disapprove the action of the Congress only on the ground that the Congress was mistaken on the constitutional issue. In other cases, where the Congress itself wished to enact a bill into law, they might disapprove either on the ground that the proposed act of Congress would be in their opinion unconstitutional or because they regarded it as inexpedient.

This feature of the Virginia plan would have involved the judges

284

deeply in politics. It was opposed for that reason by some of the more experienced lawyers among the delegates, particularly those with judicial experience, who were determined to keep the judges out of politics as much as possible. They recognized, however, that the judges could not avoid responsibility for deciding questions of conflict between ordinary legislative enactments and the law of the Constitution itself, when brought before them in the process of litigation. They anticipated that cases would arise in which the interpretation of the Constitution by the lawmakers might be questioned. They intended that in such cases the judges should review acts of the Congress, involving questionable interpretations of the Constitution, as well as those of state lawmakers, and should set them aside if found to be in conflict with the fundamental law. This doctrine of judicial review prevailed in the Convention of 1787. It became the basis for the exercise of a power of judicial veto against unconstitutional legislation.

Madison was disappointed with this disposition of the controversy over the judicial power by the Convention. He believed that the chief executive would be too weak to exercise a separate executive veto effectively without the moral and political support of the judges and that the separate judicial veto would come too late in the legislative process, would be too uncertain in its operation, and too limited in its scope, to supply a satisfactory check to the lawmakers and keep the constitutional system of distributed powers in a proper balance. He was slow to perceive the advantages of a judicial veto against legislation trespassing upon the rights of the people, when formally declared in a bill of rights attached to the Constitution, and perhaps never realized the full implications of the doctrine of judicial review in the practical operation of the constitutional system of checks and balances. Jefferson, studying the original text of the Constitution from his detached position in Paris, immediately saw the possibilities of an independent power of judicial veto against unconstitutional legislation and was quickened in his desire for a bill of rights by his vision of a Supreme Court which might thereby become a powerful guardian of the rights of the common man. His distrust of an independent and powerful chief executive, fortified by an unlimited right of reëlection, which he feared might too easily produce a dangerous life tenure of the presidency, made him all the more eager for a bill of rights capable of furnishing a broad platform upon which a vigilant Court could take its stand.

The correspondence between these two eminent statesmen on the utility of a bill of rights is illuminating. Writing to Jefferson a few months after the ratification of the Constitution by the necessary number of states to put it into operation, Madison noted [1] that "among the advocates for the Constitution there are some who wish for further guards to public liberty and individual rights. As far as these may consist of a constitutional declaration of the most essential rights, it is probable that they will be added, though there are many who think such addition unnecessary, and not a few who think it misplaced in such a Constitution." After elaborating his reasons for thinking a bill of rights unnecessary in the Federal Constitution, Madison proceeded to set forth his grounds for concluding that the addition of a bill of rights might nevertheless be useful. "Wherever the real power in a Government lies," he wrote, "there is the danger of oppression. In our Governments the real power lies in the majority of the community, and the invasion of private rights is *chiefly* to be apprehended, not from acts of Government contrary to the sense of its constituents, but from acts in which the Government is the mere instrument of the major number of constituents." This, he was convinced, was "a truth of great importance, but not yet sufficiently attended to."

These considerations led Madison to a statement of his views concerning the utility of a declaration of rights in any of the American constitutions. "What use, then, it may be asked, can a bill of rights serve in popular Governments? I answer, the two following, which, though less essential than in other Governments, sufficiently recommend the precaution: 1. The political truths declared in that solemn manner acquire by degrees the character of fundamental maxims of free Government, and as they become incorporated with the National sentiment, counteract the impulses of interest and passion. 2. Although it may be generally true, as above stated, that the danger of oppression lies in the interested majorities of the people rather than in usurped acts of the Government, yet there may be occasions on which the evil may spring from the latter source; and on such, a bill of rights will be a good ground for an appeal to the sense of the community." Madison apparently possessed little confidence in the ability of judges to check the abuse of power by legislative majorities, when supported by the prejudices of the general public. He put first in his list of the public services, which might be rendered by a formal declaration of rights, the educational value of the good advice to the people contained in such a declaration; and second, the more immediate utility of a bill of rights in cases where power might be abused by persons in authority contrary to the popular wishes. It was to the people and to public opinion rather than to the Supreme Court that Madison looked for the protection of popular rights against the abuse of power by the state legislatures or by the Congress.

Jefferson, on the contrary, held strong convictions about the importance of bills of rights, and could not be content with Madison's indifferent defense of their usefulness in the American federal and state constitutions. Replying to Madison's letter several months later from Paris,[2] he wrote: "In the arguments in favor of a declaration of rights, you omit one which has great weight with me; the legal check which it puts into the hands of the judiciary. This is a body, which, if rendered independent and kept strictly to their own department, merits great confidence for their learning and integrity." Jefferson conceded that there was some merit in the arguments of the aristocratic Nationalists in the Federal Convention in favor of the omission of a bill of rights. A federal government, possessing only delegated powers, should be less likely to abuse them than state governments, whose powers were less precisely defined. But the Federal Constitution was not as precise in its grants of power as could be desired by prudent friends of the rights of the states and of the people. The grant of authority to make all laws, which might be necessary and proper for the execution of the powers which were expressly granted, opened the door to an unpredictable expansion of the authority of the general government. A declaration of rights under such circumstances becomes necessary, Jefferson concluded, "by way of supplement" to the new Constitution. "This instrument," he added, "forms us into one state, as to certain objects, and gives us a legislative and executive body for these objects. It should, therefore, guard us against their abuses of power, within the field submitted to them." An independent Supreme Court would have important work to do, as Jefferson viewed its role in the government of the new and more powerful Union, in guarding the rights of the people as well as in keeping politics out of the administration of justice.

THE HAMILTONIAN THEORY OF JUDICIAL POWER

A radically different view of the role of the Supreme Court was offered by Alexander Hamilton in his commentaries on the Constitution in *The Federalist*.[3] Hamilton, who never regarded the original Virginia plan as an adequate basis for the strong executive he deemed desirable, was as quick as Jefferson to appreciate the political possibilities of the doctrine of judicial review. He perceived, however, as Jefferson at first did not, the possibility of calling in a powerful Supreme Court to redress the balance between the popular and the aristocratic branches of the government, the latter of which was gravely threatened, he believed, by the weakness of the chief executive under the Constitution. In number seventy-eight of *The Federalist*, Hamilton set forth the classic exposition of the doctrine of judicial review of state and federal legislation. In number eighty-one he came to grips with the problem of what the role of the Court should be in the practical exercise of the power of judicial review.

Hamilton was replying to the argument, advanced by opponents of unconditional ratification of the Constitution, that "the power of construing the laws according to the *spirit* of the Constitution will enable that court to mould them into whatever shape it may think proper." The argument was dangerous, since a belief that the Supreme Court would possess authority under the Constitution to veto all legislation that the judges might find to conflict with its spirit could frighten away those friends of constitutional government who wished the spirit of the Constitution to be interpreted by their representatives in the political departments of the government rather than by judges who might more easily get out of popular control. The occasion called for a reply making clear whether the spirit of the Constitution was a matter for determination by the people themselves, speaking through their chosen representatives or through the samples of the public on the trial juries, or by lawyers appointed to sit for life on the Supreme Court.

Hamilton's answer to this argument is not free from the suspicion of equivocation. "In the first place," he declared, "there is not a syllable in the plan under consideration which *directly* empowers the national courts to construe the laws according to the spirit of the Constitution, or which gives them any greater latitude in this respect than may be claimed by the courts of every state." He did not say what might be implied by the Constitution's broad grant of judicial power to the Supreme Court, nor did he say whether he thought the state courts possessed the power to construe state laws according to the spirit of the state constitutions. What he did say was not inconsistent with the opinion that the power of judicial review would be broad enough to cover a guardianship of the spirit as well as the substance of the Constitution. "I admit, however," he continued, "that the Constitution ought to be the standard of construction for the laws, and that wherever there is evident opposition, the laws ought to give way to the

Constitution." Hamilton should have known — and probably did know — that, if the members of the Supreme Court were to be the final judges in cases of conflict between the Constitution and the laws, the opinions of the judges would breathe life into the letter of the law and the character of the judges would be reflected in the character of the Constitution.

Hamilton's defense of the omission of a bill of rights from the original Constitution, contained in the eighty-fourth number of *The Federalist*, throws further light upon his concept of judicial review. He supported the familiar views of the aristocratic Nationalists in the Federal Convention concerning the needlessness of a national declaration of rights in addition to the existing state declarations. "I go further," he declared, "and affirm that bills of rights, in the sense and to the extent in which they are contended for, are not only unnecessary in the proposed Constitution, but would even be dangerous." His argument was, that the enumeration of rights reserved to the people might imply the possession of the powers to which the constitutional limitations could be attached, although not expressly granted, and that the failure to include all the rights of the people among those enumerated in a declaration of rights might endanger the preservation of those which were omitted. He cited the example of the liberty of the press. "What is the liberty of the press?" he asked with impressive rhetoric. "Who can give it any definition which would not leave the utmost latitude for evasion? I hold it to be impracticable; and from this I infer, that its security, whatever fine declarations may be inserted in any constitution, must altogether depend on public opinion, and on the general spirit of the people and of the government." Hamilton quoted the reference to the blessings of liberty in the preamble of the Constitution. "Here," he declared, "is a better recognition of popular rights than volumes of those aphorisms which make the principal figure in several of our state bills of rights, and which would sound much better in a treatise of ethics than in a constitution of government."

The contrast between Hamilton's views concerning the practical utility of a bill of rights and those of Jefferson is striking. The fact is that Hamilton was not interested in the rights of the people or of the states. He was interested in the establishment of a strong central government and in the development of a doctrine of judicial review which would enable the judges to construe the central government's authority as broadly as possible. A powerful and independent Supreme Court could still infuse into the new federal government much of that national

289

and aristocratic spirit which had animated the Virginia planners and their aristocratic Nationalist collaborators in the Federal Convention of 1787. The educational uses of a national bill of rights made no appeal to him. He set little store by the possibility that liberal judges might find in such a bill of rights principles which they could take hold of and turn to good account in keeping the political departments of the government from abusing their powers and trespassing upon the rights of the people. Like Jefferson, he wanted a Supreme Court which could become an influential shareholder in the power to interpret the Constitution and the laws, but, unlike Jefferson, he did not want a Supreme Court which would make the new political system more popular than the framers had designed it to be.

The fundamentally conflicting viewpoints of these two statesmen is best revealed by their opinions concerning the usefulness of a bill of rights. What Hamilton wanted was a Supreme Court which could mold the new constitutional design more nearly in the aristocratic image originally cherished by the Nationalist members of the Federal Convention. Hamilton wanted a doctrine of judicial review which would enable the Court to function as the guardian of the Constitution in the interest of the particular class which, he believed, was most likely to be the victim of the abuse of power by legislative majorities. He wanted a doctrine which could strengthen the influence of the rich in their perennial struggle, as he imagined, with the poor. Hamilton understood both the natural conservatism of most successful lawyers and the natural tendency of appointment to the judiciary for life to confirm their conservatism. He foresaw correctly the conservative influence of such a judiciary, when acting last in the process of constitutional interpretation without appeal except to the people by the difficult process of amending the Constitution. The value of an unpopular judicial decision as a precedent could be destroyed by a constitutional amendment but such destruction of a judicial precedent would require the initial approval of two-thirds majorities in both branches of the Congress. Hamilton might well have expected that the constitutional opinions of the Supreme Court would be definitive in all cases which might come before the Court, involving issues between different social classes or which deeply divided the people. Such a court could become an important bulwark of the rights of property and of the special interests of the "opulent."

The majority of the framers could not have approved Hamilton's doctrine of judicial supremacy. The original Federalists, who had most to do with the preparation of the plan for an independent and powerful Supreme Court, were most scrupulous in restricting it to judicial functions. They wanted a Federal Government of limited powers, strictly construed, and believed that a Supreme Court, divorced from politics, would be the most reliable and efficient guardian of such a Constitution. The various kinds of Unionists, particularly John Rutledge and Dr. Johnson, who were most responsible for the final form of the provisions, defining the jurisdiction of the Supreme Court, were determined to give it complete and untrammeled authority over all cases arising under the Federal Constitution. They understood that this Court would be responsible for maintaining the supremacy of the Constitution over the ordinary laws of the Congress and of the states and also over the state constitutions, and that the fundamental law could not always be strictly construed. But they hoped that the Supreme Court would not meddle with questions of legislative policy. They believed that the doctrine of judicial review, if not the Constitution itself, should be strictly construed They desired the supremacy of the Supreme Court in what they regarded as its proper sphere. But they did not consider the policy of ordinary legislation a part of that sphere.

Whether a clear distinction between constitutional principles and ordinary legislative policy could be maintained in the practice of judicial review was a question beyond the range of the framers' vision. If such a distinction could not be readily maintained, able judges would naturally develop the doctrine of judicial review into a doctrine of judicial supremacy and partisan judges could easily convert the doctrine of judicial supremacy into a powerful instrument for action in national politics. That part of the business of administering justice, which involves the interpretation of the Constitution, would then become absorbed in the regular operations of party contentiousness, and the Supreme Court, if consistently conservative, could supply the powerful check upon the popular branch of the Federal Government which the framers, as aristocrats like Hamilton and Morris believed, had failed to provide in their grant of powers to the chief executive. The power of the Congress to impeach judges and remove them from office should not be a serious check on a conservative Supreme Court, if the Senate should be as much more conservative than the House of Representatives as the aristocratic Nationalists hoped. But not all the framers could have shared these expectations of judicial ultraconservatism. The original Federalists, many of whom were inclined toward a democratic political system, seem to have put their trust for protection against the abuse of judicial power for partisan purposes in the good sense and self-restraint of the judges themselves. In general the framers seemed unaware of the full extent of the opportunity for conflict in the interpretation of the judicial power under the Constitution. The contest between the Hamiltonian and the Jeffersonian version of the doctrine of judicial review remained to be fought out by future generations of legislators and judges.

THE IMPACT OF
PARTISANSHIP ON THE JUDICIAL PROCESS

The differences of opinion among the framers of the Constitution concerning the application of the principle of a separation of powers insured the development of different attitudes toward the interpretation of the Constitution by the Supreme Court. Those who were able to control the political departments of the government of the Union were likely to assert the supremacy of those departments under the Constitution in so far as might be necessary or convenient for the success of their political programs. Those who happened to dislike the measures of the Congress and the President were likely to be more interested in a doctrine of judicial supremacy. The latter, like Madison in the Convention of 1787, would be more disturbed at the threat of encroachment by popular majorities on the rights of individuals or minorities than of trespasses against them by national political leaders. The former, like Luther Martin, would view with alarm the possibility that judicial review might become too political in spirit. Altered circumstances could easily alter the attitude of practical politicians. The same Madison, who in 1787 deplored the lack of security in the Constitution for the interests of the "opulent," was a leader among the Jeffersonian Republicans in 1798, who lamented the failure of the federal courts to protect Democratic-Republican newspaper editors and publishers against persecution under the Alien and Sedition Acts and appealed to the states to stop the alleged violation of popular rights under the Constitution. The place of judges, armed with a judicial veto, in the constitutional system of checks and balances was certain to become a bone of contention among politicians.

It is evident that the exercise of the power of judicial review would raise controversial issues, which might come before the Supreme Court in justiciable form but which could not be kept out of politics unless the decisions of the Court should meet with popular approval. The distinction between justiciable and political questions may be clear in the minds of logical judges, but it is not easy to convince the interested members of the public that a question is not political, if they think it of sufficient importance to be decided by themselves. This problem was most clearly presented to the people of the United States by the Dred Scott decision. There has never been an effective answer to Abraham Lincoln's statement in his "First Inaugural Address," [4] delivered in the face of the Chief Justice, who had written the most offensive opinion in support of the decision and who had then administered the oath of office to its foremost critic. "The candid citizen must confess," Lincoln declared, "that if the policy of the Government upon vital questions affecting the whole people is to be irrevocably fixed by decisions of the Supreme Court the instant they are made in ordinary litigation between parties in personal actions, the people will have ceased to be their own rulers, having to that extent practically resigned their Government into the hands of that eminent tribunal." Lincoln immediately defended himself against the obvious rejoinder of unreflecting advocates of the independence of the judiciary under the American system of constitutional government. "Nor is there in this view," he added, "any assault upon the court or the judges. It is a duty from which they may not shrink to decide cases properly brought before them." Clearly the role of the Supreme Court as the guardian of the Constitution cannot be intelligently investigated without some consideration of the political character of the judges.

The importance of appointing to the Supreme Court persons with a proper attitude toward the political questions which might come before it in justiciable form was well understood by the former Nationalists who furnished the effective leadership in national politics during the presidency of General Washington.[5] The first Chief Justice, John Jay, had been Secretary for Foreign Affairs under the Congress during the struggle for a new and more powerful Union and was one of Washington's staunch supporters in that struggle. All five of the associate justices were reliable Administration men. Three of them, Wilson, Rutledge, and Blair, had been members of the Federal Convention, where Blair had loyally sustained Washington's leadership within the Virginia delegation, while Rutledge and Wilson had taken principal parts in the actual framing of the Constitution. The other original associate justices, Cushing and Iredell, were state judges who had worked hard for the new Constitution in their respective states. Oliver Ellsworth, who was Chief Justice at the time of the most important of the early decisions by the Federalist Supreme Court, was the Administration leader in the Senate when appointed to the Court. Washington was plainly determined to man the Court with firm friends of the new Constitution. He manifestly believed that political considerations would influence the judicial interpretation of the fundamental law and recognized the importance of judges with a proper understanding of politics.

The later history of the Supreme Court discloses the same careful attention to the political qualifications of its members. Of the Chief Justices, Marshall, Taney, Chase, and Vinson were, or recently had been, leading members of the President's Cabinet at the time of their appointments, Taft had been President, and Hughes had been a major-party candidate for the presidency and an influential Cabinet officer. White was a party leader in the Senate, when originally appointed by President Cleveland, and his promotion to the office of Chief Justice attested President Taft's high opinion of his attitude toward the controversial issues of the day. Stone was Attorney General at the time of his original appointment to the Court, and his promotion to the chief justiceship was in recognition of his judicial services as partisan within the Court of constitutional principles espoused by the New Deal Administration. Only two of the Chief Justices, Waite and Fuller, had not qualified for their appointments by significant political services to a partisan Administration.

The selection of associate justices teaches a similar lesson. The membership of the New Deal Court, when Chief Justice Vinson succeeded to its leadership, included three Justices who were Cabinet officers at the time of their appointment, two who were holding other important executive offices, two who were Senators when appointed, one who held a judicial post, and one who was a teacher of law. The previous Conservative Republican Court was only a little less political in composition. When Chief Justice Hughes succeeded Chief Justice Taft, there were three associate justices whose appointments had followed important political services. Two had been Cabinet officers and one a party leader in the Senate. Three others had been judges of lower courts and two had been lawyers who distinguished themselves without holding any important political office, but not without significant partisan services. Chief Justice Taft himself valued previous judicial experience for membership in the Supreme Court perhaps as highly as any President, and certainly more highly than most, but of the eight appointments which he personally made or influenced the most successful were those made most definitely on political grounds.[6]

The influence of partisanship upon the relations between the Supreme Court and the political branches of the federal government has been at times a hotly controversial question. For the purpose of investigating the record of these controversies the history of the Supreme Court may be conveniently divided into five periods, corresponding to the domination within the Court of judges appointed by Presidents of different parties. Judges appointed by the Federalists formed a majority of the Court until the end of Jefferson's second term. Judges appointed by the Jeffersonian Republicans formed a majority of the Court until the latter part of Jackson's second term. Judges appointed by the Jacksonian Democrats formed a majority of the Court until near the end of Lincoln's first term. Judges appointed by the early Radical and later Conservative Republicans formed a majority of the Court until near the end of Franklin D. Roosevelt's second term. Since then so-called New Deal judges have formed a majority of the Court.

THE STRUGGLE FOR JUDICIAL SUPREMACY

The first period in a partisan history of the Supreme Court began with the appointment of John Jay as Chief Justice and continued through the terms of Chief Justices Rutledge and Ellsworth and the first part of the term of John Marshall. It was characterized by the leadership of judges who believed that they might properly exert an active influence in national politics and who were determined to support the measures of the Federalist Party. As early as 1796 they served notice on the politicians of all parties and on the general public by their opinions in the case of *Hylton* v. *United States* [7] that they would not hesitate to declare unconstitutional any act of Congress which they might find to be in conflict with the fundamental law. Two Chief Justices even accepted diplomatic missions for the purpose of promoting Administration policies at critical stages in the nation's foreign relations. Jay's mission to England resulted in the negotiation of a treaty which became a leading political measure of Washington's Administration, and Ellsworth's mission to France was designed to perform a similar function for the Administration of John Adams. On the other hand, the Supreme Court under Jay's leadership refused to render to President Washington at his request a formal opinion on a question of law. Jay's Court would not pass judgment on questions of law except in the course of deciding cases actually before them in their judicial

295

capacity, but they did not oppose his personal performance of political duties at the request of the President. Both Jay and Ellsworth obviously regarded themselves as leading members of the Administration, well qualified for acting as the right hand of the President in matters of sufficient importance.

John Marshall became Chief Justice too late to continue the practice of functioning as a principal leader of the party in power, but at precisely the right time to establish the precedent of leading the opposition to the Administration. The case of *Marbury*, one of the Federalist "midnight" justices, v. *Madison*, Marshall's successor in the office of Secretary of State, gave him the opportunity to assert the supremacy of the judiciary in a matter which was a subject of bitter partisan controversy.[8] Marshall declared that the delivery of Marbury's commission as justice of the peace, which he himself had not had time to deliver in the rush of business at the close of his term as Secretary, was a ministerial duty which the Supreme Court might have commanded Madison to perform, if the provision of the act of Congress which purported to give the Court original jurisdiction over the case had not itself been in conflict with the Constitution. Marshall was thus enabled to assert the supremacy of the Court's interpretation of the Constitution over both the executive and the legislative interpretations. He might have easily avoided this clash with the political departments of the government by recognizing that the delivery of the commission was a discretionary act, which Madison could refuse to perform in compliance with the policy of his chief, the new President. Evidently Marshall was eager to assert the supremacy of the judiciary in the field of constitutional interpretation.

It is not surprising that Jefferson should have denounced the Federalists for seeking to exploit the political power of the judicial department of the government after having lost control of the political departments. The Federalists, moreover, had sought to prolong their control of the Court by reducing its membership to five, so that Jefferson would not have an opportunity to make a fresh appointment at the first vacancy. Jefferson, however, had means at his disposal for maintaining the authority of the political departments of the government. He could recommend to the Congress that they repeal the legislation under which the "midnight" judges were appointed, and the Congress could pay to the Republican newspaper editors and campaign orators, convicted under the Federalist Sedition Act of libeling the President by their caustic criticisms of him and his measures, the fines imposed upon them by Federalist judges. Jefferson could also recommend an increase in the size of the Court to seven, in order to make room for a judge representing the new states of the West, and incidentally permit the appointment of two Jeffersonian judges without awaiting the occurrence of a vacancy by resignation or death. He could also urge the impeachment of Federalist Justice Chase of the Supreme Court, who had made himself exceptionally obnoxious to the Jeffersonians by his grossly partisan charges to grand juries. The impeachment came near enough to success to cause alarm in the Federalist Court and the possibility of swamping its Federalist majority by the creation of additional judgeships emphasized the folly of offensive partisanship by the judiciary. John Marshall's Court never again declared an act of Congress unconstitutional or issued orders to the executive branch of the government except in support of the judicial process. Its Federalist members ceased their practice of delivering political speeches to the grand juries, and tacitly consented to leave politics to the politicians.[9]

During the second period in the partisan history of the Supreme Court, when a majority of Marshall's colleagues were Jeffersonians, the Court under his leadership distinguished itself by asserting the propriety of a broad interpretation of the Constitution and by maintaining the authority of the federal government against unconstitutional encroachments by the states. The leading decision was rendered in the great case of *McCulloch* v. *Maryland*.[10] In this case the Supreme Court sustained the constitutionality of the second Bank of the United States and denied the right of the Maryland legislature to tax its operations in that state. But the policy of a broad interpretation of the Constitution had been adopted by a Jeffersonian President and Congress before it was officially approved by the Supreme Court, and the effect of the decision was to exalt the authority of the political departments of the federal government rather than that of the judges. Jeffersonian Presidents might still denounce the construction of internal improvements at national expense and veto appropriations for that purpose on the ground of unconstitutionality, but the majority of the Jeffersonians in the Congress were content to deal with such measures on grounds of expediency regardless of constitutional scruples. Jefferson himself might complain that the Jeffersonian judges, once safely established in the Court, tended to become the followers of Marshall, but the members of his party, whether in the Congress or on the Court, seemed to be in harmony with the spirit of the times. Jefferson would have pre-

ferred to save the faces of the strict constructionists by a formal amendment of the Constitution, but, since the approval by the Congress of
his purchase of Louisiana without explicit constitutional authority, his
followers, whatever their views on questions of states' rights, were
disposed to leave the Constitution to the Court as long as the judges
personally kept out of partisan politics.

Marshall ended his judicial career, as he began it, in a conflict with
the President. Jackson, like Jefferson, resented judicial interference
with what he regarded as political questions. Since the Supreme Court
would not declare the power of the Congress unequal to the creation
of a national bank — a decision which Jackson apparently would have
approved — he would act upon his own interpretation of the Constitution. In vetoing the act of the Congress extending the charter of the
Bank of the United States, and subsequently in removing the government's deposits to state banks, he asserted the equal right of the three
coördinate departments of the government to act upon their own
opinions concerning their powers under the Constitution. Again like
Jefferson, he persuaded the Congress to enlarge the Supreme Court.
The ostensible reason, as in Jefferson's time, was to provide additional
judges for circuit duty in the new states of the West. The practical
result was to enable the President to appoint additional judges of his
own political persuasion. Meanwhile, the opportune death of the Chief
Justice enabled him to appoint his trusted adviser, Roger B. Taney,
former Attorney General and Secretary of the Treasury, to head the
Court, and a new period began in the history of the relations between
the judiciary and the political departments of the government.

The third period in the partisan history of the Supreme Court was
practically coterminous with Taney's chief justiceship. During this
period only one judge was appointed who was not a Jacksonian Democrat. This lone Whig judge, Benjamin R. Curtis, served with distinction,
but a few years after the Dred Scott decision, which he strongly opposed, voluntarily resigned. Taney himself had originally been a Federalist and joined the Jacksonians only when the Federalist Party had
finally expired. He never was a Jeffersonian. An able lawyer and, like
Marshall, a strong personality, he generally dominated his colleagues
and made the period of the Jacksonian Democratic Court, as Marshall
had that of the Jeffersonian Republican Court, something different
from what might have been expected at its beginning.[11]

Taney's chief justiceship should have been devoted to the maintenance of the principle of the coördinate authority of the separate

departments of the government to interpret the Constitution, at least in matters affecting their own powers. The doctrine of judicial supremacy, as originally expounded by Hamilton, and applied by Marshall, which had been left in innocuous desuetude by the Jeffersonian Court under Marshall's leadership, should logically have been repudiated by the Jacksonian Court. And so for a score of years it seemed to have been. Then came the Dred Scott decision.[12] Not only the Missouri Compromise but also the principal plank in the platform of the new Republican Party were declared unconstitutional. A favorite doctrine of the Northern Democrats, popular sovereignty, was also seriously damaged by the decision. According to Taney's opinion neither the Congress nor a territorial legislature could exclude slavery from a territory of the United States. When President Buchanan announced in his inaugural address a hope that the decision of the Supreme Court would put an end to further political controversy over the question of slavery in the territories, the Court was plunged into the midst of a bitter struggle over the paramount issue in national politics. The advocacy of Andrew Jackson's theory of the coördinate authority of the political and judicial branches of the government became the task of Abraham Lincoln, while Taney championed the Hamiltonian doctrine of judicial supremacy. Taney, like Marshall, ended his judicial career in sharp conflict with the political head of the government.

The fourth period in the partisan history of the Supreme Court lasted for three-quarters of a century. It began with the appointment of Chief Justice Chase and ended shortly before the resignation of Chief Justice Hughes. President Lincoln appointed altogether five members of the Court and imparted to its deliberations a firm yet moderate antislavery Republican character which on the whole dominated its proceedings through the terms of Chief Justices Chase and Waite. The only other Republican President who had an opportunity to appoint both a Chief Justice and a majority of the Court was William H. Taft. This injudicious politician and politic judge successfully imparted to the Court's deliberations under Chief Justice White and later under his own personal leadership both a conservative Republican temper and the appropriate judicial doctrines. The term of Democratic Chief Justice Fuller, who presided over a Court the majority of whose members were always Republican appointees, covered the transitional phase between the Court's original antislavery Republicanism and its final procapitalism Republicanism. Throughout this entire period the Supreme Court, if it be classified in partisan terms, must be described as a Republican Court.

During this long period of Republican supremacy the Supreme Court exercised its power of judicial review more vigorously than in the earlier period.[13] In seventy-five years the Federalist, the Jeffersonian Republican, and the Jacksonian Democratic Courts had ventured to declare only two acts of Congress unconstitutional. The results in both cases had been unhappy. During an equal period the Lincoln Republican Court and its successors under Republican domination declared seventy-seven acts of Congress, in whole or in part, unconstitutional. The judicial veto was exercised ten times in nine years by Chase's Court. It was exercised eight times in fifteen years by Waite's Court. It was exercised fourteen times in twenty-two years by Fuller's Court. It was exercised twelve times in eleven years by White's Court and sixteen times in nine years by Taft's Court. Its exercise reached a climax under Chief Justice Hughes. In the first seven years of his Court seventeen acts of Congress were declared null and void. Some of these decisions were salutary and were well received by the interested portions of the public and with a decent show of respect by the makers of the laws. But in a significant number of cases the results were as unhappy as in the earlier periods. The relations between the judges and the legislators consequently suffered great vicissitudes of fortune.

The Lincoln Republican Court abandoned the policy of avoiding judicial interference with the political branches of the government, studiously practiced by the Jeffersonian and Jacksonian judges during the half century between the Marbury and Dred Scott cases except for a brief interval when Marshall clashed with Jackson. At first it tried to respect the distinction between political and justiciable acts, but its antipathy to the Radical Republicans' policy for reconstructing the South threatened the leadership of the Congress in the process of reconstruction. The Radical Republicans retaliated by amending the Judiciary Act so as to deny to the Court jurisdiction over a case which might have enabled it to declare the Reconstruction Act of March 2, 1867 unconstitutional.[14] When a bare plurality of the judges ventured to declare the Legal Tender Act unconstitutional,[15] two fresh appointments to the Court by President Grant were promptly followed by a reversal of the obnoxious decision.[16] The congressional leaders, however, were never able to bring the Court into such abject subjection to the Congress as that which they imposed upon the presidency under Andrew Johnson and General Grant. Eventually, by a series of bold decisions,[17] Waite's Court knocked the teeth out of the Civil Rights Act and loss of control of the Congress by the Radical Republicans prevented further retaliation.

The Republican Court again became involved in partisan politics in the eighteen-nineties. Its decision in the sugar-trust case [18] seemed to draw most of the teeth from the Sherman Antitrust Act. Big businessmen were pleased, but little businessmen were filled with dismay. Its decision in the Debs case [19] gratified an unpopular Administration and pleased large employers, made anxious by labor troubles, but organized labor was outraged. Its decision in the income-tax cases,[20] however, was the principal cause of the politicians' displeasure. The Democratic Congress, which under the spur of the second Cleveland Administration had falteringly reduced the tariff, sought compensation for dwindling federal revenues by reintroducing an income tax. The Supreme Court at its first hearing of the case could not make up its mind whether to give its sanction to an act denounced as socialistic and communistic by the legal spokesmen for the "opulent," or to deny the power of a Democratic Congress to impose a tax which, when adopted by an earlier Republican Congress, the Court had not disapproved. Not since the legal-tender cases had there been such an opportunity to revive the Hamiltonian doctrine of judicial supremacy. After a second hearing a Justice who previously had been undecided finally joined with those who would hold the main provisions of the act constitutional, but another Justice, who had previously been of that same opinion, changed his mind and gave a majority to the judicial faction in favor of a judicial veto.

The income-tax decision arrayed a predominantly Republican Court against a cherished policy of the Democratic Party. Since there was difference of opinion concerning the decision among Republican as well as Democratic judges, it could not be called a partisan decision in the political sense. On the contrary, the decision tended to array the partisans of the "opulent" against those of the "indigent" regardless of ordinary political partisanship. The situation seemed to be precisely the kind of class contest which the aristocratic Nationalists in the Convention of 1787 had foreseen and with which the Hamiltonian doctrine of judicial supremacy was designed to deal. But the Democratic factions, which presently seized control of their party and nominated William Jennings Bryan for the presidency, took the lead in denouncing the decision, and Republican politicians naturally gravitated toward the other side. The Democrats officially demanded a constitutional amendment which would clearly grant to the Congress the disputed power, and eventually after thirteen years of agitation a Republican Congress, in which Republicans joined with Democrats to furnish the necessary two-thirds majority, submitted the desired amendment to the states for ratification. Meanwhile the decision gave Bryan an unparalleled opportunity to restate the doctrine of departmental parity in the interpretation of the Constitution.

Bryan's version of the doctrine of departmental parity was set forth in his sensational "cross-of-gold" speech at the Democratic National Convention of 1896.[21] He added nothing to the substance of the doctrine as expounded by Jefferson, Jackson, and Lincoln. But he made a significant contribution to what may be called the documentation of the argument. "They criticize us," he cried, meaning by "they" the Gold Democrats and Republicans and by "us" other Democrats, Silver Republicans, and Populists, "for our criticism of the Supreme Court. My friends, we have not criticized; we have simply called attention to what you already know. If you want criticism, read the dissenting opinions of the Court." Delegates to the convention, who had read these opinions, could only marvel at Bryan's moderation. Justice White, later Chief Justice, in his dissenting opinion in the income-tax cases, deplored the action of the majority of the Court in denying the power of the Congress to pass an income-tax law. It seemed to him that the majority of the Court showed too little respect for long-settled precedents and were too much influenced by personal opinions based on economic theories, political creeds, and other nonjudicial materials. "If the permanency of its conclusions," he stated,[22] "is to depend upon the personal opinions of those who, from time to time, may make up its membership, it will inevitably become a theater of political strife, and its action will be without coherence or consistency." Justice Harlan, who had been originally appointed by a Republican President, expressed himself more forcibly. The action of the majority, he declared,[23] "is deeply to be deplored. It cannot be regarded otherwise than as a disaster to the country." Justice Jackson was even more emphatic. The decision, he asserted,[24] "is the most disastrous blow ever struck at the constitutional power of Congress." The plain citizen, who knew no more about the constitutionality of an income-tax law than the fact that Congress had passed such a law a generation earlier without encountering the disapproval of the Supreme Court, noted the closeness of the division of opinion within the Court and, if a Democrat, was likely to be unconvinced that the Congress had abused its power, when so many respectable judges were charging their judicial colleagues with having abused their power.

The insular cases, following the Spanish-American War, raised constitutional issues which might easily have involved the Court in political controversy. President McKinley had plausibly asserted in a speech, dealing with the constitutional status of newly acquired dependent territories overseas, that the Constitution followed the flag. This was a popular doctrine, but it did not furnish a clear rule for determining the extent of congressional power over such territories. Were they, or were they not, a part of the United States? Were, or were not, their inhabitants entitled to the privileges and immunities of American citizens, or at least to the benefits of the due-process clause of the Fifth Amendment like other persons under the protection of the federal Bill of Rights?

The Supreme Court was unable to dispose of these questions in a forthright manner. In two early cases,[25] involving the collection of revenue on imports from Puerto Rico after the destruction of Spanish authority in that island, the Court decided by a majority of five judges to four that Puerto Rico ceased to be foreign territory when the American flag was raised over the island. At the same time the Court decided that the territory had not become part of the United States, since the Congress had not seen fit to incorporate it into the territory regarded as a part of the United States. Only one of the nine judges concurred with the majority in both of these decisions. The other eight were evenly divided between two judicial factions, one of which favored the former and opposed the latter, while the other took the opposite side in both cases. The result was convenient for the politicians, who wished as free a hand as possible in dealing with the new territorial possessions, but damaging to the prestige of the Court, which was so conspicuously unable to find a generally acceptable formula for determining the constitutional status of the new policy of territorial expansion overseas. The mental agility of one judge enabled the Court to avoid an awkward conflict with imperialistic politicians, but the Court kept out of politics at the cost of its reputation for consistency in dealing with a fundamental constitutional issue.

Other contentious issues, which the Republican Court did not succeed in avoiding, arose out of the growing demand for legislation regulating conditions of employment in capitalistic industry. The Fifth Amendment provided, among other procedural limitations on the legislative power of the Congress, that no person should be deprived

303

of life, liberty, or property without due process of law. This is a constitutional provision which lends itself to various interpretations. Liberty, for instance, is a word of many different meanings, and a deprivation of liberty therefore may mean different things to different men. Sir William Blackstone,[26] whose definitions were more familiar to the framers of the Constitution than those of any other writer on the law of the English-speaking lands, defined "personal liberty" as the power "of moving one's person to whatever place one's inclination may direct, without imprisonment or restraint, unless by due course of law." The great bulwark of this liberty, of course, was the Habeas Corpus Act. But Blackstone used the word also in a more general sense. "Political liberty," he wrote, "is no other than natural liberty, so far restrained by human laws, and no further, as is necessary and expedient for the general advantage of the public." Was the "liberty" of the Fifth Amendment Blackstone's political liberty, or was it Blackstone's personal liberty, or was it something different from either?

Whatever might be the proper answer to that question, the Fifth Amendment clearly implied that a person could be lawfully deprived of his liberty, if the requirements of due process were satisfied. But what was due process of law? Was any act of the Congress, not otherwise objectionable under the Constitution, to be deemed to have satisfied this requirement, if passed through each branch of the Congress and approved by the President in the manner provided in the Constitution? Or would a failure on the part of the lawmakers to interpret the word "liberty" in a manner that would seem reasonable to the Supreme Court make the legal process so defective as to constitute a denial of the protection promised by the due-process clause of the Amendment? An affirmative answer to the former question would give the Congress and the President a free hand in determining the policies to be embodied in whatever labor legislation might be enacted under the power to regulate interstate and foreign commerce. An affirmative answer to the latter question would enable the Supreme Court to review the wisdom of such legislation, whenever a majority of the judges should find the liberty of either an employer or his employees affected by legislative restraints, and to interpose a judicial veto, if the restraints should seem to the judges to constitute an unreasonable interference with the liberty of either party, as liberty might be defined by the Court. It is evident that a proper answer to these questions was a matter of the utmost importance in the development of the relations between the judges and the legislators, particularly in that field of legislation in which wage earners employed in capitalistic industry were becoming deeply interested.

Toward the end of Fuller's chief justiceship two cases came before the Supreme Court which gave it a convenient opportunity to answer these questions. The first arose under the Federal Employers Liability Act of 1906,[27] a favorite measure of the Theodore Roosevelt Administration. This enactment sought to establish a more generous rule than that of the common law for compensating railroad employees for injuries suffered while at work. It raised the question whether the Congress has the power to abridge the freedom of railroad companies and railroad workers to make contracts providing for methods of compensation for industrial accidents other than that prescribed by the Congress. The members of the Supreme Court required five separate opinions to set forth their views on the proper disposition of this case.

The view that freedom of contract is a part of the liberty protected by the Fifth Amendment was strongly urged upon the Court by counsel for the railroad companies. Chief Justice Fuller, together with Justices Brewer and Peckham, believing that the Act was an unreasonable limitation of freedom of contract and therefore, as it appeared to them, an unconstitutional deprivation of liberty without due process of law, would have preferred to dispose of the case on this ground. None of the other judges, however, would agree to such a disposition of the case. Justices White and Day thought the law was bad because it did not clearly distinguish between railroad workers engaged in interstate commerce and employees not so engaged. In this view Chief Justice Fuller and Justices Brewer and Peckham also concurred, and on this ground accordingly the law was declared unconstitutional.

Four judges dissented. Justice Moody set forth his reasons for dissenting in an elaborate opinion which now seems completely convincing. He argued that the Act could easily be so interpreted as to restrict its benefits to workers engaged in interstate commerce, over whom the Congress had unquestionable jurisdiction, and that it was the duty of the Court to put such an interpretation on the Act. He could not admit that the policy embodied by the Congress in the Act was unreasonable, but, he contended, even if a majority of the judges thought it was unreasonable, it should be enforced by the Court. "The economic opinions of judges and their views of the requirements of justice and public policy," he declared, "even when crystallized into well-settled doctrines of law, have no constitutional sanctity. They are binding upon succeeding judges, but, while they may influence, they cannot control, legislators. Legislators have their own economic theories, their own views of justice and public policy; and their views, when embodied in a written law, must prevail." Justice Harlan, with whom Justice McKenna concurred, and Justice Holmes also wrote dissenting opinions. Without specifically endorsing all of Justice Moody's remarks about the economic theories of judges and legislators, they joined in his conclusion concerning the disposition of the case. These judges were not prepared to limit the power of judicial review as narrowly as Moody desired to limit it, but they were determined to show more respect for the judgment of the legislators than was the majority of the Court. The result of the various opinions was that the Congress could discover how to write an employers' liability law which the Supreme Court would sustain. But the public could not fail to note the wide variety of opinion among the members of the Court concerning its proper attitude toward the legislators, and the workers could hardly escape a feeling that there was an ominous lack of sympathy in high places for their particular point of view concerning the wisdom of controversial labor legislation.

The other case, which enabled the Supreme Court at this time to consolidate its position respecting the application of the Fifth Amendment to labor legislation, arose under the Railroad Labor Disputes Arbitration Act of 1898.[28] This Act was designed to foster the settlement of labor disputes on interstate railroads by arbitration between the companies and the labor unions. In order to make the policy of arbitration more effective, the Act prohibited the discharge of railroad workers on account of membership in a union. Such a prohibition abridged the freedom of the companies to discharge workers for any reason they pleased and practically outlawed contracts of employment by which the workers agreed or were forced to renounce their right to join a union. Six members of the Court joined in declaring this Act unconstitutional.

The opinion in this case, the so-called "yellow dog" contract case, was written by Justice Harlan. He declared flatly that "there is a liberty of contract which cannot be unreasonably interfered with by legislation." He proceeded to make clear the application of this general proposition to the particular case before the Court. "The right of a person to sell his labor upon such terms as he deems proper," Justice Harlan declared, "is, in its essence, the same as the right of the purchaser of labor to prescribe the conditions upon which he will accept such labor from the person offering to sell it. So the right of the employee to quit the service of the employer, for whatever reason, is the same as the right of the employer, for whatever reason, to dispense with the services of such employee . . . In all such particulars the employer and the employee have equality of right, and anv legislation that disturbs that equality is an arbitrary interference with the liberty of contract which no government can legally justify in a free land." Thus at one stroke the majority of the Court repudiated Justice Moody's plea for judicial toleration of the economic thought of legislators and committed itself to the conflicting economic theories of Chief Justice Fuller and Justices Brewer and Peckham. In vain Justice McKenna, in a persuasive dissenting opinion, expounded the policy of the Act, based on the belief that capital and labor did not meet on terms of equality in the bargaining over contracts of employment on the interstate railroads and that strengthening the unions of the workers would check the abuse of power by the stronger party to the contract and tend to establish more equitable relations between the workers and the operators of the railroads. "Liberty," Justice McKenna declared, "which is exercised in sheer antipathy does not plead strongly for recognition." But this argument made no impression on the majority of the Court.

Justice Holmes also dissented, writing one of the terse but cogent arguments which eventually won for him his high reputation as the great dissenter. "I confess that I think," he wrote, "that the right to make contracts at will that has been derived from the word 'liberty' in the Amendments has been stretched to its extreme by the decisions; but they agree that sometimes the right may be restrained. Where there is, or generally is believed to be, an important ground of public policy for a restraint, the Constitution does not forbid it, whether this Court agrees or disagrees with the policy pursued. It cannot be doubted that to prevent strikes, and, so far as possible, to foster its scheme of arbitration, might be deemed by Congress an important point of policy, and I think it impossible to say that Congress might not reasonably think that the provision in question would help a good deal to carry its policy along. But suppose the only effect really was to tend to bring about the complete unionizing of such railroad laborers as Congress can deal with, I think that object alone would justify the act. I quite agree that the question what and how much good labor unions do, is one on which intelligent people may differ . . . but I could not pronounce it unwarranted if Congress should decide that to foster a strong union was for the best interest, not only of the men, but of the railroads and the country at large." But this philosophical plea for judicial self-restraint in exercising the power of judicial veto, like the more practical argument of Justice McKenna, fell on deaf ears.

It was such decisions as this that led Theodore Roosevelt to a spectacular outburst of criticism of the judges in his last regular message to the Congress.[29] "Every time they interpret contract, property, vested rights, due process of law, liberty," he wrote, "they necessarily enact into law parts of a system of social philosophy . . . The decisions of the Courts on economic and social questions depend upon their economic and social philosophy; and for the peaceful progress of our people during the twentieth century, we shall owe most to those judges who hold to a twentieth-century economic and social philosophy, and not to a long-outgrown philosophy which was itself the product of primitive economic conditions." But President Roosevelt was no more capable than Justice Holmes of stemming the tide of judicial opinion, then running so strongly toward the incorporation of the economic philosophy of modern capitalism into the federal Bill of Rights. The Hamiltonian doctrine of judicial review was moving into a phase of unprecedented authority.

Theodore Roosevelt made what he regarded as the abuse of the judicial veto a leading issue in the Bull Moose campaign of 1912. The defeat of the Progressives broke the force of the attack upon the doctrine of judicial review, as expounded by the Conservative Republican Court. More and more resolutely the majority of the judges claimed for themselves a free hand not only in the interpretation of freedom of contract and due process of law but also in construing other provisions of the Constitution affecting the power of the Congress to regulate the conditions of employment in capitalistic industry and to make laws particularly for the protection of labor. In 1917 and 1922, respectively, the Supreme Court declared unconstitutional the first and second federal child-labor laws,[30] and in 1923 the federal minimum-wage law.[31] The commerce and tax powers of the Federal Government as well as the due-process clause in the Fifth Amendment received such strict constructions as greatly to limit the practical capacity of the Congress to make laws deemed necessary and proper in the interest of industrial wage earners and of the general public. The official opinions for the Court did not hesitate to denounce the legislation as unreasonable and therefore unconstitutional despite the manifestly contrary opinions of the legislators. The Hamiltonian doctrine of judicial review was clearly in the ascendant.

The climax of the struggle between the judges and the legislators over the exercise of the power of judicial review came when the Conservative Republican Court began to wreck the legislative program of the New Deal Democrats. In 1935 first the Hot Oil Act and then the entire National Industrial Recovery Act were declared unconstitutional; [32] so were the Railroad Retirement Act,[33] the Federal Farm Mortgage Act,[34] and the Municipal Corporations Bankruptcy Act.[35] In the following year the Court struck down the Agricultural Adjustment Act [36] and the Bituminous Coal Conservation Act.[37] These decisions seemed to threaten destruction also to the National Labor Relations Act and the whole of the Social Security Act, and to the proposed Fair Labor Standards Act. The doctrine of judicial supremacy had brought the country at last to the plight against which Lincoln had solemnly warned in his "First Inaugural." [38]

Franklin D. Roosevelt's attack upon the Supreme Court stimulated a resolute defense by its friends. Among the friends of the Court were many who disliked its recent provocative decisions but disliked even more a threat to the Court's freedom of action. The issue was shifted from the doctrine of judicial supremacy to the principle of judicial independence. Meanwhile, unexpected shifts of opinion within the Court took place in the pending National Labor Relations Act [39] and Social Security Act cases,[40] and a new majority was found to sustain the constitutionality of the remaining fragments of the Administration's legislative program. Chief Justice Hughes preserved the independence of his Court, but the Court paid a high price for victory in the form of a humiliating reversal under political pressure in its attitude toward the paramount questions of constitutional interpretation. President Roosevelt lost his battle for the court-packing bill, but won the war for the salvation of the New Deal.[41]

Republican supremacy in the Supreme Court did not long survive the change of attitude under the impact of Roosevelt's proposals for judicial reform. Like the impeachment of Justice Chase by the Jeffersonians at the close of the first period in the political history of the Court, this spectacular struggle between the judges and the legislators marked the actual end of an era. Under the judicious leadership of Chief Justice Hughes, as under that of Marshall during the latter part of Jefferson's presidency, the transition from the fourth to the fifth period in the partisan history of the Court was skillfully accomplished. It was still true, as Marshall had declared more than a century earlier, that the Constitution was intended to "endure for ages to come,"

309

and hence should be "adapted to the various crises of human affairs." The New Deal Court without too sharp a break with the past addressed itself to the perennial problem of adapting the constitutional system to the changing circumstances of the American people. The changes in those circumstances had been great and were rapidly becoming greater. The separation of powers, however, remained one of the principles of the Constitution, and the Supreme Court continued to play the role of guardian of the system of checks and balances in so far as that system might be involved in what the Court recognized as justiciable questions raised by cases brought before it for adjudication.

The fifth period in the political history of the Supreme Court had already opened, when President Roosevelt raised Justice Harlan F. Stone, the most consistent and persuasive protagonist of judicial self-restraint in the exercise of the power of judicial review, to the leadership of the Court. The Hamiltonian doctrine of judicial supremacy was again abandoned, but it was not clear precisely what would take its place. The doctrine of departmental parity requires a degree of self-denial in the use of judicial power beyond what is to be expected of most successful jurists, endowed with security of tenure and responsible for passing final judgment on all questions of law. On the other hand, the Hamiltonian doctrine of judicial supremacy can carry a Court further than prudent judges who have witnessed such a struggle as that of 1937 would ordinarily wish to go. Responsibility for the guardianship of the Constitution cannot be lightly shifted by conscientious judges, not even to legislators as highly placed as the leaders in the White House and on Capitol Hill. Neither can it properly be made the pretext for irresponsible adventures in national politics. The Court under Chief Justice Stone signalized its refreshened sense of responsibility by breathing new life into the guarantees of the Bill of Rights in cases involving the fundamental freedoms of the common man.[42] But it found no clear path to the goal of nonintervention in the political acts of the legislators.[43]

In the use of its power of judicial veto the New Deal Court under Chief Justice Stone showed great restraint. Only one act of Congress was declared unconstitutional.[44] This was a measure by means of which Congress sought to force the discharge of certain administrative officers whom it disliked by forbidding payment of their salaries. The Court found that such a measure was in effect an act of attainder, which is specifically prohibited by the Constitution. Other legislative measures, which raised important constitutional issues, were the

Emergency Price Control Act of 1942, the Economic Stabilization Act of the same year, and the provisions of the Priorities Statute and of the Second War Powers Act governing the production and distribution of articles and materials required for the national defense and found to be in short supply. The essential features of this legislation were declared to be constitutional,[45] but not without dissent by the lone survivor of the former majority in the Conservative Republican Court, which had struck down so many New Deal measures prior to President Roosevelt's attack upon the Court. Apparently the Conservative Republican Court, if it had been the guardian of the Constitution during the crisis of World War II, would have disallowed the essential features of the Administration's program for the management of the national economy in time of war. Happily the New Deal Court was able to adapt the Constitution to this crisis in the nation's affairs without repudiating the principle of the separation of powers or destroying the practical utility of the system of checks and balances.

The New Deal Court manifestly took to heart Justice Holmes's often-quoted dictum: "it must be remembered that legislatures are ultimate guardians of the liberties and welfare of the people in quite as great a degree as the courts." A due remembrance of this elementary truth should foster a proper humility on the part of Supreme Court judges in the exercise of their high function of declaring the fundamental law of the land. Yet the judges cannot divest themselves of their final responsibility for giving to the Constitution the character of a layman's instrument of government, as Franklin D. Roosevelt phrased it,[46] rather than that merely of a lawyer's contract. This responsibility necessarily involves the judges in a constant appearance before the ultimate court of public opinion. Doubtless no final judgment can be passed on the performance of the judiciary, regarded as an integral part of a working system of checks and balances, without considering their exercise of the power of judicial review of executive as well as legislative acts and also their role in maintaining the stability of the system of federalism. Nevertheless certain tentative conclusions are in order concerning the relations between the Supreme Court and the legislative branch of the Federal Government.

THE ROLE OF JUDGES
IN THE SYSTEM OF CHECKS AND BALANCES

In the first place, the history of the Supreme Court discloses an uneven record of partisanship. At times the Court has audaciously,

311

indeed almost recklessly, plunged into the midst of the struggles between the major political parties. A Federalist Court under Marshall's
leadership challenged the Jeffersonians, and later a Jeffersonian Court
under Marshall's leadership challenged the Jacksonians, a Jacksonian
Court challenged the Antislavery Republicans, a Lincoln Republican
Court challenged the Radical Republicans, and a Conservative Republican Court successively challenged the Populistic Democrats, the
Progressives, both Republican and Democratic, and the New Deal
Democrats. These clashes between the Court and the political departments of the government were not always avoidable, but they were
always injurious, in the long run if not immediately, to the Court's
prestige. The judges did not succeed in settling permanently the
political issues in which they became involved, and the permanent
settlement was invariably contrary to the Court's wishes.

It did not escape the notice of the legislators or of the public that
the Court in these controversies was invariably on the side of the
parties which had been in power in the age that was passing away and
was in opposition to the spirit of the age that was coming to power.
Its function in the scheme of checks and balances seemed to have been
to delay the process of change from an old order to a new. If the
framers had possessed a definite theory of progress, the conclusion
would logically follow that such delay must have been their intention,
and that the power to enforce a reasonable delay, in order that the
people might make sure of their desire for change, held an important
place in their system of checks and balances. Since the principal advocates of a strong and independent Supreme Court, consistently with
their eighteenth-century philosophy, sought stability rather than
progress, their purpose must have been to maintain an equilibrium
rather than to regulate the rate of evolutionary change. If these controversial decisions with their partisan implications constituted the
whole of the record of the use of the judicial veto, it would be difficult
to dissent from the implications of Justice Holmes's frank avowal in a
speech delivered shortly after Theodore Roosevelt's campaign for limitations upon the judicial veto. "I do not think," he said,[47] "the United
States would come to an end, if we lost our power to declare an Act
of Congress void." One vigorous and salutary veto, however, like that
of the New Deal Court in the Lovett case, gives pause to those who
would condemn the doctrine of judicial review.

The full record of judicial review of acts of the Congress shows that
controversial decisions on partisan issues have formed only a part of

the total. There have been times when the Supreme Court has studiously avoided involvement in partisan issues, particularly after a specially unpopular decision has injured its prestige, but it has not hesitated to use its power to disapprove and render void objectionable measures which were not important subjects of contention between the major parties. To be sure, the Court under the leadership of Marshall and Taney exercised the judicial veto only twice against acts of the Congress, and the results were in each case unfortunate. But under the later Chief Justices the acts of the Congress have more frequently encountered the veto of the Court and the results have been a mixture of good and bad fortune. It was not only in the Lovett case that the Supreme Court protected the system of constitutional government against serious damage by unwise use of legislative power.

There is no part of the system of checks and balances which in its practical operation furnishes clearer evidence in support of the framers' belief that those who possess political power are likely to abuse it. The exercise of the power of judicial review involves a perennial inquiry into cases of alleged abuse of power. If the Supreme Court majorities have frequently, if not always, been right, there has been a good deal of abuse of power by the federal lawmakers. If the dissenting minorities within the Court have occasionally been right also, there has been some abuse of power by the Supreme Court itself. As Justice Stone pertinently observed in his dissenting opinion in the Agricultural Adjustment Act case, "Congress and the courts both unhappily may falter or be mistaken in the performance of their constitutional duty." The system of checks and balances contains within itself the means of correcting the mistakes of judges as well as of legislators. The very vicissitudes in the relations between judges and legislators, and the persistent uncertainty over how far judges should go in dealing with legislation believed by them to be unreasonable, supply the most convincing arguments in justification of this feature of the framers' original plan of government.

In reviewing the constitutionality of acts of the Congress, it must be noted, the judges have repeatedly been caught so far behind the march of public opinion that, in default of a humiliating about-face on their part, only an amendment to the Constitution could bring the necessary adaptation of the instrument of government to the needs of a changing order. These amendments have taken time and the need for them has caused criticism of the judges. Nevertheless, the framers deliberately planned substantial barriers against too facile alteration

313

of the fundamental law. They also intended that what they liked to call a government of law be reconciled somehow with the requirement that it be at the same time a government of the people. An instrument of government must be able to serve the purposes of those for whose use it is designed.

The decisions against which the two Roosevelts strenuously protested, like the earlier income-tax, legal-tender, and Dred Scott decisions, revived the perennial argument over the propriety of keeping judges out of politics. The defenders of the Supreme Court could point out that the decisions certainly were not political in any partisan sense. There was no Republican judge on the Court at the time of the Dred Scott case, but in all the later highly controversial decisions both judges appointed by Republican Presidents and judges appointed by Democratic Presidents were divided in their opinions. The division of opinion within the Court tended to run along the line foreshadowed by the original cleavage between the Hamiltonian and the Jeffersonian doctrines of judicial review. The Hamiltonians would have smiled serenely at decisions so generally favorable to the interests of the "opulent," but the Jeffersonians could only have been filled with dismay that so many judges, who seemed to merit great confidence for their learning and integrity, should nevertheless have used the legal check, which the principle of the separation of powers put into their hands, to tip the balance so heavily against what some of them regarded as not unreasonable measures of legislators representing numerical majorities of the people. The separate and independent power of judicial veto, despite Madison's unsanguine attitude in the Convention of 1787, had proved a surprisingly effective substitute for the aristocratic devices which had been rejected by the framers. But how could Jefferson have been so wrong in his expectations of a body which, "if rendered independent and kept strictly to their own department," should have merited great confidence from those who, like himself, set a high value on the judicial protection of fundamental freedoms and basic human rights?

Two facts about Supreme Court judges stand out in the records of the Court. One is, that they have been lawyers; the other, that the periods when the Court has been most conspicuously conservative in its attitude toward the work of the legislators have been periods when the judges were elderly lawyers. The average age of the original judges appointed by President Washington was under fifty. By the end of the first period in the partisan history of the Court their average age had

314

risen to the middle fifties. Fresh appointments brought down the average again to under fifty at the beginning of the Jeffersonian Republican period. By the end of Marshall's tenure of office as Chief Justice the average had risen to almost sixty-five. Fresh appointments to the Jacksonian Court brought the average down again to the middle fifties. It had risen by the end of Buchanan's Administration to the high sixties. Lincoln's appointments brought it down to the low sixties. At the time of Franklin D. Roosevelt's attack on the Court the average had risen above seventy.[48] The New Deal Court once more was a comparatively young Court.

The careers of extraordinarily liberal-minded judges such as Holmes and Brandeis forbid a general indictment of elderly lawyers on a charge of excessive conservatism. Nevertheless the opinions of many competent observers since Edmund Burke support the view that lawyers naturally tend toward conservatism and that the older lawyers tend to be the more conservative. The "aristocracy of the robe" is no novel concept. Hamilton, in *The Federalist*, obviously anticipated the development of such an aristocracy. De Tocqueville, writing in the age of Jackson, included the conservative character of the legal profession among the principal factors tending to prevent the abuse of power by representatives of popular majorities in a democracy, and assigned to the influence of the judges great weight in maintaining the equilibrium of the American system of checks and balances. A half-century later John W. Burgess described the "aristocracy of the robe" as "the truest aristocracy for the purposes of government which the world has yet produced." [49] He considered the vigorous exercise of its conservative influence an essential feature of the American political system. "I believe," he declared, "that the secret of the peculiarities and excellencies of the political system of the United States, when compared with those systems founded and developed by priests, warriors, and landlords, is the predominant influence therein of the jurists and the lawyers." The record of the exercise of the power of judicial review shows that the influence of the "aristocracy of the robe" has indeed been great. Has this powerful aristocracy intervened too much in politics? And what precisely has been the nature of its influence?

There can never be any altogether satisfactory answer to the question, how free shall the judges be to disallow acts of the Congress which seem to some of them an abuse of the legislative power vested in the Congress by the Constitution. There is no better advice for Supreme Court judges, tempted to assert their authority against that of the legislators in close and doubtful cases, than the advice offered by Justice Stone, with the concurrence of Justices Brandeis and Cardozo, to the willful majority of the Court in the Agricultural Adjustment Act case. "The power of courts to declare a statute unconstitutional," he wrote,[50] "is subject to two guiding principles of decision which ought never to be absent from judicial consciousness. One is that courts are concerned only with the power to enact statutes, not with their wisdom. The other is that, while unconstitutional exercise of power by the executive and legislative branches of the government is subject to judicial restraint, the only check upon our own exercise of power is our own sense of self-restraint. For the removal of unwise laws from the statute books appeal lies not to the courts but to the ballot and to the processes of democratic government." Stone laid great stress on the last point, returning to it again near the close of this masterly opinion. "Courts," he asserted, "are not the only agency of government that must be assumed to have capacity to govern." The power of the judges to veto acts of the Congress involves power to check, but not to overbalance, that of the legislators to enact the measures they deem necessary and proper.

The record of the Supreme Court shows that the judges have not always been able to exercise the self-restraint deemed desirable by the great dissenters in the last years of the Conservative Republican Court. It is unlikely that the future will be greatly different from the past. Supreme Court judges are apt to be strong-minded men with a keen sense of duty and an eager desire to make the most of their role in the system of checks and balances. In the nature of things they will not see eye to eye in matters concerning which reasonable men are unable altogether to agree. Even judges who wish to avoid unseemly contentiousness will take different views of controversial issues.[51] Judicial factions within the Court seem inevitable. Some judges will steadily incline to views favorable to the interests of that class of people which the aristocratic Nationalists had hoped to protect through the agency of an aristocratic Senate and a power of joint executive-judicial veto. Others will not be so inclined. In the Conservative Republican Court the former type of judge predominated. In the New Deal Court the latter type has been stronger. Yet the influence of elderly lawyers on the Court seems generally to have made it disposed rather to a Hamiltonian than to a Jeffersonian version of the doctrine of judicial review. Hamilton judged the nature of judges on the whole more correctly than Jefferson. The struggle to keep the Hamiltonians on the Court from getting too much the better of the Jeffersonians seems likely to be perennial.

This of course is as it should be in a system of constitutional government based upon the principle of the separation of powers. It is desirable therefore to rationalize the political function of judges in such a system. Charles P. Curtis has done it most acceptably.[52] The Supreme Court, although in name a court of law, has become also, by virtue of the power of judicial review, an organ of government which, like other political organs, necessarily chooses between competing interests and competing policies. In making its choices it should be guided by the best current philosophy of the time. It does not need to pay as much attention to the election returns as the more obviously political branches of the government, but it must manage somehow to provide for each age an acceptable interpretation of fundamental political principles. It should not reflect as quickly as ordinary legislators the popular responses to the challenge of changing conditions. It should be more concerned with general principles than with special interests. It should no more be a pro-labor Court than a pro-capital Court. But neither should it get too far out of touch with the temper of the times. Elderly judges are likely from time to time to commit this error. Fresh appointments of younger men should ordinarily bring the needed correction to the tone of the Court. In short, as Hamilton intimated, it is a function of the Supreme Court to interpret the spirit of the Constitution. Nevertheless, the spirit, as Jefferson ventured to hope, may at times be Jeffersonian rather than Hamiltonian.

In this aspect of its operation the system of checks and balances seems shrewdly designed to accomplish its purpose. The threat of impeachment has not had to be invoked for the purpose of restraining judges in the use of their political powers since the last years of the Federalist Court. On only three occasions has it been necessary to correct judicial errors in the use of the power of judicial review by the adoption of constitutional amendments establishing the interpretation of the Constitution rejected by the Court. Resort to the threat of packing the Court has been more frequent; yet the Court remains of a convenient and suitable size. The periodic vicissitudes in the legislative influence of the Court offer the most convincing evidence of the success of the framers in contriving this feature of their general scheme. There has been ample room within the apparently rigid framework of the Constitution for great ups and downs in the practical capacity of the judges to assert their authority and make their opinions of sound public policy felt in the operations of government. They have been able to respond to the demands of certain times for the vigorous exercise of judicial power in the process of legislation without so far upsetting the balance as to destroy the possibility of regaining under altered circumstances a more tranquil relationship with the legislators.

The framers manifestly built better than they knew. Both the doctrine of judicial supremacy and that of departmental parity have made important contributions to the theory of constitutional government. The rigid constitutional framework has been sufficiently flexible to permit the interdepartmental give-and-take essential for the adaptation of a Constitution originally designed for an eighteenth-century agricultural economy to the more exacting requirements of a twentieth-century urban and industrial world. The judges have been kept out of politics to a greater extent than the aristocratic Nationalists believed would be compatible with due security for the property of the "opulent." They have not been so completely excluded from politics as to render them incapable of intervening in the legislative process, when necessary, to protect what has seemed to a majority of them to be the essential rights of both rich and poor. Their intervention has served to protect the interests of the rich more frequently than those of the poor, but the perpetual possibility that the Court, under the stimulus of Jeffersonian doctrines, will put a new spirit into the Constitution helps to reconcile the peculiarities of a government of law with the requirements of a government of the people.

The success of this feature of the system of checks and balances throws further light on the Hamiltonian theory of social and political dichotomy. At times it has seemed to some critics of the Supreme Court's decisions affecting political controversies that they were unduly favorable to the interests of the rich. Such critics have been prone to denounce the Court as a special agency of that particular minority of the people. The current form of this criticism is the Communist denunciation of the Court as the agent of the capitalist class. There can be no doubt that the Court has at times been more mindful of the interests of property owners of various kinds than one or both of the contemporary major political parties. But the Court has also failed at times to give to powerful groups of property owners the amount of protection they have demanded. On this point the decision affirming the validity of the Gold Clause Resolution of 1933 affords convincing evidence.[53] A Court which could have connived at the destruction of the system of private property would be inconceivable in a land where most of the people have owned moderate amounts of property or have been able to hope that they or at least their children would become property owners. On the other hand, a Court which would deliberately surrender the fundamental freedoms of the common man is equally inconceivable, while the common man and the average man are so nearly the same person as in the United States.

The truth is, that the record of the Supreme Court, like that of the political parties, is unintelligible on the assumption that there is a sharp division of the population into the rich and the poor. It becomes intelligible only when the fact is recognized that in the United States there is no such social division of the people, but on the contrary the poor and the rich gradually merge into one another through a great intermediate middle class the interests and attitudes of which in the long run have dominated the social and political thinking of both legislators and judges. The perennial conflict between Hamiltonian and Jeffersonian doctrines of judicial review is persuasive evidence of the paramount influence of the American middle class in maintaining the equilibrium of the more perfect Union.

CHAPTER TEN

Judges and Administrators

THE CONSTITUTIONAL THEORY OF ADMINISTRATION

THE importance of right relations between the executive and judicial branches of the government was well understood by the framers of the Constitution. Edmund Burke's reflections on the subject, expressed in 1770 in his *Thoughts on the Cause of the Present Discontents*, must have been familiar to many of them, and his analysis of the problem of judicial checks on executive power would have seemed reasonable to all. *"The discretionary powers which are necessarily vested in the monarch,"* Burke had written,[1] *"whether for the execution of the laws, or for the nomination to magistracy and office, or for conducting the affairs of peace and war, or for ordering the revenue, should all be exercised upon public principles and national grounds, and not on the likings or prejudices, the intrigues or policies, of a court.* This, I said, is equal in importance to the securing a government according to law. The laws reach but a very little way. Constitute government how you please, infinitely the greater part of it must depend upon the exercise of the powers which are left at large to the prudence and uprightness of ministers of state. Even all the use and potency of the laws depend upon them. Without them, your commonwealth is no better than a scheme on paper; and not a living, active, effective constitution. It is possible, that through negligence, or ignorance, or design artfully conducted, ministers may suffer one part of government to languish, another to be perverted from its purposes, and every valuable interest of the country to fall into decay and ruin, without possibility of fixing any single act on which a criminal prosecution can be justly grounded. The due arrangement of men in the action part of the state, far from being foreign to the purposes of a wise government, ought to be among its very first and dearest objects."

The framers had little desire for either a monarch or a court, but the discretionary powers vested in the independent and "high-toned" chief executive, which the Convention was persuaded to approve as a part of its last great compromise, were wide. There were doubtless limits to the executive power, as ultimately established, but these limits were not defined in the Constitution or indicated except in the most general way in the debates of the Convention. If the nature of the executive power was to be found in the spirit of the Constitution and could not be determined by act of Congress — the executive veto was authorized primarily in order to make that difficult — its limits would have to be determined by judicial action or depend on the interior arrangement of the executive branch itself. What might be accomplished by judicial action the framers did not venture to say. What might be accomplished by the interior arrangement of the executive offices was to be inferred from the provisions concerning the power of appointment, from the lack of provisions concerning the power of removal except by impeachment, and from the stipulation that instead of ministers, responsible to Congress, there should be heads of departments from whom the chief executive might require opinions in writing.

The uncertainty of the framers concerning the relations between the executive and judicial branches of the government was most plainly disclosed in their discussion of proposals for an executive council. Early in the proceedings of the Federal Convention the defeat of the advocates of a plural executive and the decision to vest the executive power in a single person raised the questions whether, and if so to what extent, the action of the president should be conditioned upon the advice and consent of a council. In general the advocates of a plural executive wanted a strong executive council, while the leading Nationalists opposed it, fearing that a council would stand in the way of the strong and independent chief executive which they desired. But the position of the Nationalist leaders was not altogether clear, since, fearing also that any chief executive would not be strong enough to stand alone against the representatives of the people in the Congress, Madison and Wilson were eager to associate with the chief executive in the exercise of his proposed veto against acts of the lawmakers, both national and state, a "suitable number of the judges." This proposal for a joint executive-judicial veto indicated that the Nationalist leaders were more deeply interested in an effective system of checks and balances than in any logical separation of powers and would be governed in their attitude toward proposals for an executive council by expediency rather than by principle. But the Nationalist scheme for a council of revision was rejected by the Convention, and efforts by leaders among the original Federalists to establish a council of any kind came to nothing with the collapse of the New Jersey plan.

Later in the proceedings of the Convention the question of an executive council was revived. On August 18th Ellsworth proposed a council, which should include the chief justice with the heads of departments, but Gerry was opposed to letting the chief justice have anything to do with the formation of policy and Dickinson renewed the earlier suggestion that the ministers be appointed by the Congress. Four days later Rutledge reported for the Committee of Detail a proposal for a privy council, to include the president of the Senate and the speaker of the House as well as the chief justice and the principal executive officers. This proposal, despite the weight of its sponsors, was ignored by the Convention and no more was heard of the subject until September 7th, when Mason, seconded by Franklin, moved the establishment of an executive council. Morris, speaking for the grand committee whose plan for a strong and independent chief executive was then pending before the Convention, explained that the kind of president they hoped to see at the head of the more perfect Union would be able to organize for himself such a body of advisers as he might find helpful. More specific provision in the Constitution for a presidential cabinet, he argued, would be incompatible with the strong and independent chief executive called for by their plan. This view was accepted by the Convention. A system of checks and balances was set up, based upon a more logical application of the principle of the separation of powers than had originally been contemplated by the aristocratic Nationalist leaders, but the further reconciliation of logic and expediency was left to the statesmanship of the future in the light of experience under a living Constitution.

THE ACTUAL RELATIONS
BETWEEN JUDGES AND ADMINISTRATORS

The development of the constitutional relationship between the administrators and the judges, like that between the legislators and the judges, responded to the impact of the party system upon the administrative and judicial establishments. In the period of Federalist supremacy, as Professor White has reminded us in a magisterial study of its administrative history, the question whether or not the new general government would even endure "was much in men's minds." He makes clear that Washington brought to his new task of chief administrator the same fine personal qualities which had marked his successful leadership of "the great rehearsal" in 1787. "Twelve years of experience under the Constitution," White concludes,[2] "sufficed to reveal much difference of opinion and considerable variation in practice on the administrative arrangements implementing the constitutional decisions. But good will and restraint on both sides" — a reference to the struggles between the Federalists and the Jeffersonian Republicans — "marked the initiation of the new order." Washington, of course, regarded a well-conducted judicial establishment as an essential, if not an integral, part of a well-conducted administration. His own relations with Chief Justices Jay and Ellsworth were intimate and cordial, and the contretemps with Chief Justice Rutledge, growing out of Rutledge's intemperate attack against the Jay treaty, afforded further evidence, if such evidence were needed, of Washington's conviction that the Chief Executive and the Chief Justice should stand together in politics and presumably also in administration. "His principal success," White testifies,[3] "was to plant in the minds of the American people the model of a government which commanded respect by reason of its integrity, energy, and competence."

In the Federalist period the essence of the relationship between judges and administrators was that between the Chief Justice and the Chief Executive. Under John Adams the relations with Ellsworth and his Court were no less intimate and in general no less cordial than under Washington. But under John Marshall the emphasis shifted from a decorous adherence to the principle of the separation of powers to a strenuous application of the system of checks and balances. Marshall in the Marbury case intimated that his Court had a right to command the heads of executive departments, and by implication the Chief Executive himself, to perform administrative duties of a ministerial character and also to determine which of the executive duties were ministerial and which were discretionary. This claim of power would have precipitated a head-on collision with Jefferson but for Marshall's happy discovery that the act of Congress under which the case had been brought into court was itself unconstitutional. Marshall's threat to dictate to the President in matters which Jefferson deemed strictly executive provoked retaliation, culminating in the impeachment of the politically most offensive of Marshall's judicial associates. The acquittals of Justice Chase and of Aaron Burr ended the open conflict between Chief Justice and Chief Executive and ended also the confusion of politics and administration in the relations between the judicial and the executive branches of government.

The frustration of the Federalist effort to sustain their declining political fortunes by calling the judiciary into the field of politics forced the Federalist judges to fall back upon strictly judicial processes in order to preserve a proper influence for the Court in the government of the more perfect Union. Chief Justice Marshall, in the "Flying Fish" case,[4] committed his Court to the general propositions that all public officers, military and naval as well as civil, are bound to obey the ordinary law of the land, and are personally amenable to the jurisdiction of the ordinary courts of law for their official acts. But he failed in his effort to compel President Jefferson to appear as a witness in the trial of Aaron Burr and thereafter was more cautious in asserting responsibility for a reign of law in the executive branch. President Jefferson, on the other hand, presently decided to content himself with protecting the independence and authority of his Administration by appointing suitable judges, as vacancies occurred, and relying upon their sound judgment for the development of a proper relation between the executive and judicial branches of the government. After the failure of the attempt to remove Justice Chase there were to be no more impeachments of judges for political reasons and much greater circumspection and self-restraint by politically minded courts. Thus by the end of the period of Federalist supremacy in the Supreme Court the foundations of a practical system of executive-judicial checks and balances had been laid upon a logical interpretation of the principle of the separation of powers.

The second period in the history of the Supreme Court, during which John Marshall headed a Jeffersonian Republican Court, was marked by the avoidance of clashes between the judiciary and the executive until the arrival at the White House of the pungent personality of Andrew Jackson. In cases arising out of the troublesome international situation after the failure of Jefferson's embargo and the military operations in the War of 1812 the Court actually handed down decisions which strengthened the discretionary authority of the executive in dealing with foreign affairs and in making war.[5] For the most part during this period the Supreme Court was concerned with the distribution of legislative powers between the states and the Union. A series of great decisions laid the foundations for a strict construction of the authority of the state governments and for a broad construction of that of the government at Washington. In adapting the Constitution to the various crises of the times the Jeffersonian Republican Court under Marshall's leadership gave the federal system a nationalistic character well suited to the sound growth of the nation. Even Jacksonian Democrats did not object to the strengthening of the federal executive and judiciary. Jacksonians, who insisted that the President had a constitutional right to order the removal of the Government's deposits from the Bank of the United States, had previously denounced the Court for its refusal to declare unconstitutional the act of Congress by which the Bank obtained its charter. They would have preferred a stricter construction of the legislative authority of the Congress, but yielded nothing to Marshall in their claims of power for the Chief Executive and for the Supreme Court itself.

The third period in the history of the Supreme Court, during which Roger B. Taney headed a Jacksonian Court, was less important for its contribution to the relations between judges and administrators than for its contributions to the relations between judges and legislators and to those between the nation and the states. In the Dred Scott case the Court asserted its supremacy over the Congress in the interpretation of the provisions of the Constitution relating to the legislative power as boldly as Andrew Jackson would have liked it to do in the great case of *McCulloch* v. *Maryland*. Roger B. Taney had been a Federalist, as long as there had been a Federalist Party, and was less hostile to the established traditions concerning the judicial power than might be supposed from his participation in Jackson's attack upon the Bank of the United States. As the head of the Jacksonian Court, however, he had to find a suitable formula for reconciling Jackson's claim for the President of an equal right with the Court to construe the Constitution, at least those provisions of the Constitution affecting the executive power, and Marshall's claim for the Court of final authority in all questions of law which might arise under the Constitution. The logical incompatibility of an unqualified doctrine of judicial supremacy and an unqualified doctrine of the equal right of each of the three coördinate departments of government to interpret its authority under the Constitution could not escape a legal mind as keen as Taney's.

The Jacksonian Court's solution of this constitutional dilemma was both ingenious and practical. The occasion arose in a case growing out of the overheated, but happily not sanguinary, political controversy in Rhode Island known to history as Dorr's rebellion.[6] The President of the United States refused to interfere on behalf of the rebels, holding that the government under the old constitution was the lawful govern-

325

ment of the state. The partisans of the new "People's Constitution" appealed to the courts for a review and reversal of the President's decision, claiming a right under the Federal Constitution to a republican form of government. Taney's Court refused to intervene, asserting that the question presented to it was essentially political and hence unsuited for determination in a court of law.

This distinction between political and justiciable questions enabled the Court to maintain its claim to supremacy in the decision of questions of law without clashing with the President in matters of policy concerning which the Chief Executive necessarily possesses a wide discretionary authority. It was not a new distinction, but it was a distinction which Taney's Court put to a new and significant use. Marshall's Court had never ventured to interfere with what it recognized as a political decision by the Chief Executive. It had not interfered, for instance, when President Monroe vetoed an act of Congress (the Cumberland Road Act) on constitutional grounds which Marshall could not have regarded as valid, though it did offend both President Jefferson and President Jackson by intervening in cases involving executive acts which they, though not the Court, regarded as clearly within the ambit of their discretionary authority. Taney's new emphasis on this distinction enabled both Court and President to retreat with honor from untenable positions. It was a brilliant strategic move in the perennial give-and-take between the judicial and the executive branches in the adaptation of the principle of the separation of powers to the requirements of a serviceable system of checks and balances.

Taney's Court did not allow the doctrine of political questions to impair its jurisdiction over those so-called ministerial acts of administrative officers in the performance of which their discretionary authority is reduced to a minimum. Postal officials too deeply engrossed in "politics," who were reluctant to discharge their legal obligations to those having business dealings with the post office, found the Court an insuperable obstacle to the improper mingling of politics and administration.[7] In a period marked by the progressive decentralization and disintegration of the administrative systems of the state governments the power of the courts to enforce the performance of routine duties by state administrative officers was indispensable for a tolerably fair and efficient administration of state laws. In the judicial task of holding administrative officers to a strict performance of clearly defined duties Taney's Court set a salutary example. The judicial power imposed necessary limits on the operation of the spoils system in the executive branch of government. It was not until the outbreak of civil war near the end of the Jacksonian period in the history of the Supreme Court that Taney discovered limits to the judicial authority over administration with which he did not know how to deal.[8] He could not recognize President Lincoln's decision to suspend the privilege of the writ of habeas corpus as political, and he was too old to redetermine the limits of presidential authority under the war power. The Jacksonian period in the history of the Court came to an end amidst growing confusion under the challenge of doctrines which would have been more gratifying to the robust temper of Andrew Jackson than they could be to the more legalistic mind of his frustrated Chief Justice.

THE RECORD OF THE REPUBLICAN COURT

The period of Republican supremacy in the history of the Supreme Court, like the three earlier periods, was marked by a perennial struggle to reconcile a serviceable system of checks and balances with a logical theory of the separation of powers. The further development during this period of the working relations between judges and administrative officers, like the development of the relations between judges and legislators, fell into three well-defined stages, which together covered three-quarters of a century, a period as long as the first three periods together. The first of these stages was coterminous with the terms of Chief Justices Chase and Waite, during which the Court was engaged in restoring the balance between the executive and the judicial power, so greatly disturbed by the vigorous use of the war power under President Lincoln. The second stage, which corresponded with the term of Chief Justice Fuller, was marked by the growth of new problems of administration which put the doctrine of the separation of powers to a new test and forecast a new phase in the development of the system of checks and balances. The third stage, corresponding with the terms of Chief Justices White and Taft and most of that of Chief Justice Hughes, saw the emergence of a new doctrine of judicial supremacy which, in the field of administration as in that of legislation, provoked a fresh conflict with the coördinate branches of government and resulted in another readjustment of the relations between them.

The first task of the new Republican Court, in restoring the balance between the executive and the judicial power, was to redefine the war power and reëstablish the authority of the Court over the acts of public officers, military as well as civil. The leading case was that of Milligan,[9] involving the legality of the trial of a civilian outside the theater of active military operations by a military tribunal. During the war President Lincoln had repeatedly ordered the suspension of the privilege of the writ of habeas corpus in the border states, thereby clearing the way for a military trial of persons suspected of rendering unlawful aid and comfort to the enemy. This he had done on the plea that in extraordinary emergencies, such as those created by underground plotting in the interest of the Southern Confederacy, the President and Commander in Chief should be guided by the maxim, *Salus populi suprema lex.* For some of these executive orders he had subsequently received the sanction of a congressional act of indemnity. But in Milligan's case the trial remained without congressional sanction. Milligan thus could become the passive agent of those champions of the constitutional principle of the separation of powers who were determined that dubious precedents created under pressure of an emergency should not stand unchallenged as guides for the future.

The Supreme Court had no difficulty in reaching a unanimous decision that the President had no right to suspend the privilege of the writ of habeas corpus without authority from Congress. But there was sharp disagreement concerning the implications of this decision. The majority of the Court joined in an opinion that Milligan, being a civilian under the jurisdiction of a loyal state government, had a right to be tried in a regular criminal court and punished, if guilty, under the ordinary law of the land. But four of the judges, including a majority of those appointed by President Lincoln, deemed it important not to seem to limit unduly the power of Congress, while imposing a necessary limitation on the executive power. They therefore subscribed to a separate concurring opinion, written by Chief Justice Chase.

"Where peace exists," the new Chief Justice declared, "the laws of peace must prevail." But he maintained that "when the nation is involved in war, and some portions of the country are invaded and all are exposed to invasion, it is within the power of Congress to determine in what states or districts such great and imminent public danger exists as justifies the authorization of military tribunals for the trial of crimes and offences against the discipline or security of the army or against the public safety." He was as firm as the majority of the Court, however, on the main point, holding that "there was no law for the government of the citizens, or the armed forces of the United States, while they were within American jurisdiction, which was not contained in or derived from the Constitution. And wherever our army or navy may go beyond our territorial limits, neither can go beyond the authority of the President or the legislation of Congress." These remarks were doubtless what the lawyers call *obiter dicta*, since they were not required to support the decision in the case actually before the Court, but Chief Justice Chase and those judges who concurred in his opinion were obviously mindful of the high function of the Court to give the American people sound advice concerning their constitutional rights as well as to justify its disposition of the actual case. They were determined that a war fought to free the slaves should not incidentally have the effect, even in the smallest measure, of enslaving the free.

Half a century later, when the exigencies of the first World War again caused the war power to be pressed to its limit, the meaning of the precedent established by the Supreme Court in Milligan's case became a matter of immediate interest. Charles E. Hughes, later the greatest of the Republican Chief Justices but then temporarily in private life, discussed the nature of the war power in a report to the American Bar Association.[10] He, like all the members of the Court in 1867, recognized the necessity of furnishing a substitute for the civil authority, when overthrown, in order to preserve the safety of the army and the nation. But he could not accept the majority's test of necessity, the actual closing of the civil courts. The test, Hughes believed, should not be merely physical, such as the fact that the civil courts are open or closed, nor should the Supreme Court attempt to indicate in advance the kinds of circumstances which would justify the substitution of military for civil tribunals. It is for Congress to determine such questions of expediency. To this extent he agreed with the opinion of Chief Justice Chase. But he could not give an unqualified approval of Chase's views. "If this necessity actually exists," Hughes concluded, "it cannot be doubted that the power of the Nation is adequate to meet it, but the rights of the citizen may not be impaired by an arbitrary legislative declaration. Outside the actual theater of war, and if, in a true sense, the administration of justice remains unobstructed, the right of the citizen to normal judicial procedure is secure." This opinion touches the relations between the judges and the lawmakers, as well as those between the judges and the commander in chief, in time of war, but it confirms the importance of the precedent established in Milligan's case as a means of redressing the balance between the judges and the coördinate departments of the American Government, both executive and legislative.

Several years after the Milligan decision the Supreme Court found a convenient opportunity to assert its power to keep public officers within the law over administrative officers employed by the Congress. The case of *Kilbourn* v. *Thompson* [11] grew out of the arrest by the sergeant at arms of the House of Representatives of a witness before a congressional committee who had refused to answer questions which, he contended, the committee had no right to put to him. The sergeant at arms defended himself on the ground that he was acting by direction of the House and should not be held responsible for the order of his superiors, which he felt bound to obey. The Supreme Court found, however, that the committee was investigating a matter which lay outside the constitutional jurisdiction of the Congress. The opinion for the Court was written by Justice Miller, probably the ablest of the Supreme Court justices during this period in its history. "The House of Representatives," Justice Miller declared, "not only exceeded the limit of its own authority, but assumed power which could only be properly exercised by another branch of the government, because it was in its nature clearly judicial." The sergeant at arms was held personally responsible for his action, even though performed in pursuance of his official duty, and the Court won another round in its struggle to regain a proper position in the constitutional system of checks and balances.

A more sensational case in which the judges asserted their authority to correct abuses of power by public officers was that of *United States* v. *Lee*.[12] This case arose out of an action for ejectment by the son of General Robert E. Lee against the commandant of Fort Myer and the superintendent of the national cemetery at Arlington, formerly the property of the Lee family. The Lee estate had been acquired during the Civil War by officers of the War Department for the use of the Government, taking advantage of the nonpayment of taxes on the property by the owners. General Lee during his lifetime never contested the transaction, but after his death the legal heir claimed the property on the ground that, in taking possession for the Government, the officers of the War Department had not respected the law relating to the seizure of such property for nonpayment of taxes. The fact of noncompliance with the law was clear. On behalf of the War Department, however, it was argued that in an emergency public necessity or convenience justified the procedure of the War Department officials and furthermore that the suit was in effect a suit against a sovereign state, which should not be permitted without its expressed consent. The case was complicated by sentimental considerations. In the Arlington cemetery lay buried the bodies of thousands of Union soldiers, and the possibility of the desecration or at least the neglect of their graves in consequence of the restoration of the land to a man who had taken up arms against the United States caused deep concern throughout the northern part of the Union.

In this case the Supreme Court was closely divided. A majority, however, joined in a judgment for the plaintiff. Their opinion, again written by Justice Miller, declared that the suit was not to be regarded as one against the United States but rather against the particular persons who were in actual possession of the property. It declared further that the property legally belonged to Mr. Lee. "We are told," Justice Miller continued, "that the Court can proceed no further, because it appears that certain military officers, acting under the orders of the President, have seized this estate, and converted one part of it into a military fort and another into a cemetery. It is not pretended, as the case now stands, that the President had any lawful authority to do this, or that the legislative body could give him any such authority except upon payment of just compensation. The defense stand here solely upon the absolute immunity from judicial inquiry of every one who asserts authority from the executive branch of the government, however clear it may be made that the executive possessed no such power." Justice Miller made short work of this argument. "Not only no such power is given, but it is absolutely prohibited, both to the executive and the legislative, to deprive any one of life, liberty, or property without due process of law, or to take private property without just compensation."

Justice Miller then announced in imperishable language the principle of the supremacy of law and the authority of the courts to maintain that supremacy even against the highest public officers. "No man in this country is so high as to be above the law. No officer of the law may set that law at defiance with impunity. All the officers of the government, from the highest to the lowest, are creatures of the law, and are bound to obey it. It is the only supreme power in our system of government . . . Courts of justice are established, not only to decide upon the controverted rights of the citizens as against each other, but also upon rights in controversy between them and the government." There is no case in the reports of the decisions of the Supreme Court in which its proper authority under the principle of the separation of powers is asserted with more impressive logic and dignity.

By the end of this stage in the period of Republican supremacy in the history of the Supreme Court, firm and prudent judges had re-

331

covered the prestige and power lost to the other branches of the government during the last years of the Jacksonian Court and the early years of the Republican Court itself.[13] The success of the Republican Court in redressing the balance between the judiciary and the coördinate branches was even more impressive in its dealings with executive officers than in its dealings with the lawmakers. Judicial errors of judgment had brought its prestige low and seriously impaired its practical capacity to maintain the system of checks and balances in good working order. Popular passions, inflamed by bitter partisan controversy and the sanguinary appeal from the political forum to the battlefield, increased the difficulties which stood in the way of a greater influence for moderate and conciliatory men on the bench. In the struggle to bring executive officers back under the law, however, no blunder was committed such as the judicial veto of the legal-tender act. The theory of the separation of powers continued to furnish a broad and solid foundation for the exercise of an effective power of judicial review of executive as well as of legislative acts. The Supreme Court successfully reasserted its right to share in the power to govern. It was on the whole successful also in manifesting a judicious self-control in its exercise of that right.

The chief justiceship of Melville W. Fuller marked the transition between the earlier stage in the history of the Republican Court, when it was struggling to regain an equal position in the system of checks and balances, and the later stage, when its growing prestige enabled it to achieve unprecedented victories in a struggle for judicial supremacy in the exercise of self-determined judicial power. The attitude of the Chief Justice toward the new issues which came before the Court made him a fitting symbol of the trend of the times, though a lack of personal force, rather than the fact of his appointment by a Democratic President, prevented him from becoming the Court's real leader. The record of the Republican Court during this stage of its history shows the same trend in the development of the relations between the judges and the executive branch of the government as in that of the relations between the judges and the legislative branch. There was, to be sure, no case involving judicial review of administrative acts in which the Court so boldly exploited its enhanced prestige and so grievously abused its growing power as in the judicial veto of the income-tax law of 1894. But the inauguration of government by injunction in the Debs case also provoked passionate controversy. These questionable decisions increased the reputation of the Court as the guardian of the rights of property, but by thrusting it again into the midst of political and partisan controversy they revived the memory of former errors and again unsettled its position in the system of checks and balances. Meanwhile, the process of transformation from a Radical Republican to a Conservative Republican Court continued.

The growing power of the Court was not the result alone of the natural tendency for men with power to press their power to its limit. It was also a reasonable and desirable response on the part of the judges to the growth of the executive power, which at this time was beginning the great expansion that has continued down to the present. The opportunity for the Court to expound more precisely and more generously the nature of the executive power grew out of the new legislation enacted by the Congress to deal with the new problems of the times. But the very circumstance that the Court was called upon to redefine the executive power enabled it also to redetermine the relations between the executive branch of the government and the judiciary. A serviceable system of checks and balances required a parallel growth of executive and judicial power, which in turn was dependent upon a suitable interpretation of the principle of the separation of powers. In the development of the new legislation Congress was likely to be guided rather by experience than by logic. In developing the principle of the separation of powers so as to maintain a serviceable system of checks and balances, the Court would have to be mindful of experience also, but could not altogether neglect the claims of logic.

The new age in the development of executive and judicial power under the Federal Constitution began with the establishment of the Interstate Commerce Commission in 1887. Nineteen years later President Roosevelt put teeth into the Interstate Commerce Act when he persuaded the Congress to give the Commission authority definitely to fix railroad rates. In 1910, at President Taft's instigation, the Congress recognized the importance of a distinction between the quasi-legislative powers, as the phrase was then, of a rate-regulating agency and its quasi-judicial powers, and established the Commerce Court to relieve the Interstate Commerce Commission of much of its responsibility in the field of administrative adjudication. It was evident that the new policy of federal regulation of interstate railways was creating some new problems in the practical application of the principle of the separation of powers. Did the logic of the principle require the separation of the Commerce Court from the Interstate Commerce Commission, as President Taft argued, or would a greater respect for the teachings

333

of experience suggest that the Supreme Court rather than the Congress should make the necessary readjustment in the relations between the judges and the administrators?

The early demise of the Commerce Court increased rather than diminished the uncertainty concerning the effect of the railroad rate regulation laws upon the established system of checks and balances.[14] The judges, like the politicians, were confused about the nature of the regulatory process. In 1877 the Supreme Court had declared that the regulation of the rates of businesses "affected with a public interest," whatever that might mean, was a legislative function, and that persons who might feel aggrieved at the results of such rate regulation should appeal to the voters at the polls for the election of wiser lawmakers rather than to the judges in their courts for a review and revision of the legislative product.[15] But in 1890 the Supreme Court reversed itself, holding that the regulation of rates was a judicial process, in which the judges were bound to have the last word.[16] Several of the surviving members of the Court as it was in 1877 protested strenuously at the new decision of 1890, but the general public, distrustful of the practical capacity of the voters to hold the members of regulatory commissions responsible at the polls for the use of the wide discretionary authority conferred upon them by the lawmakers, and obviously incapable of attending personally to the details of effective railroad rate legislation, seemed content to let the Supreme Court work out a satisfactory relationship in the regulatory process between the three branches of government.

The Sherman Antitrust Act of 1890 provided the judges with an excellent opportunity to develop an ancient principle of the law into an effective instrument of judicial control over administrative action under the new regulatory legislation. This ancient principle was the rule of reason. The new regulatory laws were alike in authorizing administrative officers to find the facts upon which regulatory action should be based and in granting them further wide discretionary authority to make the action fit the facts, as found. It was not difficult for the judges to insist that the administrative officers should be guided by reason in the exercise of their wide discretionary authority. It took longer for the judges to conclude that they themselves, rather than the administrators, should be the final arbiters of what was reasonable.

The justification for the establishment of regulatory commissions was that experience would give their members greater expertness in the determination of the reasonableness of action under the new regulatory laws than could ordinarily be acquired by legislators or judges. They would also enjoy better opportunities for finding the facts upon which alone reasonable action could be based. It was not until 1911 that the Supreme Court ventured to apply the rule of reason in its new form to the enforcement of the Sherman Act.[17] Its extension to the problem of rate regulation would naturally follow, judges could logically conclude. Administrators, it was obvious, would hold a different opinion, particularly if they were conscious of possessing special technical qualifications for their work.

The reciprocity provisions of the McKinley Tariff Act of 1890 gave the judges another opportunity to sanction the expansion of the discretionary authority of the executive and to redefine the relations between executive and judicial power. The Congress was persuaded that the President should have more effective powers of retaliation against foreign countries which discriminated against American manufacturers and exporters under their tariff laws, in order to protect the American interest in foreign markets. The McKinley Act therefore provided maximum and minimum schedules of tariff rates and authorized the President to impose the maximum rates on imports from countries which refused to grant the same treatment to exports from America as was granted to the exports of the most favored nation. Such a delegation of authority, it was argued by the opponents of the policy of reciprocity, was in effect a delegation of legislative power by the Congress to the executive branch of the government, which would be in conflict with the theory of the separation of powers. The Supreme Court, however, took the contrary view.[18] The Congress, the Court decided, had by law established two alternative general policies, and had then merely authorized the President to determine the facts in the light of which he was to select the proper policy for regulating the trade with a particular country in accordance with standards of judgment prescribed by the law itself. This process, the Court concluded, was by nature strictly executive.

It was evident that such a method of expanding the discretionary authority of the executive could result in an unpredictable growth of the executive power. How specific must the Congress be in designating the facts which, as found by the President, should be the basis for exercising the discretionary authority to be conferred upon him? And how much latitude did the Congress possess in prescribing standards for the guidance of the executive in the exercise of discretionary authority under such legislation? Could the Congress authorize the President

335

to exercise his discretion to act, whenever he should find action to be in the public interest? And would a general statement of the policy which the Congress wished to pursue, contained in the preamble of a statute, be a sufficient formulation of the standards guiding the discretionary authority of the executive? These were questions to which the Supreme Court would eventually give the final answers. In so doing it would necessarily claim for itself the power to make such adjustments in the system of checks and balances as might be required by its interpretation of the principle of the separation of powers.

The historic mission of the Conservative Republican Court under Chief Justices White, Taft, and Hughes was to extend the executive and judicial powers no less resolutely than it restricted the legislative powers of the Federal Government. This process resulted not only in a shift of power from the legislative branch to the coördinate branches of the government, but also in the more vigorous exercise than ever before of judicial control over the executive. Great changes were brought about in the practical operation of the system of checks and balances. The Conservative Republican Court sought to justify these changes by what it declared to be a logical interpretation of the principle of the separation of powers. Since not logic but experience gives life to the fundamental law, final judgment on the Court's performance must rest on the consequences of the changes in the operation of the check-and-balance system.

The outstanding contribution of the Conservative Republican Court to the logical development of the relations between the three branches of the Federal Government was its definition of the executive power. The occasion was a conflict of opinion concerning the power to remove postmasters before the expiration of their terms of office. The Congress had passed a law in 1876, providing for the appointment of postmasters for terms of four years and for their removal before the end of their terms in the same way in which they were appointed, that is, by the President with the consent of the Senate. President Wilson removed a postmaster for what he considered due cause without waiting for the Senate's consent. The vacancy was not filled in such a way as to imply the consent of the Senate to the removal and the aggrieved postmaster brought suit in the Court of Claims for the unpaid salary during the balance of his term.[19]

The framers of the Constitution made no explicit provision for the removal of public officers except by the process of impeachment. One inference is that their intention was to exclude all other processes of

336

removal. Another is that the failure to specify any other method of removal left the Congress free to act under its grant of power to make all laws necessary and proper for carrying into execution the powers vested by the Constitution in the Government of the United States. This inference, if well founded, would enable the Congress to make such arrangements for the removal of executive officers, appointed under the authority of acts of Congress, as might be agreeable to a majority of the Representatives and of the Senators, if the President approved, or as might be agreeable, without the President's approval, to two-thirds of the Representatives and of the Senators. A third inference is that the power of removal is an incident of the power of appointment, and accordingly executive officers, if appointed by the President with or without the consent of the Senate, or by a department head or a court of law, should be removable in the same way, or by impeachment, but in no other way. A fourth inference is that the power of removal is a part of the executive power, vested by the Constitution in the President, and that consequently, in default of any explicit limitation in the Constitution other than the establishment of tenure during good behavior for judges and of four-year terms for the President and Vice-President, it is not to be abridged by an act of Congress. The duty of the Supreme Court to interpret the Constitution compelled it to choose among these four versions of the power of removal.

Chief Justice Taft, who presided over the Court when this case came before it, having been himself President, was deeply impressed with the importance of interpreting the power of removal in such a way as to afford the Chief Executive the greatest possible assistance in performing his constitutional duty to take care that the laws be faithfully executed. From this point of view the fourth version of the power of removal was most eligible. An unrestricted discretionary power to remove any subordinate officer in the executive branch of the government, though subject to abuse for partisan purposes by an excessively partisan President, is most favorable to the efficient discharge by a competent chief executive of his responsibility for the faithful execution of the laws. Such a power of removal seemed to a majority of Taft's Court the most logical corollary of the principle of the separation of powers. This was also the conclusion of the First Congress, when establishing the executive departments at the original organization of the Federal Government.

This had not been the opinion of Chief Justice Marshall, however, when deciding the case of *Marbury* v. *Madison*. That decision made sense only on the assumption that President Jefferson did not have the power to remove Marbury from his office, once the commission was in Marbury's possession. It had not been the opinion of the Radical Republican Congress when it passed the Tenure of Office Act, designed to prevent President Johnson from removing members of his Cabinet in whom the Congress had more confidence than in the President himself. It had obviously not been the opinion of the Congress when it passed the Act which had given rise to the case pending before the Court. It was viewed with misgiving by government employees and friends of the merit system in the civil service, since under the interpretation of the Constitution favored by Taft's Court there was nothing to prevent the removal of efficient civil servants on purely political grounds by a partisan chief executive. It was viewed with misgiving also by members of the regulatory commissions and advocates of the method of regulation by independent administrative agencies, which would be exposed to dangerous political interference, specially in the performance of their quasi-judicial duties. But this version of the executive power made for a more powerful chief executive than any of the other versions.

The nature of the executive power of removal from office was reconsidered by the Conservative Republican Court under Chief Justice Hughes.[20] President Roosevelt had removed a Republican member of the Federal Trade Commission on the ground, as the President put it, that this commissioner's mind did not go along with his own. He wished to bring the Commission into closer harmony with the Administration by appointing a new member with greater sympathy for the policies of the New Deal. He did not contend that Commissioner Humphrey was inefficient. His only complaint was that, as Chief Executive, he was entitled to have a Commission which in the exercise of its wide discretionary authority could be trusted to support the Chief Executive's measures. In so far as the work of the Commission was purely executive in character, or lay within the field of administrative law-making, there was obviously much to be said for the President's point of view. But in so far as the Commission's work consisted of administrative adjudication, there was surely something to be said in favor of an interpretation of the executive power which would secure to the Commission greater independence of action.

The act creating the Federal Trade Commission made careful provision for its protection against what might be considered undue

338

political influence. No more than three of the five members were to belong to the same political party. Their appointments were for terms of seven years, not more than one member would reach the end of his term in any one year, and the only causes for removal specified in the act were inefficiency, neglect of duty, and misfeasance. The question was, therefore, whether the President might remove a commissioner for any other cause. Under the precedent established by Taft's Court the answer would have to be in the affirmative. But two members of Hughes's Court, Justices Brandeis and McReynolds, had dissented in the earlier case, and none of its members could be unmindful of the words of Justice Holmes, who had also dissented in the earlier case. The arguments of Chief Justice Taft, he had written, "seem to me spiders' webs inadequate to control the dominant facts." And he had tersely declared his preference for a different theory of the executive power. "The duty of the President to see that the laws be executed is a duty that does not go beyond the laws or require him to achieve more than Congress sees fit to leave within his power."

Justice Sutherland, in his opinion for a unanimous Court in the Humphrey case, did not go as far as Holmes would have gone in redressing the balance between the legislative and the executive powers. But he went far enough in his revision of the Taft theory to secure for the judges a greater voice in checking the abuse of power by either of the other branches of government. "Whether the power of the President to remove an officer shall prevail over the authority of Congress to condition the power, by fixing a definite term and precluding a removal except for cause, will depend upon the character of the office; the Myers decision, affirming the power of the President alone to make the removal, is confined to purely executive officers; and as to officers of the kind here under consideration, we hold that no removal can be made during the prescribed term for which the officer is appointed, except for one or more of the causes named in the applicable statute." Justice Sutherland recognized that his opinion left much room for doubt concerning the nature of a purely executive office. On that point he contented himself with saying: "To the exent that . . . there shall remain a field of doubt, we leave such cases as may fall within it for future consideration and determination as they may arise."

This important decision in the development of the judicial theory of a separation of powers offered little comfort to ordinary government workers employed under the merit system. It did not even indicate clearly where the members of the great regulatory commissions stand in the tripartite structure of the Federal Government. Are they a part of the executive branch, or, since they act also both "as a legislative agency" and "as an agency of the judiciary," do they belong to either or both of those coördinate branches of the government? Or do they constitute, as some writers have suggested, a "fourth branch" of government? The Court did not say. But it did disclose its purpose to consider and determine the degree of independence to be enjoyed by many of the most powerful civil officers whom the Congress may authorize the President to appoint. May the President remove a member of one of the great regulatory commissions before the expiration of his statutory term on the alleged ground of inefficiency when in fact the President merely wishes to create a vacancy in order to fill it with an officer whose mind goes along together with his own on the policies of the Administration? Sutherland's opinion did not face this question. All that is clear is that with respect to appointments and removals the Court decided to occupy a stronger position in the practical operation of the system of checks and balances than it had ventured to claim for itself since Marshall's futile decision in the Marbury case.

The effect of this decision was not only to secure to members of regulatory commissions greater freedom of action but also to increase the sense of independence on the part of other important administrative officers. Presently the chairman of the Tennessee Valley Authority fell out with two of his colleagues and refused to admit the right of the President to hold him accountable for the charges which he brought against them. He was accountable, he declared, only to the Congress. The President rejected this view and removed him for contumacy and insubordination.[21] In this case the Supreme Court refused to intervene. The T.V.A. was presumably a purely executive agency. The Congress could not be permitted to embarrass the President in the proper performance of his duty to take care that the law be faithfully executed.

The Tennessee Valley Authority Act raised some other interesting questions concerning the lawful distribution of the power to remove administrative officers. It provided that any member of the board of directors of the T.V.A. might be removed from office at any time by a concurrent resolution of the Senate and the House of Representatives. It provided also that any member of the board whom the President might find guilty of appointing or promoting officers or employees of the corporation for political reasons, or for any reason other than merit or efficiency, should be removed from office by the President. If the members of the board were purely executive officers, by what right did the Congress presume to direct the President when to remove them, or reserve to itself authority to make removals at pleasure? Evidently the logic of the Court's interpretation of the nature of executive power was not clearly understood in the other branches of the government. But its disposition to protect the Chief Executive against what it considered undue interference by the Congress was plain enough. In maintaining the place of the executive in the system of checks and balances, the Court reserved to itself the right to have the last word.

The disposition of the Conservative Republican Court to sanction the shifting of power, within limits to be fixed by itself, from the legislative to the executive branch of the government was further illustrated by its treatment of cases involving the exercise of contingent powers of administrative lawmaking. The problem of determining the limits of allowable administrative lawmaking is one to be settled ordinarily between the judges and the lawmakers in the legislative branch of the government. But there remains to be settled between the judges and the administrators the administrative procedures in this field of administrative action which shall be deemed consistent with the constitutional requirement of due process of law. In the first place, the administrative agency must find the facts, which are the justification for administrative action, in a proper manner. Secondly, it must be guided in its action by a reasonable interpretation of the standards of administrative discretion contained in the "intelligible principle" prescribed for its guidance by the Congress.[22]

As in dealing with the power of removal, the Conservative Republican Court began by sustaining the executive in its claims of wide discretionary authority in the choice of procedures and ended by a strict enforcement of judicial methods of proceeding upon administrative agencies. The trend of the Court's thinking is well illustrated by its action in cases involving the kind of hearing to which parties interested in a proposal for some administrative legislation may be entitled. In a case which arose under the flexible tariff law the Court held that the Tariff Commission had satisfied the requirements of due process of law respecting the kind of hearing to which an importer should be entitled, before the duty on imports of a certain chemical could be raised, by granting him such a hearing as he might have had before the Ways and Means Committee of the House of Representatives.[23] But in cases arising a few years later under the Packers and Stockyards Act the Secretary of Agriculture was held to a stricter compliance with

341

methods of conducting hearings favored by the judges.[24] The Court twice decided that Secretary Wallace's methods of hearing commission merchants, before reducing the rates charged in certain stockyards, were so defective as to cast doubt on the validity of the entire proceedings. Since the Congress had not prescribed any particular procedure, the controversy lay entirely between the Court and the Department of Agriculture and resulted in the assertion of judicial supremacy over the administrators in the choice of a method of administrative law-making.

The most extreme interference by the Conservative Republican Court with the administrative processes of an agency to which wide discretionary authority had been granted by the Congress involved a proceeding before the Securities and Exchange Commission. An oil-stock vendor, who had filed a registration statement with the Commission, learning that the Commission contemplated a further investigation before permitting the applicant to offer the stock for sale to the public, sought to prevent the investigation by withdrawing the questionable statement. This the Commission refused to permit him to do, alleging that the ends of justice might thereby be defeated. The Supreme Court decided that the applicant's notice of withdrawal should stop the Commission from further proceedings in the matter.[25] Justice Sutherland declared bluntly for a majority of the Court that "the action of the Commission finds no support in right principle or in law. It is wholly unreasonable and arbitrary. It violates . . . allowable official discretion."

Justices Brandeis, Stone, and Cardozo dissented, the latter writing an opinion in which all three joined. "The rule now assailed," he declared with bluntness not inferior to Sutherland's, "was wisely conceived and lawfully adopted to foil the plans of knaves intent upon obscuring or suppressing the knowledge of their knavery." The majority opinion, denouncing what it called the Commission's "unlawful inquisitorial investigation," had compared its action to the proceedings of the infamous royal court of the Star Chamber under the Stuarts. Justice Cardozo remarked that "historians may find hyperbole in the sanguinary simile." But the majority, without questioning the power of the Congress to authorize the Commission to protect the public against fraudulent promoters, persisted in its determination to review, and, if deemed desirable, to disallow the Commission's methods of proceeding in such cases.

A dissent by the same three judges in another case, decided by the

Court at this time, in which the opinion was also written by Justice Cardozo, throws a clear light on the different attitudes then existing in the Court concerning the proper role of administrators and judges, respectively, in the administration of modern legislation conferring wide discretionary authority on special regulatory agencies. This case grew out of an effort by the New Dealers to salvage something from the wreck of the National Industrial Recovery Act. Enacted shortly after the decision of the Supreme Court in the Schechter case, the Bituminous Coal Conservation Act provided for the adoption of codes of fair competition in the soft-coal-mining industry. Appropriate standards were provided for the guidance of the authorities set up to administer the act, and elaborate procedures for finding the essential facts were carefully prescribed. It was the intention of the lawmakers that the codes should regulate both the prices of the coal and the wages of the miners, as far as this might be possible under the power of Congress to regulate interstate commerce, and every effort was made to avoid the fatal error, committed by the authors of the N.I.R.A., of attempting to delegate too much legislative power to administrative officers.

The majority of the Court decided, nevertheless, that this Act too was unconstitutional.[26] They found it defective, not only under the commerce and due-process clauses, but also because in their opinion the standards for administrative action were too indefinite, with the result that there had been an unlawful delegation of legislative power. Moreover, "the power conferred upon the majority [of the code authorities] is, in effect, the power to regulate the affairs of an unwilling minority. This is legislative delegation in its most obnoxious form." The majority judges seemed to put little trust in the intelligence of the administrators or in their practical capacity to use their authority under the act wisely and effectively.

The three dissenting judges believed that the Bituminous Coal Conservation Act could be easily distinguished from its unlamented predecessor. It seemed clear to them that the special conditions in the coal-mining industry made unrestricted competition an inadequate safeguard of the consumers' interests. "There has been no excessive delegation of legislative power," Justice Cardozo categorically declared. "The standards established by this Act are quite as definite as others that have been approved by this Court." Then he went on to indicate the grounds for his greater confidence in administrators than in judges for such work as that of the National Bituminous Coal Commission. "Certainly a bench of judges, not experts in the coal business,"

343

he insisted, "cannot say with assurance that members of a commission will be unable, when advised and informed by others experienced in the industry, to make the standards workable, or to overcome through the development of an administrative technique many obstacles and difficulties that might be baffling or confusing to inexperience and ignorance." But the majority of the Court rejected this faith of the minority, and of the majority of the Congress, in the competence and potential usefulness of administrative *expertise*. The majority judges would sanction the delegation of some legislative power, but not too much, to administrators, and they reserved to themselves the right to determine how little would be too much.

The disposition of the Conservative Republican Court to exalt the executive power at the expense of the legislative, and the judicial power at the expense of both, was most clearly revealed in its treatment of cases involving the power to regulate "businesses affected with a public interest." There had been much controversy since 1890 concerning the line of division between the legislative and the judicial power in this field of governmental action, and a growing realization of the necessity of entrusting a greater share of the power to executive officers, particularly in the regulation of railroad rates and those of other public utilities. Logic seemed incapable of furnishing a practicable rule for the distribution of rate-regulating power between the three principal kinds of public officers. Long years of contention, however, over the valuation of property for rate-making purposes and the determination of a proper rate of return on the property "devoted to the public use" had brought increasing dissatisfaction with the established checks against the abuse of power in this field of action. The owners of property subject to regulation seemed to have more confidence in judges than in administrators as arbiters of the reasonableness of rates. The users of the services of these public utilities were inclined to put their trust chiefly in the administrators. Experience indicated the need for a better balance among the various kinds of authorities concerned with the regulatory process.

The Conservative Republican Court's theory of rate regulation was most clearly expounded, and most forcefully challenged, in another case which grew out of the efforts of the Department of Agriculture to regulate the charges of commission dealers in the stockyards.[27] Chief Justice Hughes, speaking for the majority of the Court, conceded that the fixing of rates is a legislative act. Legislative action, however, the Chief Justice insisted, "is necessarily subject to independent judicial review upon the facts and the law by courts of competent jurisdiction to the end that the Constitution as the supreme law of the land may be maintained." Administrative bodies acting as legislative agents would of course be subject to the same kind of judicial review for the same purpose. The Chief Justice felt strongly on this point. "Legislative agencies, with varying qualifications, work in a field peculiarly exposed to political demands. Some may be expert and impartial, others subservient. It is not difficult for them to observe the requirements of law in giving a hearing and receiving evidence. But to say that their findings of fact may be made conclusive where constitutional rights of liberty and property are involved, although the evidence clearly establishes that the findings are wrong and constitutional rights have been invaded, is to place those rights at the mercy of administrative officials and seriously to impair the security inherent in our judicial safeguards." The judges, in Hughes's opinion, could not escape the responsibility for guaranteeing a correct determination of whatever they might regard as "constitutional" facts. It would not be enough that the judges should review and approve the procedures of the administrators. They must make sure that the substance of the administrators' findings is also correct. Nor did the Chief Justice stop with judicial review of administrative fact finding. He went further, insisting that the duty of the judges to exercise an independent judgment in rate cases requires them likewise to assess the "weight" to be attached to the administrative finding of facts, and to take into account the entire process, including the "reasoning" upon which the action rests.

Justice Brandeis stated the views of the minority of the Court, who were disposed to put greater trust in the administrators. He could think of no good reason why findings of fact by the Secretary of Agriculture should not be as conclusive in cases where a constitutional issue is involved as in other cases. "Is there anything in the Constitution," he inquired, "which expressly makes findings of fact by a jury of inexperienced laymen, if supported by substantial evidence, conclusive, that prohibits Congress making findings of fact by a highly trained and specially qualified administrative agency likewise conclusive, provided they are supported by substantial evidence?" He thought not. Moreover, in his opinion, "the Court must consider the effect of our decisions not only upon the function of rate regulation, but also upon the administrative and judicial tribunals themselves. Responsibility is the great developer of men. May it not tend to emasculate or demoralize the rate-making body, if ultimate responsibility is transferred to others?

To the capacity of men there is a limit. May it not impair the quality of work of the courts, if this heavy task of reviewing questions of fact is assumed?" Justice Brandeis's answers to these questions are implied in an observation by Justice Stone in a dissenting opinion for the same minority of the judges in another case decided at this term of the Court. "Courts," according to Justice Stone, "are not the only agency of government that must be assumed to have capacity to govern." [28]

THE RECORD OF THE DEMOCRATIC COURT

The disposition to redress the balance between administrators and judges by discouraging such vigorous use by the courts of their power to check the actions of the new regulatory agencies, as Chief Justice Hughes deemed necessary and proper, was a leading trait of the New Deal. President Roosevelt's attack upon the Court was directed against what New Dealers believed to be the abuse of the judicial power to review and veto the acts of administrators in whom wide discretionary authority was vested, as well as against the abuse of the power to review and veto acts of Congress. Under the New Deal Court the views of the judges who had been the great dissenters under the Conservative Republican Court tended to prevail in the field of administrative law as in that of constitutional law.[29] President Roosevelt's promotion of Justice Stone to the office of Chief Justice was the clearest expression of New Deal approval for the general attitude of Justices Holmes, Brandeis, and Cardozo as well as for that of Stone himself. The perennial problem of reconciling a serviceable system of checks and balances with a logical theory of the separation of powers would be approached from a new point of view. The doctrine of judicial supremacy would be deflated. But the struggle for power between judges and administrators would continue to rage under new ideological devices, and different opinions concerning the requirements of a stable equilibrium between the separate branches of government would continue to contend for acceptance.

The first decade of the New Deal Court witnessed a revolution in the attitude of the judges toward the exercise of wide discretionary powers by administrators. Chief Justice Stone spoke for the Court in the leading cases which sanctioned the establishment of the new administrative procedures and reconciled them with the constitutional requirements of due process of law. In the leading case on administrative procedure under the Fair Labor Standards Act of 1938 the Court sustained the proceedings of the administrator of the Wage and Hour

Division of the Department of Labor in fixing minimum wages and maximum hours in the textile industry.[30] The statute provided an elaborate and complicated process for fixing minimum wages, including an Industry Advisory Committee designed to represent the various interests within the industry. Chief Justice Stone's opinion made clear the determination of the Court to approve not only the particular administrative processes which Congress had authorized under this act but also other processes which Congress might deem necessary and proper for the execution of measures conferring wide discretionary authority upon administrators. The fixing of minimum wages and maximum hours of labor in the great industries of the country had been one of the original objectives of the New Deal and this decision went far to destroy the force of the precedents established by the Court in its earlier decisions under the National Industrial Recovery and Bituminous Coal Conservation Acts.

This more tolerant judicial attitude toward administrators extended to cases involving the range of discretion as well as the procedures of the new administrative agencies. In the field of administrative legislation there was a long series of decisions, affirming the validity of general orders and regulations establishing new policies for the management of business within the limits of the discretionary authority delegated by Congress to the members of the independent regulatory agencies. Outstanding among these decisions were those approving the regulation of national broadcasting chains by the Federal Communications Commission,[31] the readjustment of railroad rates between the major traffic regions of the country by the Interstate Commerce Commission,[32] and the abolition of the basing-point price system by the Federal Trade Commission.[33] In the last decision Justice Black patted the administrators on the back, saying: "The Commission has exhibited the familiarity with the competitive problems before it which Congress originally anticipated the Commission would achieve in its experience." The great regulatory commissions had at last come of age and were to be trusted with a major share of the responsibility for translating public policy into the law of the land and taking care that this part of the law be faithfully executed.

In the field of administrative adjudication also this more tolerant judicial attitude toward administrators was made manifest. Chief Justice Stone carefully reviewed the proceedings and findings of the Federal Power Commission under the Natural Gas Act of 1938 and concluded that its order in the case of the Natural Gas Pipeline Company was valid.[34] "The courts cannot intervene," he declared, "in the absence of a clear showing that the limits of due process have been overstepped." Justice Black, speaking for himself and Justices Douglas and Murphy, criticized the majority of the Court for inquiring in such detail into the methods of the Commission in reaching its decision. The Act, he noted, provides that "a finding of the Commission as to facts, if supported by substantial evidence, shall be conclusive." Therefore, "it is not the function of the courts to prescribe what formula should be used . . . The rate of return to be allowed in any case calls for a highly expert judgment. That judgment has been entrusted to the Commission. There it should rest." No member of the Court dissented from the decision. In the next important case under the Natural Gas Act Justice Douglas wrote the opinion for the Court.[35] "The fixing of 'just and reasonable' rates," he pointed out, "involves the balancing of the investor and the consumer interests." This was work, obviously, for administrators rather than for judges. Justice Jackson took the trouble to write a separate opinion, expressing the thought that the Commission might have done its work better than it did. But, as Justice Cardozo had intimated in an earlier case, "unwisdom" is not equivalent to "abuse" of power.[36]

In later cases the New Deal Court went far beyond its Conservative Republican predecessor in its refusal to substitute its own discretion for that of administrative officers whom it found to have kept within the bounds of their administrative powers. In one case, involving a decision by the National Labor Relations Board that suspension of employees for solicitation on the employer's premises during the employees' own time was an unfair labor practice, Justice Roberts complained in a dissenting opinion that the Board had no right to reach its decision in the light of its own knowledge of industrial conditions without more substantial evidence of the unfairness of the particular labor practice at issue. But the newer members of the Court found no difficulty in approving an administrative decision based on the administrators' own *expertise*.[37] Again, the Court approved an order of the Securities and Exchange Commission disallowing an objectionable feature of a reorganization plan for a business which had been in financial difficulties.[38] Justices Jackson and Frankfurter dissented, with an opinion by the former [39] denouncing the decision of the majority for fostering an administrative process which in this case, they thought, was no better than "a method of dispensing with law." Justice Murphy defended the Court's decision, declaring that "the Commission's conclusion [was] . . . the type of judgment which administrative agencies are best equipped to make, and which justified the use of the administrative process. Whether we agree or disagree with the result reached, it is an allowable judgment which we cannot disturb."

The rejuvenated Supreme Court, in adjusting the relations between legislators and administrators and between both and the general public, eventually secured a constitutional place for economic planners and for centralized economic planning in the government of the more perfect Union. The Conservative Republican Court would have made the execution of economic plans, if not the process of planning, unconstitutional. The New Deal Court successfully adapted the Constitution to the crisis of modern capitalism in a democratic republic. The management of capitalistic industry under a system of unrestrained enterprise tends to be dictatorial. Workers in industry under such a system, accustomed to a more democratic regime in politics, demand more democracy also in industry. Consumers demand better order in industries where the relations between management and labor become too disorderly, and greater influence over the pricing and distribution of their products. These purposes cannot be achieved, as Walter Lippmann seems to argue, in one of the most significant of his books, that they should,[40] by legislation and judicial proceedings alone. Better order in industry means, under modern conditions, not only more law in industry. It means also wider discretionary authority in the administration of the law.[41]

The government of the more perfect Union in modern times has rightly assumed greater responsibility for the efficient functioning of the economic order. It has accepted and will continue to accept more onerous duties concerning the production and distribution of economic goods and the adjustment of the conflicts between various groups of producers and consumers. Labor-management relations and consumer-producer relations seem destined to occupy an ever larger part of the attention of both legislators and administrators. The expansion of administrative functions and of the administrative organization inevitably follows. The liberty of the individual is not necessarily increased by the extension of greater administrative authority over capitalistic industry. Neither is it necessarily diminished. The problem of securing the blessings of liberty is merely changed. The danger of the abuse of power arises where power resides, whether in the hands of private capitalists and businessmen or in those of the administrators of so-called public affairs. There still is no better assurance of safety for the members of the public against the abuse of power than the time-honored principles of government which seem so well fitted to sustain the faith of the people in the stability of the more perfect Union.

The more liberal attitude of the New Deal Court toward the expansion of administrative powers and also toward experiments in administrative procedure proved timely and helpful when the involvement of the United States in World War II created an extraordinary need for swift and energetic administrative action. Chief Justice Stone again took the lead in justifying unprecedented legislation, designed to meet the emergency effectively, particularly legislation delegating wide discretionary authority to special war agencies. The Emergency Price Control Act of 1942 not only delegated extraordinary powers to administrative officers, but also established novel procedures for the enforcement of its provisions. The Chief Justice's opinion in a leading case committed the Court to an unqualified approval of the measure.[42] Justice Roberts, the last survivor on the Court of the majority which had struck down the Bituminous Coal Conservation Act, dissented on the ground that in this case also there was an unconstitutional delegation of legislative power to administrative officers. Justice Roberts also dissented in a case which raised the question of the validity of the whole system of planning and directing war production under the provisions of the Second War Powers Act.[43] The peculiar theory of the separation of powers upon which the Conservative Republican Court had relied a few years earlier in support of its adverse action against leading New Deal measures would apparently have made the conduct of the war impossible without doing violence either to the Constitution or to the war plans of the Roosevelt Administration.

More difficult questions were presented to the Supreme Court by the use of military tribunals for administering justice in cases where the ordinary courts were capable of trying by due process of law persons accused of criminal misconduct. In the case of the Nazi saboteurs who had been put ashore within the United States from a German submarine, the President ordered a secret trial before a special military court. There were doubtless good reasons for not wishing to publish the evidence against the saboteurs at that stage of the war, or to disclose the manner in which it had been obtained, but the saboteurs had been arrested by civil police officers and were not originally in the custody of the military police. The Supreme Court decided that a public trial by the ordinary legal processes was not necessary under

350

the circumstances,[44] but a majority of the judges were unable to agree upon the grounds for their decision. Thus the public was left with no satisfactory explanation of the reasons for disregarding what seemed to be the constitutional requirement of due process of law in favor of a special criminal procedure ordinarily reserved for the trial of prisoners of war and other persons under the jurisdiction of the military authorities.

After the close of active hostilities, however, as after the Civil War, the Supreme Court was able to establish a better precedent for future guidance in time of war. The system of military justice which had been put into effect in the Hawaiian Islands after Pearl Harbor had been continued long after there seemed to be any real danger of invasion by the enemy, and had provoked bitter controversy between the military and the civil authorities. Cases were eventually brought before the Supreme Court [45] which enabled it to declare the prolonged jurisdiction of the military tribunals over civilians unauthorized by law. The authority of the Milligan case was expressly reasserted, and the untimely actions of the military tribunals declared invalid. The liberal attitude of the New Deal Court toward civil administrators was not extended to military authorities operating outside their proper field.

In the twilight region where military and civil administration merge, the New Deal Court found its greatest difficulties. Members of the intractable sect of Jehovah's Witnesses contested the right of local draft boards under the Selective Service Act to classify them as conscientious objectors, bound to serve in work camps if not on the field of battle, rather than as ministers of the gospel, entitled to exemption from the draft.[46] A majority of the Court sustained their conviction for absence without leave from the work camps on the ground that their classification was an act of administrative discretion which "is reviewable only if there is no basis in fact for the classification." Local draft boards, the majority of the Court believed, as well as their administrative superiors, have a right to make mistakes of judgment, provided that they do not fail to observe the prescribed requirements of the administrative process. Justices Douglas and Black dissented, contending that the administrators had misunderstood what Congress meant by ministers of religion. Justices Murphy and Rutledge also dissented, contending that the administrators had acted without sufficient evidence to support their classification of the stubborn sectaries as conscientious objectors only, and not ministers of religion. But the majority of the Court would not let these members of Jehovah's Witnesses escape punishment on such grounds. Their theory of the judicial review of administrative action compelled them to respect a normal result of the administrative process, even when the Court itself was deeply divided concerning the wisdom of that result. The Court had left far behind that acute sense of judicial responsibility for the correctness of administrative decisions which had lain so heavily on the conscience of Chief Justice Hughes.

Yet the New Deal Court could crack down as harshly upon errant administrators, when they saw fit to do so, as ever did the Conservative Republican Court. The determination of a majority of the Seventy-sixth Congress to bring about the deportation of Harry Bridges afforded the occasion for the most impressive manifestation of judicial capacity to intervene in the administrative process when sufficiently aroused by the facts of a particular case. This Congress provided for the deportation of any alien who had been, when he entered the country or at any subsequent time, a member of, or affiliated with, an organization believing in or advocating the overthrow by force or violence of the government of the United States. The Attorney General, after careful investigation, was unable to find satisfactory evidence of Bridges's membership in the Communist Party, but upon the basis of evidence of "affiliation" with that party ordered him deported. The Supreme Court by a vote of five to three reversed the order.[47] Chief Justice Stone, dissenting with the concurrence of Justices Roberts and Frankfurter, argued that the Court was not authorized to determine the weight and credibility of the evidence against Bridges, but merely to decide whether there was substantial evidence to support an order of deportation. The record disclosed the existence of such evidence, and the deportation order, in their opinion, was therefore valid. But Justice Douglas, for a bare majority of the Court, declared that the Department of Justice had erred in putting a wrong interpretation upon the word "affiliation." Bridges's affiliation with the Communists had consisted only in accepting their aid for his own lawful purposes. The evidence failed to show coöperation with Communists for their peculiar purposes. Since, according to the majority of the Court, this was not what the Congress had meant by affiliation, the deportation order was based upon an erroneous interpretation of the law and could not stand.

The New Deal Court was clearly committed to giving the administrators a more important place in the general scheme of government than had been deemed proper by the Conservative Republican Court.

Judges and Administrators

Was this development in the art of public administration logically consistent with the principle of the separation of powers? On this point there were persistent differences of opinion among the New Deal judges as among their predecessors.[48] Did it make for a more serviceable system of checks and balances? To this question there could be only one answer. The public evidently wanted a readjustment of the relations between the executive and the judicial power; the administrators were ready and able to assume a larger share of the responsibility for the administration of justice; the legislators were willing to approve the resulting changes in the system of checks and balances. The equilibrium of power, far from being upset, seemed more stable than before.

UNSOLVED PROBLEMS IN JUDICIAL REVIEW OF ADMINISTRATION

The new trend in the development of the relations between the executive and the judiciary was consistent with the essential character of the American political process. "The middle class," a thoughtful political analyst pointed out [49] in an early stage of this development, "must not only create public opinion but administer organized institutions." Corbin's conception of the middle class doubtless had been too narrow, but his insight into the nature of the changes which were taking place in the American body politic was clear and penetrating. The dominant influence of the middle class on the formation of political opinion has been an outstanding fact of American politics since the adoption of a federal Bill of Rights was made the decisive condition for the ratification of the Constitution. Corbin, thinking particularly of the members of the middle class belonging to the learned professions, declared the formation of opinion to have been their principal function in the nineteenth century. In the twentieth century, he believed, the proper field for the influence of this portion of the middle class would be public administration. The further development of the administrative services of the Federal Government, he expected, would strengthen the political influence of the middle class.

In fact the growth of this field of middle-class influence in the government of the more perfect Union has exceeded Corbin's expectations. Not only the recruitment of the higher echelons of the administrative services from the upper levels of the middle classes, but also the general dependence throughout the upper and middle grades of the services on the support of the middle classes, tend to enhance the influence of these classes in the American system of government. As the executive branch of the government grows in numbers and in power, this trend becomes more significant. The Hatch "Pure Politics" Act was a conspicuous expression of the changing attitude toward professional administrators based on growing confidence in the partisan disinterestedness and technical competence of trained experts. The disposition of New Deal legislators and judges alike to exalt the power and prestige of such administrators is perhaps the most important of all the contemporary factors tending to maintain and even to expand the political influence of the middle classes.

Invidious talk about bureaucracy is an important sign of the times. Some of the criticism of the bureaucratic thirst for power and much of the criticism directed against the imperfections of contemporary administrative organization and procedure are well founded. John H. Crider's incisive analysis of the administrative function, as developed at Washington under the sharp spur of economic crises and war emergencies, and his justified strictures against the abuse of power by incompetent and partisan administrative officials, furnished the most effective statement of problems which cannot be ignored.[50] But a great deal of the denunciation of the bureaucrats has been exaggerated, and in many cases has served mainly to disclose a politician's lack of understanding of the reasons why the spoils system had to give way to a new and better order in the administrative services, and his suspicion of a shift in the balance of power between the branches of government which threatened some of the traditional privileges of his own profession. Behind much of the invidious talk about bureaucracy has lurked the begrudging recognition that the professional administrator is bound to take a more important place in the scheme of government alongside the politician.

A more significant sign of the times is the Atomic Energy Act of 1946. This epoch-making piece of legislation, supported by both major parties in the Congress and adopted despite the persistent opposition of military officers in the executive branch of the government, furnished impressive evidence of the need for delegating the broadest discretionary powers to highly trained technicians and administrators. The general plan for this new agency and appropriate administrative techniques were derived from the experience of the Tennessee Valley Authority. Like that energetic and enterprising government-owned corporation, the Atomic Energy Commission was designed to operate with a huge capital, supplied by the public treasury, subject to such

354

control as might be exercised by the Congress through its power of the purse and by the ordinary courts through their jurisdiction over suits against federal administrative agencies. To facilitate such control, the Act established a Joint Committee on Atomic Energy, representing both branches of the Congress and both political parties, and instructed it to supervise the work of the Commission. Ample authority was granted to the Joint Committee to employ experts, consultants, technicians, and other assistants, and to conduct such investigations as it might deem advisable. Judicial review of the Commission's activities was specifically authorized in accordance with the provisions of the Administrative Procedure Act of 1946. It was clearly the intention of the Congress that this powerful administrative agency should not get out of control. Whatever might be the logical position of administrative officers, endowed with extraordinarily wide discretionary authority, under the principle of the separation of powers, they were to remain, if possible, within the confines of the system of checks and balances.

Nevertheless, the proliferation of administrative agencies exercising wide discretionary authority over increasingly important areas of government and business, and the frequent delegations of wide discretionary authority also to the President, in response to the impact of business depressions and of war, added to the traditional fear of bureaucratic inefficiency and waste a new fear that the executive branch of the government would grow too strong and get out of hand. The federal budget after World War II had swollen to ten times its size before the Great Depression. The army of federal civil employees, as well as the peacetime military establishment, had enormously increased. The influence of governmental taxation and expenditures on the national economy had become much greater than ever before in time of peace. The time had passed when ordinary reforms in the field of administrative economy and efficiency could meet the demand for effective action. The creation of the Hoover Commission on Organization of the Executive Branch of the Government gave evidence of the interest of the Eightieth Congress in improving not only the organization of the executive office of the President but also the relations between the President and the new administrative agencies and those between the administrators generally and the other branches of the government. The time had come for a review of this part of the system of checks and balances under the altered conditions of the modern neotechnic age.

The wartime expansion of the authority of the President as Com-

mander in Chief and the impressive example of governmental management of a planned economy during the war stimulated reflection
upon the whole experience with the administration of national affairs
since the framers of the Constitution, mindful of Burke's observations
on the importance of sound administrative arrangements, settled upon
a plan for the exercise of the executive power. Professor Corwin stated
with a more impressive display of evidence than other writers the
growing opinion that the powers delegated to, or assumed by, the
President have virtually ended the balance of powers originally set
forth by the Constitution.[51] He was particularly concerned with the
practical capacity of the judges to restrain the President and other
powerful executive officers from the abuse of their authority. He became convinced that the power of judicial veto was no longer equal to
the task of keeping the executive branch within its proper limits. The
doctrine of judicial review, he feared, had lost its effective authority.

The argument is not convincing as applied to the exercise of the
executive power over domestic affairs. The Administrative Procedure
Act of 1946 has not been in effect long enough to enable any but the
most tentative conclusions to be drawn concerning its effect upon the
relations between judges and administrators. But it evidently offers the
former a favorable opportunity to develop a rational system of judicial
review of administrative action. It is not necessary to abandon the
New Deal Court's preference for a tolerant attitude toward the use of
administrative discretion. It is enough that the judges retain the power,
and possess convenient processes, to restrain administrators from grave
abuses of their authority. Doubtless the Courts themselves are restrained by the dominant political ethics of the age from interfering
too vigorously with the choice of policies and administrative methods
by the executive branch, as they are so restrained also in their exercise
of the power of judicial review of acts of the Congress. Congress too
possesses ways and means of checking the executive and restoring the
balance of the governmental system. The Legislative Reorganization
Act of 1946 introduced only a part of the reforms advocated by the
La Follette-Monroney Committee into the practice of the two houses.
Much more may be done, as Professor Corwin himself recognizes, to
improve the relations between the political branches of the government. It is too soon to conclude that the balance of the constitutional
system has been irretrievably disturbed by the recent expansion of the
executive power in the area of domestic affairs.

The argument is more persuasive as applied to the exercise of the executive power over foreign affairs. The authority of the President to conduct the relations between the United States and foreign powers is not derived, the Supreme Court has declared,[52] from the Constitution, but from the law and customs of the nations of the world. "The powers of external sovereignty," Justice Sutherland wrote in an opinion for the Court, ". . . if they had never been mentioned in the Constitution, would have vested in the federal government as necessary concomitants of nationality." Sutherland was arguing in favor of the authority which had been delegated by the Congress to the President to impose an embargo on shipments of munitions of war to South American governments, when he should find such an embargo likely to preserve or restore the peace. He was hampered in developing his argument by his unwillingness to sanction the delegation of wide discretionary authority to the President in domestic affairs by such New Deal legislation as the Bituminous Coal Conservation Act. Those of his judicial colleagues who were more tolerant of New Deal legislative experiments might not have found such an argument necessary as Sutherland was making for the constitutionality of the delegation of wide discretionary authority in the field of foreign affairs. They might have considered such a conception of the presidential office excessively Hamiltonian,[53] and not well suited to an age in which Jeffersonian concepts were again coming into favor. Be that as it may, both the law governing the executive power to conduct international relations, as expounded by the Court, and the practice, as manifested by the President during and since World War II, make clear the greater freedom of action possessed by the President as Commander in Chief and Head of the State in its relations with foreign powers, than that possessed as Chief Executive under the Constitution in the conduct of government at home.[54]

Perhaps no single incident better illustrates the kind of constitutional problem which the new technological age tends to produce than the decision to develop, if possible, a hydrogen bomb. An instrument of such titanic destructive force can be used only for military purposes. It appears to possess no practical utility in time of peace except to intimidate a possible enemy from resorting to war. Even in war it appears to have little utility except as an offensive weapon. Its usefulness for purposes of defense seems questionable. A decision to proceed with the development of such a weapon may impress a foreign power as a manifestation of an aggressively unfriendly disposition. Should such a decision be made by the Chief Executive, acting in his role as Commander in Chief or director general of diplomatic negotiations? Or should he first procure the advice and perhaps also the consent of the Congress? And to what extent should the public be advised of the facts in the light of which the decision should be made and enjoy an opportunity to influence the decision by an expression of public opinion? Moreover, if the President is to make such decisions under the executive power, how should the facts be presented to him? What arrangements should be made for collecting the opinions of competent technical experts and enabling the President to act upon the best professional advice? The reservation to the Congress of the power to declare war seems a very inadequate safeguard against the possible abuse of the executive power in dealing with the problems created by modern advances in military science. Political science, as well as military, needs to advance, if the equilibrium of the constitutional system is to be maintained.

It may well be doubted whether the executive power over external affairs can be effectively checked by the legislative and judicial powers under the Constitution. It does seem likely that, as Corwin fears, the lack of constitutional restraints upon the action of the President in the conduct of foreign relations threatens the balance of the American political system.[55] Though the power to declare war and to conclude peace is reserved to the Congress, the practical capacity of the President to commit the United States by unilateral action to policies and measures which force the hands of the legislative branch and of the judiciary is ominously great. The remedy, happily, is equally clear. If the President derives his authority over external affairs from the law and customs of the nations, the restraints which are necessary and proper to keep him from abusing his power should be derived from the same source.

The American people should look to improvements in the law of nations, and particularly to improvements in the institutions for making and enforcing international law, for compensation for the lack of balance in the system of constitutional government which results from the lack of control over the President, regarded as Head of the State in its international relations, by the other branches of government under the Constitution. World federalism supplies the principle, and a world federation would supply the institutions, which are essential if the American people are to enjoy in due measure the security against the abuse of power which they originally sought under the approved principle of the separation of powers and under the planned arrangements for an effective system of checks and balance. To secure the

358

blessings of Franklin D. Roosevelt's fourth freedom, the freedom from fear, something more is necessary than to arm the country against the danger of foreign invasion. Bigger armaments are not likely to be big enough to intimidate potential enemies abroad without at the same time becoming so big as to revive ancient fears of uncontrollable power at home. To restore general confidence in the stability of the American system of checks and balances, it is indispensable to introduce more law and order into the relations between our more perfect Union and the rest of the world.

CHAPTER ELEVEN

The Supreme Court
and the States

CONFLICTING THEORIES OF FEDERALISM

THERE is nothing in the record of the debates in the Convention of 1787, or in those of the state ratifying conventions, to indicate that the framers of the Constitution expected as much from the Supreme Court as from the Senate in the role of guardian of the rights of the states. The original Federalists probably expected the most from the Supreme Court, though their expectations must be inferred from their votes rather than from their speeches. The aristocratic Nationalists, if Madison can be presumed to have spoken their thoughts on this point, held the opinion that a judicial veto exercised in the course of litigation after the enactment of proposed legislation into law would be a poor substitute for a powerful executive veto, or joint executive-judicial veto, while proposed legislation was under consideration by the Congress. But the aristocratic Nationalists in the Federal Convention had not been much interested in protecting the rights of the states. A powerful and independent Supreme Court attracted their support because of its possible utility as a defender of exposed minorities such as the "opulent" against the abuse of power by factious majorities in the Congress rather than as a guardian of the rights of the states against encroachments by the Federal Government. Whether the Supreme Court was expected to be more useful as a guardian of the reserved rights of the states and of the people or as a protagonist of the authority of the general government cannot be determined from the debates in the Federal Convention. Certainly the decision to establish such a Supreme Court had not been as unpalatable to the Nationalists in the Federal Convention as that to establish a Senate in which each state would have equal representation regardless of differences in population and wealth.

The role of the Supreme Court in the federal system has been different from its role in the system of checks and balances. Justice Holmes, who did not think that the United States would come to an end if the Court lost its power to declare an act of Congress void, was convinced that the Union would be imperiled if the Court could not continue to exercise a similar power over the laws of the states. "For one in my place," he declared,[1] "sees how often a local policy prevails with those who are not trained to national views and how often action is taken that embodies what the commerce clause was meant to end." Justice Holmes evidently believed that there was still much independence of thought and action in the state governments and abundant vitality in the federal system. Other critics of American political institutions, however, have taken a different line. Harold J. Laski, for instance, suggested [2] that "the classic theory of federalism is obsolete in its historic American form," and Professor Corwin lends the weight of his great authority to the more discriminating view [3] that "federalism in any sense has ceased to be capable of obstructing through the processes of judicial review the continued centralization of governmental power in the hands of the National Government." The conflicts of opinion among the political critics concerning the role of the judges in the federal system and the present status of the system itself cannot be settled without investigating the record of the Supreme Court in the adjustment of disputes over the nature of the more perfect Union and the management of the relations between the parts and the whole. The development of the principle of federalism, like that of the principle of the separation of powers, falls into five stages corresponding to the five major periods in the partisan history of the Supreme Court.

The first period in the history of the Court saw the emergence of two sharply conflicting views concerning the nature of the federal system. One of them has been associated with the name of Hamilton, who was the first to develop it theoretically in the eighteenth and thirty-third numbers of *The Federalist* and practically in his legislative program while Secretary of the Treasury under Washington. The Hamiltonian concept of federalism was a concept of a nationalistic federalism, which would make the federal system under the Constitution as nearly as possible the equivalent of the centralized political system which Hamilton had advocated in the Federal Convention. Under such a view of federalism the function of the Supreme Court in the interpretation of the Constitution, as Hamilton intimated with a suitable degree of obfuscation in the seventy-eighth and eighty-first numbers of *The Federalist*, would be to assert the supremacy of the government of the Union to the extent that might be found necessary and proper in the national interest. Hamilton was not interested, like Madison, in a form of federalism which, under the guise of protecting the rights of the states, would really be protecting the interests of minorities, particularly the "opulent," who might take shelter behind the rampart of states' rights. Hamilton was hopeful that the "opulent" would be able to take care of themselves through their influence in the more powerful branches of the national government, the Senate, the Presidency, and now, thanks to this new doctrine of judicial review, the Supreme Court. In the hands of bold and independent judges judicial review could become a formidable weapon in the political arsenal of aristocracy. The Supreme Court might interpret the principle of federalism to put constitutional limitations upon the powers of the states as well as upon those of the national government and thereby make the Union better serve the purposes of masterful national leaders.

The opposing view has been associated with the name of Jefferson. He, better than Madison, had understood the possibilities of the judicial veto for the guardianship of the rights of the common man and, more clearly than any member of the Federal Convention except possibly Mason, had perceived the value of a bill of rights as the basis for an effective performance in this role by the Supreme Court. In Washington's Cabinet he was the first to challenge Hamilton's theories of constitutional interpretation and, as leader of the opposition to the Federalist Administrations, he was the first to appreciate the importance of an appeal to states' rights as a means of checking the abuse of power by those in control of the Federal Government. Jefferson was not opposed to the judicial veto of unconstitutional acts by the political departments of the government. What he objected to was the failure of the judges to protect the constitutional rights of his followers, when threatened by the Alien and Sedition Acts. The Virginia and Kentucky resolutions of 1798 and 1799 were astutely vague in describing the remedies which the states were to employ in order to check the abuse of power by the national government. A constitutional amendment might be necessary, but perhaps criticism of the obnoxious decisions and an appeal to public opinion would be sufficient to restrain the trial judges in their charges to the juries or to encourage the juries to refuse to convict under the detested laws. In fact the people at the next general election turned the Federalists out of office and put the

Jeffersonians in power. The detested laws expired or were repealed and the fines collected from their victims were eventually refunded. The only change in the Constitution was that incorporated in the Twelfth Amendment. The federal system was allowed to develop in the channel made by the politicians and judges who were engaged in its operation. In Jefferson's opinion there was nothing wrong with the federal system, if its implications could be spelled out by right-minded judges.

JUDICIAL VERSUS POLITICAL
GUARDIANSHIP OF THE FEDERAL SYSTEM

That the guardianship of the federal principle in the American Constitution could not be exclusively a judicial function was a lesson which the Supreme Court learned early in its career.[4] In the leading case of *Chisholm* v. *Georgia*,[5] the Court took jurisdiction over a suit against one of the states by a citizen of another state and gave judgment in favor of the plaintiff. From the viewpoint of the nationalistic framers of the Constitution, the possibility of such interference with the right of a state not to be sued without its own consent, as it had existed before the adoption of the Constitution, was an essential feature of a satisfactory federal system. The decision, however, was obnoxious to those who had originally been anti-Nationalists and had later become anti-Federalists, and also to many others who became Federalists. It proved so unpopular that the Congress promptly proposed and the necessary number of states duly ratified the Eleventh Amendment to the Constitution, denying to the Supreme Court in the future jurisdiction over such cases. The question of jurisdiction was transformed from a justiciable into a political question, because public opinion made it so, and the episode was never forgotten by either judges or politicians.

That the Supreme Court, despite its humiliation by the politicians in the Chisholm case, would continue to use whatever authority it might claim under the Constitution in justiciable cases to establish a nationalistic interpretation of federalism was made clear by the judges at the earliest opportunity. The opportunity came with little delay in the case of *Ware* v. *Hylton*,[6] involving a dispute over a title to land. One of the claimants based his claim on an act of the Virginia legislature, passed during the Revolution, authorizing the settlement of debts due to English creditors by payments to the state. The other rested his case on the plain language of the Treaty of Peace between

363

Great Britain and the United States, protecting English creditors against unfriendly state legislation. The Supreme Court's decision, asserting the supremacy of the treaty made under the authority of the United States over the act of the Virginia legislature, was widely unpopular. It was clearly evident that the Court intended to put the states into what the judges regarded as their proper place in the new Union. But this time the politicians did not interfere with the judicial interpretation of the Constitution. The decision became the cornerstone of the federal system.

The contribution of the Federalist period in the partisan history of the Supreme Court to the development of the federal system had been made before Marshall became Chief Justice. The Court had established its right to treat as justiciable questions the problems which might arise in cases brought before it concerning the relations between the Union and the states under the Constitution. It had declared its intention to maintain the supremacy of the Constitution and of the laws and treaties of the United States over conflicting acts of the state legislatures. But it had made no effort, in construing the powers of the Congress, to mediate between the strict and the broad constructionists; nor had it given any indication concerning the kinds of minorities which might shelter themselves successfully behind the ramparts of states' rights, or behind the constitutional limitations upon the powers of the states which might be imposed by the decisions of the Supreme Court. The struggle between the Hamiltonian and the Jeffersonian versions of the federal system had only begun.

The contributions of the Jeffersonian Republican Court under the leadership of John Marshall to the development of the federal system were more pleasing to the Hamiltonians than to the Jeffersonians. In the Yazoo land-grant case,[7] involving the title to land obtained from the Georgia legislature by bribery and corruption, the Supreme Court held that the constitutional prohibition against state legislation impairing the obligation of a contract prevented the legislature from voiding the tainted title and making a fresh sale to honest purchasers. In the Dartmouth College case [8] the contract clause was employed to give further protection to vested interests against legislation by state lawmakers attempting to give effect to popular reforms. But Marshall's Court refused to carry the protection of vested interests so far as to protect a New York state steamboat monopoly against the competition of outsiders claiming a right under the Federal Constitution to navigate New York territorial waters when engaged in interstate commerce.[9]

This was Marshall's most popular decision. Vested interests could shelter themselves behind the contract clause against assaults by state politicians in the name of reform, but could not find immunity against the commerce power of the national government. In general the Supreme Court's loose interpretation of the contract clause was a triumph for the Hamiltonian concept of federalism.

The most important contribution of Marshall's Court to the development of the federal system was the decision in the great case of *McCulloch* v. *Maryland*.[10] The state legislature had imposed a tax on the operations of the Baltimore branch of the Bank of the United States for the purpose of protecting the state banks against what it considered unfair competition. The refusal of the United States Bank to pay the tax enabled the Supreme Court to affirm the twin principles of a broad construction of the legislative powers of the Congress and a strict construction of those of the state legislatures. Maryland could not tax the instrumentalities of the Federal Government, but the Congress could establish a national bank to compete with the banking systems of the states. This decision vindicated the Hamiltonian version of federalism in theory as the grant of a charter to the second Bank of the United States by a Jeffersonian Congress and President had already vindicated it in practice. The state banking interests were forced to share their privileges with the more highly privileged interests connected with the Bank of the United States. It was not vested interests of every kind that were protected by the Supreme Court's guardianship of the federal system but particularly those vested interests which were nationalistic in character. It is not surprising that Jefferson in his old age should have deplored the tendency of Republican judges, once appointed for life to the Supreme Court, to fall under the influence of the nationalistic Chief Justice.

The break between the Jeffersonian Republican Court under Marshall and the Jacksonian Democratic Court under Taney can easily be exaggerated. Jacksonian Democrats approved most heartily the decisions of Taney's Court which sustained the executive power of the President and strengthened the practical capacity of the Federal Government to enforce its laws without interference by unfriendly state governments. The sharpest issues arose over the enforcement of the fugitive-slave laws. In an early case [11] the Court made short work of a Pennsylvania statute which put obstacles in the way of the recovery of escaping Negroes under the Fugitive Slave Act of 1793, though the judges could not agree concerning the proper role of the states in the rendition of such Negroes. In a later case [12] the Court effectively checked the efforts of the government of Wisconsin to obstruct the enforcement of the more drastic Fugitive Slave Act of 1850. These decisions tended to exalt the President's executive power as those of Marshall's Court had tended to exalt the legislative powers of the Congress. Both Courts were firmly resolved to keep the state governments in their places and to maintain what they regarded as the proper authority of the government of the Union.

The rights of property also received more considerate treatment from Taney's Court than was anticipated by many property owners, shocked by the virulence of Jackson's attack upon the Bank of the United States. Taney's Court strengthened the position of the states in the banking business [13] by sanctioning the issue of bank notes by banks in which state governments were stockholders, but it was the political departments of the Federal Government which put an end to the monopolistic privileges of the Bank of the United States by refusing to extend its charter. Taney's Court also restricted the privileges of business corporations under state charters [14] by insisting that such charters be strictly construed, but the state legislatures had already discovered how to keep their own corporations under control by granting the charters for limited terms and reserving the right to alter or repeal them. Taney's Court interpreted the commerce power of the Federal Government [15] so as to permit the states to regulate interstate and foreign commerce when uniform national regulations were not necessary or appropriate, but this stricter interpretation of the commerce clause did not impair the authority of the Federal Government to make such laws regulating interstate and foreign commerce as it might deem desirable. The vested interests did not at first fare so well under Taney's Court as under Marshall's, but they did not fare badly.

The great favorites among the vested interests appear to have been the big plantation and slave owners. Taney did not altogether have his way in the matter of the fugitive-slave laws. Although he agreed with the majority of the Court that state legislatures had no right to make laws penalizing efforts to recover fugitive slaves, he could not concur in their view that the Federal Government possessed an exclusive power to make laws providing for their rendition. [16] But he had his way in the matter of the laws governing the status of slavery. The Dred Scott decision [17] not only denied the power of the Congress to enact the Missouri Compromise, but by its logical implications affirmed the power of the slaveholding states to fix the status of the Negro everywhere throughout the Union. This decision recognized greater authority in the favored state governments over the Negro than Jefferson had supposed them to possess even under the feeble Articles of Confederation. It marked a venture into the political arena which was as shocking to genuine Jeffersonians as it was gratifying to those who, like the aristocratic Nationalists of 1787, looked to the Federal Government for the ultimate security of their property. It was a decision no more to be expected from a genuine Jacksonian Democratic than from a Jeffersonian Republican Court.

While rashly braving the tempests of the political arena in the Dred Scott case, the Taney Court was prudent to the point of timidity in dealing with the quaint case of Dorr's rebellion.[18] The constitutional guarantee of a republican form of government to the states would seem broad enough to furnish solid ground on which the Court might stand in determining which of two governments, claiming the right to govern a state at the same time, might administer justice to the people thereof. It is easy to imagine that a Hamiltonian Court would not have hesitated to pronounce judgment in favor of the government with a vested right to rule. It is even possible to suppose that a Jeffersonian Court might have found some way to lend encouragement to the rebellious reformers. But Taney's Court took refuge in the distinction between justiciable and political questions and left the determination of the rights of the reformers to the President and the Congress. Twenty years later came a more severe test of the Court's ability to reconcile the rights of the states and the supremacy of the Federal Union in the face of bitter controversy concerning the nature of the federal system. With the constitutional issues raised by the advocates of secession Taney's Court found itself unable to deal in any effective manner. Whether the federal system should be mended or ended was left to the arbitrament of civil war.

JUDICIAL CENSORSHIP OF LEGISLATIVE POLICY

The beginning of the long period of Republican supremacy in the political history of the Supreme Court coincided with the radical alteration of the federal system by the process of reconstruction after the war. The Thirteenth Amendment destroyed the most powerful special interest which had ever sought judicial protection under the cover of states' rights against the legislative authority of the Congress. The

Fourteenth and Fifteenth Amendments limited the power of the states to discriminate against the freedmen and put their rights under the protection of the Supreme Court. The Reconstruction Act of 1867 provided a system of military government for the people of the South regardless of the state governments which they claimed a right to establish under the Constitution. In short, the process of reconstruction raised constitutional issues which seemed calculated to test the power of the new Republican Supreme Court as severely as that of secession had tested the power of Taney's Court.

Some contemporary observers, noting the reckless disregard both of states' rights and of judicial authority by the Republican Congress, concluded that the federal system would not survive the centralizing measures of the Radical Republicans. The Supreme Court, they ventured to predict, would not be able to preserve the remaining rights of the states or maintain the balance between the national and state governments which had been the original object of the framers of the Constitution. Federalism would cease to be a political principle from which disciples of Madison could derive an argument for faith in the durability of the traditional Union. President Lincoln had manifestly believed in a Federal Union, organized on the basis of a genuine system of federalism, and had inaugurated a method of reconstruction consistent with the theory that the Union was an indestructible Union of indestructible states. But the new Republican Court, loyal though it might be to the Lincoln policies and constitutional theory, was gravely handicapped by the political recklessness of the Congress and the political ineptitude of Lincoln's unhappy successor.

The relations between the Supreme Court and the political departments of the national government during the period of reconstruction have been discussed in connection with the principle of the separation of powers. The effect of reconstruction upon the federal system needs to be separately noted. The immediate effects were less damaging than appeared likely to the pessimists. The more remote effects were different from what was anticipated by any of the contemporary observers. Eventually, though not at first, the role of the Supreme Court in the development of the federal system was profoundly altered by the reconstruction amendments to the Constitution, particularly the Fourteenth Amendment.

The new constitutional amendments gave power to the Supreme Court the full implications of which it was slow to exploit. At first the Court was inclined to minimize the extent of the changes which had been made by these amendments in the federal system. It decided that they did not authorize the Congress to make general laws for the protection of the freedmen's civil rights and that they did not authorize the Court to interfere with the policies of the states except to prevent discrimination by law against the freedmen. The Civil Rights Act, as applied to the ordinary relations between the races within the states, was declared unconstitutional in 1883.[19] As late as 1913 the Supreme Court refused to enforce that part of the Civil Rights Act which seemed to protect the rights of citizens of African descent to equal treatment in situations which were clearly within the power of the Congress to regulate.[20] The Court held in a case where a Negro passenger on a vessel of the Merchants and Miners Transportation Company, traveling from Boston to Norfolk, demanded the right to eat in the same dining room with other first-class passengers that, since the rest of the Act had been declared unconstitutional, it would not presume to suppose that the Congress had intended to make this part of the Act effective by itself alone. A third of a century passed before the Court ventured to set aside the Virginia Jim Crow law, as applied to passengers on busses between Washington and points within the state of Virginia, on the ground that it trespassed on the authority of the Congress to regulate such commerce.[21] With discrimination against Negroes not expressly authorized by laws of the states the Republican Supreme Court firmly refused to interfere.

The Republican Supreme Court was equally reluctant to interfere with state election laws designed to exclude the Negroes from state and local politics. For years the grandfather clauses, designed to discriminate against Negro voters, were tolerated because they did not explicitly deny the vote to Negroes, and for a longer period the exclusion of Negro voters from the primary elections of the Democratic Party, in states where the Democratic Party primaries were more important than the final elections, was permitted on the ground that the amendments did not apply to such elections. It remained for the New Deal Court with a Democratic majority among its members to find that the primaries were a part of the public electoral system [22] and to declare that Democratic Party committees could not be allowed to impair the Negroes' right to vote by excluding them from primary elections.[23] Efforts by the Court to prevent discrimination by state officers against Negroes in the operation of the jury system and in other features of the administration of justice have become more effective in recent years,[24] but much remains to be done before Negroes will enjoy in all states the

369

actual equality before the law which it was the manifest purpose of the reconstruction amendments to secure to them.[25]

The most important development in the judicial interpretation of federalism by the Republican Supreme Court was the exploitation of the new constitutional limitations upon the legislative powers of the states for the purpose of imposing national principles of economic and social policy upon the state governments. The guarantee of the privileges and immunities of national citizens to all persons born or naturalized in the United States, regardless of efforts by particular states to discriminate on grounds of race or color, and the further guarantee that no person, whether citizen or alien, should be deprived by any state of life, liberty, or property without due process of law or be denied by any state the equal protection of the laws, created a tempting opportunity for the Court to breathe a new national spirit into the old federal principle. It was reluctant at first to take full advantage of this opportunity. In 1873 the Court refused to disallow a Louisiana statute establishing a monopoly of the slaughter-house business in New Orleans,[26] since it was ostensibly a measure to protect the public health, despite a plea that such a monopoly would take away the liberty of ordinary butchers to pursue their callings and impair the value of the property used in their businesses without due process of law. In 1932, however, the Court declared to be in violation of the Fourteenth Amendment an Oklahoma statute,[27] authorizing the grant of monopolistic privileges to ice manufacturers, on the same plea of lack of due process of law, despite an argument, supported by substantial evidence, that such a monopoly under proper official supervision would serve the public interest in obtaining pure ice at reasonable prices. Times had changed and judicial theories of constitutional interpretation had changed with them. An interpretation of the due-process clause which was rejected by the Lincoln Republican Court became a generation later in the hands of the Conservative Republican Court the cornerstone of the new federalism.

The method by which the Republican Supreme Court made itself the censor of state legislative policies involving restrictions upon the freedom of contract of business corporations as well as of natural persons was to change the judicial interpretations of two words and a phrase in the Fourteenth Amendment. The words were "person" and "liberty." The former the Court interpreted to include corporations; the latter the Court eventually transmuted by giving it a new philosophical, instead of its old juristic, meaning. The phrase was "due process of law." This the Court transformed from a procedural limitation upon the legislative methods of the states into a substantive limitation upon the choice of policies by state lawmakers.

The nature of the change is illustrated by the action of the Court upon two state laws regulating the hours of labor in certain industries in which the conditions of employment were deemed by state lawmakers such as to require some restrictions upon the freedom of contract between the employers and the workers. In 1898 the Court sustained the constitutionality of a Utah statute establishing an eight-hour day in coal mines.[28] In 1905 it declared unconstitutional a New York statute limiting the length of the working day in bakeries to ten hours.[29] In the former case the Court found nothing in the Fourteenth Amendment to require judicial interference with the labor policy of the Utah lawmakers, but in the latter it discovered that the act of the New York lawmakers deprived both workers and their employers of "liberty" without "due process of law." The latter decision was an exercise of the power of judicial veto which would have surprised no less than it would have gratified those aristocratic Nationalists in the Convention of 1787 who thought they had lost their fight for effective means of protecting the interests of property owners against the trespasses of popular majorities in the state legislatures.

The conflict between the original juristic interpretation of "liberty" and the new philosophical interpretation of the term was clearly revealed and emphasized in Justice Holmes's dissenting opinion in the New York bakers case. Justice Peckham, speaking for the majority of the Court, had bluntly declared: "There is no reasonable ground for interfering with the liberty of person or the right of free contract . . . in the occupation of baker." Holmes replied that "a constitution is not intended to embody a particular economic theory, whether of paternalism and the organic relation of the individual to the state or of *laissez faire*. It is made for people of fundamentally differing views, and the accident of our finding certain opinions natural and familiar or novel and even shocking ought not to conclude our judgment whether statutes embodying them conflict with the Constitution of the United States." The word "liberty" in the Fourteenth Amendment, he contended, "is perverted when it is held to prevent the natural outcome of a dominant opinion." He thought that a reasonable man might think a law limiting the hours of labor in bakeries "a proper measure on the score of health," and that the Court should therefore uphold the law. "The Fourteenth Amendment," he roundly asserted, "does not enact

Mr. Herbert Spencer's Social Statics." But the majority of the Court appeared to think that this was precisely what the Fourteenth Amendment had done.

The decision of the Republican Supreme Court in the Lochner case opened a new era in the development of the federal system. It was evident that state legislatures could not adopt policies founded on new concepts of social and industrial justice which in the opinion of the Supreme Court would involve unreasonable restrictions upon the freedom of contract of employers and workers. State courts which, unlike those in New York, Illinois, and a few other states, had not already ventured to disallow such state legislation under provisions of the state constitutions, took their cue from the federal Supreme Court and proceeded to disallow them under the due-process clause of the Fourteenth Amendment. The arbitrariness of many of these decisions, as it seemed to the friends of the measures thereby rendered invalid, caused widespread criticism, notably by dissenting judges within the courts themselves. Justice Holmes's magisterial criticism of the Lochner decision was greatly admired by a later generation, but did not stop the growing subjection of state legislative policies to the legislative policy of the Supreme Court. Justice Harlan's farsighted warning in a separate dissenting opinion in the same case, that the exercise of such a censorship by the Supreme Court would surely involve its members in controversial legislative activities for which ordinary lawmakers were better equipped, attracted less attention, but proved to be equally judicious. Nevertheless, the majority of the judges persisted in their determination to write a new theory of legislation into the Federal Constitution.

Popular criticism of the legislative policies of the Supreme Court stimulated demands for a curb on the power of judicial veto. Some critics called for a constitutional amendment which would prevent courts from declaring such legislation unconstitutional by less than a two-thirds or some other special majority of the judges. Others, more radical, advocated the recall of judges by popular vote. A few state constitutions, in states where judges were elected by popular vote, were amended so that judges could be called to account for unpopular decisions. Theodore Roosevelt suggested what he called the recall of judicial decisions as a substitute for that of judges, in order to keep the judges out of politics as much as possible. His thought was that the voters should be enabled to authorize a new interpretation of the offending constitutional provision in objectionable cases by a simplified process of constitutional amendment.

The popular discussion of these proposals produced for a time greater judicial self-restraint in the exercise of the power of judicial veto. Judges protested that they were not giving effect to their personal views concerning questions of legislative policy, but were merely acting upon the view which might be attributed to any reasonable man in interpreting the language of the Constitution. In 1917 the Supreme Court went so far toward a reversal of its previous negative policy in reviewing state labor laws as to approve an Oregon measure establishing a universal ten-hour day for industrial workers.[30] But the self-restraint of the judges in reviewing state legislation adjusting the conflicting interests of employers and workers was not lasting. The Court was unable to make up its mind what to do with another Oregon measure fixing minimum wages for working women.[31] Its members were evenly divided in opinion, and those judges who were opposed to the policy of the minimum-wage law refused to concede that there was sufficient doubt concerning its unconstitutionality to require them to yield to the judgment of the lawmakers. Supreme Court judges seemed reluctant to admit that state legislators as well as federal judges might possess the capacity to govern.

At this time the Supreme Court seemed extraordinarily irresolute in its use of the judicial veto. Compulsory workmen's-compensation acts from the states of New York and Washington were twice argued before the Court, once in 1916 and again in 1917, before it could decide that they did not involve an unreasonable limitation of the freedom of contract guaranteed by the Constitution, as the Court interpreted it, to the employers and their employees.[32] Four judges dissented in the Washington case, believing that a compensation law which required employers to contribute to a state compensation fund instead of insuring against the risk of injury to their employees with private insurance companies was an unconstitutional abridgment of freedom of contract. At the same time the Supreme Court, also by a majority of five to four, decided that a Washington statute establishing a state employment agency with exclusive authority over the placing of certain kinds of labor was unconstitutional.[33] This was the period when the Court was having much trouble making up its mind what to do with the first federal child-labor law and with the Adamson Act, adopted to prevent a nation-wide strike on the steam railroads. Leading judges held strong but conflicting convictions concerning the reasonableness of state legislation abridging the freedom of contract, and Holmes's vigorous dissenting opinions made the Court seem excessively inept in the exercise of its judicial veto against such legislation.

Later the Taft Court provoked a new outburst of criticism by dissenting judges against judicial censorship of state legislation. Statutes involving novel restraints upon the power of businessmen and corporations to do as they pleased in the management of their businesses were brought before the Courts under the due-process clause of the Fourteenth Amendment in increasing numbers. The Kansas Industrial Relations Act of 1920, designed as an experiment in the settlement of wage disputes, was declared unconstitutional in a decision which gave Chief Justice Taft an excellent opportunity to set forth the *laissez faire* view of freedom of contract.[34] Subsequent noteworthy decisions by the Conservative Republican Court struck down a New York experiment in the regulation of theater-ticket agencies,[35] a New Jersey experiment in the regulation of employment agencies,[36] a Tennessee experiment in the regulation of gasoline filling stations,[37] and an Oklahoma experiment in the regulation of the artificial-ice business.[38] Justices Holmes, Brandeis, and Stone wrote dissenting opinions in these cases, strongly critical of the action taken by the majority of the Court. It was impossible for the authors of these legislative experiments and other interested members of the public to read these opinions without feeling that the Court was deeply involved in controversies over questions of policy which the Supreme Court had formerly preferred to leave to the political branches of the government. Constitutional historians could recognize in these decisions the kind of action for which the aristocratic Nationalists had originally hoped to open the way by the device of a joint legislative-judicial veto. Hamiltonians were naturally delighted at such impressive evidence of judicial capacity to protect the rights of property against what seemed to them reckless experimentation by state legislators.

The Conservative Republican Court in its devotion to a Hamiltonian doctrine of judicial review departed far from the Hamiltonian theory of federalism. Marshall's Court, which had done most to reduce the Hamiltonian theory to practice, had adopted a broad construction of the legislative powers of the Congress, while adhering to a strict construction of the legislative powers of the state governments. Under Chief Justices Taft and Hughes the Conservative Republican Court construed the legislative powers of the states more strictly than ever before, but at the same time tended also to construe the legislative powers of the Congress strictly, when the rights of property seemed to be in jeopardy. The Tenth Amendment gained new significance when the Court struck down the second federal child-labor law [39] and the judicial veto of the Agricultural Adjustment Act [40] added unpredictable importance to the new "dual federalism." [41] These decisions, if allowed to stand unchallenged as precedents for the future, threatened to cause grave embarrassment to legislators seeking to develop national policies for the solution of emerging national problems of social and industrial justice. Yet it was clear that it was no longer possible for the state governments to deal effectively with these problems. Foreign critics of American political institutions began to speak of the "astonishing phenomenon of the rule of judges," and expressed amazement at "the spectacle of the American people living its political life according to canons laid down in the late eighteenth century to secure the political ideals and the economic rights of the American bourgeosie." [42] At long last the principle of federalism was again, as toward the end of Taney's Court, furnishing a strong bulwark for the defense of the interests of that particular minority, the "opulent," which had seemed to the authors of The Federalist so greatly in need of better protection against the abuse of legislative power by the representatives of numerical majorities in a democratic republic.

The casual nature of some of the most controversial of these decisions is well illustrated by the history of the minimum-wage cases. The Supreme Court was unable to decide the first of these cases which came before it,[43] because one of the judges disqualified himself and the other eight were evenly divided in opinion. Consequently the decision of the state court, which was favorable to the constitutionality of the law, was allowed to stand. In 1923 a federal minimum-wage law, applying to the District of Columbia, came before the Court, which was enabled by changes in its membership since the decision in the earlier case to disallow the act by a vote of five to three.[44] This precedent was followed by the Court in cases which came up subsequently from the states of Arizona [45] and Arkansas,[46] and the issue, despite the remonstrances of the dissenting judges, seemed to have been settled adversely to the constitutionality of minimum-wage laws for women in industry. In 1936 another minimum-wage case came to the Supreme Court from the state of New York,[47] involving a law which had been drafted with extraordinary care in order to avoid these constitutional difficulties, and the issue was reopened. This law also was declared unconstitutional. However, the vote of the Court was close, and among the four dissenting judges was Chief Justice Hughes, who wrote an opinion marked by sensitive feeling and strong conviction, protesting against the decision of the majority. A year later, after President Roosevelt had made a political issue out of the Court's exercise of its power of judicial veto, a minimum-wage law of the state of Washington, which had long been moribund, was revived and brought before the Court to give it the opportunity to reconsider its previous decisions. On this occasion one of the judges who had found the New York minimum-wage law unconstitutional the year before changed his mind and made a new majority of five in favor of the constitutionality of such legislation.[48]

Such an extraordinary record of judicial uncertainty and vacillation vindicated the judgment of those framers of the Constitution who originally opposed judicial intervention in the legislative process. Twenty-four years had passed since the enactment of the first mandatory minimum-wage law for women. During the first four of these years the constitutionality of such laws had been in doubt, while action by the Court was awaited. Then for six years they had been regarded as constitutional. Thereafter for fourteen years they had been considered unconstitutional. Finally by the action of a bare majority of the Court they became constitutional again. During these twenty-four years seventeen different judges had sat on the Court, when minimum-wage law cases were under consideration, of whom eight had made known their favorable opinion of the minimum-wage laws, five had declared themselves against their constitutionality, one had been on both sides of the question, and three had managed to keep their opinions to themselves. In the face of such a record it was impossible to contend that the judges were better qualified than the legislators for determining the course of legislative policy.

This paradox of the federal system, as interpreted by the Conservative Republican Court, was strikingly illustrated by the problem of legislating effectively against the evil of unregulated child labor. State legislators found difficulty in dealing effectively with this evil because of the advantage possessed by the employers in states with the lowest legislative standards in competition with employers in states with higher standards. The first federal child-labor law, however, was declared unconstitutional [49] on the ground that the Congress, in forbidding the transportation across state lines of the products of factories and mills employing children of tender years, or employing any children for excessively long hours, had exceeded its power to regulate interstate commerce. The decision was not made any more palatable to the friends of effective child-labor legislation by the fact that the Court was divided five to four in this case. Justice Holmes utilized the occasion to write one of his most powerful dissenting opinions.

The grievance of the friends of the law was further aggravated by the action of the Court at about the same time in sustaining the Adamson Act,[50] fixing hours of labor and incidentally raising wages for railroad workers, who were mostly grown men. This decision was reached by another close vote in which eight of the judges were evenly divided in the same way as in the child-labor case. Chief Justice White, who held the balance of power in these two cases, saved the Adamson Act by voting with one set of four judges, while voiding the child-labor law by joining the other set of four judges. It seemed that the Chief Justice, like the President, had become one of the chief legislators in the field of labor legislation. A few years later, when former President Taft had become Chief Justice, the Conservative Republican Court struck down the second federal child-labor law.[51] This measure undertook to do no more than use the tax power to tax out of existence the offending evil of excessive child labor. The tax power had been used in this way without incurring the displeasure of the Court in several earlier cases, but the Taft Court decided to draw the line at regulating the employment of children by this means.

The tendency to take a narrow view of the power of the Congress to regulate interstate commerce as well as of its tax power reached a climax at the time of the Conservative Republican Court's attack upon the legislative program of the New Deal. The interpretation of the commerce power in the N.I.R.A. case seemed irreconcilable with that in the earlier packers and stockyards case.[52] The interpretation of the tax power in the A.A.A. case revived the theory, strongly favored in certain quarters before the Civil War, that "the general government" and the states, being both of them "sovereign," faced each other as equals across the boundary line between their respective jurisdictions. This theory, which Professor Corwin has termed "dual federalism," it had once been the mission of the Lincoln Republican Court to dispel. But times had changed and the Conservative Republican Court's conception of federalism had changed with them.

There has been much argument concerning the nature of the beneficiaries of this judicial activity in the field of legislative policy.[53] The spokesmen for organized labor were most critical of the Court, while the advocates of the causes in which businessmen and business

377

corporations were specially interested were readiest to defend its decisions. It was an era in which the Court seemed to be fulfilling the hopes of the Hamiltonians for the establishment of a doctrine of judicial review which would protect the interests of the "opulent" against political attacks by the representatives of the "indigent." The federal system, despite the lugubrious predictions of those who imagined that it could not stand under the economic and social changes of modern times, was certainly an important part of the general system of constitutional government. Its importance, moreover, was manifestly contingent in no small measure upon the power which its existence gave to the Supreme Court to discover justiciable questions in the political problems of the day.

JEFFERSONIANISM VERSUS HAMILTONIANISM

The fifth period in the judicial development of the federal system has seen a strong reaction against the Hamiltonian doctrine of judicial review.[54] The opinions of the great dissenters in the last years of the Conservative Republican Court became the foundation of the political philosophy of the New Deal Court. In no field of the Court's action was this constitutional revolution more effective than in the application of the principle of federalism. Justice Brandeis, in his great dissent in the Oklahoma ice-utility case,[55] expressed with transcendent clarity the neo-Jeffersonian attitude. The state legislators had decided to treat the ice business as a public utility and regulate it accordingly, but the majority of the Court deemed such a policy inadvisable and declared the statute unconstitutional under the due-process clause. Justices Brandeis and Stone found that the measure bore a substantial relation to the evils the legislators had discovered and wished to correct. "Under these circumstances," Justice Brandeis wrote, "to hold the act void, as being unreasonable, would in my opinion involve the exercise, not of the function of judicial review, but the function of a super-legislature."

Justice Brandeis expounded in luminous prose both the neo-Jeffersonian doctrine of judicial review and the neo-Jeffersonian principle of federalism. "To stay experimentation in things social and economic is a grave responsibility. Denial of the right to experiment may be fraught with serious consequences to the nation. It is one of the happy incidents of the federal system that a single courageous State may, if its citizens choose, serve as a laboratory, and try novel social and economic experiments without risk to the rest of the country. This Court has the power to prevent an experiment. We may strike down the statute which embodies it on the ground that, in our opinion, the measure is arbitrary, capricious or unreasonable. We have the power to do this, because the due-process clause has been held by the Court applicable to matters of substantive law as well as to matters of procedure. But in the exercise of this high power, we must be ever on our guard, lest we erect our prejudices into legal principles. If we would guide by the light of reason, we must let our minds be bold."

The New Deal Court did not fail in boldness.[56] As opportunities arose, it overruled the decisions of the Conservative Republican Court adverse to state experimentation in the fields of labor and social-welfare legislation. It also overruled decisions which, by unduly narrowing the concept of interstate commerce in the alleged interest of protecting the rights reserved to the states in the field of commercial regulation, had hindered experimentation by the national government in the fields of labor and social-welfare legislation. It overruled decisions which had further exploited the concept of federalism in pursuance of a Hamiltonian concept of judicial review by denying to the national government the use of the tax power in aid of nation-wide social and economic experiments by the New Deal. The result of these decisions was to enlarge the practical capacity of both national and state governments to perform legislative experiments and to increase their usefulness to the peoples of the states and of the nation. The power of judicial veto was not abdicated. But the character of the federal system was made more positive and its reputation was greatly improved.

The New Deal Court has accepted the Conservative Republican Court's interpretation of the due-process clause of the Fourteenth Amendment as an instrument for applying the provisions of the federal Bill of Rights to the states, but has changed the emphasis on the implications of due process. It has consistently refused to substitute its judgment for that of the state legislatures in the adjustment of conflicts between different economic and social interests, particularly in cases involving restrictions upon the freedom of contract of employers and wage earners, but on the other hand has gone beyond the Conservative Republican Court in finding reasons for vetoing legislative acts abridging the fundamental freedoms of the common man.[57] In the Gitlow case, where a Communist Party official appealed from a conviction by a state court for violation of a statute penalizing certain abuses of the freedom of speech and of the press, the Taft Court had held for the first time that the general liberty of the Fourteenth Amendment included the particular liberties set forth in the First Amendment.[58] Although Gitlow did not obtain judicial approval of the liberty to incite sedition, which he sought, the precedent became the point of departure for a series of decisions in which the Jeffersonian version of the doctrine of judicial review tended to prevail. Chief Justice Hughes, despite the opposition of his more conservative colleagues, led the way in broadening the due-process clause to protect freedom of the press, and freedom of speech and public assembly, against restrictive state legislation.[59] The New Deal Court gladly followed these liberal precedents as opportunity offered. The effect was to include under the protection of the Fourteenth Amendment the guarantees of personal liberty contained in the First Amendment.

Early beneficiaries of the New Deal Court's preference for a Jeffersonian version of the doctrine of judicial review were the Negroes. In a sensational Alabama case the Court insisted that under the due-process clause criminal proceedings in state courts must be so conducted as to satisfy the requirement of a fair trial according to a nationally acceptable standard of fairness.[60] In an equally sensational Florida case it insisted that due process included fair treatment of persons under arrest by the police before trial.[61] In another sensational case where a Negro arrested on a charge of stealing a tire was beaten to death by the sheriff, assisted by a special deputy and a policeman, a majority of the judges sought to breathe new life into the remains of the old civil-rights acts.[62] Brushing aside the contention of a minority that the theft of a tire was a local offense and should be dealt with by the state courts in accordance with state laws, they held that the Negro had a right under the Fourteenth Amendment not to be beaten to death while in the custody of state officers. It was clear that the New Deal Court was determined to do more for the protection of the civil rights of Negroes under the Fourteenth Amendment than had been done by its predecessors, and would presumably sanction more effective legislation than had yet been enacted by the Congress. Dissenting judges, clinging to an earlier conception of federalism, objected to the new trend, but the majority of the judges found nothing incompatible with a serviceable federal system in giving Negroes better protection for their procedural rights under the due-process clause.

The New Deal Court's preference for the Jeffersonian version of the doctrine of judicial review was put to a severe test by the aggressive activities of the dogmatic sect known as Jehovah's Witnesses.[63] These zealous sectarians believed that the only true government was a dictatorship of the saints and that they were bound to spread their gospel by all Christian means. In the earliest cases arising out of their activities, the Supreme Court decided that the right of the Witnesses to distribute tracts and other religious literature on the public streets could not be made dependent upon previous permission by municipal officers, claiming a discretionary authority to grant or withhold permission in the interest of clean streets, free from waste paper and other litter. The Court protected also the right of the Witnesses to sell propagandist pamphlets and books without paying municipal license fees required of commercial booksellers and agents. The Court even sustained an appeal by the Witnesses against a municipal ordinance prohibiting the ringing of doorbells for the purpose of summoning householders to receive propagandist literature. But the Witnesses were restive under restraints of any kind upon their propagandist zeal and persistently resorted to methods of proselytizing that were deeply offensive to members of other faiths. Within a few years they had appealed no less than sixteen controversial cases to the Supreme Court, in disposing of which the judges had written twenty-seven separate opinions. In several cases the judges had been closely divided in opinion, and twice the Court had reversed itself, seeking a serviceable rule for drawing the line between the freedom of the Witnesses to propagate their religion, on the one hand, and, on the other, the right of other persons to be free from excessively aggressive solicitation and other objectionable interferences with their own religious liberty. Despite the impatience of state and local authorities with the provocative behavior of the sect the Supreme Court persisted in its search for a proper adjustment between conflicting claims to freedom in the exercise of religion.

The compulsory-flag-salute cases offered the New Deal Court its finest opportunity to establish the Jeffersonian doctrine of judicial review.[64] Justice Frankfurter's opinion for the Court in the first of these cases and his dissenting opinion in the second case contain a classic statement of the modern doctrine of states' rights. But his contention that state elections furnish the proper forum for the protection of the rights of the people against the abuse of power by state legislatures was not Jeffersonian. The dissenting opinion of Chief Justice Stone in the first case, and Justice Jackson's opinion for the Court in the second, sounded the keynote of the new era inaugurated by the New Deal Court. "The very purpose of a Bill of Rights," Justice Jackson declared, "was to withdraw certain subjects from the vicissitudes of political controversy, to place them beyond the reach of majorities and officials, and to establish them as legal principles to be applied by the courts." Justice Jackson also stated another Jeffersonian principle, which the Court was determined to maintain, with cogent eloquence. "If there is any fixed star in our constitutional constellation," he concluded, "it is that no official, high or petty, can prescribe what shall be orthodox in politics, nationalism, religion, or other matters of opinion, or force citizens to confess by word or act their faith therein."

The decisions of the New Deal Court suggest that there is firmer ground than the due-process clause on which the Court can stand when vindicating the fundamental freedoms of the individual. The clause of the Fourteenth Amendment which guarantees the privileges and immunities of national citizenship was long neglected by the Supreme Court. Since business corporations, whether or not they were persons, were certainly not citizens, it did not offer the same attraction as the due-process clause to the spokesmen for business interests seeking protection from the Court against restrictive state legislation. It remained for the Hughes Court to find in this clause the means of protecting property against discriminatory taxation by state legislatures.[65] But this decision seemed to Justice Stone to open the door too wide for judicial review of such legislation and eventually he persuaded his associates to repudiate this new departure in judicial participation in the state legislative process.[66] The New Deal Court was quick to abandon a doctrine which might involve the judges in a new series of decisions as impolitic as those of the Conservative Court under the Hamiltonian doctrine of judicial review.

The practical utility for the protection of personal rights of the clause covering the privileges and immunities of citizenship was discovered and brought to public attention in the Jersey City free-speech case.[67] The Supreme Court had no difficulty in finding that Mayor Hague's claim to be the law could not stand against the right of C.I.O. organizers to harangue the public at suitable times and places, but its members found great difficulty in agreeing upon reasons for its decision. Justice Black ventured the suggestion, in which Justice Roberts and also Chief Justice Hughes concurred, that the right to discuss national issues in public was one of the privileges of national citizenship and that a citizen who exercised that right in a proper manner was entitled to protection against interference by ill-advised local police. The utility of the privileges and immunities clause was further developed by Justices Douglas and Jackson in the "Okie" case.[68] The migration of indigent citizens from Texas to California could not be stopped at the state line by any state legislative enactment, the Court unanimously declared. A majority of the Court professed to believe that such legislation would be an unconstitutional encroachment on the power of the Congress to regulate interstate commerce. But the minority could not agree that the conveyance of an impecunious American in his brother-in-law's automobile is analogous to the transportation of cattle or coal. An American citizen, Justice Jackson asserted, who may be required by law to fight for his country, surely cannot be restrained from settling in any part of it he chooses on the shabby ground that he might become a public charge.

The boldness of the New Deal Court under Chief Justice Stone in protecting the personal rights of unpopular minorities against the abuse of legislative power by state lawmakers and local police officials has continued to be manifest under Chief Justice Vinson. The New Deal judges have insisted that the right of Negroes to equality of opportunity for higher education shall be respected in fact as well as in principle.[69] They have forbidden state and local officials to enforce the provisions of restrictive covenants in contracts for the sale of land designed to prevent Negroes and others from making their homes in residential areas preëmpted by members of more privileged classes.[70] They have also, at the instance of a parent, forbidden state and local school authorities to release any part of the time of pupils in the public schools for religious training under the instruction of priests and other ministers of religion, in order to maintain a strict separation of church and state.[71] They have even disallowed a local ordinance regulating the use of sound trucks, in order to protect the right of Jehovah's Witnesses to preach the gospel on the public streets.[72] Jeffersonianism has continued to triumph over Hamiltonianism. The doctrine of judicial review, as applied to legislation affecting the principle of federalism, despite the New Deal Court's reluctance to interfere with novel experiments in the field of social and economic policy by state legislators, has manifestly been strengthened by the Court's action in cases affecting the fundamental freedoms of Americans under the Bill of Rights.

The Jeffersonian doctrine of judicial review, however, is no more favorable than the Hamiltonian doctrine to unanimity of opinion within the Court and no more likely to put an end to doubt and uncertainty in adapting a Constitution, intended to endure for ages, to the changing conditions of a changing world. A majority of the Court consented to the appropriation of public money for the transportation of pupils to parochial schools in New Jersey,[73] brushing aside the objection that such payments would violate the provision of the First Amendment prohibiting legislation affecting an establishment of religion. The transportation of pupils to such schools, the majority of the Court seemed to hold, could be treated as a part of a state system of public education, if a state legislature deemed such treatment in the public interest, rather than as a part of a religious establishment. A majority of the Court consented also to the use of "blue-ribbon" juries for the trial of labor leaders charged with extorting money from contractors under threats of calling strikes against them,[74] despite the objection that such a form of trial would deny the offending labor leaders their right to trial by a jury of their peers. Due process of law, the majority of the Court declared, did not require a uniform legal procedure in all states. But in these and other important cases dissenting judges wrote opinions as strongly critical of the majority as those written by the great dissenters in the Conservative Republican Court. The differences of opinion among the judges were as spectacular as at any period in the Court's history.[75]

The general tendency of the decisions by the New Deal Court affecting the operation of the federal system has been to carry the centralization of power at Washington further than under the Conservative Republican Court. This is particularly true in cases involving the use of money. The Sixteenth Amendment enormously increased the practical capacity of the national government to raise money by taxation and threatened to disturb the equilibrium of the federal system by greatly extending the practice of financing the public services of the state governments through grants-in-aid from the Federal Treasury. The attachment of conditions to the expenditure of these grants can be the means of shifting power to determine policy to the national from the state governments. In a suit brought by the state of Oklahoma against the United States Civil Service Commission,[76] the Supreme Court refused to set aside an order of the Commission, issued under the Hatch "Pure Politics" Act, withholding highway funds from the state while a member of the state highway commission continued to hold the chairmanship of the Democratic state central committee. The tax power also has been interpreted less favorably to the states than before. A long series of uncertain and vacillating decisions led eventually to the conclusion that, while federal officers should not be exempt from state income taxes, neither should state officers be exempt from the federal income tax.[77] The same trend was illustrated by the Saratoga Springs case, in which it was finally established that the business operations of the state governments should not escape taxation by the federal government.[78] The Court decided also that state-owned businesses were bound to respect the price ceilings established by the O.P.A., despite the alleged "sovereignty" of the owner.[79] In some of these cases the judges were divided in opinion; in other cases they could agree on the decision, though not on the reasons for it. It remained as clear as ever, since President Washington had first acted upon the principle that judges should be politically sound, that the further development of the federal system by the Supreme Court would reflect the political attitudes of the judges.

The importance of judicial review of state legislation does not seem great, if measured by the bare number of acts of the state legislatures vetoed by the Supreme Court. Before the adoption of the Fourteenth Amendment the number of such judicial vetoes averaged less than one a year. After the adoption of the Fourteenth Amendment the number jumped to around five a year under the Antislavery Republican Court. Under the Conservative Republican Court it averaged around ten a year. The number of judicial vetoes fell off sharply under the New Deal Court. At no time was the number of such vetoes considerable in comparison with the number of vetoes of state legislation by the state governors. Compared with the total volume of state legislation it seems negligible.

The effect of judicial review upon the legislative policies of the states, however, has been greater than the number of judicial vetoes would suggest. Marshall's Court and Taney's Court used their power of judicial veto to maintain the authority of the Federal Government in what the Court deemed its proper sphere. Marshall's Court protected particularly the legislative authority of the Congress and Taney's put greater emphasis on the protection of the federal executive power. The Conservative Republican and New Deal Courts have used their veto power to establish and maintain national policies in matters previously regarded as reserved to the states. The Conservative Republican Court was particularly solicitous for the protection of property rights against shocking and also merely novel experiments by the states and the New Deal Court has put greater emphasis on the protection of human rights against the injurious results of local hostility or indifference. The state courts have generally taken their cue from the Supreme Court and the policies favored by the federal judges have tended to prevail in the states. The effect on state legislative policy has been strongly influential, if not always decisive. The federal judges, despite the ups and downs of judicial prestige, have been the major force in the development of the federal system.

Federalism has become something radically different from what it was in the minds of the original Federalists in the Convention of 1787. The place of the states in the constitutional system of government, as judicially construed, is not what it was before the adoption of the Fourteenth Amendment, or the Sixteenth, to say nothing of the changes wrought by the subsequent amendments to the Constitution. But the state governments still have an independent place in the political system, and their practical importance in the life of the people is greater than ever before. The loss of power to the national government has been more than compensated, from a pragmatic point of view, by the gain of functions and prestige from the local governments within the states. Professor Laski's view that the so-called sovereign states are a luxury of an expanding capitalist system, which can no longer be afforded in a stage of capitalist contraction and decline, does not square with the actual condition of the states in the more perfect Union. "The small unit of government," he has insisted, is "impotent against the big unit of giant capitalism." [80] But the state governments have much to do besides contending with great industrial corporations. They have roads and other public works to maintain, the children of the people to educate, the delinquents to restrain, and in many cases the defectives to support. They spend more money, they employ more officials and workers, and they render greater services to the people, than ever before. Their mere existence, as independent agencies for the administration of public affairs and the expression of public opinion, constitutes an important limitation upon the authority and activities of the national government. The new federalism is different from the old, but it is no less real and no less rational.

There seems no good reason for dissenting from the opinion of Professor Carl B. Swisher concerning the present status of the American federal system.[81] Discussing the "shifting boundaries of federalism," he recognized that the normal development of modern capitalistic industry, together with the consequences of a great depression and a great war, have caused the exercise of an amount of power by the national government which was unimaginable by conservative judges in the age of Calvin Coolidge. Federal grants-in-aid and other novel developments have enabled the national government to become "in

many matters the architect of the policy administered by the states."
Nevertheless, "the states remain the custodians of power not merely
commensurate with that exercised in earlier years but substantially
greater." The maintenance of the federal system, he wisely concludes,
"is essential to the highest welfare of the people of the United
States." [82]

The federal principle still requires not only that the state governments be kept within their proper sphere of action but also that the
national government be kept within its proper sphere. Madison might
think, if he could view the present political scene in the United
States, that the particular minority which he hoped might gain additional protection under the federal system — that is, the "opulent" — is
not benefiting from it as much as other minorities whose exposure to
oppression in a democratic republic he would have viewed with less
alarm. But times change and the working of an institution changes
with them. The New Deal judges, like their predecessors, will grow
older, and, again like their predecessors, will grow more conservative.
Hamiltonian versions of the doctrine of judicial review will again
contend with the Jeffersonian, and doubtless will again gain ground.
As long as the middle classes continue to dominate the political scene,
such contention among the judges will continue to make for the
stability and durability of the more perfect Union. Benjamin F. Wright's
conclusion, that under the New Deal Court the law of the Constitution
is in a healthier condition than it was under the Conservative Republican Court, is sound in its application to federalism as well as to the
separation of powers.[83] The function of judicial review remains
the cornerstone of constitutional government in the more perfect
Union.

Madison's original opposition to the principle of federalism illustrates the blindness which can afflict even the most intelligent political
thinker when he undertakes to plan institutions in the interest of a
public including generations yet unborn. How long would national
politicians, supported by victorious national parties, have resisted the
temptation to meddle intolerably with the domestic affairs of the
states, if the Congress had possessed the powers of reviewing and
disallowing state legislation which the original Virginia plan proposed
to confer upon it, to say nothing of Charles Pinckney's and of Hamilton's schemes of centralized power? How long would a system of
national government have lasted under which the Congress was authorized to veto any act of a state legislature which in its judgment con-

387

flicted with the letter, or perhaps even with the spirit, of the Constitution, as interpreted by itself? Not even the elaborate defenses for the rights of the states which were contained in the finished Constitution gave a sense of security strong enough to prevent the secession of eleven states and an attempt to establish a separate confederacy. Experience has vindicated the judgment of the original Federalists in insisting upon an independent and powerful organ of judicial review, in addition to a Senate elected by the state legislatures, for the purpose of keeping the national and state governments within their proper fields of action.

The gravest danger to the federal system does not arise from any failure of the political branches of the national government to understand the advantages of decentralization in the management of public affairs in a country as big and diversified as the United States or of the judiciary to draw a suitable line of division between national and state powers under the changing conditions of modern times. It arises from the inordinate growth of the national military establishment and the complete destruction of the balance which once existed between the armed forces under the direction of the President and those of the states. It has not been possible to transform the United States into an arsenal of democracy with a view to securing the blessings of freedom from fear for peace-loving peoples abroad without jeopardizing the equilibrium of the federal system at home. Adequate security for the rights of the states and of the people becomes increasingly contingent upon a redistribution of power over armaments between the national government and a general international organization. Under the strenuous conditions of the contemporary world it is necessary to extend the principle of federalism to the area of world government in order to redress the balance between the states and the Union in the government of the nation. The principle of federalism, like that of the separation of powers, seems still to be well suited to the needs of the American people in the management of their domestic affairs. But in the conduct of their foreign relations new conditions have brought such a great expansion of the central executive power as to threaten the stability of the federal system as well as that of the system of checks and balances. Unless it becomes possible to look to the government of a world federation to take some of the pressure off the national government for the protection of the nation against the menace of war, the equilibrium of the whole constitutional system will be unstable.

THE ADJUDICATION OF INTERSTATE DISPUTES

The role of the Supreme Court in the federal system has been determined mainly by its action in cases in which it has exercised appellate jurisdiction. These are cases between natural persons, including both private individuals and public officers, together with cases involving voluntary associations, business corporations, and criminal prosecutions against individuals in the names of states. The Supreme Court has defined the meaning of federalism as an incident to the adjudication of private rights. Cases between states, and other cases in which the Court has original jurisdiction, have been of minor importance in the development of the federal system. This part of the Court's record, however, is of greater significance in applying the lessons of American experience with the principle of federalism to the problem of forming a general international organization suited to the requirements of the family of nations.

In the adjudication of disputes between states the Supreme Court has been most successful in cases where its judgment could be executed by proceedings in inferior courts involving primarily the rights of private persons. The earliest and most numerous disputes between states — those that have arisen over boundaries — have been of this nature. State lines have been uncertainly defined or, when following the courses of rivers, have shifted with the shifts in their channels. Many boundary disputes have been settled by the Supreme Court and little difficulty has been found in procuring the compliance of all the interested parties. These disputes have rarely raised political controversies of general public interest or otherwise tested the capacity of the Court to enforce its decisions against the opposition of state governments.

The Supreme Court has been successful also in settling disputes between states, involving the acts of public officers, where the execution of its decisions involved nothing more on the part of state officials than willingness to desist from some objectionable action. An excellent illustration of this kind of interstate dispute was the suit of Pennsylvania and Ohio against West Virginia to cause the public service commission of the latter state to cease its discrimination against out-of-the-state consumers in the distribution of natural gas.[84] The West Virginia state officials abandoned their discriminatory practices at the order of the Supreme Court without objection on the part of the state government or consumers of natural gas within the state. Another success for the Supreme Court was scored in the complicated litigation between the state of Illinois and the other Great Lakes states over the diversion of water from Lake Michigan through the Chicago drainage canal.[85] In order to maintain the water level of the Great Lakes at a satisfactory height, the Court enjoined the authorities of the drainage canal from diverting more than a limited amount of lake water. The city of Chicago was left to solve its problem of sewage disposal as best it could under the circumstances. The state of Illinois acquiesced in the Court's decision and the execution of its judgment presented no special difficulty.

The Supreme Court has been less successful in settling interstate disputes where the enforcement of its decisions has required positive action by state officials. Several awkward disputes of this kind have arisen out of conflicting plans for the use of water from interstate rivers for purposes of irrigation. In the original case of Kansas against Colorado the Supreme Court committed itself to the principle of an equitable apportionment of the water of the Arkansas River, but avoided responsibility for an actual redivision of the water between riparian users in those two states.[86] In later cases, involving the apportionment of the waters of the North Platte River between Wyoming, Nebraska, and Colorado, and the apportionment of the waters of the Colorado River between the states of the Southwest, the Court appeared to temporize in the hope that the problems could be solved by interstate compacts. On the more difficult case of the Colorado River water, where Arizona was arrayed in a stubborn contest against the other Southwestern states, a settlement was finally reached by political action in the shape of an act of Congress.[87] In the North Platte case the Court eventually faced its responsibility for an equitable apportionment of the water and authorized a specific plan for the development of irrigation systems in the three states.[88] But the states remained free to institute further proceedings with a view to the modification of the prescribed plan. It cannot be said that the dispute has been finally settled by the Court. The Court's function in these cases seems to have been that of mediation and conciliation rather than of genuine arbitration or adjudication.

The Supreme Court has been least successful in settling interstate disputes where the enforcement of its decisions has involved positive action by the political branches of a state government. The outstanding illustrations of cases of this kind have been interstate suits for the recovery of debts. Since judgments against a debtor state could ordinarily be satisfied only by a legislative appropriation of money and the levying of a tax or other political action in order to cover the appropriation, a recalcitrant debtor would be in a position to raise the questions whether the Supreme Court possessed authority to enforce its decision and, if so, how it should be done. Several suits in which state governments sought to collect defaulted state bonds on behalf of private persons were dismissed by the Supreme Court on the ground that the plaintiff states were not directly interested in the recovery of the debts.[89] The leading case of this kind in which the Supreme Court gave judgment to a state was one in which the owner of the bonds had given them unconditionally to the state which brought the suit.[90] The bonds, when originally issued, had been secured by the deposit of collateral with state officers who could turn over the collateral at the order of the Court without specific authorization by the state legislature. Whether the value of the collateral was sufficient to discharge the whole of the debt seemed to be immaterial.

The most significant episode was the interminable suit of Virginia against West Virginia.[91] In this case the plaintiff asked the Supreme Court to make the defendant assume its fair share of the Virginia state debt, as it stood at the time of the separation of West Virginia. The plaintiff appeared nine times before the Court in prosecution of its suit. The Supreme Court decided that Virginia's claim was just and determined the amount of debt to be assumed by West Virginia, but persistently postponed facing the problem of enforcing its judgment. It displayed a patience which almost ceased to be a virtue in avoiding definitive action in the hope that West Virginia would come to a friendly understanding with its neighbor. After many years of inconclusive litigation West Virginia finally settled out of court. The outcome of the proceedings was a triumph for the Supreme Court in its self-assumed role of mediator and conciliator rather than a triumph of justice under law.

The record of the Supreme Court in the exercise of its original jurisdiction over interstate disputes reveals that it has not yet learned how to settle political disputes by judicial processes. It has no adequate means of coercing a so-called sovereign state. Disputes that a state is determined to regard as political cannot be settled by judicial processes. Disputes that a state might regard as political may nevertheless be settled by judicial processes, if they can be transformed into disputes between persons, private, corporate, or official, so as to become justiciable. The distinction between justiciable and political is decisive

391

in determining the limits of the Supreme Court's practical capacity to settle disputes among the members of the more perfect Union. But what is the nature of this distinction the Court has found great difficulty in saying precisely.[92] Experience shows that it is for the political branches of government to say finally what shall be deemed to be political. In the nature of things the judges cannot resolve an appeal from the politicians concerning the meaning of politics.

The significance of the Supreme Court's action in disputes between the states is emphasized by its action in disputes between a state and the United States. After the Civil War both Mississippi and Georgia tried to stop the enforcement of the Reconstruction Act by suits in the Supreme Court against President Johnson and Secretary of War Stanton, respectively.[93] The Radical Republicans, who controlled the legislative, if not the executive, branch of the Federal Government, insisted that the suits were political, and the Court adopted their view. Later suits by states to stop the expenditure of public money for purposes which the states regarded as beyond the proper authority of the Federal Government came to a similar end.[94] Suits to stop federal taxation of state businesses have likewise failed. Both South Carolina and New York have sought to avoid payment of federal taxes on businesses conducted by the state governments, or for their account, but the Supreme Court has refused to recognize a state immunity against federal taxation of such enterprises.[95] The Court also has recognized the priority of federal claims against an insolvent debtor over those of a state where both claims seemed to be equally valid.[96] The states have not fared well in the Supreme Court when their interests have conflicted directly with those of the Union.

The record of litigation in the Supreme Court between state governments and that of the Union discloses a surprising indifference on the part of the former to the possibility of appearing in court as the protector of the interests of its citizens against discriminatory action by federal officers and administrative agencies. Recently the state of New York brought a suit against the United States for the purpose of checking alleged discrimination against New York shippers by the Interstate Commerce Commission in regulating freight rates on interstate railroads.[97] The Commission had acted in response to complaints by Southern and Western states that the freight-rate structure was unduly favorable to the Northeastern section of the country. State governments sponsored the various interests of their own shippers and the dispute took the form of a struggle between the sections. The

Court decided that the Commission had not exceeded its discretionary authority under the Transportation Act and refused to interfere·with its action. Justice Jackson, who happened to be a citizen of New York, and Justice Frankfurter, residing in Massachusetts, dissented, protesting that the Commission's decision was political. But the majority of the judges did not find it objectionable on that ground, and the aggrieved shippers were left to take their grievance, if they wished, to the Congress.

In the case of *United States* v. *California,* decided at the same term of the Court, the Federal Government claimed title to submerged oil lands under coastal waters within the three-mile limit and challenged the right of the state government to grant leases of such lands to approved oil companies.[98] The Court decided in favor of the United States, and the aggrieved oil companies, disappointed in their hope that the state government could protect their interests by judicial proceedings, showed greater faith than the New York shippers in the political process and carried their appeal to the Congress. In general the Supreme Court has recognized that the states have a right to do as they please in matters which they regard as political, that the Federal Government has the same right in matters which it regards as political, and that in the nature of things the right of the lesser power in case of conflict must yield to that of the greater. Such conflicts are finally settled by political instead of judicial processes. Justice must be sought through wise arrangements for the distribution of legislative power between the federal and state governments and through intelligent campaigns for the choice of representatives in the political branches of these governments. If justice be defined as the adjustment of conflicts of interest among the people of a state in such a way as to promote the best interests of the whole body of people, it is best established by adherence to sound principles of constitutional government rather than by juristic formulas. In the government of the more perfect Union, instead of an abstract theory of justice there is due process of law.

Ordinarily, special interests which wish to check what seem to them abuses of power by the Federal Government do not look to their state governments for the desired protection. They seek protection through the judicial process by proceedings in their own names or through political action by their representatives in the political parties or in their own special-interest organizations. Milling interests, which objected to the Agricultural Adjustment Act, paid the tax assessed

393

against them under protest and then sued in the federal courts for the recovery of the money.[99] Mining interests, which objected to the Bituminous Coal Conservation Act, initiated a suit in the federal courts to restrain their own company from paying the tax to be assessed against them.[100] Electric-power interests, which objected to the sale of power in their territory by the Tennessee Valley Authority, proceeded by a suit in the federal courts directly against the T.V.A.[101] When, as in the latter case, the judicial proceedings fail to bring the desired protection, the "interests" can put pressure on legislators through the agency of the lobby or, in special cases, through a political party in which they may possess some influence. The president of the Commonwealth and Southern Power Company, the leading competitor of the T.V.A., was actually nominated for the presidency of the United States by the Republican Party, though he had only recently become a Republican, as the best available symbol of opposition to the New Deal. Original suits in the Supreme Court in the name of a state have been among the least important of the methods for adjusting important conflicts between special interests which are strong enough to influence the action of politicians, either national or state.

The record of the Supreme Court in the adjudication of disputes between the federal and state governments, like that in the adjudication of strictly interstate disputes, is not encouraging for those who would cite its performance as an example for an International Court of Justice under the authority of the United Nations. It is clear that a world court must have jurisdiction over individuals, if it is to function effectively as the arbiter of disputes between nations. National governments, like state governments, if free to choose between submitting to unpopular judicial decisions and treating them as political, are likely to choose the latter course. Judicial knowledge of their natural preference in such cases discourages positive judicial action. The judicial power cannot deal with political questions effectively, it can hardly deal with them at all, except in cases where private parties alone are directly involved. If governments become involved in international conflicts of interest, they will naturally try to settle them by political methods. Among the members of the family of nations, as among the states of the American Union, important disputes must ordinarily be recognized as political, and political disputes are settled better by politicians than by judges.

Federalism, regarded as one of the political principles which

American experience has shown to be sound, possesses some important advantages. It helps to divide power so as to diminish the liability of corruption, which accompanies its possession, without impairing too much the practical capacity of those who hold it to use it for the public good. With the enormous growth of political power in modern times the need for its wide distribution becomes greater than ever before.[102] Moreover the distribution of power as widely as possible among the people for whose benefit it should be used brings certain practical benefits. Democracy is justified less by efficiency of administration than by the development of character through the performance of the duties of citizenship. Federalism lives on the belief that the problems of government are likely to be solved most satisfactorily if the responsibility for solving them is placed as directly as possible on those particular bodies of people who are most concerned with the problems and best capable of judging when they are solved effectively. The experience of the American people suggests that the very process of seeking a solution, where the power to act and the responsibility for action are joined as closely as possible together, encourages the development of the best qualities of citizenship throughout the whole body of the people.[103]

Federalism, which was originally a principle of government forced upon the framers by the constraint of circumstances, and which owes its survival in no small part to the unanticipated solicitude of the Supreme Court judges, has justified by its fruits its reluctant inclusion by Madison among his basic principles of constitutional government. The judges have been able to safeguard the essential processes of a serviceable and durable federal system, and have done much to secure the reasonable objectives of both the Hamiltonian and the Jeffersonian versions of the doctrine of judicial review. But it has been the politicians, both national and state, operating through the political branches of government and complying with the requirements of due process of law as determined by the judges, who have been most successful in adjusting the important conflicts of interest among the people of the more perfect Union. This is one of the most valuable lessons about constitutional government to be learned from American experience in the management of the more perfect Union. It is a lesson of prime significance in planning the institutions of a more perfect international organization.

CHAPTER TWELVE

To Perfect the
More Perfect Union

A CRITIQUE OF MADISON'S THREE PRINCIPLES

THE experience of the American people since the formation of the more perfect Union confirms what most of the framers of the Constitution believed to be the experience of the ages. Those who possess power are prone to abuse it. Congressmen have many times exploited the power of numerical majorities to make laws in the interest of particular factions or combinations of factions, with too little regard for other interests. Presidents have repeatedly stepped over the line which divides governing from domineering. Even the Supreme Court has at several crises in the life of the nation yielded to the temptation to write its own views of public policy into the fundamental law of the land under cover of questionable decisions in cases arising out of ordinary litigation. Men in power press on until they reach the limit of their power. This seems to have been as true of Americans under the Federal Constitution as of other men.

American experience has shown also that Madison was right in his analysis of the problem of government. It is necessary that the men in the government should be able to control the governed. It is necessary also that they should control themselves. Since the framers could not rely upon the rulers' powers of self-control to protect the governed against oppression, they sought to define the authority of public officers of all kinds as precisely as possible, and to give to those in charge of the different departments of the government the means, as well as an interest, to prevent the abuse of power by others. The aristocratic Nationalists put greater trust in the principle of the separation of powers than most of the other members of the Convention of 1787. The plans which they originally devised were not acceptable to a majority of the framers without substantial changes, but the system of

396

checks and balances which was finally adopted has served its purpose remarkably well. Each of the constitutional organs of government in the more perfect Union has at times seemed to grow so strong as to upset the balance of the system and make impossible the recovery of its equilibrium. But each overweening Congress or President or Supreme Court has eventually been succeeded by another which has seemed to threaten the stability of the system through excessive weakness rather than excessive strength. Legislators, executives, and judges have at various times seemed dangerously deficient both in the power to control others and in that of self-control. Up to now, however, the powers of mutual control vested in the different parts of the system have sufficed to prevent its destruction.

It was no part of the Nationalists' original plans that the authority of the government of the Union as a whole should be precisely defined or that its powers should be checked and balanced by those reserved to independent state governments. The enumeration of the powers granted to the Congress, insisted upon by the original Federalists and the various kinds of Unionists, and the more explicit reservation of rights to the people, insisted upon by the representatives of the middle classes in the state ratifying conventions, strengthened the judicial branch of the government of the Union and created a more stable equilibrium of power than the aristocratic Nationalists had planned or would have adopted, if left to their own devices. But the system of checks and balances was greatly improved by the invention of the principle of federalism. This principle, too, has not worked out in the way expected by its original advocates in the Convention of 1787. The Senate, like the House of Representatives, has served to protect local interests, though in different proportions, rather than the particular rights of the states regarded as political entities. In fact, because of its participation in the executive power, the Senate has become a more important protector of local interests than the House of Representatives. It has been the Supreme Court which has protected the constitutional authority of the state governments.

Though the Federal Government has become far more active and energetic in modern times than could have been anticipated by the framers, the balance of the federal system has not been thereby destroyed. The state governments also have become more active and energetic than could have been anticipated by the framers. All the state governments are still able to make an independent contribution to the actual government of the American people, and the larger and stronger state governments seem likely to sustain indefinitely a federal system which would doubtless be precarious if dependent solely on the support of the smaller and weaker states. Doubtless the tremendous growth of the national military establishment in recent years compels the attachment of reservations to this forecast. Nevertheless, it is plainly too soon to speak of the obsolescence of federalism.

Most unexpected in the development of the government of the more perfect Union has been the effect of the natural limits to the practical capacity of numerical majorities of the people to govern. No part of the political philosophy of the aristocratic Nationalists seemed more speculative and questionable in 1787 than Madison's theory of natural limits to the power of popular majorities. None of Madison's aristocratic colleagues openly endorsed his speculations concerning the obstacles to the organization of popular majorities into effective governing parties. None seemed to share his confidence that these obstacles would add much to the difficulties to be put in the way of majority rule by the systematic distribution of the authority of the national government under the Constitution. The democratic Nationalists certainly hoped that these obstacles would prove less formidable barriers than they seemed to Madison to the advance of democracy in national politics. The aristocratic Federalists and Unionists obviously put their trust mainly in the principle of federalism for the protection of minority interests against the abuse of power by reckless national majorities. The democratic Federalists and Unionists may have shared Madison's distrust in the practical capacity of numerical majorities in the country as a whole to get together for the efficient exercise of power, but what he hoped for, as a further check against the abuse of power by the poor and indigent, they must have feared as an additional weakness in a political system already overloaded, in their opinion, with checks on the authority of popular majorities in the interest of the rich and opulent.

The experience of more than one hundred sixty years shows clearly both how right Madison was in his analysis of American politics and how limited is the foresight of even the most acute political analyst. It has certainly been more difficult to organize popular majorities on the great scale of national politics than on the more modest scale of politics within the states. The diversity of interests among the representatives from the different sections of a large country restricts the practical capacity of a majority of the representatives to use their power for private ends. Majorities may be found for particular purposes but precisely the same majority is not likely to be greatly interested in many different purposes. The necessity of finding different majorities for different purposes breeds respect for adverse opinions in particular cases, or at least a greater tolerance of diversity of opinion than would exist if a clear majority of the representatives were united in promoting numerous legislative measures in which all members of the majority felt an equal interest in overpowering the opposition. The legislative process in such a legislative body is not a simple matter of vindicating the right against the wrong. It is the more complex business of adjusting conflicts of interest with a view to the greatest advantage of the greatest number. The greater the variety of particular interests which may come in conflict and require adjustment, the greater the probability that the adjustment of these interest conflicts will promote the best interests of the whole body of people. Madison rightly argued that such a legislative process should afford the rich and opulent, who form a permanent minority of the American people, substantial protection against the abuse of power by the poor and indigent who, he assumed, would form a permanent majority of the people.

The limitation of the power of popular majorities which Madison expected from the nature of the legislative process has been further secured by the nature of the electoral process on the great scale of national politics. Money and leisure for attention to public affairs — the peculiar advantages of the opulent — have been indispensable for the conduct of national elections and for the maintenance of national parties. The first national party was definitely aristocratic in leadership and spirit, as Madison and his closest political associates in the Federal Convention clearly anticipated. Yet, as the Jeffersonian Republicans, the Jacksonian Democrats, and their various successors have demonstrated, resolute and persistent popular leaders are able to create parties which can overpower those in possession of the national government, regardless of their original advantages in wealth and numbers. Madison did not foresee the normal operation of a bipartisan system in national politics. The "ins" always seem to possess adequate wealth for the purpose of maintaining a national organization as well as the advantage of superior numbers, but the "outs" have never been kept out of the presidency for more than a single generation at a time. Partisan success uniformly creates conditions favorable to the reorganization of defeated parties or to the organization of new popular majorities on a new partisan basis. The formation of national parties, as of durable and effective majorities in the Congress, has always been difficult, but it has been successfully accomplished often enough to demonstrate the essential nature of major parties in national politics.

In the nature of things national parties must be leagues of local factions as well as organizations in which the influence of wealth is combined with the influence of numbers. They are certainly more heterogeneous in their composition than parties which are contained within the borders of particular states. They are also more dependent upon a proper combination of wealth and numbers. If one result — as Madison foresaw — is to limit the power of numbers by the difficulty of uniting a majority of the people in support of the special interests of the various factions of which it is composed, another equally important result — which Madison did not clearly foresee — is the limitation of the influence of wealth as well as numbers by the impossibility of getting office with the support of either alone. These circumstances tend to reduce the danger that power will be abused in the interest either of particular localities or of special classes of the people. Madison rightly emphasized the limitations on the power of national leagues of local factions, growing out of the natural differences between their various special interests. American experience emphasizes also the dependence of parties for success in national elections upon a proper blending of the influence of wealth and numbers. The former condition tends to exalt the influence of the middle sections in national politics; the latter, to exalt the influence of the middle classes. These natural tendencies have given a greater importance in the more perfect Union than even Madison could foresee to his third principle of government.

THE PARAMOUNT PRINCIPLE OF THE POLITICAL MEAN

This principle, which from being the least of Madison's three principles has gained greater importance by the development of organized partisanship, must now be appraised in connection with its companion principle, an unforeseen product of the political system devised by the framers, the principle of the political mean. In the period of predominantly agrarian politics the middle sections of the country generally held the balance of power. The strategic position of the middle sections in national politics meant the actual ascendancy of the middle-class graingrowers among the various rural factions. In more recent times the rise of an industrial city-dwellers' world has been reflected in the growing influence of the urban middle class. At all times the sectional and class structure of the national parties has greatly influenced the character of the actual government of the more perfect Union. Madison foresaw the importance of economic and social factors in the organization of a governing party under the Constitution. He did not foresee the development of a two-party system which would foster and preserve the influence of the political mean in national politics.

The American form of the two-party system is a natural response of a democratic people to the challenge of the constitutional method of electing Presidents. There is no practical alternative to the organization of the bulk of the "outs" for the purpose of winning presidential elections, if a majority of the people are to have an effective voice in the choice of the officer who is in practice the chief legislator as well as the chief executive. The system of bipartisanship which has developed is often criticized on the ground that the differences between the two major parties are unimportant and even unreal. Such criticism misses the point. If there were no differences between the parties except the personal differences between their candidates for the presidency, the system would still serve its essential purpose. Both parties would strive to find the candidates who would seem most attractive to the kinds of voters holding the balance of power in the big doubtful states. The safeguard against a perpetual monopoly of power by the "ins" would be the disposition of those voters least dominated by habit and tradition to make a rational choice at the polls. A bipartisan system, uncomplicated by important economic and social differences between the parties, would offer these voters the kind of choice they are most competent to make intelligently.

In fact there have always been substantial differences between the major parties with respect to sectional and class structure. The normal operation of the bipartisan system tends to enhance the influence of the intermediate sections and middle classes. It militates against the abuse of power by the extremes of sectional and class interest. Under modern conditions it works steadily for the success of the more moderate and conciliatory types of politicians. Doubtless under these conditions, too, partisan differences on the factitious issues of a campaign are less important than inconsiderate critics may think desirable, and the practical capacity of the voters to settle partisan controversies over the questions of the day by their choice between candidates may be small. But the system makes for moderation in politics. It tends to prevent, as Madison foresaw, the abuse of power by the many, who are poor, at the cost of the rich, and also — the prospect of which troubled him less — the abuse of power by the rich at the cost of the poor.

The principle of the political mean works in various ways. It may be applied by combining a democratic with an oligarchic (aristocratic or plutocratic) element in a political process. The collaboration of judge and jury in the administration of justice in common-law courts offers the best illustration of such a combination. The jury is or should be a fair sample of the general public. The judge introduces an aristocratic, or under less favorable conditions a plutocratic, element into the judicial process. De Tocqueville regarded the system of trial by jury as one of the most important factors in stabilizing the American political system in the age of Jackson.[1]

The aristocratic Nationalists in the Federal Convention were more interested in the legislative than in the judicial process. They would have liked a bicameral legislative system in which the Senate represented the opulent, while the voice of the people spoke through the House of Representatives. The necessity of compromise between the two chambers of such a Congress, in order that controversial legislation might be adopted, would favor a course of action representing a mean between the extremes which the chambers would naturally prefer, if free to act alone. But such a combination of aristocratic and democratic elements in the legislative process could result in no legislation at all, if the natural conflicts between the two chambers, instead of ending in rational compromises, produced nothing but interminable deadlocks. The refusal of the original Federalists and of the various kinds of Unionists to consent to such an arrangement and their insistence upon a different kind of Senate, in view of the natural tendency of politicians to abuse their powers, even when the limits of power have not been reached, was surely one of the happy developments in the framing of the Constitution.

Another method of applying the principle of the political mean is to take purely democratic and oligarchic elements and blend them into a single political process. This method is best illustrated by the normal operation of the system of nominations and elections in national politics. Universal, direct, and equal suffrage furnishes a powerful democratic element in the electoral process. The great need for money in the organization of parties and the conduct of elections introduces a powerful oligarchic element in the same process. These two elements are thus blended into a nominating and electing process which the American tradition describes as democratic, the Marxist higher criticism insists is plutocratic, and the facts reveal as a smooth and astonishingly satisfactory blend of democracy, plutocracy, and aristocracy. Both the system of electing the House of Representatives and that of electing the Senate, since the introduction of direct popular elections, exemplify in the same way the operation of this method of applying the principle of the political mean. It has been operating in presidential elections ever since the eclipse of the electoral colleges. This development in the government of the more perfect Union has greatly strengthened the moderating and stabilizing factors which Madison dimly and only partly foresaw but rightly appraised at a high value.

A third method of applying the principle of the political mean is to give disproportionate power to that portion of the people which is neither very rich nor very poor, but falls between the extremes of opulence and indigence. This method is best illustrated by the normal operation of the party system in national politics. The predominance of the rural middle class, that is, of the independent farmers operating family-size farms, was most conspicuous in the times of the Jeffersonian Republicans, the Jacksonian Democrats, and the radical Antislavery Republicans. But the decisive influence of this class was evident from the beginning of national politics, as the record of the framing and adoption of the Constitution, including the Bill of Rights, clearly reveals. In recent times the rise of an important urban middle class has complicated the partisan pattern without greatly altering its essential character. As long as the great states of New York, Pennsylvania, Ohio, Illinois, and California continue to form the principal battleground in the presidential campaigns of the major parties, the influence of the middle classes can hardly fail to remain decisive. Demagogues may try to exploit the passions of the very poor, enemies of the people may seek to turn against them the wealth of the very rich, but, barring unpredictable calamities ruinous to the class structure of the American economy, such efforts to abuse power cannot succeed under the established conditions of American politics.

It is not only the middle-class basis of national politics, but also the moderate temper of American politicians, that insure the effectiveness of the principle of the political mean in the government of the more perfect Union. The leading framers of the Constitution, notably Washington and Franklin, earnestly desired that a spirit of moderation should prevail in the administration of the new government. This they regarded as more important than the adoption of particular expedients among their proposals for a Constitution. They deliberately set what they believed to be a proper example by their own conduct in the Federal Convention. They furthermore agreed, reluctantly but consistently, to a frame of government which neither of them altogether liked, but which possessed what both regarded as the essential characteristic of a durable constitution — a system of distributed powers which could be operated efficiently only by reasonable politicians of moderate temper and conciliatory disposition. By a happy accident rather than by design this system of constitutional government was completed and made suitable for a democratic people by the development of a system of party government which Washington at least would have deplored. Franklin, with his greater practical experience in the working of popular government, may have expected something like the two-party system in national politics, and would have liked its encouragement of middle-class influence, but he could hardly have anticipated the peculiar manner of its operation, so favorable to the blending of the influences of wealth and of numbers in a political system which is at the same time both democratic and aristocratic. The framers built better than they knew.

The superiority of a political system which tends to exalt the influence of the middle classes of the people and to foster the success of public-spirited politicians of moderate temper and conciliatory disposition was thoroughly understood by the wisest of the founding fathers. John Adams's ponderous arguments in favor of a form of government in which true aristocrats would be able to prevail over both plutocrats and demagogues, and to secure the interests of the "middling sort" of people as the most practicable approximation to the public interest itself, fell generally on deaf ears.[2] His *Defense of the Constitutions of Government of the United States* doubtless exerted some influence over the framers of the Constitution and would have exerted a greater influence, if they could have understood it more easily. Jefferson, despite his denunciation of Adams's "monocratic" notions, not only understood Adams better than did most contemporary politicians, but felt a greater sympathy with his peculiar political ideas. Writing to his old friend several years after their retirement from active politics, Jefferson declared:[3] "I agree with you that there is a natural aristocracy among men. The grounds of this are virtue and talents . . . There is also an artificial aristocracy, founded on wealth and birth . . . The natural aristocracy I consider as the most precious gift of nature for . . . the government of society." This, of course, was also John Adams's opinion.

The differences between the two great political thinkers had been pointed out by Jefferson in an earlier letter of the same correspondence.[4] Adams's son, John Quincy Adams, had by then already gone over to the party of the Jeffersonians and the father had broken long before with the faction of the Hamiltonians. "The same political parties which now agitate the United States," Jefferson wrote with understandable exaggeration, "have existed through all time . . . We broke into two parties, each wishing to give the government a different direction; the one to strengthen the most popular branch, the other the more permanent branches, and to extend their permanence." The roots of partisanship, it is now clear, grew deeper, but Jefferson was right in emphasizing the desire of the Federalists to strengthen the executive and judicial departments of the government under the Constitution, while his party sought to extend the authority and influence of the Congress. Adams's insistence in his reply to Jefferson [5] that his own views should be distinguished from those of the Hamiltonians rested on the distinction which Jefferson promptly recognized between the artificial and the natural aristocracy. It is a valid distinction. The government of the more perfect Union was certainly not in the beginning, and is not now, a democracy in the strict sense of the term, as used by Adams and Jefferson. Nor was it such an aristocracy as Hamilton would have liked, in which the artificial aristocracy, that is, the plutocracy, possesses a preponderance of power. It was, and it is, a combination of democracy, artificial aristocracy, and natural aristocracy. Jefferson and Adams were quick to recognize its true character. They differed somewhat in the proportions of each element which they would have liked in the mixture, but they agreed in thinking that the public interest would be best protected and preserved by a suitable mixture of all three elements. This the application of the principle of the political mean tends to establish.

Lowell's observations concerning the parliamentary system of government in Great Britain [6] may well be applied with the proper qualifications to the government of the more perfect Union under the Constitution of 1787. The American political system, as it now stands, was by no means contemplated by the men who planned it; it is in fact quite contrary to the ideas of many of the framers; the steps they took were consciously and rationally taken to meet certain immediate needs without much thought of possible ultimate consequences; but they naturally led to the system which has evolved. It is a system which is singularly consistent in the interrelations of its several parts and harmonious in its operation, when men of moderate temper are in power. To be sure, countries like Mexico, Brazil, and Argentina, which have copied most closely the characteristic features of the written American Constitution, have not obtained equally harmonious results in the actual operation of their constitutions. It is evident that the American system has been particularly well suited to the conditions of the country as well as to the temper of the people. The principles of the separation of powers and of federalism, as embodied in the Constitution by the framers, appear to have been justified by the results which have been attained. But it is the principle of the political mean, as it has come to be applied on the great scale of American national politics, even though the framers did not contemplate it and the result is contrary to the preconceived ideas of many of them, that contributes most to the explanation of the stability and capacity for growth of the government of the more perfect Union.

The constitutional system of checks and balances was constructed under the aegis of the Newtonian physics. The laws of motion, the principles of celestial mechanics, the grand conception of the equilibrium of the sidereal universe, cast a spell over the minds of intelligent men. Political philosophers dreamed of perpetual harmony between the various elements of states and of the permanent stabilization of their governments. But the eighteenth century passed away in the midst of sanguinary revolutions and violent warfare of unprecedented extent and destructiveness. To the widespread belief in the natural perfectibility of men and states succeeded an uneasy feeling that all attempts to improve the lot of mankind by political methods would be frustrated by the consequences of their own vices and follies. The conception of a rational world to be quickly perfected by reasonable men, who, having lost their faith in princes, would at last be free to act consistently with their faith in themselves, gave way to a more romantic universe in which perfection awaited the end of a long process of gradual improvement through a natural process of progressive change. The nineteenth-century doctrine of evolution, like the eighteenth-century laws of motion, cast a spell over the minds of intelligent men and inspired new dreams of progress in politics as well as in other branches of human thought and action.

A system originally derived from the established principle of the separation of powers was strengthened and improved, so American political philosophers could believe, by the happy discovery of the new principle of federalism. How, it may now be asked, can a constitutional system, so firmly stabilized, be flexible enough to be capable of the changes which are the essence of progress? Or, if capable of such changes, how can it retain its original stability? The Supreme Court has shown a beneficent talent for gradual and moderate adaptation of the written constitution to the requirements of new times and altered circumstances, and other more difficult changes in the government of the more perfect Union have been accomplished by the costly violence of civil war. But there is a further answer to these questions. It is a vital part of the American contribution to the science of government. The most important single force in the process of stabilization has been the membership of the middle classes, as they have developed with the development of the country, operating through the unplanned institution of organized partisanship. The special political role of the middle classes has been a guaranty of constitutional stability. It has also been a guaranty of political progress.

The principle of the political mean is a progressive as well as a conservative principle, because in the nature of things the political mean itself changes in response to the challenge of a changing economic and social order. The experience of the American people has already borne witness to its changeable character. The urban middle class has risen to the occasion caused by the rise of urban industrial civilization. The nature of the urban middle class itself changes as urban industry and society evolve. Skilled labor makes an ever larger place for itself in the middle class, attracting to it also a substantial portion of the semiskilled. The special political role of the middle classes may be an unarticulated major premise in the subconscious thinking of middle-class Americans. It is, nevertheless, in a progressive society an indubitable guaranty of political progress as well as order.

THE QUEST FOR GREATER PERFECTION

The ordinary argument in favor of the American system of government under the Constitution is purely pragmatic. Under this political system the American people have grown numerous, prosperous, and powerful. Why take thought, therefore, concerning the basic principles upon which the national government was originally constructed? Even if a political analyst should view the contemporary political scene with a philosophical eye and conclude with Lowell that the British parliamentary system is more harmonious in its operation than any other system now existing, or perhaps that ever did exist, the difficulty of

407

amending the Constitution of the United States, particularly for reasons which are purely theoretical and highly speculative, would dictate the conclusion that it is more practical to keep the system which exists, improving it from time to time in matters of detail as circumstances permit, rather than to scrap it and substitute a system based upon different principles. This indeed was Lowell's conclusion, reached early in life and never abandoned.[7]

Political critics who, like Lowell, have devoted years to the systematic and purposeful study of political structures and political processes may agree with him that a system of government to which a people have become adjusted through the experience of successive generations is not to be changed for reasons less weighty than those which persuaded the generation of the founding fathers to exchange the Articles of Confederation for the Constitution of the more perfect Union. Yet critics who believe that the basic principles, or any of them, upon which the American national government rests are unsound, or at least untimely, will continue to discuss the desirability of amendments which, without destroying the general character of the system, might bring it more nearly into line with what they consider the best thinking of contemporary political science. In fact, all three of Madison's principles are under attack. Neither the separation of powers nor federalism escapes criticism from one quarter or another. Most persistent and determined of the criticism is that directed against the principle of the political mean, which has come to take so important a place alongside Madison's original doctrine of the natural limits to the power of popular majorities.

The principle of the separation of powers is obviously open to criticism by those who challenge the logical basis of the existing distribution of power between the three departments of the national government. The Supreme Court patiently struggles with its perennial task of giving a rational interpretation to arrangements which were originally adopted on empirical grounds. It succeeds in maintaining a serviceable system of checks and balances without ever putting an end to the problems of definition which the practical operation of the system continually produces. The record of the Supreme Court, though not free from marks of confusion and irresolution, suggests that the judges of this eminent tribunal, with its peculiar mixture of political and judicial duties, will continue to prove capable of maintaining the balance of the system. In so doing they will doubtless continue to vindicate Justice Holmes's profound judgment that experience, not logic, is the life of the law — particularly, it may be added, of constitutional law.

The aspect of the system of checks and balances which has attracted the most attention from leading students of American politics, though not from students of constitutional law, is the relationship between the President and the Congress. Walter Lippmann has stated the problem with exemplary lucidity in his comment, already quoted, on the lend-lease bill.[8] What he called "the perennial difficulty" was certainly familiar enough. Conflict between the President and the Congress had begun with the first President and there was no sign of its end. It is clear that under the American system neither the President nor the Congress can be sure of getting the legislative action which it wants. But there is a more important question. Can the American people get the legislation they want under such a system?

The critics of the principle of the separation of powers thought not. Woodrow Wilson was the first to state their case effectively. His *Congressional Government*, written in a period when Presidents were exceptionally weak and Congresses were strong but undisciplined, drew a sensational contrast between the systems of congressional and parliamentary government. "Congressional government," he wrote,[9] "is Committee government; Parliamentary government is government by a responsible Cabinet Ministry." The former system, he argued with persuasive rhetoric and impressive illustrations, made for irresponsibility, confusion, inefficiency, and popular dissatisfaction. The latter, as expounded in Bagehot's luminous essay on the English Constitution, seemed its direct opposite in all these respects. Wilson did not explicitly advocate the introduction of the British parliamentary system into the American government. He did make clear his conviction that the American system of divided power and responsibility could not long endure. Either the President must submit to the supremacy of the Congress, or the Congress must accept the leadership of the President, or both must acknowledge their common subjection to the authority of a governing party. In Great Britain instead of the traditional system of constitutional government there was in fact, Bagehot argued, party government. In the United States constitutional government could not so easily be replaced by party government, but might not there be a greater concentration of authority and responsibility in the members of the majority party, both at the Capitol and in the White House? And might not the addition of more effective party government to the constitutional system abate the evils of which Wilson so eloquently complained?

Wilson's indictment of the system of checks and balances, as applied to the relations between the President and the Congress, has been found a true bill by a long series of subsequent writers on American politics.[10] But there has been no agreement among them concerning the manner in which harmony should be established between the executive and legislative departments and clear responsibility for the efficient use of power should be enforced. Some of the critics of the American system have wanted a parliamentary system for the United States as a means toward more effective control of the President by the Congress. Others have preferred greater control of the Congress by the President. All have agreed that the British system of parliamentary government is one in which the problem of the right relations between the executive and legislative departments has been solved by entrusting great power to the political parties, but they have had different views concerning the redistribution of power between the President, the Congress, and the kind of parties operating in American national politics.

The meaning of the example of England since the development of parliamentary government has been by no means clear. In Bagehot's time parliamentary government meant the actual supremacy of the majority party in the Parliament. In contemporary Britain the House of Lords has lost most of its political importance and the House of Commons seems to be tending to become a kind of electoral college which, in giving its support to a particular Prime Minister and Cabinet, merely registers a decision previously reached outside of the Parliament. Since the Parliament Act of 1911 ushered in the present phase of the British system there have been thirteen different ministries in Great Britain. Five of these ministries were supported by a party with a clear majority in the House of Commons. They qualify as cabinet governments of the type admired by Bagehot, but they have held office for only about one-third of this period. Five were coalition ministries, supported by two or more parties and containing ministers belonging to all the parties in the coalition. They held office for more than a third of the period. Three ministries were formed by parties which did not possess a majority of the votes in the House of Commons and held office only by the tolerance of other parties. Their tenure of office was naturally shorter than that of the other ministries.

It is the exception rather than the rule that a Cabinet is overthrown by an adverse vote in the House of Commons. Cabinets may be overthrown by the breakup of a coalition, or by the voluntary retirement or death of the Prime Minister, but most often in recent years they have been overthrown by the people at a general election. Parliamentary government has become cabinet government, and the working of the system evidently depends not only on the state of parties in the House of Commons but also on the state of mind of the people in the country. The system works best when one party holds a clear majority of the seats in the House of Commons, and another party holds a practical monopoly of the opposition in the House and in the country. But recent experience shows that there can be no certainty of the continuous existence of these favorable conditions. The uncertainty seems more favorable to the authority of Cabinets and Prime Ministers than to that of Parliaments or majority parties in the House of Commons.

Woodrow Wilson, the theorist and critic of American politics, wanted an improved form of party government at Washington. Apparently from the beginning he preferred presidential to congressional leadership of the governing party. In a new preface to a later edition of his first book, published soon after the Spanish-American war,[11] he recorded his pleasure at the signs of increasing presidential authority, and in a later book, published on the eve of his entrance into active politics,[12] he emphasized the role of the President as leader of his party. In the White House himself he made a gallant and for six years an extraordinarily successful effort to play such a role. Woodrow Wilson, the practical politician, did not seek new powers for the President by changes in the Constitution, but he exploited to the utmost the new opportunities for the development of presidential leadership afforded by the changing conditions of his time.

Wilson's solution for the problem of good working relations between the President and the Congress has commended itself to other vigorous Presidents. Theodore Roosevelt before him, and Franklin D. Roosevelt afterward, sought, like Wilson, to make themselves the masters of their parties and through partisan control of the Congress to dominate the political processes of the national government. All of them succeeded for a time and distinguished their periods of effective party leadership by the skillful promotion of bold and imaginative legislative programs. All of them found their positions as party leaders and chief legislators increasingly difficult after they had achieved their early objectives and new issues called for new policies. They were eventually forced to seek congressional support wherever they could

411

find it, regardless of party. Partisan majorities in the Congress were unable to take the initiative in the development of policy or, as in Wilson's case, disappeared. Party government became more and more inadequate.

Some of the critics of American politics who have believed with Wilson in the desirability of an improved form of party government at Washington have concluded that effective presidential leadership requires additional power for the presidential office.[13] They have noted the weakness of strong Presidents in the latter part of their terms and the incapacity of ordinary men in the presidency to lead their parties effectively at any time. They have been appalled at the irresponsibility and weakness of the Government itself at times when the capture of one or both branches of the Congress by the opposition party has deadlocked the legislative process in matters of partisan controversy before the end of a presidential term. They have desired that the American President, like the British Prime Minister, should be able to dissolve the Congress in order to terminate the frustration and futility caused by the distribution of governing power between a President and a Congress who are unable to work together harmoniously and effectively. To this end they have advocated constitutional amendments extending the term of Representatives to equal that of Senators and authorizing the President at his discretion to call a fresh election of Congressmen before the expiration of their regular terms.

Other critics have feared the consequences of vesting such extensive power in the hands of a single person at the head of a triumphant political party. Such a President would be a more powerful leader than any British Prime Minister. He would combine the authority and prestige of both prime minister and king. His party, once firmly established in power, could monopolize the patronage and other perquisites of government. Party government, when the governing party becomes too strong, can open the way to tyranny. It is evident, as the examples of Fascist and Communist dictatorships have convincingly demonstrated again to the contemporary world, that there was good reason for the founding fathers' belief in an effective system of checks and balances. The proper question is, how should the principle of the separation of powers be applied in order to secure the happiest mean between a dangerous concentration of political power in too few hands and a dangerous distribution of power among too many hands. The conversion of a President with limited powers into a President-King with powers which might get out of control does not seem a rational answer to the question.

The case for the supremacy of the Congress and the subordination of the President has been put most adequately by Henry Hazlitt.[14] He recognized that the fusion of the executive and the legislature, which he desired, could not be brought about without profound changes in the constitutional position of the President. He proposed therefore [15] that the President should be deprived of his power to veto acts of Congress, and that the power to execute the laws, to make treaties, and to direct military and naval policy should be transferred from the President to a chosen congressional leader or premier. The President would thus cease to be chief executive, except for ceremonial purposes, and would no longer function as commander in chief or as principal manager of foreign relations. These were the least constitutional changes in the presidency which would be necessary to establish the parliamentary system in the United States in such a form that the Congress could formulate the policies of the government under leadership of its own selection and that the selected leadership would be responsible for executing the congressional policies. It would be necessary also to extend the term of the House of Representatives, subject to the power of the premier to dissolve the House at any time and order a fresh election of Congressmen, and to reduce the authority of the Senate so that the responsibility of the premier and cabinet would be clearly due to the House alone. By the adoption of such changes, Hazlitt argued, a parliamentary system of government could be introduced under which the voters would choose between the leaders of the two major parties in the House of Representatives. The evils denounced by Woodrow Wilson could thus be cured, Hazlitt believed, without transforming the President into a dictator who might get out of control and become a tyrant.

Hazlitt's proposals evidently leave a great deal to the imagination. How does he know that the American people would be willing to surrender again to Congressional Caucuses the power to nominate the candidates for the presidency or, what would be more important under his system, the candidates for the great office of premier? The Congressional Caucus was rejected by the people as a nominating agency a century and a quarter ago, and its grave limitations as an agency for devising legislative programs does not inspire confidence in its capacity for more important functions. How does he know that the American people would even accept the issues put forward by the party

413

leaders in the House of Representatives as the paramount issues in national campaigns? The voters in the states and congressional districts have long claimed, and since the adoption of the direct-primary system of nominating candidates for Congress have asserted with greater success than before, a right to determine for themselves the weight to be assigned to the various issues involved in a general election. How does he know that there would be greater harmony between the various local factions which compose a national party after an election than before? The example of cabinet government in the French Republic and other states in Continental Europe where the parliamentary system has been introduced demonstrates that imitations of the British system may work very differently under different conditions. It might prove as difficult for Americans as for Frenchmen, Germans, or Italians to maintain the two-party system, if the attempt were made to establish party government upon an alien model. None of the critics of the American system argues that the multiparty system and factional politics, as developed in Continental European parliaments, would be an improvement over the system that now exists, to say nothing of what this system might be made to be, with much less effort than would be required to introduce the parliamentary system in any form, British or Continental.

A more recent proponent of a scheme of cabinet government for the United States, Thomas K. Finletter,[16] shows a greater respect for the realities of American politics. Unlike most advocates of cabinet government he is not interested in altering the relative influence in national politics of the President and the Congress. He does not desire that either should be able to dominate the other. He accepts the principle of the separation of powers as a fundamental principle in American politics. But he shares the great faith held by all the American advocates of responsible party government in the practical utility of lengthening the terms of Representatives to equal those of Senators, and of providing for the dissolution of the Congress when there is urgent need for harmony between it and the President. However, Finletter insists upon the importance of a simultaneous judgment by the voters on the work of both President and Congress. He contends that at a dissolution the office of the President as well as those of the Congressmen should become vacant and all alike should stand for reëlection.

Finletter proposes that the right of mutual dissolution should be conferred upon both the President and the Congress in order that the balance of power between them may not be destroyed in the process of improving the harmony of their joint operations. He does not repudiate the Madisonian principle of the separation of powers but aims rather to perfect the system of checks and balances resulting from its practical application. He is particularly concerned over the deadlocks in the legislative process which threaten the competence of the national government whenever neither President nor Congress will yield to the leadership of the other. "The mere existence of the right of dissolution," he thinks,[17] "should break these deadlocks immediately." He understands that the expected results from his suggestions for a new kind of party government are contingent upon the development of a more rational form of the bipartisan system. He appreciates the importance of strong national parties, based upon principles in support of which their members are united, instead of the leagues of local interests which now dominate the political scene. "If the right of dissolution existed," he believes,[18] "this emphasis on local issues would largely disappear." In this faith he rests his case. "Strong national parties," he concludes,[19] "would constitute the link between the Executive and the Congress, which would fuse them into a team."

THE DOMINANT INFLUENCE OF MIDDLE-CLASS PARTIES

The advocates of strong party government as the proper remedy for the inconveniences and evils of the established system of relations between the President and the Congress seem to take for granted that the kind of parties which would exist, if their proposals were adopted, would be the idealistic kind described in Burke's familiar definition. There would be two great parties, they assume, each consisting of persons united for the purpose of promoting the national interest upon some particular principle in which they all agree. The record, however, shows that up to now not even those members of the parties who have been elected to the Congress on the regular party tickets are united on the policies which were public issues during the electoral campaigns, to say nothing of uniting on new policies required to meet the new issues which arise after the elections. They are generally united on the fundamental principles of American government, but these issues are beyond ordinary partisanship and the members of both major parties are equally devoted to them. The great bond of union between partisans is devotion to the particular interests of those groups of voters who have been traditionally affiliated with their

415

party, and desire to appease those groups of voters who appear to hold the balance of power between the major parties. The record shows further how complex is the resulting basis of partisanship and how confused the tangle of loyalties attached to the various special interests and modified by the paramount importance of the intermediate sections and middle classes. It is impossible for realistic political analysts to accept the view that parties will be more idealistic in the future than in the past.

There can be no doubt that the great national parties are something more than mere combinations of politicians for the purpose of getting into office and power. They are far from being unprincipled conspiracies against the public interest. But expediency rather than principle is the life of partisanship. It is hard to see how it can be otherwise under any kind of party system. Surely as long as Congressmen are nominated at direct primaries and elected at free elections in their states and districts, local issues and special interests are bound to dominate the calculations of the candidates, regardless of party, and strong national parties of the kind envisaged by the advocates of an improved system of party government will continue to be an iridescent dream. Other changes besides granting to the President and the Congress the right of mutual dissolution are indispensable if an end is to be put to the influence of local interests in national politics. At least the right of nomination, covering candidates for the Congress as well as for the presidency, would have to be vested in permanent national party organizations rather than in temporary conventions and local primaries.

That such a concentration of partisan power is possible, where the natural conditions are favorable and appropriate measures are adopted, is demonstrated by the monolithic parties which have dominated the governments of great nations for considerable periods of time in the Fascist and Communist states of Europe. Such concentrations of power, however, are clearly incompatible with the present system of constitutional government in the United States. Constitutional changes, going much further than those suggested by American critics in the Wilsonian tradition, would be necessary if national parties of much greater strength than those now existing were to be established. If the necessary constitutional changes were made, there can be no assurance that the two-party system would survive. If the influence of local interests in the national parties were greatly reduced and groups of people were still free to pursue their special interests in their own way, a great expansion of the lobby and a great growth of lobbying would follow. How a high-powered system of group representation in the legislative process at Washington could be adjusted to a system of strong party government is not easy to foresee. In short, the consequences of great changes in the party system defy prediction.

Foreign critics of American institutions have been more concerned than those born and bred in the United States about the future of the American way of political life. The American tradition has been to take a better future for granted. The first generations under the government of the more perfect Union possessed a natural self-reliance, fostered by their successful struggle to subdue the wilderness, which encouraged them to believe that the vigorous enterprise of intelligent politicians under a freely competitive party system, like that of farmers, workers, and businessmen in the ordinary course of making a living, would insure the full utilization of the opportunities for advancement offered by a richly endowed country with liberty and justice for all. Later generations were able to reënforce this traditional faith in the future with a conscious belief in progress as the natural tendency of a rational universe. But European scholars and political analysts, armed with a more exact knowledge of the conditions and problems of older countries, were more disposed to think that these conditions and problems would eventually be reproduced in the new world. They could easily imagine the difficulty of making American institutions work as satisfactorily in the old world as in the new. It was not difficult for them to imagine also that dissatisfaction would arise with the traditional political ideas and methods in America as European economic and social conditions and problems began to develop in response to the reckless exploitation and closer settlement of the newer country.

The trend of foreign criticism is noteworthy for its increasing challenge to American self-confidence. De Tocqueville, the first competent foreign scholar to publish a systematic and purposeful analysis of the government and politics of the United States under the Constitution, recorded some impressions of the future of democracy in America, which remain after more than a century of more than ordinary interest to Americans. But de Tocqueville seems not to have been seriously concerned about the future of the Americans. It was the future of Frenchmen, and the possibility of their profiting by American experience in developing a democratic republic at home, that obviously constituted his primary interest. Bryce, a half century later, was a more sophisticated observer than de Tocqueville, equally sanguine

417

by nature and no less sympathetic with the Americans of his time. He took impressive pains in making his analysis of the strength and weakness of what he happily termed the American Commonwealth. His attitude was more somber than de Tocqueville's. Nothing could be certain about the future, he concluded, except that it would be different from the present.[20] Now another half-century and more has passed. The democratic republic in America has survived some of the graver perils anticipated by de Tocqueville. It has survived changes as great as any anticipated by Bryce. It is not yet demonstrably the worse for the experience. On the contrary, its claim to the character of a commonwealth seems stronger than in Bryce's time. The growth of the American people in population, wealth, and power now attracts more attention from foreign critics than ever before. Most articulate among them was the late British political theorist, Harold J. Laski.

The contrast between Laski's prognostications and those of his predecessors is striking. He was positive in his conviction that it is for Americans to learn the lessons of recent political changes in Europe rather than for Europe to learn from America. The economic changes of our time, he was confident, would impose stresses and strains upon the traditional way of American political life as they had upon the European ways. He had observed their effects upon the organization of political parties and the development of the forms of political power in Europe and he expected similar results in America. The chief political need of the new age, he thought, is a stronger executive.[21] This need in his opinion could best be met by introducing the British system of cabinet government. Recognizing, however, the practical impossibility of making extensive changes in the written constitution on theoretical grounds, he did not advocate any form of the parliamentary system for the United States. He was content to suggest minor changes in the constitutional powers of the President, trusting to the emergence of stronger leadership in the presidency through the development of stronger national parties.

The realignment of parties, Laski thought, would result from the inevitable growth of governmental action in economic affairs. "The point at which this development is likely to emerge," he asserted in his last book,[22] "is set by the experience of Europe. Where the period of economic expansion reaches its limit there emerges always a disparity of opportunity which results, sooner or later, in an antagonism of interest. And where that antagonism begins to take a conscious form the result is always that a party is formed to safeguard interests, on both sides, which feel themselves to be in jeopardy." This meant to Mr. Laski the emergence of two great parties in the United States confronting each other in much the same way as the Labour Party and the Conservatives do in Great Britain. "It is even possible," he added,[23] "that the arrival of this situation may be quickened by the influence of the Soviet Union."

There is no reason for questioning Laski's opinion concerning the continued growth of governmental action in matters affecting the national economy. A free-enterprise system, such as that to which the American people are committed, is not identical with a system of exclusively private or corporate enterprise. It is a system big enough to include public enterprise as well as private and corporate, and is by no means incompatible with the vigorous development of public undertakings in the public interest. The government of a country in which public spirit is as widely and energetically manifested as in the United States will certainly respond to the challenge of the economic changes of modern times with ambitious plans for promoting the general welfare by political action. When Theodore Roosevelt declared that "strenuous battling for the right is the noblest sport the world affords," he was speaking for more than one generation of eager young American politicians. He was sounding the keynote for the new order in American politics. The settled purposes of the American people, asserted in the preamble to the Constitution of the more perfect Union, insure a bright future for political parties which can capture the spirit of American life and give it effective expression.

But there is no discernible room in this future for powerful proletarian or other narrowly class-conscious parties. Barring unpredictable national disasters, ruinous to the rational aims and moderate temper of the middle classes, the major parties of the future will not be greatly different from those of the past. There can be no electoral majorities in national politics for parties which scorn the support of the middle classes. The proper strategy for major-party leadership was discovered early in the history of national politics. The aristocratic Nationalists could not put together a victorious combination of factions in the Federal Convention without including rural and urban middle-class elements. When the Federalist Party, which emerged from the factional conflicts in the Convention under Washington's skillful leadership and gained its great triumph by timely concessions in the matter of a bill of rights to the middle-class agrarians in the state ratifying conventions, neglected the interests of the rural middle class under Washington's less competent successors, it lost its majority to the Jeffersonian Republicans. Jefferson built his party around the middle classes. Up to now this has been the time-honored formula for success in national politics.

There have been no recent changes in the structure of the national economy which render the traditional strategy of national party leaders obsolete. There is nothing in the contemporary political scene to suggest that the Marxist partisan strategy can be more successful under the existing economic and social conditions than it could have been under those of the past. Proletarian parties, like strictly capitalistic parties, cannot meet the requirements of national politics. Communism, like Fascism, is a European political movement which cannot be successfully introduced into the United States without first Europeanizing American life by excessive indulgence in war or in preparation for war. The various theories of class struggle, whether advanced by Communists or by Fascists, make too little allowance for the observable facts of American social and political life. Above all, they make too little allowance for the existence and the power of the middle classes. They can be supported only by political theorists who do not understand the American principle of the political mean.

Every party which remains long in power requires rejuvenation. The alternations between the "ins" and the "outs," characteristic of a healthy two-party system, facilitate this essential process. The perennial response of each new generation to the enterprising leadership of those who bravely evoke fresh visions of national grandeur will always supply the basis for new political movements under a freely competitive political system. Whether such new political movements succeed, as the Antislavery Republicans did, in smashing one of the former major parties and forming a new opposition party, or, as the Free Soilers and the Populists did, fail to upset the established partisan alignment, they help to infuse a new spirit into the opposition to the party in power, and stimulate the latter to greater efforts to retain the confidence of a majority of the people. But no new political movement can become a major party and gain power under the Constitution without broadening its appeal and diversifying its program sufficiently to win the confidence of the various special interests and particular attitudes required to form a majority of the American people. The British system of bipartisan politics has not been reproduced on the Continent of Europe, despite much admiration for British political methods and practices and a parallel growth of governmental intervention in the economic affairs of the inhabitants. The Laskian argument that the British form of bipartisanship will necessarily develop in the United States cannot convince Americans who understand the foundations of American politics.

American experience has demonstrated that by taking thought intelligent citizens can bring about substantial improvements in their political methods and institutions. The record of achievement since the time of Bryce, for instance, shows gratifying changes for the better in several areas of political action where he found much to criticize. There is good reason to believe that the flow of improvements in the practical working of the national government will be maintained indefinitely by the same painstaking attention to matters of detail on the part of intelligent citizens. The Presidency, as President Roosevelt's Committee on Administrative Management and the recent Hoover Commission on the Organization of the Executive Branch of the Government have shown, can be strengthened and made more efficient by the adoption of improvements in administrative organization and procedure, which have already been tested and found good by state governments or are clearly indicated as necessary and proper by the experience of the national government itself. Minor changes in the President's constitutional authority, such as the extension of his veto power to items in appropriation bills and perhaps also to parts of other public bills, would also be helpful. But no major change in his constitutional position is called for by past experience with the system of checks and balances.

The Congress, it is becoming clear also, will never grow strong by striving to weaken the President, but only by strengthening itself. The investigations and report of the La Follette-Monroney Committee have revealed to the politicians — what was already well understood by disinterested observers [24] who had closely studied the legislative process at Washington — that the way to maintain the authority of the legislative branch of the national government is not to deprive the President of power, but to increase that of the Congress to perform its own essential functions. The reform of the rules of debate in the Senate so as to enable a majority after due deliberation to take timely action, the control of the Committee on Rules in the House so as to enable a majority there also after due deliberation to take timely action, the abolition of the oppressive seniority system in both houses of the Congress so that talented members may rise more rapidly to positions of leadership: these are some of the changes which the

421

lawmakers can wisely employ to improve their methods of action. The resulting improvement also in the position of their leaders in dealing with the President would make for better relations between the two chief policy-determining branches of the government. It is not drastic changes in the basic principles of the national government that are needed at this time, but only those modest improvements that moderate leadership could readily accomplish with the means already at its disposal.

There is no rational basis for loss of confidence in the soundness and practical utility of the three great principles upon which the government of the more perfect Union was established. The relations between the President and the Congress, which have put the American system of checks and balances to its severest trial, form no exception to this general conclusion. It is not possible to show that Americans would be better governed if Presidents were able to dominate the Congress, or the Congress to dominate Presidents, more consistently and more completely than heretofore. It is desirable that both the President and the Congress should be able to function more effectively than has been necessary up to now under normal conditions. But this can be accomplished by the cumulative effect of gradual changes without abandoning the fundamental principles of the government of the more perfect Union.

The principle of federalism, like that of the separation of powers, has stood the test of time. These principles, as applied by successive generations of American legislators, administrators, and judges, have served the purposes of the framers. They have given character to a system of government under which the men in power have been able to control one another without losing their ability to control the governed. It is too soon to say that the conception of constitutional government as a system of checks and balances — the three departments of government checking one another and the federal and state governments checking each other — is obsolete. The practical application of these principles has brought many changes in the details of the original arrangement of the constitutional structure and processes. Further changes are desirable and to be expected. Corwin was right when he said that "individual rights cannot rely in this period of our history upon governmental stagnation for their protection." [25] He indicated the proper way to improve the system of government when he called for such constitutional arrangements "as best promise that necessary things be done in time, but that the judgment that they are necessary be as widely representative as possible." He himself wisely emphasized the importance of a better relationship between the President and the Congress in the legislative process. But surely such a relationship can be achieved without sacrificing either the principle of the separation of powers or that of federalism as these two principles are being adapted to the novel conditions of a changing social and economic order by a rejuvenated Supreme Court.

The principle of the political mean, regarded as the consummation of Madison's third principle of government, if due heed be paid to its essential character as modified by the development of party government under the Constitution, has more than justified its author's expectations. It may be that Madison's contribution to the understanding of this principle does not exceed that of other framers, notably Franklin, whose insight into some aspects of the political process in a democratic republic penetrated more deeply than his. Be that as it may, it is clearly more realistic and useful to arrange the various social and economic groups into three main classes than, like Communists and Fascists in modern times and some of the original aristocratic Nationalists in 1787, into no more than two. No major party, since the definite establishment of the two-party system, has been exclusively an upper-class party or a lower-class party. All major parties have been more or less effectively dominated by the middle classes. Through the party system, which many of the framers distrusted, the middle classes have maintained a kind of political equilibrium, which all of them desired. The middle classes have thus succeeded in performing the constitutional function which some of the eighteenth-century political philosophers assigned to the independent chief executive or "patriot king."

In American national politics the most important single force in the process of political stabilization has been the membership of the middle classes operating through the political parties. The maintenance of political stability in the future clearly depends upon the preservation of the strength and self-confidence and public spirit of these same classes. This will naturally be a principal objective of the most successful politicians, who in their competitive struggle for power will tend under ordinary circumstances to promote policies suitable for this purpose. The economic underwriting of the Constitution, to borrow Beard's expressive phrase,[26] means the adoption of political programs designed to preserve and strengthen the economic and social forces which give the political system its character and vitality. The natural

423

operation of the government of the more perfect Union should normally produce an economic underwriting of the Constitution which will promote the general welfare by serving the general public interest, when practicable, and, when that is impracticable, by preserving and strengthening the social and economic character and the political authority of the middle classes.[27]

THE CLEW TO A STILL MORE PERFECT UNION

The most serious defect in the government of the more perfect Union is exposed by the conduct of foreign relations. The framers of the Constitution recognized that there are important differences between foreign and domestic affairs which require that they be conducted in a different manner. In dealing with domestic affairs the executive power is with minor exceptions exercised according to law and the President can under normal circumstances be prevented from grave abuse of his power by a wise exercise of the lawmaking and enforcement-supervising powers of the Congress. But in dealing with foreign affairs the President possesses powers not so effectively controlled by the Congress. The House of Representatives is excluded from a share in the treaty-making power, and the Senate, though it must be consulted by the President, cannot act by an ordinary majority vote. The requirement that a two-thirds majority of the Senators consent to the ratification of treaties puts the exercise of the treaty-making power outside the area of partisan responsibility and compels a different relationship between the President and the Senate from that obtaining in domestic affairs. Since the treaty-making power cannot be exercised effectively except on a bipartisan basis, the conduct of foreign relations becomes excessively difficult whenever a partisan Administration seeks to execute important controversial policies by means of treaties. A system of party government for internal affairs and bipartisan government for external affairs is a logical solution of the problem, but experience shows how difficult it may be to hold the President accountable for his policies without destroying the basis of bipartisan collaboration.

The paralysis of foreign policy by the intrusion of partisanship may be avoided in two ways. The President may proceed by means of an executive agreement instead of a treaty, and as long as the Supreme Court is willing to respect such an agreement, as if it were a part of the law of the land, the President can take a course in foreign affairs independent of the Congress, unless an appropriation of money is needed to give effect to his policy. Doubt concerning the willingness of the Congress to make necessary appropriations and the willingness of the Supreme Court to deal with executive agreements as it would with treaties introduces deplorable elements of uncertainty into the conduct of foreign relations, if a determined President persists in pursuing an independent course. The doubts can be dissolved only by granting a degree of independence to the President which is incompatible with such protection of the people against arbitrary and oppressive action by public officers as was a primary objective of the framers of the Constitution. The President, moreover, possesses a further advantage over the Congress by virtue of his great authority as commander in chief of the armed forces of the United States. The framers hoped to keep the authority of the commander in chief within safe limits by limiting strictly the size of the standing army, but the exigencies of the modern world have enormously increased the forces at the disposal of the President and visibly created a military power which, if it could have been foreseen, would have been viewed with grave alarm by many of the founding fathers. It is easy to imagine what George Mason or Elbridge Gerry would say, if they could witness the present tremendous military establishment under the orders of the President as commander in chief.

The alternative is for the Congress, or one of its branches, to participate in the determination of foreign policy by means of such acts and resolves as may be within its constitutional powers. The Wilmot proviso and the Fulbright and Vandenberg resolutions reflect the practical capacity of Congressmen to warn or to encourage a President bent on the development of a new foreign policy. How Congressmen can even take control of policy into their own hands is demonstrated by the annexations of Texas and of Hawaii. But the Congress is handicapped in its efforts to assert its authority over the conduct of foreign relations by its inferior knowledge of foreign affairs and its inability to act as swiftly and as secretly as the President. Under the exigent conditions of modern times the authority of the President as director general of international negotiations is not much less arbitrary than that as commander in chief of the armed forces. He cannot declare war without the consent of the Congress, but he can create situations which force the hand of the Congress and compel it to follow his lead. He cannot make peace without the consent of one or both of the branches of the Congress, but he can commit the country to courses of action which they cannot repudiate without grave injury to national prestige and incalculable effects on the nation's vital interests. In short, neither the system of constitutional government, provided by the framers, nor the system of party government, added by their posterity, can give the people of the United States the security against the abuse of power in the conduct of foreign relations that they enjoy in the management of their domestic affairs. The President, if he will, can act almost as promptly and vigorously as any foreign chief executive, but such a development of the executive power is not what the people of the Revolution fought for and the framers of the Constitution planned.

The method of conducting foreign relations discloses a fundamental defect in the American political system. Madison once described the whole problem of government as consisting of two parts: first, how to enable the government to control the governed, and second, how to compel the government to control itself. The problem has been well, if not perfectly, solved under the government of the more perfect Union in the field of domestic affairs. But it has not been solved satisfactorily under the exigent conditions of modern times in the field of foreign affairs. The explanation is clear.

In the management of domestic affairs all the substantial private and local interests that may be concerned in a particular affair are represented in the governmental processes. Action in the public interest means an adjustment of the conflicts between special interests in such a way as best to serve the common good of the whole body of people. The public interest is more than a particular special interest which is able to prevail in the adjustment of a conflict with other special interests. It is more than the sum of the special interests which gain recognition in a particular process of adjustment. It is more than the bare fact of a temporary equilibrium among a group of special interests. It is nothing less than such an adjustment of conflicting special interests as can give the people durable confidence in the stability of the state itself. The government of the more perfect Union in accordance with the three major political principles affords adequate security for such adjustments of interest conflicts in domestic affairs.

In the conduct of foreign relations the necessary conditions for the protection of the public interest are not satisfied. The world has developed a sense of common interests that cannot be duly represented in the governmental processes of any national state, not even one as well organized as the United States. Those interests may easily conflict with the special interests of particular states, and processes for the satisfactory adjustment of such interest conflicts cannot be maintained by the governments of such states. The rights of men, for example, regarded as citizens of a world community, tend to conflict with the supposed interests of sovereign states, intent on protecting national interests by the means at the direct disposal of their governments.[28] The right of the people of a particular nation to know what is going on at the seat of government of the United Nations, to discuss publicly the policies under consideration there, and to criticize the attitude of their own government toward the proceedings of the United Nations, may conflict with the supposed requirements of the national defense and be abridged by the unilateral action of a national government incapable by its very nature of representing the common interests of mankind. The international community alone is capable of creating processes for the adjustment of conflicting national interests which can serve the common good of all the nations. The government of a particular national state can serve efficiently only the special interests of that state. The more capable it is, in consequence of its political structure and processes, of acting as an instrument of its own national interests, the less competent it must be to serve those interests of its people which they hold in common with other members of the community of nations. There is no satisfactory solution of this problem short of applying the principle of federalism to the organization of mankind.

To bring the authority of the American presidency under an effective reign of law in the field of foreign affairs, it is necessary to delegate to a world federation the powers which are appropriate for the protection of the rights of men regarded as citizens of the world. How effective such a reign of law might be is clearly forecast by the steps which have already been taken to make the President more accountable for his conduct of foreign relations under the United Nations Participation Act of 1945. The American representatives in the Security Council, the Economic and Social Council, and the Trusteeship Council are appointed with the approval of the Senate and are subject in their action to such instructions as the Senate or the Congress may issue by due process of law. The President himself in his management of affairs within the jurisdiction of the United Nations is bound to act in accordance with the processes established under the authority of its Charter. Open debate in the Security Council affords a better basis for making any national executive responsive to world opinion in matters of interest to all mankind than can ever exist where the executives of the nations are free to pursue their special national interests by the methods of secret diplomacy. The greatest defect in the American political system can best be remedied by bringing to bear upon the operations of the President in the area of international affairs processes for the adjustment of international interest conflicts which may rest upon the consent of the governments of the civilized nations and be sustained by the organized opinion of mankind.

A political study of the American Constitution leads inevitably to a fresh view of Lowell's hypothesis that "men, like animals, may attain a self-consistent and harmonious system of conducting their affairs by a process of striving for immediate intentional objects, if the conditions happen to be such as to lead to a system of that kind; and this although the actors themselves do not contemplate it, or even if the result is quite contrary to their preconceived ideas." It is clear from the experience of several generations that the self-consistency and harmony of the American political system will not be complete until the conduct of foreign relations is brought within the scope of a system based upon similar principles and that in the nature of things this cannot be accomplished without the establishment of a suitable government for the community of nations. Thus the improvement of the American system tends naturally to coincide with the improvement of the political structure and processes of the civilized world. The American people cannot perfect their own Federal Union without at the same time forming a more perfect Union of all mankind. It is a conclusion which adds to the authority of Kant's great hypothesis concerning the natural principle of the political order. Americans above all other men have a right to believe that the history of the world should be regarded as the realization of a hidden plan of Nature to bring about a more perfect Union of the Nations as the only state in which all the capacities implanted by Her in mankind can be fully developed.

Americans may well believe also that the example of the framers should encourage the peoples of the contemporary world to believe that a more perfect Union of the Nations can be brought about by rational reflection and choice and need not be dependent upon either accident or force. The awful spectacle of a world without a world government can be ended by means of plans which moderate and conciliatory politicians are capable of making. Such plans should be

428

based upon the principles of government which American experience has demonstrated to be sound. The principles of the separation of powers and of federalism seem well suited to the task of forming a more perfect Union of the Nations through reflection and choice. Equally important, however, is the principle of the political mean, if the establishment of law and order in the world is not to be the result of accident or force. This does not mean that the frame of government of a World Federal Union must be similar to that of the American Federal Union. It does mean that the principles of government accepted by the framers of the American Constitution, if employed by statesmen of conciliatory dispositions and moderate tempers following the methods of 1787, can furnish a trustworthy foundation for a similar triumph of human reason over the rival agencies of accident and force in the evolution of political society.

Notes

1. Publius, *The Federalist*, No. 85 (New York, 1788). Publius was the pen name of three collaborators, Alexander Hamilton, James Madison and John Jay. No. 85 was written by Hamilton. There has been considerable controversy over authorship of certain numbers of *The Federalist*. Hamilton planned the series of papers and wrote most of the numbers, but James Madison wrote a considerable number and John Jay a few. For a discussion of the evidence concerning the authorship of the disputed numbers, see Douglass Adair, "The Authorship of the Federalist Papers," *The William and Mary Quarterly*, I, 97–123, 235–265 (April and July 1944). There are many editions of *The Federalist*. Convenient and inexpensive editions are those published by E. P. Dutton and Co., Everyman's Library, No. 519 (first printing, 1911); and by Random House, the Modern Library (first printing, 1937). The first edition containing what now appears to be the correct identification of authors is *The Federalist, or The New Constitution*, edited by Carl Van Doren (New York: The Heritage Press, 1945). For the latest edition see *The Federalist, or The New Constitution*, edited by Max Beloff (Oxford: Blackwell, 1948). Beloff adds an instructive introduction which is an important contribution to the literature concerning *The Federalist*.

2. Carl Van Doren, *The Great Rehearsal; the Story of the Making and Ratifying of the Constitution of the United States* (New York: Viking Press, 1948). For a well-informed discussion of the differences between the problem of forming an American federal union in 1787 and a world federal union at the present time, see John C. Ranney,

"The Bases of American Federalism," *The William and Mary Quarterly*, III, 1–35 (January 1946).

3. Letter from Benjamin Franklin to Ferdinand Grand, October 22, 1787. See *The Works of Benjamin Franklin*, John Bigelow, ed. (New York: Putnam, 1904), XI, 389; and *The Writings of Benjamin Franklin*, A. H. Smyth, ed. (New York: Macmillan, 1907), IX, 619.

4. There has been no dispute over Hamilton's authorship of the first number of *The Federalist*.

5. *Debates in the Federal Convention of 1787 as Reported by James Madison*, Sept. 17, 1787. Madison's *Debates* was first published in 1845 as vol. V of the second edition of Jonathan Elliot's *The Debates in the Several State Conventions on the Adoption of the Federal Constitution, Together with the Journal of the Federal Convention*, etc. (Philadelphia, 1836). There was no official record of the debates in the Federal Convention of 1787. Private notes were taken independently by several of the delegates and have been published both separately and in collected editions. Besides Madison's *Debates*, the most useful set of notes is that of Robert Yates, *Secret Proceedings and Debates of the Convention Assembled at Philadelphia in the Year 1787 for the Purpose of Forming the Constitution of the United States of America* (Albany, 1821).

The quotations in this book from Madison's *Debates* and from Yates's *Secret Proceedings and Debates* have been taken from a volume entitled *Documents Illustrative of the Formation of the Union of the American States*, published by direction of the Congress under the editorial super-

431

vision of the Legislative Reference Division of the Library of Congress, Sixty-ninth Congress, First Session, House Document No. 398 (Washington: Government Printing Office, 1927). This edition will be cited hereafter as *Documents*. Franklin's speech appears on pp. 739–740. The text of Madison's *Debates* published in *Documents* follows the text published by the Carnegie Endowment for International Peace, *Debates in the Federal Convention of 1787 as Reported by James Madison*, Gaillard Hunt and James Brown Scott, eds. (Washington, 1920). Other sets of notes published in *Documents* are those of Rufus King, William Paterson, Alexander Hamilton, Dr. James McHenry, and Major William Pierce. The notes of John Lansing were discovered subsequently and edited by J. R. Strayer and published under the title, *The Delegate from New York or Proceedings of the Federal Convention of 1787 from the Notes of John Lansing, Jr.* (Princeton: Princeton University Press, 1939).

Another collected edition of the various sets of notes on the debates in the Federal Convention is that of Max Farrand, *Records of the Federal Convention*, 3 vols. (New Haven: Yale University Press, 1911; 2nd ed., 4 vols., 1937). For a rearrangement of Madison's *Debates* so as to bring together all the scattered passages relating to the same topic see A. T. Prescott, *Drafting the Federal Constitution* (Baton Rouge: Louisiana State University

Press, 1941). An account of the work of the Convention, which gives a convenient summary of the material in Madison's *Debates*, is Charles Warren, *The Making of the Constitution* (Boston: Little, Brown, 1928; new ed., 1937).

6. *Documents*, p. 742.

7. This is one of the numbers of *The Federalist* the authorship of which has been disputed. The evidence in favor of Madison's authorship is set forth by Professor Adair in the article cited above. His argument that Madison was the author of this number seems to me convincing.

8. A. Lawrence Lowell, "An Example from the Evidence of History," *Factors Determining Human Behavior*, Harvard Tercentenary Publications, No. 1 (Cambridge: Harvard University Press, 1937), pp. 119–132.

9. James Bryce, *The American Commonwealth* (New York: Macmillan, 1888), III, 648.

10. Harold J. Laski, *Parliamentary Government in England* (New York: Viking Press, 1938), pp. 19–23.

11. Immanuel Kant, *The Natural Principle of the Political Order* (1784). See *Eternal Peace and Other International Essays* (Boston: World Peace Foundation, 1941), pp. 1–25. See also C. J. Friedrich, ed., *The Philosophy of Kant* (Modern Library, 1949), pp. 116–131.

12. C. J. Friedrich, *Inevitable Peace* (Cambridge: Harvard University Press, 1948).

CHAPTER TWO

1. Standard accounts of the framing of the Constitution are Max Farrand, *The Framing of the Constitution of the United States* (New Haven: Yale University Press, 1913) and his *The Fathers of the Constitution: A Chronicle of the Establishment of the Union* (New Haven: Yale University Press, 1921). See also Charles Warren, *The Making of the Constitution* (Boston: Little, Brown, 1928; new ed., 1937); Hastings Lyon, *The Constitution and*

the Men Who Made It; The Story of the Constitutional Convention, 1787 (Boston and New York: Houghton Mifflin, 1936); Fred Rodell, *Fifty-five Men* (New York: Telegraph Press, 1936); Fred T. Wilson, *Our Constitution and Its Makers* (New York: F. H. Revell, 1937). The liveliest account of the framing of the Constitution is Carl Van Doren's *The Great Rehearsal, The Story of the Making and Ratifying of the Constitution* (New York: Viking

Press, 1948). The latest account is that by Irving Brant in the third volume of his magistral life of Madison. See Brant, *James Madison, Father of the Constitution, 1787–1800* (Indianapolis: Bobbs-Merrill, 1950); chaps. i – xii, pp. 11–60. This excellent work did not appear in time for use in preparing the present book.

2. Irving Brant, *James Madison, The Nationalist, 1780–1787.* (Indianapolis: Bobbs-Merrill, 1948); see esp. chap. xxvi, "Prologue to the Constitution," pp. 414–415.

3. The evidence in support of the opinion that Madison was the principal author of the Virginia plan is convincingly presented by Irving Brant, *James Madison, The Nationalist,* p. 416.

4. *Documents,* pp. 116–119.

5. *Ibid.,* p. 131.

6. *Ibid.,* pp. 174, 390–391.

7. *Ibid.,* pp. 605, 979–980.

8. *Ibid.,* pp. 204–207.

9. *Ibid.,* p. 204n.

10. *Ibid.,* pp. 208–210.

11. *Ibid.,* pp. 304, 316.

12. *Ibid.,* pp. 387–388.

13. *Ibid.,* pp. 323–324.

14. *Ibid.,* pp. 337–338.

15. *Ibid.,* pp. 522–523, 528–535, 546–547, 667, 671.

16. Jonathan Elliot, *The Debates in the Several State Conventions on the Adoption of the Federal Constitution, Together with the Journal of the Federal Convention,* etc., 4 vols. (Philadelphia, 1836), I–IV, *passim.*

17. *Documents,* pp. 161–163, 279–281. Cf. *The Federalist,* No. 10.

18. *Documents,* pp. 215–223, 776–783; see esp. p. 221. See also Nathan Schachner, *Alexander Hamilton* (New York: Appleton Century, 1946).

19. *Documents,* pp. 319–321, 838–839. See Daniel Walther, *Gouverneur Morris, Witness of Two Revolutions,* tr. by Elinore Denniston (New York and London: Funk and Wagnalls, 1934), esp. chap. iii, "At the Philadelphia Convention," and chap. iv, "Morris's Principles."

20. *Documents,* p. 373.

21. See my *The Middle Classes in American Politics* (Cambridge: Harvard University Press, 1940), pp. 3–12, 28–30, 132–137, 149–157.

22. For the view of the latest biographer, see Carl Van Doren, *Benjamin Franklin* (New York: Garden City Publishing Co., 1941).

23. *Documents,* pp. 351–360.

24. *Ibid.,* pp. 374–375, 638–639.

25. *Ibid.,* pp. 828, 379–381.

26. *Ibid.,* pp. 360–368, 495–498.

27. This phase of the struggle for a more perfect Union is vividly described in Carl Van Doren, *The Great Rehearsal;* see chap. x, "The War of Words and Ideas," pp. 176–193.

28. Montesquieu, *Spirit of Laws,* Book XI, chap. v. The ideas of Montesquieu were best known to the framers through the references in Sir William Blackstone's *Commentaries on the Laws of England,* of which the first American edition, reprinted from the fourth English edition, was published at Philadelphia in 1771. The first reference to Montesquieu appeared on the last page of Book I, chap. i. The substance of Montesquieu's doctrine of the separation of powers appeared also in chap. ii. See the first Worcester edition (reprinted from the 11th London edition at Worcester, Mass., 1790), I, pp. 145, 154–155.

29. See *The Federalist,* No. 51.

30. *Documents,* pp. 127–128.

31. *Ibid.,* pp. 371–372; see also pp. 673–675.

32. *Ibid.,* pp. 131–146, 392–399, 408–432, 442–458, 662–665, 668–680.

33. *Ibid.,* pp. 659–661, 153–154, 198–199, 400–403, 429–432.

34. *Ibid.,* pp. 660–661, 690–692.

35. *Ibid.,* pp. 147, 152, 165–167, 547–551, 624.

36. *Ibid.,* pp. 390–392.

37. *Ibid.,* pp. 422–429.

38. *Ibid.,* p. 548.

39. Elliot, *Debates,* II, p. 196.

40. *Documents,* p. 423.

41. *Ibid.,* p. 547.

42. *Ibid.,* p. 424.

43. *Ibid.,* pp. 128, 196.

44. Notably the old Revolutionists, Franklin and Sherman; see *Documents*, p. 148.

45. Notably George Mason; see *Documents*, pp. 652, 737.

46. *Documents*, p. 716.

47. *Ibid.*, p. 597.

48. Charles Francis Adams, *The Works of John Adams, Second President of the United States* (Boston: Little, Brown, 1850–56), V, p. 90.

49. Elliot, *Debates*, II, pp. 248, 281.

50. *Documents*, p. 751.

51. *The Writings of Thomas Jefferson* (Washington: Thomas Jefferson Memorial Association of the United States, 1907), VII, pp. 309–315.

52. *Documents*, pp. 739–740. See my *Human Rights in the Modern World* (New York: New York University Press, 1948), pp. 37–39.

CHAPTER THREE

1. In a letter from Jefferson, then in Paris, to Madison, December 20, 1787. See *The Writings of Thomas Jefferson*, published by order of Congress, H. A. Washington, ed. (New York and London, 1853), II, pp. 327–333.

2. *Ibid.*, IV, p. 463.

3. Jonathan Elliot, *The Debates in the Several State Conventions on the Adoption of the Federal Constitution, Together with the Journal of the Federal Convention*, etc., 4 vols. (Philadelphia, 1836), II, pp. 243–248. See also my *Middle Classes in American Politics* (Cambridge: Harvard University Press, 1940), pp. 4–6.

4. Elliot, *Debates*, III, p. 54.

5. John Adams, *A Defense of the Constitutions of Government of the United States of America* (London, 1787–88).

6. Charles Francis Adams, *The Works of John Adams, Second President of the United States* (Boston: Little, Brown, 1850–56), V, pp. 90, 183. See C. M. Walsh, *The Political Science of John Adams* (New York: Putnam, 1915).

7. Adams, *The Works of John Adams*, V, p. 458.

8. Elliot, *Debates*, I, pp. 503–505.

9. Adams, *The Works of John Adams*, IX, p. 570.

10. The National Resources Committee, *Report on the Structure of the American Economy*, pt. I. (Washington: Government Printing Office, 1939).

11. Nikolai Bukharin, *Historical Materialism, A System of Sociology* (New York: International Publishers, 1925), p. 276.

12. *Ibid.*, pp. 282 ff.

13. Lewis Corey, *The Crisis of the Middle Class* (New York: Covici, Friede, 1935), p. 274.

14. See the discussion of this topic in my book, *The New Party Politics* (New York: W. W. Norton, 1933), pp. 101–107.

15. George Gallup and S. F. Rae, *The Pulse of Democracy; the Public-Opinion Poll and How It Works* (New York: Simon and Shuster, 1940), p. 169.

16. "The Fortune Survey," No. 27, *Fortune* (February 1940).

17. *Sixteenth Census of the United States: 1940. Population: Comparative Occupation Statistics of the United States, 1870–1940* (Washington: Government Printing Office, 1943).

18. Lewis Mumford, *Technics and Civilization* (New York: Harcourt Brace, 1934), p. 229.

19. Alfred W. Jones, *Life, Liberty and Property* (New York: Lippincott, 1941), p. 354.

20. *Ibid.*, p. 349.

21. For a suggestive discussion of this whole subject, see Richard Centers, *The Psychology of Social Classes, A Study of Class Consciousness* (Princeton: Princeton University Press, 1949). Class consciousness of all kinds is doubtless less clearly defined in the United States than in Europe, and middle-class consciousness in particular certainly takes a different form. See, for an in-

teresting treatment of the middle class in English politics, Roy Lewis and Angus Maude, *The English Middle Classes* (New York: Knopf, 1950). The traditional English middle class is far from identical with the middle class in America.

22. For more detailed treatments of this subject, see my earlier books, *The Political Parties of Today* (New York: Harpers, 2nd ed. 1925), chap. iii, "The Economic Basis of National Politics," chap. iv, "The Sectional Basis of National Politics"; and *The Middle Classes in American Politics* (Cambridge: Har-

vard University Press, 1940), pt. II, chap. i.

23. For the results of a recent inquiry into the politics of this section, see V. O. Key, Jr., *Southern Politics in State and Nation* (New York: Knopf, 1949). This excellent volume should be compared with Gunnar Myrdal, *An American Dilemma; The Negro Problem and Modern Democracy* (New York and London: Harpers, 1944), pt. V; and John Gunther, *Inside U.S.A.* (New York: Harpers, 1947), chaps xl–xlix.

CHAPTER FOUR

1. *The Federalist* (Modern Library ed., 1937), No. 10, pp. 53–62.

2. *Documents*, p. 415.

3. *Ibid.*, p. 669.

4. For interesting speculation on the consequences of the Democratic Party split in 1948, see W. B. Hesseltine, *The Rise and Fall of Third Parties from Anti-Masonry to Wallace* (Washington: Public Affairs Press, 1948). Cf. Louis H. Bean, *How to Predict Elections* (New York: Knopf, 1948).

5. Alexis de Tocqueville, *Democracy in America*, Bowen ed., 2 vols. (Cambridge, 1862), I, p. 226.

6. Graham Wallas, *Human Nature in Politics* (Boston: Houghton Mifflin, 1909), p. xi.

7. Charles A. Beard, *Economic Origins of Jeffersonian Democracy* (New York: Macmillan, 1915).

8. Martin Van Buren, *Inquiry into the Origin and Course of Political Parties in the United States* (New York, 1867).

9. See A. M. Schlesinger, Jr., *The Age of Jackson* (Boston: Little, Brown, 1945).

10. Irving Stone, *They Also Ran; The Story of the Men Who Were Defeated for the Presidency* (Garden City: Doubleday Doran, 1943), p. 367.

CHAPTER FIVE

1. The South, regarded as a political section, has been the subject of more interest to students of American politics than any other section. For the latest in a series of valuable studies, see V. O. Key, Jr., *Southern Politics in State and Nation* (New York: Knopf, 1949).

2. Based on official election returns compiled by The Associated Press and published in *The New York Times*, December 11, 1948.

3. *The Congressional Directory, 81st Congress, 1st Session* (Washington: Government Printing Office, 1949).

4. Bureau of the Census, *Vote Cast in Presidential and Congressional Elections, 1928–1944* (Washington: Government Printing Office, 1946). For the results of earlier elections see Edgar E. Robinson, *The Presidential Vote, 1896–1932* (Palo Alto: Stanford University Press, 1934). Figures for still earlier elections were published in *The Tribune Almanac* and its predecessor, *The Whig Almanac*. See also Cortez Ewing, *Presidential Elections, 1860–1936* (Norman: University of Oklahoma Press, 1940).

5. For a statistical analysis of the problem of forecasting the results of presidential elections, see Louis H. Bean, *How to Predict Elections* (New York: Knopf, 1948). For a different view, see Arthur M. Schlesinger, *Paths to the Present* (New York: Macmillan, 1949), chap. iv, "The Tides of National Politics," pp. 77–92. For a study of the process by which a voter makes up his mind in a presidential campaign, see Paul F. Lazarsfeld and Associates, *The People's Choice* (New York: Columbia University Press, 2nd ed., 1948).

6. For statistical analyses of national elections, see my *The Political Parties of Today* (New York: Harpers, 2nd ed., 1925), and *The Middle Classes in American Politics* (Cambridge: Harvard University Press, 1940).

7. *Sixteenth Census of the United States: 1940. Housing: First Series Supplement, Block Statistics*; and *Analytical Maps.*

8. H. L. Moon, *Balance of Power:* *the Negro Vote* (New York: Doubleday, 1948).

9. Peter Odegard, *Pressure Politics, the Story of the Anti-Saloon League* (New York: Columbia University Press, 1928).

10. See V. O. Key, Jr., *Politics, Parties, and Pressure Groups* (New York: Crowell, 2nd ed., 1947).

11. See my "The Changing Outlook for a Realignment of Parties," *The Public Opinion Quarterly*, X, no. 4 (Winter, 1946–47).

12. See E. P. Herring, *The Politics of Democracy* (New York: Norton, 1940), and compare E. E. Schattschneider, *Party Government* (New York: Farrar and Rinehart, 1942).

13. This development has not only dispelled such fears as those of Madison but also seems likely to frustrate such hopes as those of Professor Laski. See Harold J. Laski, *The American Democracy* (New York: Viking Press, 1948), pp. 134–137.

CHAPTER SIX

1. *United States Code — Congressional Service*, 1948, no. 6, pp. xviii–xix.

2. The best description of existing congressional procedure will be found in Floyd M. Riddick, *Congressional Procedure* (Boston: Chapman and Grimes, 1941), and in the same author's *The United States Congress, Organization and Procedure* (Washington: National Capitol Publishers, 1949).

3. Henrietta and Nelson Poynter, eds., *The Congressional Quarterly, A Service for Editors and Commentators* (Washington: Press Research, Inc., 1945). Quotations by permission of the editors and publishers.

4. See, for the case in support of this view, Robert Luce, *Congress, An Explanation* (Cambridge: Harvard University Press, 1926). Paul De W. Hasbrouck, *Party Government in the House of Representatives* (New York: Macmillan, 1927).

5. See, for the case for greater partisan control and responsibility in the legislative process, W. F. Willoughby, *Principles of Legislative Organization and Administration* (Washington: Brookings Institution, 1934). E. E. Schattschneider, *Party Government* (New York: Farrar and Rinehart, 1942) and the same author's *The Struggle for Party Government* (College Park: The University of Maryland, 1948).

6. *The Congressional Quarterly.* See note 3 above.

7. Robert Luce, *The Science of Legislation* (Boston: Houghton Mifflin, 1935), IV, "Legislative Problems," p. 732.

8. See Roland Young, *This Is Congress* (New York: Knopf, 1943). George B. Galloway, *Congress at the Crossroads* (New York: Crowell, 1946). James M. Burns, *Congress on Trial* (New York: Harpers, 1949). Stephen K. Bailey, *Congress Makes a Law* (New York: Columbia University Press, 1950).

9. Harold J. Laski, *The American Democracy* (New York: Viking Press, 1948), p. 72.

10. Alexis de Tocqueville, *Democracy in America* (Bowen ed., 1862), I, chap. viii, "The Federal Constitution."

11. *Ibid.*, I, p. 227–229.

12. Matthew Josephson, *The Politicos* (New York: Harcourt Brace, 1938).

13. James Bryce, *The American Commonwealth* (New York: Macmillan, 1888), III, chap. cxv, p. 655.

14. See George B. Galloway, *Congress at the Crossroads* (New York: Crowell, 1946), chap. iii.

15. Woodrow Wilson, *Congressional Government, A Study in American Politics* (Boston: Houghton Mifflin, 1885), pp. 318, 332–333.

16. *Ibid.* (15th ed., 1900), pp. xiii, xvii.

17. Floyd M. Riddick, *Congressional Procedure* (Boston: Chapman and Grimes, 1941), p. 62.

18. R. L. Neuberger and S. B. Kahn, *Integrity; the Life of George W. Norris* (New York: Vanguard Press, 1937), p. 36.

19. Woodrow Wilson, *Congressional Government* (15th ed., 1900), pp. xvi, xviii.

20. See E. P. Herring, *Group Representation before Congress* (Baltimore: Johns Hopkins University Press, 1929).

21. *The Congressional Quarterly.* See note 3 above.

CHAPTER SEVEN

1. See James Hart, *The American Presidency in Action,* 1789 (New York: Macmillan, 1948), chap. iv, "The President and the Senate."

2. Alexis de Tocqueville, *Democracy in America* (Bowen ed., 1862), I, pp. 228–229.

3. Matthew Josephson, *The Politicos* (New York: Harcourt Brace, 1938), pp. viii–ix.

4. James Bryce, *The American Commonwealth* (New York: Macmillan, 1st ed. 1888), III, p. 655.

5. *Ibid.*, III, p. 412.

6. *Ibid.*, III, p. 414.

7. *Ibid.*, III, p. 660.

8. *Ibid.*, III, p. 674. See also an essay of mine, reviewing Bryce's observations and predictions, "The Future of Democracy in America," in *The Middle Classes in American Politics* (Cambridge: Harvard University Press, 1940), pp. 226–271.

9. Bryce, *op. cit.*, III, p. 655.

10. George H. Haynes, *The Senate of the United States, Its History and Practice* (Boston: Houghton Mifflin, 1938), II, p. 1071.

11. Ernest S. Bates, *The Story of Congress, 1789–1935* (New York: Harpers, 1936), p. 421.

12. For a scholarly analysis of party government at this period, see Roy Franklin Nichols, *The Disruption of American Democracy* (New York: Macmillan, 1948).

13. Robert Luce, *Legislative Assemblies* (Boston: Houghton Mifflin, 1924); see esp. chaps. xi, xiv, and xv for his views on the character and quality of Congressmen.

14. *The Congressional Directory, 80th Congress, 1st Session* (Washington: Government Printing Office, 1947). See also George B. Galloway, *Congress at the Crossroads* (New York: Crowell, 1946), chap. ii, "How Congress is Composed."

15. A. Lawrence Lowell, *The Influence of Party Upon Legislation in England and America* (Washington: Government Printing Office, 1902).

16. *The Congressional Quarterly.* See chap. vi, note 3.

17. Lindsay Rogers, *The American Senate* (New York: Knopf, 1926), p. ix.

18. Franklin L. Burdette, *Filibustering in the Senate* (Princeton: Princeton University Press, 1940).

19. W. F. Willoughby, *The Principles of Legislative Organization and*

Administration (Washington: Brookings Institution, 1934), p. 499.

20. See Will Maslow, "F.E.P.C. — A Case History in Parliamentary Maneuver," *University of Chicago Law Review*, XIII, 407–445 (June 1946).

CHAPTER EIGHT

1. A. Lawrence Lowell, *Public Opinion and Popular Government* (New York: Longmans, Green, 1913), pt. 2, "The Function of Parties."

2. See chap. ii, note 28.

3. *Documents*, pp. 142–143.

4. *Ibid.*, p. 171.

5. James E. Pollard, *The President and the Press* (New York: Macmillan, 1947).

6. Woodrow Wilson, *Constitutional Government in the United States* (New York: Columbia University Press, 1908).

7. Robert Luce, *Legislative Problems* (Boston: Houghton Mifflin, 1935), chap. vii, "President and Congress." See esp. p. 220 where the author states: "Our Presidents still mainly acquiesce."

8. For an excellent discussion of this subject, see Clarence A. Berdahl, "Some Notes on Party Membership in Congress," *American Political Science Review*, XLIII, Nos. 2, 3, and 4 (April, June, and August 1949).

9. B. J. Hendrick, *Lincoln's War Cabinet* (Boston: Little, Brown, 1946).

10. Harold J. Laski, *The American Presidency* (New York: Harpers, 1940), p. 21.

11. See my article, "The Changing Outlook for a Realignment of Parties," *The Public Opinion Quarterly*, X, No. 4 (Winter, 1946–47).

12. Laski, *The American Presidency*, p. 251.

13. Walter Lippmann, "Today and Tomorrow," *New York Herald Tribune*, February 8, 1941.

14. See esp. E. P. Herring, *Presidential Leadership* (New York: Farrar and Rinehart, 1940), and also Roland Young, *This Is Congress* (New York: Knopf, 1943). Cf. Wilfred E. Binkley, *President and Congress* (New York: Knopf, 1947); see esp. p. 297.

15. See esp. Lawrence H. Chamberlain, *The President, Congress, and Legislation* (New York: Columbia University Press, 1946). See also, James M. Burns, *Congress on Trial* (New York: Harpers, 1949), chap. v, "The Story of Three Bills"; and E. E. Schattschneider, *Politics, Pressures and the Tariff* (New York: Prentice Hall, 1935).

16. Wesley C. McCune, *The Farm Bloc* (Garden City: Doubleday, 1943).

17. For a well-considered program of measures designed to strengthen the Presidency, see Louis Brownlow, *The President and the Presidency* (Chicago: Public Administration Service, 1949). Brownlow, who had enjoyed extraordinary opportunities to study the administrative problems of the chief executive, recommended (1) granting to the President permanent and unfettered authority to reorganize the administrative branch of the government; (2) freedom from Congressional interference in administrative detail; (3) power to veto items in appropriation bills; (4) maintenance of strict accountability for expenditures by an independent audit; and (5) some flexible system of advisory committees within the executive office to help coordinate governmental policy. Cf. *The Hoover Commission Report on Organization of the Executive Branch of the Government* (New York: McGraw Hill, 1949). See also the same Commission's *Concluding Report, A Report to the Congress, May, 1949* (Washington: U. S. Government Printing Office, 1949).

18. For a well-informed and thoughtful set of proposals designed to strengthen the Congress, see Estes Kefauver and Jack Levin, *A Twentieth Century Congress* (New York: Duell, Sloan and Pearce, 1947). Senator (then Representative) Kefauver recommended, among other changes, (1) the intro-

duction of electric voting in both branches of Congress; (2) question periods as in the British Parliament; (3) the establishment of a joint policy committee, comprising the party leaders in both branches, for the majority party and also for the minority party; (4) further consolidation of committees and use of joint committees; and (5) the abolition of the seniority system of choosing committee chairmen.

19. For a scholarly treatment of one of the possibilities of improving the position of the House, see Lucius Wilmerding, *The Spending Power, A History of the Efforts of Congress to Control Expenditures* (New Haven: Yale University Press, 1943).

20. See chap. x, note 55.

21. Edward S. Corwin, *Constitutional Revolution, Ltd.* (Claremont, Calif.: Pomona, Scripps and Claremont Colleges, 1941; rev. ed., 1946) and *Total War and the Constitution* (New York: Knopf, 1947).

22. Presented to the Convention, June 18, 1787. See *Documents*, pp. 978–988.

23. See *The Federalist*, Nos. 67–77.

24. Emery Reves, *The Anatomy of Peace* (New York and London: Harpers, 1945).

CHAPTER NINE

1. Madison's letter to Jefferson, October 17, 1788, in Gaillard Hunt, ed., *The Writings of James Madison*, 9 vols. (New York: Putnam, 1904), V, pp. 269–275.

2. Jefferson's letter to Madison, March 15, 1789, in *The Writings of Thomas Jefferson*, 20 vols. (Washington: Thomas Jefferson Memorial Association of the United States, 1907), VII, pp. 309–315.

3. Nos. 78, 81, and 84 of *The Federalist*, in which the views of "Publius" on judicial review and the utility of bills of rights were set forth, were Hamilton's.

4. *Speeches and Letters of Abraham Lincoln, 1832–1865*, Everyman's Library ed., (New York: E. P. Dutton, 1907), pp. 171–172.

5. For appointments to the Supreme Court see Charles Warren, *The Supreme Court in United States History*, 2 vols. (Boston: Little, Brown, 1922). Cf. Cortez A. M. Ewing, *The Judges of the Supreme Court, 1789–1937, A Study of Their Qualifications* (Minneapolis: University of Minnesota Press, 1938). For the qualifications of the members of the New Deal Court, see Wesley McCune, *The Nine Young Men* (New York: Harpers, 1947), and C. Herman Pritchett, *The Roosevelt Court, A Study in Judicial Politics and Values, 1937–1947* (New York: Macmillan, 1948), chap. i.

6. Henry F. Pringle, *Life of William Howard Taft; A Biography* (New York: Farrar and Rinehart, 1939), pp. 529–537.

7. *Hylton* v. *United States*, 3 Dallas 171 (1796).

8. *Marbury* v. *Madison*, 1 Cranch 137 (1803).

9. See Albert J. Beveridge, *The Life of John Marshall*, 4 vols. (Boston and New York: Houghton Mifflin, 1916); and cf. Charles G. Haines, *The Role of the Supreme Court in American Government and Politics, 1787–1835* (Berkeley: University of California Press, 1944).

10. *McCulloch* v. *Maryland*, 4 Wheaton 316 (1819).

11. B. F. Wright, *The Growth of American Constitutional Law* (Boston: Houghton Mifflin, 1942); see esp. chap. iv, "Jacksonian Judges and the Judicial Power."

12. *Dred Scott* v. *Sandford*, 19 Howard 393 (1857).

13. Wright, *The Growth of American Constitutional Law*, chap. v, "The Emergence of Modern Constitutional Law."

14. *Ex parte McCardle*, 7 Wallace 506 (1869).

15. *Hepburn* v. *Griswold*, 8 Wallace 603 (1870).

16. Legal Tender Cases, 12 Wallace 457 (1871).

17. Civil Rights Cases, 109 U.S. 3 (1883).

18. *United States* v. *E. C. Knight Co.*, 156 U.S. 1 (1895).

19. *In re Debs*, 158 U.S. 564 (1895).

20. Income Tax Cases, 157 U.S. 429 (1895); 158 U.S. 601 (1895).

21. *Speeches of William Jennings Bryan*, 2 vols. (New York and London: Funk and Wagnalls, 1909), I, p. 238.

22. 157 U.S. 651 (1895).

23. 158 U.S. 684 (1895).

24. 158 U.S. 706 (1895).

25. *De Lima* v. *Bidwell*, 182 U.S. 1 (1901); *Downes* v. *Bidwell*, 182 U.S. 244 (1901).

26. Sir W. Blackstone, *Commentaries on the Laws of England*, (T. M. Cooley's 2nd American ed., 1876), Book I, chap. i, "Of the Absolute Rights of Individuals."

27. *Howard* v. *Illinois Central Railroad Co.*, 207 U.S. 463 (1908).

28. *Adair* v. *United States*, 208 U.S. 161 (1908).

29. Theodore Roosevelt, Annual Message to the Congress, December 8, 1908.

30. *Hammer* v. *Dagenhart*, 247 U.S. 251 (1918); *Bailey* v. *Drexel Furniture Co.*, 259 U.S. 20 (1922).

31. *Adkins* v. *Children's Hospital*, 261 U.S. 525 (1923).

32. *Panama Refining Co.* v. *Ryan*, 293 U.S. 388 (1935); *Schechter Poultry Co.* v. *United States*, 295 U.S. 495 (1935).

33. *Railroad Retirement Board* v. *Alton Railroad Co.*, 295 U.S. 330 (1935).

34. *Louisville Joint Stock Bank* v. *Radford*, 295 U.S. 555 (1935).

35. *Ashton* v. *Cameron County District*, 298 U.S. 513 (1936).

36. *United States* v. *Butler*, 297 U.S. 1 (1936).

37. *Carter* v. *Carter Coal Co.*, 298 U.S. 238 (1936). For a weighty criticism of this decision, see W. H. Hamilton and Douglass Adair, *The Power to Govern; The Constitution, Then and Now* (New York: W. H. Norton, 1937).

38. Irving Brant, *Storm over the Constitution* (Indianapolis: Bobbs-Merrill, 1936).

39. *National Labor Relations Board* v. *Jones and Laughlin Steel Co.*, 301 U.S. 1 (1937).

40. The Social Security Act Cases, 301 U.S. 548 (1937); 301 U.S. 619 (1937).

41. Robert H. Jackson, *The Struggle for Judicial Supremacy* (New York: Knopf, 1941).

42. Wesley McCune, *The Nine Young Men* (New York: Harpers, 1947).

43. C. Herman Pritchett, *The Roosevelt Court; A Study in Judicial Politics and Values, 1937–47* (New York: Macmillan, 1948).

44. *United States* v. *Lovett*, 328 U.S. 303 (1946).

45. *Yakus* v. *United States*, 321 U.S. 414 (1943); *Steuart and Bro., Inc.* v. *Bowles*, 322 U.S. 398 (1944).

46. *The Public Papers of Franklin D. Roosevelt* (New York: Macmillan, 1941), VI, "1937: The Constitution Prevails," p. 362.

47. O. W. Holmes, *Collected Legal Papers* (New York: Harcourt, Brace and Howe, 1920).

48. See a memorandum from Harry L. Hopkins to the President, "Papers Relating to the Supreme Court, 1937," Roosevelt Memorial Library, Hyde Park, N. Y.

49. John W. Burgess, *Political Science and Comparative Constitutional Law*, 2 vols. (Boston: Ginn, 1890), II, p. 364.

50. *United States* v. *Butler*, 297 U.S. 1 (1936).

51. See McCune, *The Nine Young Men, passim*, and Pritchett, *The Roosevelt Court*, chap. x, "The Plight of a Liberal Court."

52. Charles P. Curtis, *Lions under*

the Throne (Boston: Houghton Mifflin, 1947).

CHAPTER TEN

1. *Works of Edmund Burke* (Boston: Little, Brown, 1839), I, p. 377. The emphasis is Burke's.
2. Leonard D. White, *The Federalists, A Study in Administrative History* (New York: Macmillan, 1948), p. 405.
3. *Ibid.*, p. 101.
4. *Little* v. *Barreme*, 2 Cranch 170 (1804).
5. *Brig Aurora* v. *United States*, 7 Cranch 382 (1813); *Martin* v. *Mott*, 12 Wheaton 19 (1827).
6. *Luther* v. *Borden*, 7 Howard 1 (1849).
7. *Kendall* v. *United States*, 12 Peters 524 (1838).
8. *Ex parte Merryman*, Fed. case 9, 487 (1861).
9. *Ex parte Milligan*, 4 Wallace 2 (1866).
10. Charles E. Hughes, "War Powers Under the Constitution," *Reports of the American Bar Association*, XLII (1917), pp. 232–248.
11. *Kilbourn* v. *Thompson*, 103 U.S. 168 (1880).
12. *United States* v. *Lee*, 106 U.S. 196 (1882).
13. See Charles Fairman, *Mr. Justice Miller and the Supreme Court, 1862–1890* (Cambridge: Harvard University Press, 1939).
14. I. L. Sharfman, *The Interstate Commerce Commission; A Study in Administrative Law and Procedure* (New York: The Commonwealth Fund, 1931), I, pt. 1.
15. *Munn* v. *Illinois*, 94 U.S. 113 (1877).
16. *Chicago, Milwaukee, and St. Paul Railway Co.* v. *Minnesota*, 134 U.S. 418 (1890).
17. Standard Oil and American Tobacco Company Cases, 221 U.S. 1 (1911).
18. *Field* v. *Clark*, 143 U.S. 649 (1892).
19. *Myers* v. *United States*, 272 U.S. 52 (1926). See, for discriminating comment on this decision, James Hart, *The American Presidency in Action, 1789* (New York: Macmillan, 1948), pp. 155–213.
20. *Humphrey's Executor* v. *United States*, 295 U.S. 602 (1935).
21. See Message of the President to the Congress, March 23, 1938, transmitting opinion of Acting Attorney General Robert H. Jackson, *Congressional Record*, March 23, 1938.
22. *Hampton* v. *United States*, 276 U.S. 394 (1928).
23. *Norwegian Nitrogen Products Co.* v. *United States*, 288 U.S. 294 (1933).
24. *Morgan* v. *United States*, 298 U.S. 468 (1936); 304 U.S. 1 (1938).
25. *Jones* v. *Securities and Exchange Commission*, 298 U.S. 1 (1936).
26. *Carter* v. *Carter Coal Co.*, 298 U.S. 238 (1936); see esp. pp. 333–334.
27. *St. Joseph Stock Yards Co.* v. *United States*, 298 U.S. 38 (1936).
28. *United States* v. *Butler*, 297 U.S. 1 (1936).
29. Edward S. Corwin, *Constitutional Revolution, Ltd.* (Claremont, Calif.: Pomona, Scripps, and Claremont Colleges, 1941; rev. ed., 1946).
30. *Opp Cotton Mills* v. *Administrator*, 312 U.S. 126 (1941).
31. *National Broadcasting Co.* v. *United States*, 319 U.S. 190 (1943).
32. *New York* v. *United States*, 331 U.S. 284 (1947).
33. *Federal Trade Commission* v. *Cement Institute*, 333 U.S. 683 (1948).
34. *Federal Power Commission* v. *Natural Gas Pipeline Co.*, 315 U.S. 575 (1942).
35. *Federal Power Commission* v. *Hope Natural Gas Co.*, 320 U.S. 591 (1944).
36. *American Telephone and Telegraph Co.* v. *Federal Communications Commission*, 299 U.S. 232 (1936).
53. *Norman* v. *Baltimore and Ohio Railroad Co.*, 294 U.S. 240 (1935).

37. *Republic Aviation Corp.* v. *National Labor Relations Board,* 324 U.S. 793 (1945).

38. *Securities and Exchange Commission* v. *Federal Water and Gas Corp.,* 332 U.S. 194 (1947).

39. *Ibid.,* 332 U.S. 209 (1947).

40. Walter Lippmann, *An Inquiry into the Principles of the Good Society* (Boston: Little, Brown, 1937).

41. See Robert E. Cushman, *The Independent Regulatory Commissions* (New York: Oxford University Press, 1941). Cf., James M. Landis, *The Administrative Process* (New Haven: Yale University Press, 1938); and Walter Gellhorn, *Federal Administrative Proceedings* (Baltimore: Johns Hopkins Press, 1941).

42. *Yakus* v. *United States,* 321 U.S. 414 (1943).

43. *Steuart* v. *Bowles,* 322 U.S. 398 (1944).

44. *Ex parte Quirin,* 317 U.S. 1 (1942).

45. *Duncan* v. *Kahanamoku,* 327 U.S. 304 (1946).

46. *Cox* v. *United States,* 322 U.S. 442 (1947).

47. *Bridges* v. *Wixon,* 326 U.S. 135 (1945).

48. C. Herman Pritchett, *The Roosevelt Court, A Study in Judicial Politics and Values, 1937–1947* (New York: Macmillan, 1948); see esp. chap. vii, "Bureaucracy: No Alien Intruder."

49. John Corbin, *The Return of the Middle Class* (New York: Scribner, 1922), p. 323.

50. John H. Crider, *The Bureaucrat* (Philadelphia and New York: Lippincott, 1944).

51. Edward S. Corwin, *Total War and the Constitution* (New York: Knopf, 1947).

52. *United States* v. *Curtiss-Wright Export Co.,* 299 U.S. 304 (1936).

53. See *The Federalist,* No. 69, "The Powers of the President." In discussing the nature of the executive power over foreign affairs, Hamilton wrote that it "arises naturally from the sovereign power which relates to treaties."

54. *In re Yamashita,* 327 U.S. 1 (1946), and *in re Homma,* 327 U.S. 759 (1946). Cf. A. Frank Reel, *The Case of General Yamashita* (Chicago: University of Chicago Press, 1949). See also *Hirota* v. *MacArthur,* 335 U.S. 876 (1948).

55. See my discussion of "The Impact of Foreign Commitments on the Presidency," in Rowland Egger, ed., *International Commitments and National Administration* (Charlottesville: University of Virginia, 1949), pp. 23–38. See also R. E. Sherwood, *Roosevelt and Hopkins* (New York: Harper, 1948), p. 264.

CHAPTER ELEVEN

1. O. W. Holmes, *Collected Legal Papers* (New York: Harcourt, Brace and Howe, 1920), p. 291.

2. Harold J. Laski, *The American Democracy* (New York: Viking Press, 1948), p. 137.

3. Edward S. Corwin, *Total War and the Constitution* (New York: Knopf, 1947), p. 173.

4. Cf. B. F. Wright, *The Growth of American Constitutional Law* (Boston: Houghton Mifflin, 1942), chap. vi, "Umpiring the Federal System."

5. *Chisholm* v. *Georgia,* 2 Dallas 419 (1793).

6. *Ware* v. *Hylton,* 3 Dallas 199 (1796).

7. *Fletcher* v. *Peck,* 6 Cranch 87 (1810).

8. *Dartmouth College* v. *Woodward,* 4 Wheaton 518 (1819).

9. *Gibbons* v. *Ogden,* 9 Wheaton 1 (1824).

10. *McCulloch* v. *Maryland,* 4 Wheaton 316 (1819).

11. *Prigg* v. *Pennsylvania,* 16 Peters 539 (1842).

12. *Ableman* v. *Booth,* 21 Howard 506 (1859).

13. *Briscoe* v. *Bank of Kentucky,* 11 Peters 257 (1837).

14. *Charles River Bridge* v. *Warren Bridge*, 11 Peters 420 (1837).

15. *Cooley* v. *Board of Wardens*, 12 Howard 299 (1851).

16. See his separate opinion in *Prigg* v. *Pennsylvania*.

17. *Dred Scott* v. *Sandford*, 19 Howard 393 (1857).

18. *Luther* v. *Borden*, 7 Howard 1 (1849).

19. Civil Rights Cases, 109 U.S. 3 (1883).

20. *Butts* v. *Merchants and Miners Transportation Co.*, 230 U.S. 126 (1913).

21. *Morgan* v. *Virginia*, 328 U.S. 373 (1946).

22. *United States* v. *Classic*, 313 U.S. 299 (1941).

23. *Smith* v. *Allwright*, 321 U.S. 649 (1944).

24. C. Herman Pritchett, *The Roosevelt Court, A Study in Judicial Politics and Values, 1937–1947* (New York: Macmillan, 1948), pp. 137–152.

25. President's Committee on Civil Rights, *To Secure These Rights* (Washington: Government Printing Office, 1947).

26. Slaughter House Cases, 16 Wallace 36 (1873).

27. *New State Ice Co.* v. *Liebmann*, 285 U.S. 262 (1932).

28. *Holden* v. *Hardy*, 169 U.S. 366 (1898).

29. *Lochner* v. *New York*, 198 U.S. 45 (1905).

30. *Bunting* v. *Oregon*, 243 U.S. 426 (1917).

31. *Stettler* v. *O'Hara*, 243 U.S. 629 (1917).

32. *New York Central Railroad Co.* v. *White*, 243 U.S. 188 (1917); *Mountain Timber Co.* v. *Washington*, 243 U.S. 219 (1917).

33. *Adams* v. *Tanner*, 244 U.S. 590 (1917).

34. *Wolff Packing Co.* v. *Court of Industrial Relations*, 262 U.S. 522 (1923).

35. *Tyson* v. *Banton*, 273 U.S. 418 (1927).

36. *Ribnik* v. *McBride*, 277 U.S. 350 (1928).

37. *Williams* v. *Standard Oil Co.*, 278 U.S. 235 (1929).

38. *New State Ice Co.* v. *Liebmann*, 285 U.S. 262 (1932).

39. *Bailey* v. *Drexel Furniture Co.*, 259 U.S. 20 (1922).

40. *United States* v. *Butler*, 297 U.S. 1 (1936).

41. Edward S. Corwin, *The Twilight of the Supreme Court* (New Haven: Yale University Press, 1934), chap. i, "Dual Federalism v. Nationalism."

42. Dennis W. Brogan, *Government of the People* (New York: Harpers, 1933), pp. 19, 35.

43. *Stettler* v. *O'Hara*, 243 U.S. 629 (1917).

44. *Adkins* v. *Children's Hospital*, 261 U.S. 525 (1923).

45. *Murphy* v. *Sardell*, 269 U.S. 530 (1925).

46. *Donham* v. *West-Nelson Manufacturing Co.*, 273 U.S. 657 (1927).

47. *Morehead* v. *New York ex rel. Tipaldo*, 298 U.S. 587 (1936).

48. *West Coast Hotel Co.* v. *Parrish*, 300 U.S. 379 (1937).

49. *Hammer* v. *Dagenhart*, 247 U.S. 251 (1918).

50. *Wilson* v. *New*, 243 U.S. 332 (1917).

51. *Bailey* v. *Drexel Furniture Co.*, 259 U.S. 20 (1922).

52. *Schechter Poultry Corp.* v. *United States*, 295 U.S. 495 (1935). Cf. *Stafford* v. *Wallace*, 258 U.S. 495 (1922).

53. Charles Warren, *The Congress, the Constitution, and the Supreme Court* (Boston: Little, Brown, 2nd ed., 1935). Cf. Irving Brant, *Storm over the Constitution* (Indianapolis: Bobbs-Merrill, 1936).

54. Robert H. Jackson, *The Struggle for Judicial Supremacy* (New York: Knopf, 1941).

55. *New State Ice Co.* v. *Liebmann*, 285 U.S. 262 (1932).

56. Edward S. Corwin, *Constitutional Revolution, Ltd.* (Claremont, Calif.: Pomona, Scripps, and Claremont Colleges, 1941; rev. ed., 1946). For a striking illustration of the new

attitude toward old issues, see Justice Jackson's restatement of the scope of the power to regulate interstate commerce in the case of *Wickard v. Filburn*, 317 U.S. 111 (1942).

57. Wesley McCune, *The Nine Young Men* (New York: Harpers, 1947).

58. *Gitlow v. New York*, 268 U.S. 652 (1925).

59. *Near v. Minnesota*, 283 U.S. 697 (1931); *De Jonge v. Oregon*, 299 U.S. 353 (1937).

60. *Powell v. Alabama*, 287 U.S. 45 (1932); *Norris v. Alabama*, 294 U.S. 587 (1935).

61. *Chambers v. Florida*, 309 U.S. 227 (1940).

62. *Screws v. United States*, 325 U.S. 91 (1945).

63. Pritchett, *The Roosevelt Court*, pp. 93–101.

64. *Minersville School District v. Gobitis*, 310 U.S. 586 (1940); *West Virginia Board of Education v. Barnette*, 319 U.S. 624 (1943).

65. *Colgate v. Harvey*, 296 U.S. 404 (1935).

66. *Madden v. Kentucky*, 309 U.S. 83 (1940).

67. *Hague v. Congress of Industrial Organizations*, 307 U.S. 496 (1939).

68. *Edwards v. California*, 314 U.S. 160 (1941). See also the discussion of this topic in my *Human Rights in the Modern World* (New York: New York University Press, 1948), chap. iii, "The Constitutional Privileges and Immunities of Americans."

69. *Sipuel v. Board of Regents of the University of Oklahoma*, 332 U.S. 631 (1948).

70. The Restrictive Land Covenant Cases, 334 U.S. 1 (1948).

71. *McCollum v. Board of Education*, 333 U.S. 203 (1948).

72. *Saia v. New York*, 334 U.S. 558 (1948).

73. *Everson v. Board of Education*, 330 U.S. 1 (1947).

74. *Fay v. New York*, 332 U.S. 261 (1947).

75. Pritchett, *The Roosevelt Court*, chap. x, "The Plight of a Liberal Court."

76. *Oklahoma v. United States Civil Service Commission*, 330 U.S. 127 (1947).

77. *Graves v. New York ex rel. O'Keefe*, 306 U.S. 466 (1939).

78. *New York v. United States*, 326 U.S. 572 (1946).

79. *Chase v. Bowles*, 327 U.S. 92 (1946).

80. Harold J. Laski, "The Obsolescence of Federalism," *The New Republic*, XCVIII, 367–369 (May 3, 1939).

81. Carl B. Swisher, *The Growth of Constitutional Power in the United States* (Chicago: University of Chicago Press, 1946), p. 44.

82. *Ibid.*, p. 25.

83. Wright, *The Growth of American Constitutional Law*, p. 259.

84. *Pennsylvania v. West Virginia*, 262 U.S. 533 (1923).

85. *Wisconsin v. Illinois* 278 U.S. 367 (1929); See also *Wisconsin, Minnesota, Ohio, and Pennsylvania v. Illinois*, 311 U.S. 107 (1940).

86. *Kansas v. Colorado*, 206 U.S. 46 (1907); Cf. *Colorado v. Kansas*, 320 U.S. 383 (1943).

87. *Arizona v. California*, 298 U.S. 558 (1936).

88. *Wyoming v. Colorado*, 259 U.S. 496 (1922); *Nebraska v. Wyoming*, 325 U.S. 593 (1945).

89. *New Hampshire v. Louisiana*, 108 U.S. 76 (1883).

90. *South Dakota v. North Carolina*, 192 U.S. 286 (1904); Cf. *North Dakota v. Minnesota*, 263 U.S. 365 (1923).

91. *Virginia v. West Virginia*, 246 U.S. 565 (1918).

92. *Coleman v. Miller*, 307 U.S. 433 (1939). In this case Chief Justice Hughes made a great effort to clarify the distinction, but only Justices Stone and Reed fully agreed with him.

93. *Mississippi v. Johnson*, 4 Wallace 475 (1867); *Georgia v. Stanton*, 6 Wallace 50 (1867).

94. *Massachusetts v. Mellon*, 262 U.S. 447 (1923).

95. *South Carolina* v. *United States,* 199 U.S. 437 (1905); *New York* v. *United States,* 326 U.S. 572 (1946).
96. *Massachusetts* v. *United States,* 333 U.S. 611 (1948).
97. *New York* v. *United States,* 331 U.S. 284 (1947).
98. *United States* v. *California,* 332 U.S. 19 (1947).
99. *United States* v. *Butler,* 297 U.S. 1 (1936).
100. *Carter* v. *Carter Coal Co.,* 298 U.S. 238 (1936).
101. *Ashwander* v. *Tennessee Valley Authority,* 297 U.S. 288 (1936).

102. For a well-informed survey of recent developments and a judicious interpretation of contemporary policy, see George C. S. Benson, *The New Centralization, A Study of Intergovernmental Relationships in the United States* (New York: Farrar and Rinehart, 1941).
103. For a skillful analysis of this experience see Jane Perry Clark, *The Rise of a New Federalism* (New York: Columbia University Press, 1938). See also for illuminating comment Paul H. Appleby, *Big Democracy* (New York: Knopf, 1945).

CHAPTER TWELVE

1. Alexis de Tocqueville, *Democracy in America* (Bowen ed., 1862), I, pp. 358–367.
2. C. M. Walsh, *The Political Science of John Adams* (New York: Putnam, 1915).
3. Letter from Thomas Jefferson to John Adams, October 28, 1813, reprinted in *The Life and Selected Writings of Thomas Jefferson* (New York: Modern Library ed., 1944), p. 632.
4. Letter of Thomas Jefferson to John Adams, June 27, 1813, *ibid.,* p. 627.
5. Letters of John Adams to Thomas Jefferson, July 9 and July 13, 1813. Charles Francis Adams, *The Works of John Adams, Second President of the United States* (Boston: Little, Brown, 1850–56), X, pp. 50–54.
6. See chap. i, pp. 8 ff.
7. A. Lawrence Lowell, *Essays on Government* (Boston: Houghton Mifflin, 1889), pp. 46–58.
8. Walter Lippmann, "Today and Tomorrow," *New York Herald Tribune,* February 8, 1941. See chap. viii, p. 270.
9. Woodrow Wilson, *Congressional Government, A Study in American Politics* (Boston: Houghton Mifflin, 1885), p. vi.
10. The latest writer in this line is C. P. Patterson, *Presidential Government in the United States* (Chapel Hill:

University of North Carolina Press, 1947); see esp. chap. x, "The Real Adjustment of the Relation of the President to the Congress," pp. 259–267.
11. Woodrow Wilson, *Congressional Government* (15th ed., 1900), p. xvi.
12. Woodrow Wilson, *Constitutional Government in the United States* (New York: Columbia University Press, 1908); see chap. iii, "The President of the United States," pp. 54–81.
13. William Y. Elliott, *The Need for Constitutional Reform; A Program for National Security* (New York: Whittlesey House, 1935), pp. 232–235. See also James M. Burns, *Congress on Trial* (New York: Harper, 1949), pp. 198–202.
14. Henry Hazlitt, *A New Constitution Now* (New York: Whittlesey House, 1942).
15. *Ibid.,* p. 105
16. Thomas K. Finletter, *Can Representative Government Do the Job?* (New York: Reynal and Hitchcock, 1945).
17. *Ibid.,* p. 112.
18. *Ibid.,* p. 119.
19. *Ibid.,* p. 128.
20. See my *Middle Classes in American Politics* (Cambridge: Harvard University Press, 1940), pt. 2, chap. iii, "The Future of Democracy in America."
21. Harold J. Laski, *The American*

Presidency (New York: Harper, 1940), pp. 243–252.

22. Harold J. Laski, *The American Democracy* (New York: Viking Press, 1948), p. 134.

23. *Ibid.*, p. 137.

24. See, for example, the valuable report, "Our Form of Government," prepared by a committee of editors of *Time, Life* and *Fortune* magazines and published as a supplement to *Fortune* (November 1943) under the title, *The United States in a New World*, pt. 5. See also Merlo J. Pusey, *Big Government: Can We Control It?* (New York: Harper, 1945).

25. Edward S. Corwin, *Total War and the Constitution* (New York: Knopf, 1947), p. 181.

26. Charles A. Beard, *The Republic* (New York: Viking Press, 1943); see chap. xix.

27. See my *The Middle Classes in American Politics* (Cambridge: Harvard University Press, 1940), pp. 31–55.

28. See my *Human Rights in the Modern World* (New York: New York University Press, 1948); see esp. chap. vi and the Epilogue.

Index

Index

Index

453

Index

457

Index

459